In the name of God, the (

Sayyid Quṭb

⁓

IN THE SHADE OF
THE QUR'ĀN

Fī Ẓilāl al-Qur'ān

VOLUME XI

⁓

SŪRAHS 16–20

Al-Naḥl – Ṭā Hā

⁓

Translated and Edited by
Adil Salahi

⁓

THE ISLAMIC FOUNDATION
AND
ISLAMONLINE.NET

Published by

THE ISLAMIC FOUNDATION,

Markfield Conference Centre,
Ratby Lane, Markfield, Leicestershire LE67 9SY, United Kingdom
Tel: (01530) 244944, Fax: (01530) 244946
E-mail: i.foundation@islamic-foundation.org.uk
Website: www.islamic-foundation.org.uk

Quran House, PO Box 30611, Nairobi, Kenya

PMB 3193, Kano, Nigeria

ISLAMONLINE.NET,
PO Box 22212, Doha, Qatar
E-mail: webmaster@islam-online.net
Website: www.islamonline.net

British Library Cataloguing-in-Publication Data
Qutb, Sayyid, 1903–1966
 In the shade of the Qur'an, Vol. 11
 1. Koran – Commentaries
 I. Title
 II. Salahi, M.A.
 III. Islamic Foundation (Great Britain)
 297.1'229

ISBN 0 86037 425 4
ISBN 0 86037 420 3 pbk

Typeset by: N.A.Qaddoura
Cover design by: Imtiaze A. Manjra
Printed by: Antony Rowe Ltd

Contents

Transliteration Table

Consonants. Arabic

initial: unexpressed medial and final:

ء	’	د	d	ض	ḍ	ك	k
ب	b	ذ	dh	ط	ṭ	ل	l
ت	t	ر	r	ظ	ẓ	م	m
ث	th	ز	z	ع	‘	ن	n
ج	j	س	s	غ	gh	هـ	h
ح	ḥ	ش	sh	ف	f	و	w
خ	kh	ص	ṣ	ق	q	ي	y

Vowels, diphthongs, etc.

short: َ a   ِ i   ُ u

long: ـَا ā   ـِي ī   ـُو ū

diphthongs: ـَوْ aw

ـَىْ ay

A Tempting Last-Minute Offer

Introduction

The woman was thin, weak, undernourished and lonely. She had spent a year in a prison wing which contained no provisions for female prisoners, and where she was for most of the time the only woman. Now, she was being received by the prison 'commander' who had been trying to persuade her that she had an important mission that could be of great benefit to her family, and to Egypt as a whole. There was nothing outwardly difficult, he said, about the mission she was expected to do. She was to talk to her elder brother, the brother who had reared and looked after her and the rest of their family ever since their father had died when she was still very young. Only a short walk separated them, for he was also in the same prison. But she knew the task was impossible and she plainly stated so.[1] Yet the 'commander' went on:

> I have already gone beyond my authority, showing you the order to carry out your brother's death sentence, approved and signed by the President. Now there is no way anyone can stop the execution except in the way I have explained. So, you owe it to him, to yourself, to your family and to Egypt as a whole. You have to understand that all of us are now on your side. We know that we have been wrong and we want to rectify things as much as possible, but those who want him dead will not stop. Therefore, we have to move

---

1. I am indebted to Mrs Hamīdah Quṭb for favouring me with the details of the events mentioned in this Introduction. She also refers to them in her book, *Riḥlah fī aḥrash al-Layl*, Dār al-Shurūq, Cairo, 1988, pp. 157–174.

gradually, and the first step is to prevent the execution. Without your help we cannot do this. You are the only one who can influence him. You are not only his sister, but more like a daughter to him. He will listen to you. And if you can get his agreement, you will be released tomorrow. He will be out of here, in your family home, within two weeks. With him though we have to go through a longer procedure, reducing the sentence first and then releasing him for health reasons. This will not take more than two weeks. What we are asking in return is no more than three lines which will not take him a minute to write. So, you go and persuade him. Help us to help you, him, your family and Egypt.

Should she smile, or be overjoyed? Should she jump at the chance being offered her that would end this year-long nightmare of imprisonment, with all the torture, isolation and humiliation that it involved? Should she dream of being reunited with her two imprisoned brothers in their family home within two weeks? Should Hamīdah Quṭb, the youngest in her family, feel that freedom was beckoning her, asking no more than a little persuasion to manipulate the tender love her eldest brother felt for her? She knew that what was being asked of her brother was false, but their jailors lived on falsehood. What would it matter if her brother gave them a little extra falsehood to spare his life and secure her release, as well as the release of her other brother? Yet she knew better. Hence, she looked at the man and said: "You know that my brother will never tell a lie. It does not matter who talks to him: if he knows something to be untrue, he will not say it. I do not think I can change his commitment to the truth, regardless of the cost."

The commander was not to be deterred. He continued trying to enlist her support:

What alternative do you leave us, then? We want to save his life, but without your help, we are powerless. Unless he writes these three lines, the execution order will have to be carried out tomorrow. No one can stop it. We have no means of even requesting a one-week postponement. Believe me, if I knew of any other way to save his life, I would do it. We want what had happened to belong to the past, and we want to open a new page where we all work together for Egypt. So, help us, and we will help you.

She knew that her brother would never agree to their request. For it meant deliberately and knowingly writing and signing a blatant lie, and he would never do such a thing. But these people were asking her to go to him to try to persuade him. This meant seeing him and speaking to him, at least for a minute or two. They would be there, watching her and listening to their conversation. But at least she would be with him, looking at his face and listening to his sweet words. If they carried out their threat tomorrow... No, she could not face such a prospect. He was dearer to her than life itself. So, let her seize the opportunity and carry their message to him. Perhaps she would prolong the meeting for a while.

She looked at the prison commander who, sensing a softening in her attitude, tried to put a smile on his face that always looked so horrid to his long suffering prisoners. She said: "I will try to persuade him, but I do not think there is much chance that he will agree."

"This is the proper attitude", he said. Now you try to persuade him, and tell him what it means for you to be released tomorrow. Assure him that he, too, will be saved, and we will release him within two weeks. Do this for him, and for your family, and for Egypt. You have to tell him that those who wish Egypt no good have been after his head, but we want to foil their efforts, save him and do what is best for Egypt, by getting rid of them. He must give us a chance to do so now by helping us to save him.

She left his office accompanied by Safwat al-Roubi, an officer of the military prison who was one of its most notorious torturers. No one had ever accused him of showing even the slightest trace of sympathy or kindness to anyone. He was leading her to her brother's cell. Just before opening the door, he said to her: "We do not have much time. The whole meeting cannot take more than half an hour." She did not reply. He opened the door and stood in the middle.

There he was: Sayyid Quṭb, her brother who, 33 years her senior, brought her up. No father could have cared for her better than he had done. How much she longed to hug him and express her feelings and her fears. But the cruel officer was there watching, and she had a task to accomplish. So she cut short the family part and proceeded to deliver her message:

> My dear, dear brother. These people want you to write a letter to the President. A short letter is enough, but you have to express your regret. It also must include something to say that your organization was financed by King Faisal of Saudi Arabia. If you write this, they will…

She did not have to continue, because her brother turned to the prison officer and said: "Had this been true, no force on earth could have prevented me from declaring it, but because it is untrue, no force on earth can force me to say it."

Al-Roubi said harshly: "But you will have to pay a heavy price, then."

Sayyid Quṭb replied: "What price? Life? This is something God gives us. He alone controls it. When He determines to take it away, we submit to His will."

The prison officer was speechless. For a moment, he did not know what to say. He then looked at her and said: "Then you have only a quarter of an hour. I will come in 15 minutes to take you away."

She talked to her brother, complaining about how she found perseverance so very hard. She said: "My dearest. I submit myself to God's will, but life without you is meaningless, empty, hard, devoid of all happiness." He reassured her saying that, even though he expected this to be his last day, he was as content, free and happy as never before. "I have no problem with whatever fate I have to face. All I am thinking of is you, and I prayed hard for you last night, and felt that my prayers were answered. This long stage of hardship will come to an end, and Islam will be triumphant as and when God wills."

She did not try to persuade him to agree to the offer she brought, because she knew he would never compromise on a matter of principle.

But she was eager to know how he was facing the prospect of his imminent death. He told her that a little over a year earlier he could have fled the country and escaped imprisonment. He had been warned of the impending trouble and a plan to take him out of the country was carefully made and its success was guaranteed. But he was not prepared to leave those who considered him their leader and had themselves no means of escape. He felt his position was with them, sharing their fate. He also told her that throughout the interrogation and the trial, he exonerated all his associates of all charges against them, taking upon himself all the blame for whatever they had done. But he assured her also that there was no truth in the charges against him or his organization. These charges were mere fabrication. No one had sought a confrontation with the government, let alone plotted to overthrow it.

Again he told her that he had never changed his views about the fact that there should be no uprising to overthrow the government by the advocates of Islamic revival. This, he argued, would be totally unproductive, and would not lead to the establishment of a proper Islamic government. The proper method was rather advocacy and education. This was the only way to bring into being a community of Muslims who were true to Islamic values and principles, and who would not barter their ideals for personal gain. Such advocates of Islam must follow the example of the Prophet's companions who withstood the hardship when it was visited on them, and who were ready to sacrifice their lives for their faith when it was threatened. Hence, when they enjoyed power, they used it for the welfare of mankind, seeking no personal gain for themselves. Islamic revival today must also follow the same lead.

She wanted this conversation to last forever, but the door was opened, and the same officer reappeared. His voice sounded heartless as he said to her: "Do not be greedy! I have given you twice the time that was allowed you." Was she greedy to want to talk to her brother for a few minutes, or a few hours, longer? How perverted were these people's thinking! She was dragged back to her own cell. The following day she learnt that the death sentences against her brother and two members of his organization had been carried out.

Was the offer of release serious? Had Sayyid Quṭb written that letter, would the Nasser regime have given him his freedom? Maybe, for they were able to use such a statement to great advantage. Relations between Egypt and Saudi Arabia were good only for brief periods during the Nasser era. In 1966, shortly before Sayyid Quṭb was executed, relations between the two countries were at their lowest point, particularly after Egypt had been dragged into the 1962-67 civil war in Yemen. Nasser might have needed such a statement from Sayyid Quṭb for political ends so as to gain the support of other powers which he desperately needed.

Some people may argue that Sayyid Quṭb should not have taken such an uncompromising stand. They would maintain that his release from prison would have ensured the release of thousands of prisoners and achieved great gains for Islam and its advocates. But such a view does not look beyond the surface. To start with, if he had written that letter, there was no guarantee that he would have been released. Indeed, Nasser's regime might not have released anyone, not even his sister. Such a letter would have been an admission of guilt which the authorities might have used against him and his fellow prisoners. The regime was fully aware that the charges they levelled at the new crop of the Muslim Brotherhood were concocted in the offices of the Egyptian military intelligence and that they carried no real substance. But for Sayyid Quṭb to express his regret and to falsely admit receiving funds from King Faisal would have endorsed all such false accusations.

On the other hand, if the authorities fulfilled their promise and released him, his sister and brother, as well as thousands of innocent detainees, they would have had to go through a long series of 'admission and regret' episodes which would have been aired on television. This would have marred the image of the Muslim Brotherhood for a long time and would have meant a serious setback for the Islamic revivalist movement throughout the world.

Even worse would have been the fact that such a letter would have branded the entire Islamic advocacy movement as a political one seeking power, and as such, it would be no different from other political parties and groupings. Indeed, its opponents tried hard to attach such an image to it.

Sayyid Qutb had the vision of a firm believer who placed his entire trust in God. If any member of the Muslim Brotherhood, or any advocate of Islam, was prepared to make such a huge sacrifice, then so be it. They would go to their Lord content and happy for having fulfilled their task to the best of their ability. For him, political gaming was too trivial for advocates of Islam to play. Instead they advocated the message God had bestowed from on high, and which He guaranteed to preserve for all time. This was the message for which the Prophet Muḥammad and his Companions advocated and sacrificed much. Its new generation of advocates must therefore follow in the footsteps of the first generation and work hard to convince their communities that only through total commitment to the implementation of Islam, conducting their lives on its basis, would they achieve all that they aspired for. This would inevitably cost them dearly, but they were to be ready to give such sacrifices as they were called upon to make, in the same way the first generation of Muslims sacrificed everything they had for the sake of Islam. When they had proved themselves before God, through the sacrifices they were willing to give, He would ensure their victory at a time He decided. Their victory, then, would not be for a political party, or an organized group of any type. It would be a victory for the message of Islam. Whether this would be in the present generation or in the future should not concern them. They were to do their duty and leave matters to God.

With such vision, saving his own neck was not a great issue for Sayyid Qutb. What concerned him instead was to ensure that he was not tempted to join a political game in which he had no personal interest, and which could not serve the cause of Islam. Hence, when the heartless prison officer threatened him with having to pay a heavy price for his refusal to write the letter to Nasser, his answer put the whole issue in the correct perspective. If he had to pay with his life, so be it. Life is granted by God and ended by Him at the moment He chooses. It was much better to die as a committed advocate of Islam than to compromise on matters of principle, even though such a compromise meant enjoying a life of comfort.

The *sūrahs* included in this volume, and those in the next two volumes, are of the first edition which Sayyid Quṭb wrote before his first imprisonment. This means that they were written before the change he introduced in his approach as a result of his long imprisonment. This change reflected his deep thinking about the lack of steadfastness shown by many who were previously seen as solidly committed to the cause. This made him realize that commitment to Islam was not as real as it appeared. Unless such commitment is deeply rooted, he argued, it cannot produce the desired results. Hence, his future work, particularly in the revised edition of *In the Shade of the Qur'ān*, aimed to ensure the strengthening of such commitment. He died however before he could complete the work.

Should he have tried to buy time so as to be able to complete his commentary on the Qur'ān? Was this not enough reason for him to jump at the offer of release? The answer is that his martyrdom speaks much louder than any words he could have written. Today, however, he is vilified as the philosopher or the theoretician whose writings encouraged the rise of Islamic extremism. Nothing though is further from the truth. Sayyid Quṭb was very clear that only through education can we hope to raise a generation of advocates of Islam who are well aware of its principles, values and teachings so as to conduct their lives on their basis. Only when they prove themselves as seeking no personal gain for themselves will God trust them with the task of implementing Islam in real life. Political gaming, or the overthrow of government by military *coup* or popular uprising, were inappropriate tools for pushing forward the cause of Islamic revival. The proper way was and is for Muslims to be more strongly convinced of, and better educated in, their faith so as to be able to implement it fully in life. Thus, their lives become practical examples of what Islam can do to ensure happiness for all of humanity.

Sayyid Quṭb's writings came alive when he refused to compromise, preferring to die rather than tell an untruth that served the narrow interests of the regime. By doing so, he added more power to his words than his great literary talent could have done.

London   **Adil Salahi**
Rajab 1425 H
August 2004

SŪRAH 16

Al-Naḥl

(The Bees)

Prologue

Although this *sūrah* enjoys a calm rhythm with a quiet, soft beat, it nonetheless tackles several main topics within its broad framework. It makes use of several sound effects and emphatic connotations to heighten its impact. Like all *sūrahs* revealed in Makkah, it discusses the main topics of faith, such as God's oneness, revelation and resurrection. But it also refers to a number of secondary topics, such as the essential unity between Abraham's faith and the faith preached by Muḥammad (peace be upon them both). It outlines the true nature of God's will, and mentions the human will with regard to accepting or denying the true faith, following divine guidance or going astray. It explains the mission of God's messengers and His law that applies to those who deny them and their messages. It discusses the question of who may forbid things or leave them lawful, and the false concepts of pagan ideologies in this regard. It speaks of leaving one's community to migrate for God's sake, the persecution Muslims may suffer at the hands of unbelievers, the rejection of faith after having accepted it and what punishment any of these situations may incur. It then adds some discussion on human dealings, such as maintaining justice, ensuring kindly treatment, giving money for good purposes and the fulfilment of promises and pledges, as well as other practices that observe the

1

principles of faith. Thus we see how the *sūrah* weaves together its interrelated subject matter.

These topics are presented within an expansive framework in which all the events take place. It includes the heavens and the earth, with the rain pouring down, the trees springing up, the day and night, the sun, the moon and the stars, the seas, the mountains and the rivers. It is indeed this whole world with all that takes place in it as well as the life to come with all its scenery and the fates of different categories of God's creatures. It also includes the realm that lies beyond the reach of our perception, and the feelings it inspires within us.

Against such a broad backdrop the *sūrah* sounds like a massive campaign aimed at profoundly influencing people's hearts and minds. It is a campaign that uses a moderate rhythm with several coherent sounds. It has nothing of the very strong beats we hear in *Sūrahs* 6 and 13, Cattle and Thunder respectively. Yet in its quiet rhythm it addresses every sense and feeling in the human soul, as well as both reason and conscience. It alerts our eyes to see, our ears to hear, our hands to touch and feel, our consciences to be alert and our minds to reflect. It portrays every aspect of the whole universe, looks at the present life and the life to come, as well as secrets of the universe and what is beyond the reach of our faculties of perception. All these are used to heighten the effect on our senses, hearts and minds. The result is a massive panorama which only a closed mind and a dead heart can ignore.

We are directed to look at the signs and messages that God has placed throughout the universe, and the great bounties and blessings He has given to mankind, and to reflect on the scenes of the Day of Judgement, the images of death, and the fate suffered by former communities. Coupled with this is a series of emotional touches that penetrate the depths of our hearts, and which refer to the different stages of human life from unborn embryos, to people in the full vigour of youth, in mid-life and in old age, as also in situations of strength and weakness, enjoying God's blessings or enduring hardship. It uses different styles and modes of expression, giving examples, drawing images, relating dialogue and presenting stories in order to make its message clear and enhance its effect.

The splendid colours that impart their shades to the whole atmosphere of the *sūrah* also highlight a number of great natural phenomena, reflecting the greatness of creation, God's bounty, His knowledge and elaborate planning. These are all intermingled. The great universe created by God is subject to God's perfect knowledge and His meticulous design and planning. Yet it is meant to be a blessing for mankind, meeting not only their needs but also their wishes and expectations. Thus all needs and necessities are satisfied; adornments provided; relaxation of body and soul ensured. It is then right that people should give thanks and express their gratitude to God.

Thus throughout the *sūrah* we see God's blessings and believers expressing gratitude. There are several directives on the need to show such gratitude, coupled with various comments. Parables are given, as well as examples. The most vivid of these is that of the Prophet Abraham who is described as showing "*his gratitude for the blessings bestowed by Him who had chosen him and guided him to a straight path.*" (Verse 121)

All this is given in a perfect harmony of image, connotation, expression, rhythm, issue and subject matter. We now hope to outline some of these as we discuss the *sūrah* in detail.

I

God the Creator of All

Al-Naḥl (The Bees)

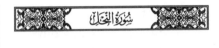

In the Name of God, the Merciful, the Beneficent

God's judgement is bound to come; so do not seek to hurry it on. Limitless is He in His glory and sublimely exalted above anything people may associate with Him. (1)

He sends down angels with this divine inspiration, [bestowed] by His will on such of His servants as He pleases: 'Warn [mankind] that there is no deity other than Me: so fear Me.' (2)

He has created the heavens and the earth in truth; sublimely exalted is He above anything people may associate with Him. (3)

He creates man out of a drop of sperm; yet this same man is openly contentious. (4)

خَلَقَ ٱلْإِنسَٰنَ مِن نُّطْفَةٍ فَإِذَا هُوَ خَصِيمٌ مُّبِينٌ ۝

He creates cattle which give you warmth and other benefits; and from them you obtain food. (5)

وَٱلْأَنْعَٰمَ خَلَقَهَا لَكُمْ فِيهَا دِفْءٌ وَمَنَٰفِعُ وَمِنْهَا تَأْكُلُونَ ۝

And you find beauty in them when you drive them home in the evening and when you take them out to pasture in the morning. (6)

وَلَكُمْ فِيهَا جَمَالٌ حِينَ تُرِيحُونَ وَحِينَ تَسْرَحُونَ ۝

And they carry your loads to distant lands, which you could not otherwise reach without much hardship to yourselves. Your Lord is certainly Most Compassionate, Merciful. (7)

وَتَحْمِلُ أَثْقَالَكُمْ إِلَىٰ بَلَدٍ لَّمْ تَكُونُوا۟ بَٰلِغِيهِ إِلَّا بِشِقِّ ٱلْأَنفُسِ إِنَّ رَبَّكُمْ لَرَءُوفٌ رَّحِيمٌ ۝

And [He creates] horses, mules and asses for you to ride or put on show. And He creates other things of which you have no knowledge. (8)

وَٱلْخَيْلَ وَٱلْبِغَالَ وَٱلْحَمِيرَ لِتَرْكَبُوهَا وَزِينَةً وَيَخْلُقُ مَا لَا تَعْلَمُونَ ۝

It is God alone who points to the right path. Yet many may swerve from it. Had He so willed, He would have guided you all aright. (9)

وَعَلَى ٱللَّهِ قَصْدُ ٱلسَّبِيلِ وَمِنْهَا جَآئِرٌ وَلَوْ شَآءَ لَهَدَىٰكُمْ أَجْمَعِينَ ۝

It is He who sends down water from the skies. From it you drink, and with it grow the plants on which you pasture your cattle. (10)

هُوَ ٱلَّذِىٓ أَنزَلَ مِنَ ٱلسَّمَآءِ مَآءً لَّكُم مِّنْهُ شَرَابٌ وَمِنْهُ شَجَرٌ فِيهِ تُسِيمُونَ ۝

And with it He causes crops to grow for you, and olive trees, and date-palms, and grapes, and all other kinds of fruit. Surely in this there is a sign for people who think. (11)

يُنۢبِتُ لَكُم بِهِ ٱلزَّرْعَ وَٱلزَّيْتُونَ وَٱلنَّخِيلَ وَٱلْأَعْنَٰبَ وَمِن كُلِّ ٱلثَّمَرَٰتِ إِنَّ فِى ذَٰلِكَ لَءَايَةً لِّقَوْمٍ يَتَفَكَّرُونَ ۝

And He has made the night and the day and the sun and the moon to be subservient to you; and all the stars are subservient to His command. In this there are signs for people who use their reason. (12)

وَسَخَّرَ لَكُمُ ٱلَّيْلَ وَٱلنَّهَارَ وَٱلشَّمْسَ وَٱلْقَمَرَ وَٱلنُّجُومُ مُسَخَّرَٰتٌۢ بِأَمْرِهِ إِنَّ فِى ذَٰلِكَ لَءَايَٰتٍ لِّقَوْمٍ يَعْقِلُونَ ۝

On the earth He has fashioned for you objects of various hues; surely in this there is a sign for people who take heed. (13)

وَمَا ذَرَأَ لَكُمْ فِى ٱلْأَرْضِ مُخْتَلِفًا أَلْوَٰنُهُ إِنَّ فِى ذَٰلِكَ لَءَايَةً لِّقَوْمٍ يَذَّكَّرُونَ ۝

It is He who has made the sea subservient to [His laws], so that you may eat fresh meat from it, and take from it gems which you may wear. You see the ships ploughing through the waves, so that you may be able to go forth in quest of His bounty, and that you may be grateful. (14)

وَهُوَ ٱلَّذِى سَخَّرَ ٱلْبَحْرَ لِتَأْكُلُوا۟ مِنْهُ لَحْمًا طَرِيًّا وَتَسْتَخْرِجُوا۟ مِنْهُ حِلْيَةً تَلْبَسُونَهَا وَتَرَى ٱلْفُلْكَ مَوَاخِرَ فِيهِ وَلِتَبْتَغُوا۟ مِن فَضْلِهِ وَلَعَلَّكُمْ تَشْكُرُونَ ۝

He has placed firm mountains on earth lest it should sway with you; and rivers and paths so that you may find your way (15)

وَأَلْقَىٰ فِى ٱلْأَرْضِ رَوَٰسِىَ أَن تَمِيدَ بِكُمْ وَأَنْهَٰرًا وَسُبُلًا لَّعَلَّكُمْ تَهْتَدُونَ ﴿١٥﴾

as well as landmarks. By the stars, too, are people guided. (16)

وَعَلَٰمَٰتٍ وَبِٱلنَّجْمِ هُمْ يَهْتَدُونَ ﴿١٦﴾

Is He, then, who creates like one that cannot create? Will you not, then, think? (17)

أَفَمَن يَخْلُقُ كَمَن لَّا يَخْلُقُ أَفَلَا تَذَكَّرُونَ ﴿١٧﴾

Should you try to count God's blessings, you will never be able to compute them. God is indeed Much Forgiving, Merciful. (18)

وَإِن تَعُدُّوا نِعْمَةَ ٱللَّهِ لَا تُحْصُوهَآ إِنَّ ٱللَّهَ لَغَفُورٌ رَّحِيمٌ ﴿١٨﴾

God knows all that you keep secret and all that you bring into the open. (19)

وَٱللَّهُ يَعْلَمُ مَا تُسِرُّونَ وَمَا تُعْلِنُونَ ﴿١٩﴾

Those beings that some people invoke beside God cannot create anything; they themselves are created. (20)

وَٱلَّذِينَ يَدْعُونَ مِن دُونِ ٱللَّهِ لَا يَخْلُقُونَ شَيْئًا وَهُمْ يُخْلَقُونَ ﴿٢٠﴾

They are dead, not living, and they do not know when they will be raised back to life. (21)

أَمْوَٰتٌ غَيْرُ أَحْيَآءٍ وَمَا يَشْعُرُونَ أَيَّانَ يُبْعَثُونَ ﴿٢١﴾

Overview

This first passage speaks about God's oneness. It makes use of all the tools we outlined in the Prologue: the numerous signs and indicators the great variety of God's creation exhibit, the countless favours He has bestowed on man in every stage of his life, His perfect knowledge of what is kept secret and what is left public, the life of this world and the life to come.

An Imminent Grave Event

God's judgement is bound to come; so do not seek to hurry it on. Limitless is He in His glory and sublimely exalted above anything people may associate with Him. He sends down angels with this divine inspiration, [bestowed] by His will on such of His servants as He pleases: 'Warn [mankind] that there is no deity other than Me: so fear Me.' (Verses 1–2)

The unbelievers in Makkah used to ask the Prophet to hasten their punishment in this life, or to hasten the punishment God has in store for them in the life to come. As time passed with no punishment being inflicted, they urged the Prophet more and more to hasten it, demonstrating that they could not care less. They thought that Muḥammad was warning them against something that would never happen. His only aim, as they imagined, was to get them to believe what he said and accept his faith. They could not understand God's wisdom in giving them time. Nor could they appreciate His grace. They would not reflect on the signs He has placed everywhere in the universe around them. Nor would they reflect on His revelations in the Qur'ān which address people's minds and hearts. That is after all a much more effective address than punishment and suffering. It is more worthy of man whom God has honoured when He gave him a mind, feelings and an independent will to study, reflect and make free choices.

The opening of the *sūrah* is very decisive: "*God's judgement is bound to come.*" It implies that the command has been given, and that God's will has been made. This is sufficient for the judgement to come to pass at the time appointed for it by God Himself. "*So do not seek to hurry it on.*" God's laws operate in accordance with His will. They cannot be hurried, nor can they be postponed to satisfy people's wishes. The statement here tells us that God's judgement, to resurrect people or to inflict His punishment on those who deserve it, has been made. It will come to pass at the time God has determined. There will be no hurrying and no delay.

The decisive nature of this statement is especially effective, even on those who try to wear a careless face. Moreover, it expresses the truth. Whatever God wills is bound to take place. The fact that He has made a judgement means that it is carried out, and that it becomes part of reality. Hence, there is neither an overstatement of facts nor a deviation from them.

Their beliefs, associating partners with God, and all the false concepts that they formulate on that basis, are far removed from God's true nature: "*Limitless is He in His glory and sublimely exalted above anything people may associate with Him.*" (Verse 1) Beliefs that ascribe divinity to anyone other than God all lack foundation. They are the result of degenerate and disgraceful thinking.

God, who does not abandon mankind to their erring beliefs and baseless concepts, sends down from on high what gives them life and saves them: "*He sends down angels with this divine inspiration, [bestowed] by His will on such of His servants as He pleases.*" (Verse 2) This is God's greatest favour and blessing. He not only sends down water from the sky to make the earth quicken and to give physical life, but He also sends down the angels with His divine inspiration. The Arabic expression uses the word *rūḥ,* which also means 'spirit', for inspiration. This adds connotations of life within people's souls, consciences and feelings, and within society so as to preserve them all from corruption. This is the first thing that God sends down to people from on high, and it is His most important blessing and bounty. God's purest creation, the angels, are sent down to His chosen servants, the prophets, giving them a message that is summed up in these words: "*Warn [mankind] that there is no deity other than Me: so fear Me.*" (Verse 2)

The emphasis here is on God's oneness, which is the central point of the Islamic faith. It breathes life into people's souls. It is also the parting point between the way which gives life and the way which destroys it. A soul that does not believe in God's oneness is lost, confused, pulled in all directions by diverse and contradictory concepts and beliefs. It cannot move with its whole being towards a definite goal. Use of the term *rūḥ* in reference to God's message implies all these. Indeed it provides a fitting reference to them at the beginning of this *sūrah* which speaks of the great variety of God's favours. It is the top of all these blessings, without which all others lose their value. Indeed man does not make a proper use or derive proper benefit from anything on earth unless his soul comes alive with the great blessing of faith.

The warning is given a special mention so as to appear to be the central point of the message, because the larger part of the *sūrah* speaks about the unbelievers who deny God's blessing, prohibit what God has made lawful, violate their covenant with God and reject faith altogether. This makes the warning more appropriate at the outset, coupled with a call to fear God and avoid incurring His displeasure.

Creation and Compassion

The *sūrah* then begins to outline the aspects of creation that emphasize the oneness of the Creator, and the aspects of blessing that confirm that it is God alone who bestows them all. These are revealed in groups that follow one another sequentially, starting with the creation of the heavens and the earth, and moving to the creation of man: *"He has created the heavens and the earth in truth; sublimely exalted is He above anything people may associate with Him. He creates man out of a drop of sperm; yet this same man is openly contentious."* (Verses 3–4)

"He has created the heavens and the earth in truth." (Verse 3) The truth is at the core of their creation and their existence. Indeed the truth is an essential element in managing their affairs and the affairs of all creation. Nothing is created in vain or idle play. Everything derives its existence on the basis of the truth, and leads eventually to the truth. *"Sublimely exalted is He above anything people may associate with Him."* (Verse 3) He is exalted above their pagan beliefs and above any creatures they associate with Him. He is indeed the One who has created the heavens and the earth and all beings that live in them. No creature is worthy of being His partner. Indeed He has no partners.

11

"*He creates man out of a drop of sperm; yet this same man is openly contentious.*" (Verse 4) The gulf is so huge between the origin and the end, between the worthless sperm and the man in open contention. He disputes with his Lord and denies Him. He argues about His existence or His oneness. Yet the way the verse runs leaves no gap between the point of origin, the drop of sperm, and the grown up man engaged in dispute and contention. This shows the contrast to be complete and the gulf too wide. Such brevity is intended for enhanced effect.

Against the expanse of the heavens and the earth man stands out. Therefore, the *sūrah* mentions some of the creation God has made subservient to man, beginning with cattle: "*He creates cattle which give you warmth and other benefits; and from them you obtain food. And you find beauty in them when you drive them home in the evening and when you take them out to pasture in the morning. And they carry your loads to distant lands, which you could not otherwise reach without much hardship to yourselves. Your Lord is certainly Most Compassionate, Merciful. And [He creates] horses, mules and asses for you to ride or put on show. And He creates other things of which you have no knowledge.*" (Verses 5–8)

In numerous situations that are similar to the environment where the Qur'ān was revealed, and in any agricultural set-up, which remains the principal one in the whole world, the value of cattle is fully appreciated. Indeed mankind cannot survive without cattle. The better known cattle in Arabia at the time were camels, cows, sheep and goats. On the other hand, horses, mules and asses were for riding and show. They were not meant to be eaten. Indeed there is disagreement among scholars on the permissibility of eating the meat of these animals. Imām Abū Ḥanīfah relies on this verse which defines the uses of these animals to say that horses may not be eaten. The majority of scholars, however, maintain that they are permissible to eat. In this they rely on authentic *aḥādīth* and on practical *sunnah*.

As the Qur'ān refers to this aspect of God's blessings, it refers to the practical needs it fulfils in human life. Cattle give warmth as we use their hide, wool and hair. These have even further benefits. We also obtain milk and meat from cattle. We are reminded that cattle provide food for people and carry their loads when they travel. Without cattle, people would until recently have found great difficulty in reaching their destination. At the same time we enjoy their beauty, particularly when we drive them home in the evening and when we take them to pasture in the morning. Just looking at them moving along, strong and full of vigour, gives us pleasure. Rural people are better able than town dwellers to appreciate the meanings to which these verses refer.

Horses, mules and asses also meet other human needs. They are used as mounts to ride or, they are put on show for their beauty: "*And [He creates] horses, mules and asses for you to ride or put on show.*" (Verse 8) Here we encounter a particularly interesting point in the Islamic outlook of life, whereby beauty constitutes an important aspect. God's blessing does not merely satisfy essential needs, such as food, drink and mounts. It also satisfies healthy desires beyond basic needs. Here we find satisfaction of the sense that enjoys beauty and seeks pleasure, and also satisfies human feelings that are more sublime than animal desires and needs.

"*Your Lord is certainly Most Compassionate, Merciful.*" (Verse 7) This comment refers in particular to the carrying of heavy loads to distant lands which people could not reach otherwise without enduring much hardship. Thus the comment directs our attention to the great blessings that God has given us by creating cattle, and to the great mercy accompanying this blessing.

"*And He creates things of which you have no knowledge.*" (Verse 8) This sentence comments on the creation of cattle, horses, mules and asses and the different uses to which they are put and the benefits they provide. Thus it invites people's imagination to look beyond their immediate environment and the time in which they live. Beyond what exists at a particular location and in a particular time there are other forms and types of life. God wants people to expect this so as to broaden their vision. He also wants them to accept such other forms of life when they are available. They must not refuse to benefit by such new types, saying that they will only use the cattle, horses, mules and asses their fathers used. Similarly, no one should be so rigid as to say that since the Qur'ān only mentioned these, no other form of transport can be used.

Islam is open minded and flexible. It equips its followers with the ability to use all potentials and resources that are available at any time. The Qur'ān thus prepares people's minds and hearts to receive whatever

God creates and science discovers or produces in the future. A proper Islamic conscience is always ready to accept any new remarkable addition to God's creation or to scientific discovery. Over the years many new means of riding and carrying loads have been added, as well as many objects of beauty. None of these were known to people when the Qur'ān was revealed. There will be many more which are unknown to us. The Qur'ān prepares us to accept these without difficulty by stating that God *"creates things of which you have no knowledge."* (Verse 8)

Within the context of carriage, riding and travelling to reach certain destinations on earth, the *sūrah* adds other objectives which we can reach by travelling along mental ways. Such is the road to faith, which is a straight way that has no turnings. It does not go beyond the defined goal. There are other ways that do not lead to the same destination. Now God has undertaken to make the way leading to Him clear and well defined. He points it out through the signs He has placed in the universe and through His messengers: *"It is God alone who points to the right path. Yet many may swerve from it. Had He so willed, He would have guided you all aright."* (Verse 9)

The right path is the straight one which does not bend here or there. It goes directly to its destination, allowing for no deviation. A swerving path may lead away from the destination, or may go beyond it, without stopping at it.

"Had He so willed, He would have guided you all aright." (Verse 9) But it has been His will that He creates man with the dual propensity to follow His guidance or to go astray, and to let him choose to follow either way. Hence, some people follow the right path and some follow swerving ways. Neither type goes beyond God's will which has determined to allow man free choice.

Blessings Galore

The second group of great signs in God's creation and His unlimited blessings then follow:

> It is He who sends down water from the skies. From it you drink, and with it grow the plants on which you pasture your cattle. And with it He causes crops to grow for you, and olive trees, and date-

palms, and grapes, and all other kinds of fruit. Surely in this there is a sign for people who think. (Verses 10–11)

Water pours down from the sky in accordance with laws that God has placed in nature and set into operation. It is these laws that control the running of such water and bring about its outcome in accordance with God's will. Indeed He initiates every movement and determines every result by a special act of will. The water is mentioned here as an aspect of God's grace. *"From it you drink."* So it has the quality of being suitable for drinking. Its other quality follows: *"And with it grow the plants on which you pasture your cattle."* (Verse 10) This reference fits in well with the earlier mention of cattle. It provides harmony between the pasture and cattle. A reference is also made to plants which serve as food for man, including olives, dates and grapes, and many other types of fruit.

"Surely in this there is a sign for people who think." (Verse 11) There is certainly a sign in the way God has designed the universe and set its laws so that they fit human life. Man would not have been able to survive on this planet had the laws of nature been unsuitable for his nature and life needs. That man is placed on the surface of the earth has not come about by blind coincidence. Nor is it a matter of coincidence that proportions and relativity between our planet and other planets and stars are as they are, or that climatic conditions are so suitable to support human life and satisfy man's needs and desires.

The people who think are the ones who understand that there is elaborate and wise planning in the universe. They relate a natural phenomenon such as rain and its effects of initiating life and helping plants and trees to grow and yield their fruit to the higher laws of existence and the evidence pointing to the Creator who has no partners. They appreciate that everything is part of His planning and under His management. The careless see such phenomena every morning and every evening, winter and summer, but it stirs nothing in their minds. They do not feel any urge to try to identify the One who has designed this unique and remarkable system.

A third group of signs are then added: *"And He has made the night and the day and the sun and the moon to be subservient to you; and all the stars are subservient to His command. In this there are signs for people who use their reason."* (Verse 12)

Another aspect of the perfect design of creation and the blessings bestowed on mankind at the same time is the creation of the night, day, sun, moon and stars. All these help to meet our needs on earth. We do not say that they have been created for man, but they are made to serve his existence and to benefit him. The phenomenon of the succession of day and night has a profound effect on human life. If anyone is in doubt, let him imagine a day that is not followed by a night, or a night not followed by a day, and reflect what that would mean to the life of human beings, animals and plants on earth.

The same applies to the sun and moon. They have a direct bearing on life on earth, its origin, maintenance and growth. Moreover, *"all the stars are subservient to His command."* (Verse 12) They serve the interests of man and other beings known only to God. All this is, again, part of the wise and elaborate planning that includes everything in the universe. The harmony and balance between all universal laws are appreciated by people who use their reason and contemplate what lies beyond these laws: *"In this there are signs for people who use their reason."* (Verse 12)

Yet another group of blessings that God bestows on mankind is also mentioned: *"On the earth He has fashioned for you objects of various hues; surely in this there is a sign for people who take heed."* (Verse 13)

What God has created and placed on the earth is fantastic in its nature and diversity. We need only to mention the metals that are available in the soil. These support the life of whole communities during different periods. It is sufficient to cast a glance at these hidden resources to appreciate the great blessing to which the *sūrah* refers. These are kept for mankind until they have achieved sufficient progress to make use of these resources when they are needed. Whenever it is said that a great treasure has been exhausted, another is discovered. All this is part of the provision God has placed at man's service. *"Surely in this there is a sign for people who take heed."* (Verse 13) Such people do not forget that it is God's able hand that has kept these treasures and resources hidden for them until they are able to make use of them.

We are then alerted to another group of God's creation which is the sea and its animal life. Its water is salty and cannot be used for drinking or irrigation. Yet it includes a fantastic range of blessings that God bestows on man: "*It is He who has made the sea subservient to [His laws], so that you may eat fresh meat from it, and take from it gems which you may wear. You see the ships ploughing through the waves, so that you may be able to go forth in quest of His bounty, and that you may be grateful.*" (Verse 14)

The sea and its life forms also meet many human needs and satisfy various human desires. From it we obtain fresh fish and other species to eat. In it we find pearls and corals which we use as ornaments. Some communities continue to use shells as personal ornaments or to make artefacts from them. The reference to ships also hints at the element of beauty and its satisfaction, not merely the use of shipping for transport. "*You see the ships ploughing through the waves.*" (Verse 14) The expression here draws our attention to the beauty we see everywhere in the universe. Such beauty stands out just as the object we are contemplating is seen to serve a definite purpose and meet a felt need. We only need to appreciate such beauty and not confine ourselves to needs that must be satisfied.

The verses here draw our attention to the fact that we should seek what God has given us of provision and bounty, and to our duty of giving thanks to Him for having placed food, ornament and beauty for us in the salty sea: "*so that you may be able to go forth in quest of His bounty, and that you may be grateful.*" (Verse 14)

The last group of God's numerous blessings mentioned in this passage refers to different aspects of God's creation: "*He has placed firm mountains on earth lest it should sway with you; and rivers and paths so that you may find your way, as well as landmarks. By the stars, too, are people guided.*" (Verses 15–16)

Modern science gives us several theories which explain the formation of mountains, but it does not mention their function to which the Qur'ān refers. The most important of these contradictory theories is that the surface of the earth shrank as it cooled down after its initial burning stage. This then led to the formation of valleys, hills and mountains on its surface. Yet the Qur'ān mentions that the mountains ensure that the earth remains well balanced. This function is not given due attention by scientists.

In contrast with the firm mountains, our attentions are drawn to the running rivers and the roads we follow. There is a direct link between the rivers and the mountains in this scene. Many a river starts at a mountain, where rain-water gathers. The roads also have a direct link with both mountains and rivers. They provide another link to the general atmosphere of movement, cattle, mounts and transport. Juxtaposed with the roads are the landmarks which people use to ensure that they are following the right way. These include hills, mountains and open spaces, as well as the stars which guide travellers on sea and dry land alike.

False Deities That Create Nothing

Now that the aspects of creation, blessings and great design have been completed in this first passage of the *sūrah*, a comment follows to emphasize the point at issue, namely the oneness of God who is sublimely exalted above all those beings people associate as partners with Him:

> *Is He, then, who creates like one that cannot create? Will you not, then, think? Should you try to count God's blessings, you will never be able to compute them. God is indeed Much Forgiving, Merciful. God knows all that you keep secret and all that you bring into the open. Those beings that some people invoke beside God cannot create anything; they themselves are created. They are dead, not living, and they do not know when they will be raised back to life.* (Verses 17–21)

This comment comes at the most opportune time. We are all ready to accept the point it makes: *"Is He, then, who creates like one that cannot create?"* (Verse 17) Could there be more than one answer? No! Of course not! They are not alike. Is it possible that a human being can equate God who has created all these with false deities that create nothing? *"Will you not, then, think?"* (Verse 17) The point needs no more than a little reflection and the whole case is set to rest.

The *sūrah* mentions a great variety of God's blessings. Now it comments on this, saying: "*Should you try to count God's blessings, you will never be able to compute them.*" (Verse 18) If people are unable even to compute God's blessings, they are much less likely to be able to thank God enough for them. Indeed most blessings remain unnoticed by man, because they are too familiar to him. He is thus oblivious to their importance. He only notices the importance of a blessing that he has taken for granted when it is withdrawn. We need only remember how oblivious we are of the importance of different organs and systems in our bodies. We only remember this when we are ill, because our organs are not functioning properly. Nevertheless, God's forgiveness ensures that man's shortcomings and lack of gratitude are overlooked: "*God is indeed Much Forgiving, Merciful.*" (Verse 18)

The Creator knows full well what He has created, what is apparent of it and what is concealed: "*God knows all that you keep secret and all that you bring into the open.*" (Verse 19) How can they equate Him with their alleged deities who neither create nor have any knowledge. They are indeed dead, having no life whatsoever. Indeed they have no feelings: "*Those beings that some people invoke beside God cannot create anything; they themselves are created. They are dead, not living, and they do not know when they will be raised back to life.* (Verses 20–21)

The reference here to the resurrection implies that the Creator must, for certain, know its time, because resurrection is complementary to creation. It is then that the living receive their reward for what they have done in life. The deities that do not know when their worshippers are raised to life are only a mockery. A true Creator determines when to resurrect His creation.

2

Divergent Outlooks and Attitudes

Your God is the One God. Those who deny the life to come have hearts that persist in denying the truth. They are full of arrogance. (22)

إِلَٰهُكُمْ إِلَٰهٌ وَٰحِدٌ ۚ فَالَّذِينَ لَا يُؤْمِنُونَ بِالْآخِرَةِ قُلُوبُهُم مُّنكِرَةٌ وَهُم مُّسْتَكْبِرُونَ ﴿٢٢﴾

God surely knows what they keep secret and all that they bring into the open. He does not love those who are arrogant. (23)

لَا جَرَمَ أَنَّ اللَّهَ يَعْلَمُ مَا يُسِرُّونَ وَمَا يُعْلِنُونَ ۚ إِنَّهُ لَا يُحِبُّ الْمُسْتَكْبِرِينَ ﴿٢٣﴾

Whenever they are asked, 'What has your Lord bestowed from on high?' they say: 'Fables of the ancients!' (24)

وَإِذَا قِيلَ لَهُم مَّاذَا أَنزَلَ رَبُّكُمْ ۙ قَالُوا أَسَاطِيرُ الْأَوَّلِينَ ﴿٢٤﴾

On the Day of Resurrection they shall bear the full weight of their burdens, as well as some of the burdens of those ignorant ones whom they have led astray. Evil is the burden they shall bear. (25)

لِيَحْمِلُوا أَوْزَارَهُمْ كَامِلَةً يَوْمَ الْقِيَامَةِ ۙ وَمِنْ أَوْزَارِ الَّذِينَ يُضِلُّونَهُم بِغَيْرِ عِلْمٍ ۗ أَلَا سَاءَ مَا يَزِرُونَ ﴿٢٥﴾

21

Those who lived before them also schemed. But God struck their edifice at its foundation, and its roof fell in upon them from above, and suffering befell them from where they did not perceive. (26)

قَدْ مَكَرَ ٱلَّذِينَ مِن قَبْلِهِمْ فَأَتَى ٱللَّهُ بُنْيَنَهُم مِّنَ ٱلْقَوَاعِدِ فَخَرَّ عَلَيْهِمُ ٱلسَّقْفُ مِن فَوْقِهِمْ وَأَتَىٰهُمُ ٱلْعَذَابُ مِنْ حَيْثُ لَا يَشْعُرُونَ ۝

Then, on the Day of Resurrection He will cover them with ignominy, and say: 'Where are those alleged partners of Mine concerning whom you have engaged in dispute?' Those who are endowed with knowledge will say: 'Ignominy and misery shall this day befall the unbelievers, (27)

ثُمَّ يَوْمَ ٱلْقِيَمَةِ يُخْزِيهِمْ وَيَقُولُ أَيْنَ شُرَكَآءِىَ ٱلَّذِينَ كُنتُمْ تُشَٰقُّونَ فِيهِمْ قَالَ ٱلَّذِينَ أُوتُوا ٱلْعِلْمَ إِنَّ ٱلْخِزْىَ ٱلْيَوْمَ وَٱلسُّوءَ عَلَى ٱلْكَٰفِرِينَ ۝

those whom the angels have gathered in death while they are still wronging themselves.' These will then offer their submission, saying: 'We have done no wrong!' [They will be answered]: 'Yes, indeed. God has full knowledge of all that you were doing! (28)

ٱلَّذِينَ تَتَوَفَّىٰهُمُ ٱلْمَلَٰئِكَةُ ظَالِمِىٓ أَنفُسِهِمْ فَأَلْقَوُا ٱلسَّلَمَ مَا كُنَّا نَعْمَلُ مِن سُوءٍ بَلَىٰٓ إِنَّ ٱللَّهَ عَلِيمٌ بِمَا كُنتُمْ تَعْمَلُونَ ۝

Enter the gates of hell, where you shall abide.' Evil indeed is the abode of the arrogant! (29)

فَٱدْخُلُوٓا أَبْوَٰبَ جَهَنَّمَ خَٰلِدِينَ فِيهَا فَلَبِئْسَ مَثْوَى ٱلْمُتَكَبِّرِينَ ۝

وَقِيلَ لِلَّذِينَ ٱتَّقَوْاْ مَاذَآ أَنزَلَ رَبُّكُمْ
قَالُواْ خَيْرًا لِّلَّذِينَ أَحْسَنُواْ فِي هَٰذِهِ
ٱلدُّنْيَا حَسَنَةٌ وَلَدَارُ ٱلْأَخِرَةِ خَيْرٌ
وَلَنِعْمَ دَارُ ٱلْمُتَّقِينَ ٣٠

But when the God-fearing are asked: 'What has your Lord revealed?' they say: 'All that is good.' For those who do good in this world, good reward [is assured]; but far better is their abode in the hereafter. Blessed is the dwelling place of the God-fearing. (30)

جَنَّٰتُ عَدْنٍ يَدْخُلُونَهَا تَجْرِى مِن تَحْتِهَا
ٱلْأَنْهَٰرُ لَهُمْ فِيهَا مَا يَشَآءُونَ كَذَٰلِكَ
يَجْزِى ٱللَّهُ ٱلْمُتَّقِينَ ٣١

The Gardens of Eden they will enter; through which running waters flow. There they shall have everything they desire. Thus shall God reward the God-fearing; (31)

ٱلَّذِينَ تَتَوَفَّاهُمُ ٱلْمَلَٰٓئِكَةُ طَيِّبِينَ يَقُولُونَ
سَلَٰمٌ عَلَيْكُمُ ٱدْخُلُواْ ٱلْجَنَّةَ بِمَا كُنتُمْ
تَعْمَلُونَ ٣٢

those whom the angels gather in death while they are in a state of purity, saying: 'Peace be upon you! Enter paradise by virtue of what you were doing [in life].' (32)

هَلْ يَنظُرُونَ إِلَّآ أَن تَأْتِيَهُمُ ٱلْمَلَٰٓئِكَةُ
أَوْ يَأْتِىَ أَمْرُ رَبِّكَ كَذَٰلِكَ فَعَلَ ٱلَّذِينَ
مِن قَبْلِهِمْ وَمَا ظَلَمَهُمُ ٱللَّهُ وَلَٰكِن
كَانُوٓاْ أَنفُسَهُمْ يَظْلِمُونَ ٣٣

Are they [who disbelieve] awaiting anything but for the angels to appear before them, or for your Lord's command to come? Those before them did the same. It was not God who wronged them, but it was they who wronged themselves. (33)

23

The evil consequences of their misdeeds overtook them, and they were overwhelmed by the very thing they used to deride. (34)

فَأَصَابَهُمْ سَيِّئَاتُ مَا عَمِلُواْ وَحَاقَ بِهِم مَّا كَانُواْ بِهِۦ يَسْتَهْزِءُونَ ﴿٣٤﴾

Those who associate partners with God say, 'Had God so willed, neither we nor our forefathers would have worshipped any other than Him, nor would we have declared anything forbidden without a commandment from Him.' Those before them said the same. Are the messengers bound to do anything other than to clearly deliver the message? (35)

وَقَالَ ٱلَّذِينَ أَشْرَكُواْ لَوْ شَآءَ ٱللَّهُ مَا عَبَدْنَا مِن دُونِهِۦ مِن شَيْءٍ نَّحْنُ وَلَآ ءَابَآؤُنَا وَلَا حَرَّمْنَا مِن دُونِهِۦ مِن شَيْءٍ كَذَٰلِكَ فَعَلَ ٱلَّذِينَ مِن قَبْلِهِمْ فَهَلْ عَلَى ٱلرُّسُلِ إِلَّا ٱلْبَلَٰغُ ٱلْمُبِينُ ﴿٣٥﴾

Indeed, We have raised a messenger in every community, [who said to them]: 'Worship God and shun the Evil One.' Among them were some whom God graced with His guidance, while others were inevitably doomed by their error. Go, then, about the earth and observe what was the end of those who denied the truth. (36)

وَلَقَدْ بَعَثْنَا فِي كُلِّ أُمَّةٍ رَّسُولًا أَنِ ٱعْبُدُواْ ٱللَّهَ وَٱجْتَنِبُواْ ٱلطَّٰغُوتَ فَمِنْهُم مَّنْ هَدَى ٱللَّهُ وَمِنْهُم مَّنْ حَقَّتْ عَلَيْهِ ٱلضَّلَٰلَةُ فَسِيرُواْ فِي ٱلْأَرْضِ فَٱنظُرُواْ كَيْفَ كَانَ عَٰقِبَةُ ٱلْمُكَذِّبِينَ ﴿٣٦﴾

However eager you may be to show them the right way, [know that] God does not bestow His guidance upon any whom He judges to have gone astray. They shall have none to support them. (37)

إِن تَحْرِصْ عَلَىٰ هُدَىٰهُمْ فَإِنَّ ٱللَّهَ لَا يَهْدِى مَن يُضِلُّ وَمَا لَهُم مِّن نَّٰصِرِينَ ٣٧

They most solemnly swear by God that God never raises the dead to life. Yes indeed! That is a promise to which He has bound Himself, even though most people do not know it. (38)

وَأَقْسَمُوا۟ بِٱللَّهِ جَهْدَ أَيْمَٰنِهِمْ لَا يَبْعَثُ ٱللَّهُ مَن يَمُوتُ بَلَىٰ وَعْدًا عَلَيْهِ حَقًّا وَلَٰكِنَّ أَكْثَرَ ٱلنَّاسِ لَا يَعْلَمُونَ ٣٨

[Thus] He will make clear to them the reality of matters over which they differ, and the unbelievers will know that they were liars. (39)

لِيُبَيِّنَ لَهُمُ ٱلَّذِى يَخْتَلِفُونَ فِيهِ وَلِيَعْلَمَ ٱلَّذِينَ كَفَرُوٓا۟ أَنَّهُمْ كَانُوا۟ كَٰذِبِينَ ٣٩

Whenever We will anything to be, We need only say, 'Be' – and it is. (40)

إِنَّمَا قَوْلُنَا لِشَىْءٍ إِذَآ أَرَدْنَٰهُ أَن نَّقُولَ لَهُۥ كُن فَيَكُونُ ٤٠

As for those who forsake their homes for the sake of God after having suffered injustice, We shall most certainly give them a fine abode in this life; yet better still is their reward in the life to come, if they but knew it. (41)

وَٱلَّذِينَ هَاجَرُوا۟ فِى ٱللَّهِ مِنۢ بَعْدِ مَا ظُلِمُوا۟ لَنُبَوِّئَنَّهُمْ فِى ٱلدُّنْيَا حَسَنَةً وَلَأَجْرُ ٱلْءَاخِرَةِ أَكْبَرُ لَوْ كَانُوا۟ يَعْلَمُونَ ٤١

[Such reward is granted to] those who, having been patient in adversity, place their trust in their Lord. (42) ⊗

ٱلَّذِينَ صَبَرُواْ وَعَلَىٰ رَبِّهِمْ يَتَوَكَّلُونَ ۝

The messengers We sent before you were but men whom We inspired. So, if you have not realized this, ask those who are endowed with knowledge. (43)

وَمَآ أَرْسَلْنَا مِن قَبْلِكَ إِلَّا رِجَالًا نُّوحِىٓ إِلَيْهِمْ فَسْـَٔلُوٓاْ أَهْلَ ٱلذِّكْرِ إِن كُنتُمْ لَا تَعْلَمُونَ ۝

[We sent such messengers] with clear proofs and divine books, and We have now bestowed on you the reminder so that you may elucidate to mankind all that has been bestowed on them, and that they may take thought. (44)

بِٱلْبَيِّنَٰتِ وَٱلزُّبُرِ وَأَنزَلْنَآ إِلَيْكَ ٱلذِّكْرَ لِتُبَيِّنَ لِلنَّاسِ مَا نُزِّلَ إِلَيْهِمْ وَلَعَلَّهُمْ يَتَفَكَّرُونَ ۝

Do those who devise evil schemes feel secure that God will not cause the earth to swallow them, or that suffering will not befall them whence they do not perceive? (45)

أَفَأَمِنَ ٱلَّذِينَ مَكَرُواْ ٱلسَّيِّئَاتِ أَن يَخْسِفَ ٱللَّهُ بِهِمُ ٱلْأَرْضَ أَوْ يَأْتِيَهُمُ ٱلْعَذَابُ مِنْ حَيْثُ لَا يَشْعُرُونَ ۝

Or that He will not suddenly take them to task in the midst of their comings and goings; for they can never frustrate His design? (46)

أَوْ يَأْخُذَهُمْ فِى تَقَلُّبِهِمْ فَمَا هُم بِمُعْجِزِينَ ۝

Or that He will seize them when they are alert and apprehensive? Surely your Lord is Most Compassionate, Most Merciful. (47)

أَوَيَأْخُذَهُمْ عَلَى تَخَوُّفٍ فَإِنَّ رَبَّكُمْ لَرَءُوفٌ رَّحِيمٌ ۝

Do people not see how every object God has created casts its shadow right and left, prostrating itself before God in complete submission? (48)

أَوَلَمْ يَرَوْاْ إِلَى مَا خَلَقَ اللَّهُ مِن شَيْءٍ يَتَفَيَّؤُاْ ظِلَالُهُ عَنِ الْيَمِينِ وَالشَّمَآئِلِ سُجَّدًا لِّلَّهِ وَهُمْ دَاخِرُونَ ۝

For, before God prostrates itself every living thing in the heavens and the earth, as do the angels. They do not behave in arrogant defiance. (49)

وَلِلَّهِ يَسْجُدُ مَا فِي السَّمَٰوَٰتِ وَمَا فِي الْأَرْضِ مِن دَآبَّةٍ وَالْمَلَٰٓئِكَةُ وَهُمْ لَا يَسْتَكْبِرُونَ ۝

They fear their Lord, who is high above them, and do as they are bidden. (50)

يَخَافُونَ رَبَّهُم مِّن فَوْقِهِمْ وَيَفْعَلُونَ مَا يُؤْمَرُونَ ۩ ۝

Overview

The first passage of this *sūrah* outlined a great many aspects of God's marvellous creation and His blessings which He bestows on His servants, and His knowledge of what is open and what is secret. The other beings which the unbelievers allege to have a share of divinity do not create anything; indeed they themselves are created. They are devoid of knowledge, dead and unlikely ever to come to life. They do not know when their servants are resurrected in order to face the reckoning. This clearly shows that they cannot be deities worthy of worship. Indeed it shows that all beliefs based on a multiplicity of deities are false. This was the first issue raised by the *sūrah* in connection with the question of God's oneness, with an added reference to the question of resurrection.

The present passage picks up where the last one left off, starting a new round which begins with a clear statement of God's oneness. It makes clear that those who do not believe in the Day of Judgement have hearts that are hardened in their denial of the truth. Blindness has become an essential characteristic that prevents them from admitting the truth to which signs clearly testify. Their arrogance stops them from acknowledging what they feel to be the truth and accepting its message. The passage concludes with a touching scene in which we see all shadows prostrating themselves, together with every living thing in the heavens and earth, as well as the angels, to God. These are free of arrogance. They fear God and obey His command without dissent. This scene of complete obedience contrasts with that of the hardened unbelievers arrogantly denying the truth at the beginning of the passage.

In between these two scenes, the *sūrah* reports what the arrogant unbelievers say about revelations and about the Qur'ān. They allege that all this is merely fables of the ancients. It also reports their claims about the reasons for their associating partners with God, their prohibition of what God has made lawful, alleging that God wants them to do what is evil and that He accepts it from them. It quotes their assertions about resurrection and judgement, as they emphatically swear that God does not bring back to life anyone who has died. It answers all their claims, portraying them as they face their death, and as they are brought back to life disclaiming their false assertions.

The *sūrah* also paints scenes of the fate of earlier communities which denied the truth like the unbelievers do. It warns them against being seized by God at any moment of the day or night, when they are totally unaware, either moving around on earth, or feeling apprehensive, expecting God's punishment to overwhelm them. In this passage the *sūrah* also reports what the believers say, and what they expect when they are gathered to God, and what awaits them of goodly reward on the Day of Judgement. The passage concludes with a scene of total serenity and complete obedience demonstrated by all, including shadows, living creatures and angels, in heaven and on earth.

Unbelief Compounded by Arrogance

Your God is the One God. Those who deny the life to come have hearts that persist in denying the truth. They are full of arrogance. God surely knows what they keep secret and all that they bring into the open. He does not love those who are arrogant. (Verses 22–23)

The *sūrah* provides a clear link between believing in God's oneness and believing in the Day of Judgement. Indeed it makes the one evidence for the other, as worshipping God alone is closely associated with belief in resurrection and reward. It is in the hereafter that God's wisdom and justice are clearly and fully manifested.

"*Your God is the One God.*" All that the *sūrah* has outlined of great signs of creation and blessing, and also of the signs of His perfect knowledge, lead to this clear truth. A truth with manifest effects seen in the harmony and complementarity of the laws of nature governing the universe.

Those who reject this great truth, and do not believe in the hereafter, are not short of proof and evidence. The fault lies rather with them and their own hardened natures. Their hearts persistently deny the very signs they see. They are arrogant, unwilling to accept clear evidence, submit to God, and believe in His Messenger.

God who has created them knows this. Indeed He knows what they keep secret and what they do and say in the open, and He does not like what He knows of them. They are full of arrogance. "*He does not love those who are arrogant.*" (Verse 23) An arrogant nature is unlikely to be convinced or to submit to the truth. It is their arrogance that makes them unloved by God.

Whenever they are asked, 'What has your Lord bestowed from on high?' they say: 'Fables of the ancients!' On the Day of Resurrection they shall bear the full weight of their burdens, as well as some of the burdens of those ignorant ones whom they have led astray. Evil is the burden they shall bear. (Verses 24–25)

Those arrogant people with hardened, unresponsive hearts are asked, '*What has your Lord bestowed from on high?*' (Verse 24) But they do

29

not give the direct and normal answer, quoting some verses from the Qur'ān or stating their import without distortion to prove their honest reporting even though they may not believe in it. They give instead a dishonest answer, saying, '*Fables of the ancients!*' (Verse 24) A fable is defined as 'a story not founded on fact, a legend or myth.' Thus do they describe the Qur'ān which addresses minds and souls, deals with life situations, human behaviour, social interactions as well as people's conditions, past, present and future. They only describe it as such because it relates some parts of the history of earlier communities. Their denial of the truth thus leads them to bear the burden of their own sins, as well as a portion of the burdens of those whom they lead astray, preventing them from believing in God and the Qur'ān, keeping them unaware of its truth and nature. The Qur'ān describes these sins as heavy burdens. Indeed, they are foul burdens. They weigh heavily on people's souls like loads weigh heavily on their backs. They trouble hearts like burdens trouble the body. Indeed they are worse and even more troublesome than physical burdens, heavy as these may be.

A Wicked Campaign

Ibn Abī Ḥātim reports: "The elders of the Quraysh met for consultation. Some of them said: 'Muḥammad is a man of fine argument. If he speaks to a man, he soon gets hold of him. Therefore, select some of your most honourable people, whose lines of ancestry are well known. Let them take their positions at every route into Makkah, at one or two day's distance, so that they turn away anyone who comes to meet Muḥammad.' People did just that. If any of them met a man sent by his people to find out about Muḥammad, he would introduce himself to him, telling him his position among his people. He would then offer to tell him about the Prophet, saying, 'He is a liar who has been followed only by slaves and ignorant people, and those who are good for nothing. All wise men among his people have taken a clear stand against him.' This would be enough to turn many people away. It is to this that God refers in the verse stating: "*Whenever they are asked, 'What has your Lord bestowed from on high?' they say: 'Fables of the ancients!*'" (Verse 24)

"On the other hand, if the man sent to find out about the Prophet is one to whom God has given insight, he would say: 'I am certainly a bad intelligence gatherer if, having reached so close, I am to return now without meeting this man and listening to what he says in order to give my people a true picture of him.' He would insist on going into Makkah, where he would meet the believers and where they would tell him that all that Muḥammad says is good and fine."

This was a well orchestrated propaganda campaign mounted by the Quraysh against Islam. A similar campaign is organized in every generation by arrogant people who do not wish to submit to the truth despite all the evidence supporting it. Indeed the arrogant among the Quraysh were not the first to deny the truth or to scheme against it. The *surah* draws for them a picture of the fate suffered by schemers before them, and their destiny in the hereafter. It shows them what they endure from the moment their souls part with their bodies until they receive their punishment in the life to come. All this is depicted in vivid images, following the inimitable style of the Qur'ān:

> *Those who lived before them also schemed. But God struck their edifice at its foundation, and its roof fell in upon them from above, and suffering befell them from where they did not perceive. Then, on the Day of Resurrection He will cover them with ignominy, and say: 'Where are those alleged partners of Mine concerning whom you have engaged in dispute?' Those who are endowed with knowledge will say: 'Ignominy and misery shall this day befall the unbelievers, those whom the angels have gathered in death while they are still wronging themselves.' These will then offer their submission, saying: 'We have done no wrong!' [They will be answered]: 'Yes, indeed. God has full knowledge of all that you were doing! Enter the gates of hell, where you shall abide.' Evil indeed is the abode of the arrogant!* (Verses 26–29)

"*Those who lived before them also schemed.*" (Verse 26) The *surah* paints their scheming as though it was a building with foundations, corners, ceiling and roof, which implies that it was a massive and well designed plot. But nothing can stand up to God's might: "*But God struck their edifice at its foundation, and its roof fell in upon them from above."* (Verse 26) This paints a picture of total destruction, overtaking them from beneath their feet and above their heads. The foundations supporting the building collapse, and the roof falls down burying them. *"And suffering befell them from where they did not perceive."* (Verse 26) Thus the building they very carefully constructed to provide them with shelter becomes their burial ground as they are overwhelmed from every direction. Little did they think that what they built for shelter would become the instrument of their own destruction.

The image we have here is one of complete destruction. This is the perfect irony directed at those who scheme and plot against God's message, believing that their scheming is too strong and elaborate to ever be foiled. But God's own scheming is far too weighty for them to oppose. This scene is often repeated. The Quraysh were not the first to take this stand, nor would they be the last. On the other hand, God's message goes on along its clear way, no matter what the plotters devise. People turn around from time to time, and they see that highly effective scene portrayed by the Qur'ān: *"But God struck their edifice at its foundation, and its roof fell in upon them from above, and suffering befell them from where they did not perceive."* (Verse 26)

All this takes place in the present life on earth. But there is something else beyond: *"Then, on the Day of Resurrection He will cover them with ignominy, and say: 'Where are those alleged partners of Mine concerning whom you have engaged in dispute?'"* (Verse 27) This is now a scene of the hereafter, where we see the plotters stand up in shame, and when their arrogance and scheming is no longer of any use to them. They stand in front of the One to whom all creation and all authority belong. He will rebuke them, asking: *"Where are those alleged partners of Mine concerning whom you have engaged in dispute?"* You were keen to dispute with My Messenger and his followers who acknowledged My oneness, claiming that your false deities were My partners. Where are they now?

In their shame and humiliation, they will remain silent. On the other hand, those endowed with knowledge, angels, messengers and true believers, whom God permits to speak, will say plainly and forcefully: *"Ignominy and misery shall this day befall the unbelievers."* (Verse 27)

Now they are taken a step backwards, and described at the moment they face death. *"Ignominy and misery shall this day befall the unbelievers, those whom the angels have gathered in death while they are still wronging themselves."* (Verses 27–28) The angels are gathering their souls which they themselves have wronged by depriving themselves of the light and reassurance of faith. By their own actions they have brought about their own ruin, and now they have to suffer punishment in hell.

The *sūrah* paints their position at the moment of their death, when they are still close to earth and to all the falsehood they asserted here, and all their evil scheming: *"These will then offer their submission, saying: 'We have done no wrong!'"* (Verse 28) Those who used to revel in their arrogance are now submissive, unable to contend. They offer complete submission! But at the same time they lie. This may be an aspect of their plotting in this life as they submissively say: *"We have done no wrong!"*

Yet the answer comes to them straightaway from God who knows their true reality: *"Yes, indeed. God has full knowledge of all that you were doing!"* (Verse 28) There is no room now for lies or deception. They have to suffer the fate of all arrogant peoples who deny the truth: *"Enter the gates of hell, where you shall abide. Evil indeed is the abode of the arrogant!"* (Verse 29)

A Perfect Contrast

On the other side stand the God-fearing. Their picture contrasts fully with that of the arrogant unbelievers, in origin and destiny:

> But when the God-fearing are asked: 'What has your Lord revealed?' they say: 'All that is good.' For those who do good in this world, good reward [is assured]; but far better is their abode in the hereafter. Blessed is the dwelling place of the God-fearing. The Gardens of Eden they will enter; through which running waters flow. There they shall have everything they desire. Thus shall God reward the God-fearing; those whom the angels gather in death while they are

in a state of purity, saying: 'Peace be upon you! Enter paradise by virtue of what you were doing [in life.]' (Verses 30–32)

The God-fearing realize that the very essence of the divine message and all that God has revealed of directives, commandments and laws is good and perfect. Hence when they are questioned about what God has revealed from on high, they sum it up in a word: *"All that is good."* They go on to outline this good that God has revealed, according to what they have learnt from God's revelations: *"For those who do good in this world, good reward is assured."* (Verse 30) They enjoy a good life and have a good position. However, *"Far better is their abode in the hereafter."* It is certainly better than all there is in this present life. *"Blessed is the dwelling place of the God-fearing."* (Verse 30) More details are now given about this abode of the hereafter, which is shown to be a goodly one indeed: *"The Gardens of Eden they will enter, through which running waters flow."* (Verse 31) In such a place and with such resources they have comforts and luxuries in abundance. *"There they shall have everything they desire."* (Verse 31) They will want for nothing. Every good thing is provided without any limit on what God grants them. *"Thus shall God reward the God-fearing."* (Verse 31)

Again the *sūrah* takes a step backwards to show the God-fearing believers as they are about to die. It is an easy scene, as they are comforted by the angels: *"Those whom the angels gather in death while they are in a state of purity."* (Verse 32) They are in a comfortable, pure condition, looking forward to meeting God, having nothing to fear. The angels greet them: *"Peace be upon you!"* (Verse 32) This is a greeting of welcome and reassurance. They follow this by delivering the happiest news of all: *"Enter paradise by virtue of what you were doing [in life]."* (Verse 32)

At the end of this scene with its two aspects of death and resurrection, the *sūrah* queries what the idolaters of the Quraysh are waiting for? Are they waiting for the angels to gather their souls, or for God's command to resurrect them? For this is what happens to them on death and then on the day when resurrection takes place by God's command. Yet they have a clear lesson in what happened to earlier communities. They have been shown two images delineating what happens to both parties:

> *Are they [who disbelieve] awaiting anything but for the angels to appear before them, or for your Lord's command to come? Those before them did the same. It was not God who wronged them, but it was they who wronged themselves. The evil consequences of their misdeeds overtook them, and they were overwhelmed by the very thing they used to deride.* (Verses 33–34)

The attitude of human beings is amazing. They see what happened to people of earlier generations who followed the same course they follow. But they do not take heed. They do not believe that what happened to earlier communities can happen to them. They do not realize that the laws of nature operate in accordance with a well defined pattern, and that premises lead to their natural conclusions, actions receive their just reward, and God's law will not be suspended to appease anyone.

"*It was not God who wronged them, but it was they who wronged themselves.*" (Verse 33) God has given them the freedom of thought and choice. He has shown them all His signs placed in the universe around them and within their own souls, warning them against the consequences of their actions. He then left them to choose, and to bear the consequences of their own doings in accordance with His laws. Thus He has not wronged them in any way. Their fate is a case of action rebounding on the perpetrator.

Indeed God does not inflict too severe a punishment on them. Instead, their own misdeeds were severe, and it is these they have to endure the natural consequences of: "*The evil consequences of their misdeeds overtook them, and they were overwhelmed by the very thing they used to deride.*" (Verse 34) This verse and similar ones are very significant. People are not punished with anything other than the natural consequences of their own actions. These are the very things which sink them to a degree lower than that of human beings. Hence they are punished with something lower than what is fitting for humans. They endure a humiliating abode and painful suffering.

Two Ways for Mankind

Now the *sūrah* reports yet another argument advanced by the unbelievers, to explain the reasons for their disbelief.

> *Those who associate partners with God say, 'Had God so willed, neither we nor our forefathers would have worshipped any other than Him, nor would we have declared anything forbidden without a commandment from Him.' Those before them said the same. Are the messengers bound to do anything other than to clearly deliver the message? Indeed, We have raised a messenger in every community, [who said to them]: 'Worship God and shun the Evil One.' Among them were some whom God graced with His guidance, while others were inevitably doomed by their error. Go, then, about the earth and observe what was the end of those who denied the truth.* (Verses 35–36)

They lay on God's will the blame for all their own and their forefathers' deviant beliefs, their worship of false deities, as also for their misguided concepts leading them to prohibit what God had made lawful without any clear authority from Him. They allege that none of them would have done anything of the sort, had God willed to prevent it. This is a grossly mistaken view of God's will and how it operates. Furthermore, it deprives man of the most important quality which God has given him in this life.

God's will is never directed so as to make His servants associate partners with Him. Nor is He ever pleased when they prohibit what He has made lawful. This is clearly stated in His law contained in His messages to mankind. The messengers were only assigned the task of delivering His message, and they were up to the task, exerting their best efforts to fulfil it: "*We have raised a messenger in every community, [who said to them]: 'Worship God and shun the Evil One.'*" (Verse 36) This is the command He issued, outlining what He wishes His servants to do. God Almighty does not order His servants to do something which He knows them to be, by nature, unable to do, or to do what He has compelled them to avoid. The clear evidence proving His displeasure with those who disobey His orders is the punishment which

He inflicted in former times on those who denied His messages and messengers. Hence He draws attention here to the fate of those disobedient communities: "*Go, then, about the earth and observe what was the end of those who denied the truth.*" (Verse 36)

God, the Creator, the Wise, has willed that human beings should have an equal propensity either to follow His guidance or to go astray, and that their choice of which way to follow should be completely free. He has also given them reason and intellect in order to be able to determine which way to choose. He has placed in the universe numerous pointers to guidance, and these signs are there for them to see, hear, sense and feel wherever they turn at any moment of the night or day, leading their minds to the right conclusion.

Out of His grace, which He gives in abundance, God has not left His servants to make their choice only on the basis of their reasoning. He has given in His laws, which were outlined by His messengers, a clear and constant standard for people to follow when they need guidance. By using this standard, which is not subject to people's wishes and desires, they are able to determine right and wrong on any matter. He did not make His messengers overbearing tyrants who used brute force to compel people to believe in Him. These messengers were only carriers of His messages, assigned only the task of delivering them. They called on people to worship God alone, to steer away from every type of belief that associates partners with Him, and to shun submission to any power other than God's: "*We have raised a messenger in every community, [who said to them]: 'Worship God and shun the Evil One.'*" (Verse 36)

Some people respond positively to God's message: "*Among them were some whom God graced with His guidance.*" (Verse 36) Another group chose error: "*Others were inevitably doomed by their error.*" (Verse 36) Neither party has broken away from God's will for He did not compel them to follow one way or the other. Each chose the way for himself after having been given sufficient guidance to distinguish between truth and error. Such guidance is placed within man himself and is also made available everywhere in the universe around him.

This statement also refutes the false argument advanced by the idolaters and repeated by many of those who commit every kind of disobedience of God. Islam is very clear on this point. God orders His servants to do only what is right and good, and He forbids them only what is evil. He may sometimes choose to inflict clear punishments which plainly reflect His displeasure. But this does not mean that He intervenes to compel them to go astray and then punishes them for something over which they claim to have no choice. This is absolutely false. They are completely free to follow the way they choose, and that freedom is given them by God's will. Whatever good or evil they do, then, takes place by God's will in this sense only.

This explains the comment given in the form of an address to the Prophet outlining the law determining what people may follow of guidance or error: *"However eager you may be to show them the right way, [know that] God does not bestow His guidance upon any whom He judges to have gone astray. They shall have none to support them."* (Verse 37) People's acceptance of divine guidance is not the result of the Prophet's deliberations and efforts. This is not his task. His mission is only to deliver the message God gave him. Guidance and error are subject to God's law which never fails, bringing the same results every time. Whoever deserves to remain in error according to God's law shall not receive His guidance. That is because of the operation of the laws God has set in nature. This is His will which is always done. Hence, *"they shall have none to support them."* Besides, who can support them against God?

The Truth of Resurrection

The unbelievers make yet another argument to justify their rejection of the divine message. *"They most solemnly swear by God that God never raises the dead to life. Yes indeed! That is a promise to which He has bound Himself, even though most people do not know it. [Thus] He will make clear to them the reality of matters over which they differ, and the unbelievers will know that they were liars. Whenever We will anything to be, We need only say, 'Be' – and it is."* (Verses 38–40)

The question of resurrection has been the main point of contention among many communities ever since God sent His messengers to mankind, commanding them to do what is good and forbidding them

38

what is evil, warning them always that they are accountable for their deeds before God on the Day of Judgement.

Yet these people from the Quraysh were ready to solemnly swear that God will not raise anyone to life after death. In other words, they acknowledge God's existence but deny that the dead will be brought back to life by Him. They consider such resurrection to be impossible after bodies have decomposed, organs separated and molecules are scattered everywhere. They overlook the miraculous nature of life in the first place. They are oblivious to the nature of God's power and the fact that it cannot be compared with that of human beings or their abilities. They do not realize that to bring anything into existence does not trouble God in any way, and does not place any burden whatsoever on His power. It is sufficient for Him to decide to bring something into existence for that thing to exist.

Human beings are also oblivious of God's purpose behind resurrection. The fact is that nothing reaches its fullness in this life. People differ on truth and falsehood, right and error, good and evil, etc. Their differences and disputes cannot be settled or reach the right conclusion in this life on earth. It is a matter of God's will that some of them live long, and that they are not held to account for their deeds during this life. Thus, reward and punishment are administered in the hereafter when everything reaches its fullness.

The *sūrah* replies to the unbelievers' assertion that the dead will not be resurrected. It dispels people's doubts with an emphatic assertion: "*Yes indeed! That is a promise to which He has bound Himself.*" (Verse 38) When God makes a promise, then that promise is fulfilled without fail. "*Even though most people do not know it.*" (Verse 38) People are rarely aware of the true nature of a promise made by God.

The whole thing has a definite purpose: "*He will make clear to them the reality of matters over which they differ, and the unbelievers will know that they were liars.*" (Verse 39) They lie when they allege that their methods are based on true guidance, when they accuse God's messengers of lying, and when they deny the life to come and entertain concepts and beliefs that are false and lack basis. Besides, resurrection is so easy: "*Whenever We will anything to be, We need only say, 'Be' –*

and it is." (Verse 40) Resurrection is one such easy thing. It will take place once God wills it to.

In contrast to those who persist in denying the truth, the *sūrah* provides a glimpse of the true believers who are prepared to abandon their homes and migrate in order to lend support to God's cause. Their only motivation is their faith in God and in the hereafter.

> *As for those who forsake their homes for the sake of God after having suffered injustice, We shall most certainly give them a fine abode in this life; yet better still is their reward in the life to come, if they but knew it. [Such reward is granted to] those who, having been patient in adversity, place their trust in their Lord.* (Verses 41–42)

These are the people who migrate, leaving their homes, abandoning all property and belongings, sacrificing an easy life with their own peoples and communities. They seek only God's reward. When they experience tyranny and injustice, they leave their homeland in order to live a life of obedience to God. Hence, God promises them in return for the loss of their homes something that they will like: *"We shall most certainly give them a fine abode in this life."* (Verse 41) They will be well compensated for their loss: *"yet better still is their reward in the life to come,"* but people are rarely aware of the fact. Such people have important qualities which deserve God's reward. Hence when they persevere in the face of hardship, and they are *"patient in adversity,"* their reward is assured. This is because they *"place their trust in their Lord."* (Verse 42) They associate no partner with Him in belief, reliance and trust.

The *sūrah* reiterates the task of God's messengers. This comes in the context of highlighting the mission of the last Messenger and the revelations bestowed on him from on high. This forms a prelude to warnings threatening the unbelievers with severe punishment.

> *The messengers We sent before you were but men whom We inspired. So, if you have not realized this, ask those who are endowed with knowledge. [We sent such messengers] with clear proofs and divine books, and We have now bestowed on you the reminder so that you may elucidate to mankind all that has been bestowed on them, and that they may take thought.* (Verses 43–44)

Those messengers We sent in former times were men too. We did not send angels or any other type of creation. They were men chosen for a task: *"whom We inspired,"* just like We inspire you. Their task, like yours, was simply to deliver their message. *"So... ask those who are endowed with knowledge"*, i.e. the people and nations to whom messengers were sent in earlier times. Ask them, *"if you have not realized this [fact]"*, to make sure whether those messengers were men or angels or belonged to some other type of creation. We certainly sent human messengers *"with clear proofs"*, and We gave divine books, and, *"We have now bestowed on you the reminder that you may elucidate to mankind all that has been bestowed on them."* (Verse 44) This applies to those who received earlier revelations but who then differed among themselves concerning the messages contained in their divine books. The Qur'ān provides a clear judgement in their disputes. This also applies to the Prophet's contemporaries, the first community to be addressed by the Qur'ān. The Prophet was there to explain it to them and to provide practical guidance on how it should be implemented in their lives. *"And that they may take thought,"* on the signs God has placed in the universe confirming the message of truth, and reflect on the Qur'ānic revelations. Indeed the Qur'ān always calls on people to reflect and use their reason.

Universal Submission to God's Power

The present passage started with a reference to those who plot and scheme. It now concludes with two highly charged emotional touches. The first warns that against God's scheme no one is safe at any time of the night or day. The other invites people to join the whole universe in extolling God's praises and worshipping Him. Only man can refuse to submit to God, while everything around him glorifies and praises God:

Do those who devise evil schemes feel secure that God will not cause the earth to swallow them, or that suffering will not befall them whence they do not perceive? – Or that He will not suddenly take them to task in the midst of their comings and goings; for they can never frustrate His design? – Or that He will seize them when they are alert and apprehensive? Surely your Lord is Most Compassionate,

41

Most Merciful. Do people not see how every object God has created casts its shadow right and left, prostrating itself before God in complete submission? For, before God prostrates itself every living thing in the heavens and the earth, as do the angels. They do not behave in arrogant defiance. They fear their Lord, who is high above them, and do as they are bidden. (Verses 45–50)

It is indeed most amazing that human beings see how God's hand is working yet they take no heed. Those of them who scheme continue their plotting, and those who thus far have been safe continue to feel secure against a strike that will overwhelm them just as happened to other people before them. They entertain no fear that God may inflict punishment on them at any moment, whether they are asleep or awake, mindful or oblivious of what is going on around them. The *sūrah* warns them of the impending danger which they may ignore at their peril: *"Do those who devise evil schemes feel secure that God will not cause the earth to swallow them, or that suffering will not befall them whence they do not perceive?"* (Verse 45) Or do they feel secure that God will not smite them at any time while they travel about on business or pleasure. *"They can never frustrate His design."* (Verse 46) They are not immune from His punishment wherever they happen to be. Or do they feel safe against a strike which *"will seize them when they are alert and apprehensive?"* (Verse 47) Their expectation of danger and alertness to it will not frustrate God's will. He is just as able to seize them when they fully expect danger as He is able to take them unawares. The fact remains that God *"is Most Compassionate, Most Merciful."* (Verse 47)

The question has to be asked again: Do those who devise evil schemes feel secure against God's punishment? They are certainly totally oblivious to what is going on around them whereby the whole universe, with all its laws and phenomena, delivers a message of submission to God and acceptance of His will: *"Do people not see how every object God has created casts its shadow right and left, prostrating itself before God in complete submission? For, before God prostrates itself every living thing in the heavens and the earth, as do the angels. They do not behave*

42

in arrogant defiance. They fear their Lord, who is high above them, and do as they are bidden." (Verses 48–50)

The image drawn here is one of shadows extending and retreating, moving and standing still. It is highly inspiring, provided that we open our hearts, alert our senses and respond to what goes on in the universe around us. The Qur'ān expresses the notion of submission to God's laws by prostration. This is indeed the most expressive aspect of submission. The *sūrah* thus alerts us to the gentle movement of shades, for it profoundly influences our feelings. It depicts all creatures, 'in complete submission'. It also adds the angels to this universal grouping. This gives us a wonderful image of living creatures, shadows, inanimate objects and angels in a position of full submission to God. It depicts their complete devotion and sincere worship. None is too proud to refuse to worship Him or to disobey His command. Only a group of arrogant human beings jarr the tune in this remarkable orchestration.

Thus this passage, having started with a reference to arrogant unbelievers, concludes with isolating such arrogant humans in a scene that comprises the whole universe.

3

The One and Only God

God has said: 'Do not take [for worship] two deities, for He is but one God. Hence, of Me alone stand in awe.' (51)

وَقَالَ ٱللَّهُ لَا تَتَّخِذُوٓاْ إِلَٰهَيْنِ ٱثْنَيْنِۖ إِنَّمَا هُوَ إِلَٰهٌ وَٰحِدٌۖ فَإِيَّٰيَ فَٱرْهَبُونِ ۝

His is all that is in the heavens and the earth, and to Him alone submission is always due. Will you then fear anyone but God? (52)

وَلَهُۥ مَا فِى ٱلسَّمَٰوَٰتِ وَٱلْأَرْضِ وَلَهُ ٱلدِّينُ وَاصِبًاۚ أَفَغَيْرَ ٱللَّهِ تَتَّقُونَ ۝

Whatever blessing you have comes from God; and whenever harm befalls you, it is to Him that you cry out for help. (53)

وَمَا بِكُم مِّن نِّعْمَةٍ فَمِنَ ٱللَّهِۖ ثُمَّ إِذَا مَسَّكُمُ ٱلضُّرُّ فَإِلَيْهِ تَجْـَٔرُونَ ۝

Yet no sooner does He remove the harm from you than some among you associate partners with their Lord, (54)

ثُمَّ إِذَا كَشَفَ ٱلضُّرَّ عَنكُمْ إِذَا فَرِيقٌ مِّنكُم بِرَبِّهِمْ يُشْرِكُونَ ۝

[as if] to show their ingratitude for what We have given them. Enjoy, then, your life [as you may]; before long you will come to know [the truth]. (55)

لِيَكْفُرُواْ بِمَآ ءَاتَيْنَٰهُمْۚ فَتَمَتَّعُواْ فَسَوْفَ تَعْلَمُونَ ۝

They assign a share of the sustenance We provide for them to what they know nothing of. By God, you shall certainly be called to account for your false inventions. (56)

وَيَجْعَلُونَ لِمَا لَا يَعْلَمُونَ نَصِيبًا مِّمَّا رَزَقْنَاهُمْ تَاللَّهِ لَتُسْأَلُنَّ عَمَّا كُنتُمْ تَفْتَرُونَ ۝

And they assign daughters to God, who is limitless in His glory, whereas for themselves they choose what they desire. (57)

وَيَجْعَلُونَ لِلَّهِ الْبَنَاتِ سُبْحَانَهُ وَلَهُم مَّا يَشْتَهُونَ ۝

And when any of them is given the happy news of the birth of a girl, his face darkens and he is filled with gloom. (58)

وَإِذَا بُشِّرَ أَحَدُهُم بِالْأُنثَىٰ ظَلَّ وَجْهُهُ مُسْوَدًّا وَهُوَ كَظِيمٌ ۝

He tries to avoid all people on account of the [allegedly] bad news he has received, [debating within himself:] shall he keep the child despite the shame he feels, or shall he bury it in the dust? Evil indeed is their judgement. (59)

يَتَوَارَىٰ مِنَ الْقَوْمِ مِن سُوءِ مَا بُشِّرَ بِهِ أَيُمْسِكُهُ عَلَىٰ هُونٍ أَمْ يَدُسُّهُ فِي التُّرَابِ أَلَا سَاءَ مَا يَحْكُمُونَ ۝

To those who do not believe in the life to come applies the attribute of evil, whereas to God applies the attribute of all that is most sublime, for He is Almighty, Wise. (60)

لِلَّذِينَ لَا يُؤْمِنُونَ بِالْآخِرَةِ مَثَلُ السَّوْءِ وَلِلَّهِ الْمَثَلُ الْأَعْلَىٰ وَهُوَ الْعَزِيزُ الْحَكِيمُ ۝

If God were to take people to task for their wrongdoing, He would not leave a single living creature on the face [of the earth]. But He gives them respite for a set term. When their time arrives, they cannot delay it by an hour, nor can they hasten it. (61)

وَلَوْ يُؤَاخِذُ اللَّهُ النَّاسَ بِظُلْمِهِم مَّا تَرَكَ عَلَيْهَا مِن دَآبَّةٍ وَلَكِن يُؤَخِّرُهُمْ إِلَىٰ أَجَلٍ مُّسَمًّى فَإِذَا جَآءَ أَجَلُهُمْ لَا يَسْتَخْرُونَ سَاعَةً وَلَا يَسْتَقْدِمُونَ ۝

They attribute to God what they hate [for themselves]. And their tongues assert the lie that theirs is the supreme reward. Without doubt, it is the Fire that awaits them, and they will be hastened on into it. (62)

وَيَجْعَلُونَ لِلَّهِ مَا يَكْرَهُونَ وَتَصِفُ أَلْسِنَتُهُمُ الْكَذِبَ أَنَّ لَهُمُ الْحُسْنَىٰ لَا جَرَمَ أَنَّ لَهُمُ النَّارَ وَأَنَّهُم مُّفْرَطُونَ ۝

By God, We have sent messengers to various communities before your time, but Satan made their foul deeds seem fair to them. He is also their patron today. A grievous suffering awaits them. (63)

تَاللَّهِ لَقَدْ أَرْسَلْنَا إِلَىٰ أُمَمٍ مِّن قَبْلِكَ فَزَيَّنَ لَهُمُ الشَّيْطَنُ أَعْمَالَهُمْ فَهُوَ وَلِيُّهُمُ الْيَوْمَ وَلَهُمْ عَذَابٌ أَلِيمٌ ۝

We have bestowed upon you from on high this book for no other reason than that you may make clear to them those issues on which they differ, and [to serve] as guidance and grace to people who believe. (64)

وَمَا أَنزَلْنَا عَلَيْكَ الْكِتَبَ إِلَّا لِتُبَيِّنَ لَهُمُ الَّذِي اخْتَلَفُوا فِيهِ وَهُدًى وَرَحْمَةً لِّقَوْمٍ يُؤْمِنُونَ ۝

And God sends down water from the skies, giving life to the earth after it has been lifeless. In this there is surely a sign for people who listen. (65)

وَٱللَّهُ أَنزَلَ مِنَ ٱلسَّمَآءِ مَآءً فَأَحْيَا بِهِ ٱلْأَرْضَ بَعْدَ مَوْتِهَآ إِنَّ فِى ذَٰلِكَ لَآيَةً لِّقَوْمٍ يَسْمَعُونَ ۝

In cattle too you have a worthy lesson: We give you to drink of that [fluid] which is in their bellies, produced alongside excretions and blood: pure milk, pleasant to those who drink it. (66)

وَإِنَّ لَكُمْ فِى ٱلْأَنْعَٰمِ لَعِبْرَةً نُّسْقِيكُم مِّمَّا فِى بُطُونِهِ مِنۢ بَيْنِ فَرْثٍ وَدَمٍ لَّبَنًا خَالِصًا سَآئِغًا لِّلشَّٰرِبِينَ ۝

And from the fruit of the date-palms and vines you derive intoxicants and wholesome food. Surely in this there is a sign for people who use their reason. (67)

وَمِن ثَمَرَٰتِ ٱلنَّخِيلِ وَٱلْأَعْنَٰبِ تَتَّخِذُونَ مِنْهُ سَكَرًا وَرِزْقًا حَسَنًا إِنَّ فِى ذَٰلِكَ لَآيَةً لِّقَوْمٍ يَعْقِلُونَ ۝

Your Lord has inspired the bee: 'Take up homes in the mountains, in the trees and in structures people may put up. (68)

وَأَوْحَىٰ رَبُّكَ إِلَى ٱلنَّحْلِ أَنِ ٱتَّخِذِى مِنَ ٱلْجِبَالِ بُيُوتًا وَمِنَ ٱلشَّجَرِ وَمِمَّا يَعْرِشُونَ ۝

Then eat of all manner of fruit, and follow humbly the paths your Lord has made smooth for you.' There issues from its inside a drink of different colours, a cure for people. Surely in this there is a sign for people who think. (69)

ثُمَّ كُلِى مِن كُلِّ ٱلثَّمَرَٰتِ فَٱسْلُكِى سُبُلَ رَبِّكِ ذُلُلًا يَخْرُجُ مِنۢ بُطُونِهَا شَرَابٌ مُّخْتَلِفٌ أَلْوَٰنُهُ فِيهِ شِفَآءٌ لِّلنَّاسِ إِنَّ فِى ذَٰلِكَ لَآيَةً لِّقَوْمٍ يَتَفَكَّرُونَ ۝

It is God who has created you; and in time will cause you to die. Some of you are left to the most feeble stage of life, so that they no longer know what they had previously known. God is indeed All-Knowing, infinite in His power. (70)

وَٱللَّهُ خَلَقَكُمۡ ثُمَّ يَتَوَفَّىٰكُمۡ وَمِنكُم مَّن يُرَدُّ إِلَىٰٓ أَرۡذَلِ ٱلۡعُمُرِ لِكَىۡ لَا يَعۡلَمَ بَعۡدَ عِلۡمٖ شَيۡـًٔا إِنَّ ٱللَّهَ عَلِيمٞ قَدِيرٞ ۝

To some of you God has given more than He has given to others. Those who are so favoured are unwilling to share their provisions with those whom their right hands possess, so that they are all equal in this respect. Will they, then, deny God's favours? (71)

وَٱللَّهُ فَضَّلَ بَعۡضَكُمۡ عَلَىٰ بَعۡضٖ فِي ٱلرِّزۡقِ فَمَا ٱلَّذِينَ فُضِّلُواْ بِرَآدِّي رِزۡقِهِمۡ عَلَىٰ مَا مَلَكَتۡ أَيۡمَٰنُهُمۡ فَهُمۡ فِيهِ سَوَآءٌ أَفَبِنِعۡمَةِ ٱللَّهِ يَجۡحَدُونَ ۝

And God has given you spouses of your own kind and has given you, through your spouses, children and grandchildren, and provided you with wholesome sustenance. Will they, then, believe in falsehood and deny God's grace and blessings? (72)

وَٱللَّهُ جَعَلَ لَكُم مِّنۡ أَنفُسِكُمۡ أَزۡوَٰجٗا وَجَعَلَ لَكُم مِّنۡ أَزۡوَٰجِكُم بَنِينَ وَحَفَدَةٗ وَرَزَقَكُم مِّنَ ٱلطَّيِّبَٰتِ أَفَبِٱلۡبَٰطِلِ يُؤۡمِنُونَ وَبِنِعۡمَتِ ٱللَّهِ هُمۡ يَكۡفُرُونَ ۝

Instead of God, they worship something that can provide them with no sustenance from the heavens or the earth. Never can they have such power. (73)

وَيَعۡبُدُونَ مِن دُونِ ٱللَّهِ مَا لَا يَمۡلِكُ لَهُمۡ رِزۡقٗا مِّنَ ٱلسَّمَٰوَٰتِ وَٱلۡأَرۡضِ شَيۡـٔٗا وَلَا يَسۡتَطِيعُونَ ۝

Do not, then, compare anything with God. Indeed, God knows all, whereas you have no knowledge. (74)

فَلَا تَضْرِبُوا لِلَّهِ الْأَمْثَالَ إِنَّ اللَّهَ يَعْلَمُ وَأَنتُمْ لَا تَعْلَمُونَ ۝

God makes this comparison between a man enslaved, unable to do anything of his own accord, and a [free] man on whom We have bestowed goodly favours, and he gives of it both in private and in public. Can these two be equal? All praise is to God alone, but most people have no knowledge. (75)

ضَرَبَ اللَّهُ مَثَلًا عَبْدًا مَّمْلُوكًا لَّا يَقْدِرُ عَلَى شَيْءٍ وَمَن رَّزَقْنَٰهُ مِنَّا رِزْقًا حَسَنًا فَهُوَ يُنفِقُ مِنْهُ سِرًّا وَجَهْرًا هَلْ يَسْتَوُونَ الْحَمْدُ لِلَّهِ بَلْ أَكْثَرُهُمْ لَا يَعْلَمُونَ ۝

And God makes another comparison between two men, one of whom is dumb and can do nothing of his own accord. He is a sheer burden to his master: wherever he sends him, he accomplishes no good. Can he be considered equal to one who enjoins justice and follows a straight path? (76)

وَضَرَبَ اللَّهُ مَثَلًا رَّجُلَيْنِ أَحَدُهُمَا أَبْكَمُ لَا يَقْدِرُ عَلَىٰ شَيْءٍ وَهُوَ كَلٌّ عَلَىٰ مَوْلَاهُ أَيْنَمَا يُوَجِّههُّ لَا يَأْتِ بِخَيْرٍ هَلْ يَسْتَوِى هُوَ وَمَن يَأْمُرُ بِالْعَدْلِ وَهُوَ عَلَىٰ صِرَاطٍ مُّسْتَقِيمٍ ۝

Overview

This third passage of the *sūrah* is again devoted to the major issue of God's oneness. The first three verses make it clear that God is one without partners, and that to Him alone the entire universe and all that it contains belong, and that He is the One who bestows all bounty and grace. The passage concludes with two comparisons between a

50

master who owns and provides, and a slave who is able to do nothing of his own accord. Can these two be equal? How is it, then, that God, the Master of all and the Provider for all, is assigned equals who have no power and provide nothing? How can it be said that He is God and they are gods like Him?

In this passage a picture is painted of people suffering affliction and turning to God alone for help. When their affliction is removed, they associate partners with Him.

The passage also portrays some aspects of the superstitious nature of pagan beliefs, in that their followers attribute some of what God has provided for them to their false deities, while they themselves do not share with their slaves anything they own. They attribute females to God as His daughters while they hate to have daughters born to themselves: "*When any of them is given the happy news of the birth of a girl, his face darkens and he is filled with gloom.*" (Verse 58) Yet at the same time they boast that they will have all the good things, and that they will be rewarded handsomely for their deeds. All these misconceptions they have inherited from earlier communities that held idolatrous beliefs.

In this passage the *sūrah* portrays a few examples of God's creation, showing how only God is able to produce such things and sustain them. In itself, this constitutes a great evidence of God's control of the whole universe. It is God who sends down water from the skies to bring life to the earth after it has been lifeless. It is He who produces pure milk from the bellies of cattle, so that people may have a wholesome drink. He it is who brings out the fruits of the date-palms and the vines, from which people make their intoxicating drinks and derive good sustenance. Through His inspiration, the bees take up their homes in hills, trees and in wooden trellises people put up, and then produce honey which provides a cure for many ailments. It is God also who creates people and then gathers them in death. Some of them He leaves to old age, when they forget what they had learnt in life and become naïve. He it is who provides for some in abundance while He gives less to others. And it is God who gives them spouses and enables them to have children and grandchildren. Yet despite all these favours, people take to worshipping beside God things that can give them no sustenance, and which are themselves powerless, claiming that such things are equal to Him. All such fabrications are indeed false.

All these aspects are within people's own environment and even within themselves. They are directed to them so that they will appreciate God's power and its work in the world around them. The conclusion depicts the two clear examples we have already referred to. Thus, the whole passage addresses the human mind and conscience, striking powerful notes that are certain to influence any human being.

All Grace Comes from God

God has said: Do not take [for worship] two deities, for He is but one God. Hence, of Me alone stand in awe. His is all that is in the heavens and the earth, and to Him alone submission is always due. Will you then fear anyone but God? Whatever blessing you have comes from God; and whenever harm befalls you, it is to Him that you cry out for help. Yet no sooner does He remove the harm from you than some among you associate partners with their Lord, [as if] to show their ingratitude for what We have given them. Enjoy, then, your life [as you may]; before long you will come to know [the truth]. (Verses 51–55)

God has commanded that people do not worship two deities, for there is only one God, without partner or equal. The style here relies on the repetition of numbers for emphasis. This is not easily reflected in translation. Arabic, the language of the original text of the Qur'ān, admits a repetition of the number two to the dual form of deity in the first sentence. If we were to give a literal translation, the sentence would read: "Do not take for worship two deities in doubles." Again repetition is employed in the next sentence to emphasize God's oneness. This is re-emphasized in the use of 'alone' in the last part of the verse: "*Of Me alone stand in awe.*" There is a sense of reiterated warning in this verse. This added emphasis reminds us that the issue in question is that of faith. God's oneness must be a concept of complete and perfect clarity in the mind of every believer.

52

God, the only deity, is also the One to whom everything belongs: "*His is all that is in the heavens and the earth.*" (Verse 52) All true faith also belongs to Him: "*To Him alone submission is always due.*" (Verse 52) It is a continuous process, ever since there was a faith and people to believe in it. Such belief means submission, and no faith is true unless it is based on submission to Him. He alone gives blessings and bestows grace: "*Whatever blessing you have comes from God.*" (Verse 53) It is also ingrained in human nature that whenever people experience hardship and difficulty, they turn to God, seeking His help. At such times, there is no room for the superstitions of idolatry or pagan beliefs. To Him alone people turn with their appeals to remove their hardship: "*Whenever harm befalls you, it is to Him that you cry out for help.*" (Verse 53)

Thus we see that Godhead and dominion in the universe belong to God alone. All submission is addressed to Him, and all grace is bestowed by Him, and to Him alone everyone should turn in all situations. Human nature is a witness to this. When it experiences affliction, harm or hardship, it returns to its purity and turns to God alone. Yet despite all this, no sooner does God save people from some type of harm that could destroy them than some of them associate partners with Him. This leads them to disbelief in God's guidance and to denying His grace. Such people should think clearly about what will happen to them after their brief enjoyment: "*Enjoy, then, your life [as you may]; before long you will come to know [the truth].*" (Verse 55)

The *sūrah* portrays here a picture of a certain type of human being which is found across every generation. When harm and affliction strikes, people's hearts turn to God for help. By nature, they know that He is the only One to protect them when no one else can. In times of comfort and pleasure, they are preoccupied with enjoyment, weakening their relationship with God: "*whenever harm befalls you, it is to Him that you cry out for help. Yet no sooner does He remove the harm from you than some among you associate partners with their Lord.*" (Verses 53–54) They deviate from His path, following diverse ways which may lead to outright idolatry, or may take the form of ascribing divinity to values and situations, even though they may not describe these as deities.

53

Indeed deviation may be even more extreme so as to prevent people from turning to God in times of hardship. Instead they may turn to some other creature, appealing to them to save their skins. They may do so under the pretext that such creatures enjoy a special position with God, or they may have some other excuse. For example, when people appeal to 'saints' to cure their illnesses or remove their afflictions. Such people are thus even more deviant than the pagan Arabs.

Common Forms of Paganism

"They assign a share of the sustenance We provide for them to what they know nothing of." (Verse 56) They thus prohibit themselves some types of cattle, not allowing themselves to ride these or to eat their meat, or they allow these animals' use to men, forbidding them to women, as we saw in *Sūrah* 6, Cattle. They do this in the name of their alleged deities of which they know nothing. They are simply false inventions which they inherited from earlier ignorant generations. It is God who gave them this bounty, the cattle which they ride and use. Yet they give a portion of these to things which are in reality unknown to them. Their false deities did not give them the cattle. The cattle were created by God who has made them available to them. He calls on people to believe in His oneness, but they stubbornly associate partners with Him. The whole situation is full of irony which no human being of sound mind can accept.

Despite the fact that the faith based on God's oneness is well established, some people continue to assign a portion of the sustenance God provides for them to beings or things similar to the idols of ignorant days. Some, for example, set loose a calf, which they call, 'Sayyid Al-Badawī's calf.' The calf is thus sanctified. It is allowed to roam freely, eat whatever it will, with no one benefiting from it in any way, until it is slaughtered in honour of Sayyid Al-Badawī, a mystic buried in Ṭanṭā, an Egyptian city. Others pledge sacrificial animals to dead 'saints' in the same way as the ignorant Arabs used to do when they assigned portions of God's provisions to their idols. Such sacrificial animals are forbidden to be pledged in this way, forbidden to be eaten when they are slaughtered, even though God's name is mentioned at their slaughter, because they have been sanctified to things other than God.

"*By God, you shall certainly be called to account for your false inventions.*" (Verse 56) This is stated emphatically, with an oath. It is an invention that destroys the very foundation of faith, because it flies in the face of the concept of God's oneness.

> *And they assign daughters to God, who is limitless in His glory, whereas for themselves they choose what they desire. And when any of them is given the happy news of the birth of a girl, his face darkens and he is filled with gloom. He tries to avoid all people on account of the [allegedly] bad news he has received, [debating within himself:] shall he keep the child despite the shame he feels, or shall he bury it in the dust? Evil indeed is their judgement.* (Verses 57–59)

Deviation from the right faith is not limited to beliefs. Indeed when people deviate from the essence of faith, their deviation spreads into their social life and its traditions. Whether faith is given prominence or kept in the background in any society, it continues to be the prime influence on living conditions. The Arabs of the days of ignorance, or *jāhiliyyah*, used to claim that God had daughters, i.e. the angels, yet they themselves hated that daughters should be born to them. Thus daughters can be assigned to God, while they give themselves the sons they love.

Such deviation from the right faith led them to bury their daughters alive, or to ill-treat or humiliate them. They feared that girls would bring them shame, if they did not guard their honour and chastity, or bring them poverty. For girls neither fought in war nor earned a living. On the contrary, they could be taken captive in the never ending tribal skirmishes, and this brought shame to the whole tribe. Alternatively, girls needed to be fed, placing a burden on family resources. The true faith is free of all such misconceptions. All sustenance is provided by God for everyone. None will take anything more than what is assigned to him or her. Moreover, human beings, male and female, are given by God a position of honour. In Islam, a woman is a human being, equal to man in status. She is the other half of the human entity, as Islam states.

The *sūrah* paints a grim picture of the practices of ignorance: "*And when any of them is given the happy news of the birth of a girl, his face darkens and he is filled with gloom.*" (Verse 58) He is sad and angry, trying to suppress his fury, as though the birth of a girl is a disaster when she is a gift from God, just like any boy. Man cannot fashion the foetus in the womb so as to determine the sex of his child. He cannot breathe life into it, or make the fertilized egg a human being. It is sufficient to reflect how life grows, by God's will, from a sperm into a human being, to make the birth of a child, of either sex, a joyous occasion. It is a miracle of creation despite the fact that it takes place all the time. Why should a man who is given a daughter feel sad and gloomy when he himself has no say in any stage of the process of creation. It is all done by God, while he himself is only the means to accomplish God's will.

It is divine wisdom that has determined that life is started with a couple: a male and a female. This means that the woman is as essential to the continuation of life as the man, indeed more so, because it is inside the woman that the first stage of life is completed. How can a man thus feel sad when given the news of the birth of a daughter? Why does he hide away, feeling ashamed, when life cannot continue and prosper without both spouses? This is obviously then a case of deviant social concepts and traditions. Hence the *sūrah* comments: "*Evil indeed is their judgement.*" (Verse 59)

Here we have a fair example of the role of the Islamic faith in establishing social norms and conditions on the right basis. We also appreciate the honourable view of women, and indeed of all mankind, that Islam propagates. For it was not only women but the whole of humanity who was treated unjustly in Arab pagan society. A woman is a human being, and humiliating or insulting her is an insult to mankind whom God has honoured. To bury a girl alive, like the Arabs did, is to kill half of mankind. It is contrary to the whole purpose of creation which necessitates that every living thing, not only human beings, comes from a male and a female.

Whenever human society deviates from the true faith, ignorant concepts begin to raise their ugly faces. In fact we see the same concepts that prevailed then creeping up again today. Many social classes do not welcome the birth of a girl. It is often the case that a woman is not treated on an equal footing with a man. She is not offered the same care or respect. This is an aspect of paganism the seeds of which were planted with the deviation from the true Islamic faith that has affected many communities.

It is amazing that some people criticize, even condemn, Islam and its laws, particularly with regard to women, on the basis of what they see in societies that have deviated from Islam. They do not trouble themselves to look at the relevant Islamic concepts and the fundamental changes they have produced in social conditions as well as in people's minds and feelings. What they should realize when they look at the true Islamic viewpoint with regard to women is that this viewpoint has not been the product of any practical necessity, human theory or social or economic need. It is a viewpoint that is inherent in the Islamic faith which was revealed by God who has given mankind a position of honour. This honour applies both to man and woman. Both have equal status and both are honoured by God.

If God Were to Inflict Punishment Now

By nature, Islam differs with all other creeds and societies in concepts and outlook. The difference between the two is as wide as the difference between the unbelievers' characteristics and God's own attributes. For He is far above all comparison: *"To those who do not believe in the life to come applies the attribute of evil, whereas to God applies the attribute of all that is most sublime, for He is Almighty, Wise."* (Verse 60)

At this point the question of associating partners with God is closely related to that of denying the life to come. Both stem from the same sort of deviation. They are interlinked in people's minds, leading to clear influences on the individual, human society and life altogether. Whilst the unbelievers are evil, in thought, behaviour, beliefs, concepts, and practices, God has the most supreme attributes. He cannot be compared with anyone, least of all those unbelievers. He is mighty, setting everything in its right place, wise, acting always on the basis of infinite wisdom.

He certainly can punish people for their wrongdoing. Had He chosen to do so, He would have brought everything down over their heads. But in His wisdom, He has decided to give them respite, for a definite term:

> *If God were to take people to task for their wrongdoing, He would not leave a single living creature on the face [of the earth]. But He gives them respite for a set term. When their time arrives, they cannot delay it by an hour, nor can they hasten it.* (Verse 61)

God has created man and bestowed on him grace and blessings of all types. Man is the only creature on earth that spreads corruption, commits injustice, denies his Creator, allows tyranny within his own social set up and inflicts harm on other species. Yet despite all this, God is merciful to him, gives him one chance after another, and never abandons him altogether. His wisdom goes hand in hand with His might; His grace with His justice. But human beings are short-sighted, deluded by the respite given them. They do not feel how graceful God is to them until His justice brings them to account at the end of the term He has appointed for them. But *"when their time arrives, they cannot delay it by an hour, nor can they hasten it."* (Verse 61)

What is even more amazing is that those who associate partners with God assign to Him what they dislike for themselves, whether daughters or other things. They then falsely claim that they will only have what is good in return for what they do and allege. The Qur'ān states what they shall have, and this differs widely from what they claim: *"They attribute to God what they hate [for themselves]. And their tongues assert the lie that theirs is the supreme reward. Without doubt, it is the Fire that awaits them, and they will be hastened on into it."* (Verse 62)

The translation of this verse here is the nearest one possible. But the original Arabic expression, *taṣifu alsinatuhum al-kadhib*, describes their tongues as though they are the lie itself, or a reflection of it giving its exact likeness, as we say of a woman walking gracefully, 'she is grace itself.' Literally, the verse states, 'their lie of a tongue asserts.' They have been lying for such a very long time that they themselves represent a symbol indicating falsehood.

Their claim that they shall have the supreme reward when they assign to God what they hate for themselves is the lie their tongues reflect. Before the verse is completed however, the Qur'ān places them face to face with the truth, namely, that their reward is undoubtedly the Fire. They deserve this because of what they have done in their lives: "*Without doubt, it is the Fire that awaits them.*" (Verse 62) They will be sent directly to it: "*And they will be hastened on into it.*" (Verse 62)

Those Arabs were not the first community to deviate from the path of the truth, nor were they the first to attribute to God what they did not accept for themselves. Other communities before them traversed the same deviation and false claims against God. Satan made their concepts and actions seem fair to them and they accepted his bidding. Thus he became their master. God, then, sent His Messenger to save them, show them the truth and judge between them in their disputes over their faith. He provided guidance to the believers and delivered a message that is an act of grace bestowed on them:

> *By God, We have sent messengers to various communities before your time, but Satan made their foul deeds seem fair to them. He is also their patron today. A grievous suffering awaits them. We have bestowed upon you from on high this book for no other reason than that you may make clear to them those issues on which they differ, and [to serve] as guidance and grace to people who believe.* (Verses 63–64)

This means that the purpose of the last message is to judge in the disputes that arise between the different peoples who claim to believe in previous messages. The original message is based on God's oneness. Yet doubts and confusion have crept into this central concept. All types of distortion of its clarity in any way or form are absolutely false. The Qur'ān clarifies all this and serves as guidance and grace to those whose hearts are willing to receive it.

Clear Signs to Reflect Upon

At this point, the *sūrah* reviews some of the aspects pointing to God's oneness in what God has created in the universe, and in the qualities and characteristics He has given man, as well as in the aspects of grace He has bestowed on him which none but God could have provided. In the verse we have just discussed He mentions His book, the Qur'ān, which is the best aspect of grace God has bestowed on man as it imparts life to souls. Now, this is followed by mentioning the water God sends down from the sky to give physical life to man and other creatures. "*And God sends down water from the skies, giving life to the earth after it has been lifeless. In this there is surely a sign for people who listen.*" (Verse 65) Water is indeed the source of life for every living thing. This verse makes it the source of life for the whole earth, implying that this includes all that exists on earth. The One who transforms death into life is indeed the One who deserves to be God and to whom worship is addressed: "*In this there is surely a sign for people who listen.*" They should indeed reflect on what they hear and listen to its message. In fact the Qur'ān repeatedly mentions the signs pointing to God and His authority, and how He brings life into what is dead. It draws people's attentions to this, because it provides irrefutable proof for anyone who reflects on what he sees and hears.

Another sign is derived from the creation of cattle and their lives: "*In cattle too you have a worthy lesson: We give you to drink of that [fluid] which is in their bellies, produced alongside excretions and blood: pure milk, pleasant to those who drink it.*" (Verse 66) How is milk produced through the udders of cattle? It is made of what remains in the bellies of cattle after they have digested their food and the absorption of the excretions in the intestines to transform it into blood. The blood is then circulated to every cell in the body, but when it reaches the milk glands or the udder, it becomes milk through a fine process set by God. This is indeed an aspect of His fine and inimitable creation.

Indeed the whole process that transforms the food intake into blood, and gives every cell what it needs of the blood's ingredients is a highly remarkable process. Yet this goes on all the time inside the body, just like the metabolism process. At every moment complicated processes of maintenance and destruction take place in this unique organism, which continue until the spirit departs from the body. No fair minded human being could contemplate such remarkable processes without feeling that every atom in his being glorifies the Creator. Even the most complex man-made apparatus fades into insignificance when compared to the human constitution or to any one of its systems or even its countless cells.

Indeed beyond the general description of the metabolism processes we find details that fill us with wonder. Within this process, the function of a single cell in the human body is remarkably wonderful.

All this has remained a secret until recently. This scientific fact mentioned in this *sūrah* about how milk is produced alongside excretions and blood was unknown to mankind. Indeed no contemporary of the Prophet could have ever imagined it, let alone described it so accurately. No self respecting human being could ever argue about this. The mention of one such fact is sufficient to prove that the Qur'ān is God's revelation. All mankind was at the time totally ignorant of such facts.

Such pure scientific facts apart, the Qur'ān carries within its own unique characteristics irrefutable proofs of its being revealed by God, provided we appreciate such characteristics as they truly are. However, one scientific fact like this, expressed with such accuracy, refutes all arguments advanced by those who are hardened in their rejection of the truth.

"*And from the fruit of the date-palms and vines you derive intoxicants and wholesome food. Surely in this there is a sign for people who use their reason.* (Verse 67) Such fruits come out of the life which is produced through the rain pouring down from the sky. From them people make wine and other intoxicating drinks, which were not forbidden at the time this *sūrah* was revealed. People also derive from such fruits wholesome food. The way this verse is phrased implies that intoxicants are unwholesome, which serves as a preliminary indication of their forthcoming prohibition. The verse describes the situation as it was in practice. It does not imply that wines and

61

intoxicants were permissible. On the contrary it hints that they will soon be forbidden. *"Surely in this there is a sign for people who use their reason."* (Verse 67) People with reason are sure to realize that the provider of all these fruits and other provisions is God, the One who deserves to be worshipped.

The Bee and Its Honey

Your Lord has inspired the bee: 'Take up homes in the mountains, in the trees and in structures people may put up. Then eat of all manner of fruit, and follow humbly the paths your Lord has made smooth for you.' There issues from its inside a drink of different colours, a cure for people. Surely in this there is a sign for people who think. (Verses 68–69)

The bees work on the prompting of their nature which God has given them. It is an inspiration that they follow. The work the bees do is so detailed, accurate and well planned that the rational mind finds it difficult to contemplate. This applies to the building of the hives, the division of the work between the bees, and to their production of pure honey.

The bees take up home, according to their nature, in hills and mountains, in trees and in structures people put up for their vines or other plants. God has smoothed things for the bees through what He has planted in their nature and through the nature of the world around them. The verse states that honey provides a cure for people. Although this has already been fully explained by some medical experts, it is also true for the simple reason that the Qur'ān states it. This is what every Muslim should believe, based on the complete truth embodied in the Qur'ān. This is what the Prophet expressed very clearly.

Al-Bukhārī and Muslim relate on the authority of Abū Saʿīd al-Khudrī that "a man came to the Prophet telling him that his brother was suffering from diarrhoea. The Prophet told him: 'Give him a drink of honey.' The man did, then he came again and said: 'Messenger of God, I have given him honey, but his complaint has worsened.' The Prophet said to him: 'Go and give him a drink of honey.' The man went away again before returning the third time to say: 'Messenger of God, that has only aggravated his condition.' The Prophet said emphatically: 'God tells the truth and your brother's belly tells lies. Go and give him a drink of honey.' The man did just that and his brother took the drink and was cured." [Related by al-Bukhārī and Muslim]

This report is so significant because it demonstrates the Prophet's complete trust in the face of the patient's seeming deterioration when given honey to drink. But the situation ended with a clear confirmation of the truth stated in the Qur'ān. A Muslim should always have such complete trust in the truth of what the Qur'ān says, even though reality may appear to contradict it at times. In other words, what is stated in the Qur'ān is more truthful than apparent reality, which could easily change, giving way to a new reality that will confirm the Qur'ānic statement.

We need to reflect a little on the fine harmony in portraying these blessings: the sending down of water from the sky, the production of milk alongside excretions and blood, the derivation of intoxicants and wholesome food from the fruits of date and vine trees, and the production of honey by bees. All are drinks produced from materials that possess totally different shapes and forms. Since the context is that of drinks, the only aspect of blessings related to cattle mentioned here is their milk. This adds to the harmony of the vocabulary employed in this panoramic scene. In the next passage we will see how the *sūrah* mentions the hide, wool and hair of cattle, because the context then is one of dwellings, homes and places of refuge. Hence the aspects of cattle mentioned there are those that fit that scene. This is an essential element of the artistic harmony evident in the Qur'ān.

The Life Cycle

The *sūrah* moves on to touch on something much closer to human beings, because it relates to their very being, their life on earth, provisions, spouses, children and grandchildren. They are more likely to feel an affinity with this and to respond positively to the message it provides:

It is God who has created you; and in time will cause you to die. Some of you are left to the most feeble stage of life, so that they no longer know what they had previously known. God is indeed All-Knowing, infinite in His power. To some of you God has given more than He has given to others. Those who are so favoured are unwilling to share their provisions with those whom their right hands possess, so that they are all equal in this respect. Will they, then, deny God's favours? And God has given you spouses of your own kind and has given you, through your spouses, children and grandchildren, and provided you with wholesome sustenance. Will they, then, believe in falsehood and deny God's grace and blessings? Instead of God, they worship something that can provide them with no sustenance from the heavens or the earth. Never can they have such power. (Verses 70–73)

The first aspect points to life and death which affect every human being. It is a simple fact that people love life, and when they reflect on this it may well bring about an appreciation of God's power and grace. Similarly, fear for one's life may engender a sense of caution and reliance on God who gives life. Furthermore, the image of the elderly, being feeble, forgetting what they have learned and languishing in a naïve state similar to that of a helpless child may make people reflect on the various stages of life and adopt a more humble attitude. They will begin to look at man's strength, knowledge and ability in a different light. The final comment of the verse is, *"God is indeed All-Knowing, infinite in His power."* (Verse 70) This portrays the fact that true, absolute and eternal knowledge belongs to God alone, as does the irresistible power which is never weakened by time. All knowledge and power people possess are imperfect, partial and limited by time.

The second aspect demonstrates what God has provided for people. In this respect people clearly differ with some having more than others. Such differences have their reason in accordance with God's law. Nothing takes place haphazardly. A man may have intelligence, knowledge and common sense, but his talent in earning a living remains limited. This does not detract from the fact that he may be talented in other areas. Another person may appear dull, lacking in knowledge or naïve, but he has an eye for what brings profit and how to make the best of any financial investment. At a casual glance, it seems that affluence has nothing to do with ability, but the fact is that it is the fruit of a special type of ability. Moreover, it may be that God gives someone in abundance to test that person, and He may test another by giving him limited provisions. Whichever test a person has to go through is determined by God's wisdom.

That people have different means is a well-known phenomenon. This is more pronounced in communities where there is much inequity. The *sūrah* refers to this phenomenon which was clearly apparent in Arabian society, and makes use of it in order to dispel those myths that had their roots in the pagan beliefs of the Arabs. These have been referred to in an earlier *sūrah*. One such myth was their practice of allocating to false gods a share of the provisions of agricultural produce God gave them. Here the *sūrah* identifies that they do not give such provisions to their slaves to establish equity. How come, then, they give a portion of what God has granted them to false gods? "*Will they, then, deny God's favours?*" (Verse 71) Instead of expressing their thanks and gratitude to God who has given them these provisions, they associate partners with Him.

The third aspect looks at people, their spouses, children and grandchildren. It begins with a statement of the relationship between the two sexes: "*God has given you spouses of your own kind.*" (Verse 72) All belong to the same human race, and the female is not an inferior species to be ashamed of when a daughter is born. He also "*has given you, through your spouses, children and grandchildren.*" (Verse 72) Humans are mortal, and so they feel that their lives continue through their children and grandchildren. Touching upon this aspect is very significant. To this blessing is added the provision of sustenance, because of the similarity between the two types of blessing: "*And [He] provided you with wholesome sustenance.*" (Verse 72) The comment at the end of the verse takes the form of a rhetorical question: "*Will they, then, believe in falsehood and deny God's grace and blessings?*" (Verse 72) Do they associate false partners with Him, in flagrant disobedience of His orders, when He has given them all these blessings? He is the Lord of all the world and His Lordship has practical manifestations in their lives at all times.

"Will they, then, believe in falsehood?" (Verse 72) Everything other than God in respect to beliefs is false. Thus, all their deities and myths are false, having no truth in them. They *"deny God's grace and blessings,"* when these are true, having practical effects in their own lives.

Incomparable Situations

Instead of God, they worship something that can provide them with no sustenance from the heavens or the earth. Never can they have such power. (Verse 73)

It is indeed amazing that human nature can become so twisted as to allow the worship of things that can provide people with nothing. They prefer such things to God, the Creator who provides them with all they have and all the blessings they enjoy. Yet they go even further, attributing to them similarities with God. Hence the commandment: *"Do not, then, compare anything with God. Indeed, God knows all, whereas you have no knowledge."* (Verse 74) God has no peers, so people must never claim that there is anyone equal or similar to Him.

The *sūrah* then gives two examples of a master who can give and provide and a disabled slave who earns nothing. These examples are given to bring the eternal truth they had overlooked closer to their understanding. That truth is that God has no peers and that they must never equate God with anyone in their worship. Everyone and everything other than God is created by Him, and all are His servants.

God makes this comparison between a man enslaved, unable to do anything of his own accord, and a [free] man on whom We have bestowed goodly favours, and he gives of it both in private and in public. Can these two be equal? All praise is to God alone, but most people have no knowledge. And God makes another comparison between two men, one of whom is dumb and can do nothing of his own accord. He is a sheer burden to his master: wherever he sends him, he accomplishes no good. Can he be considered equal to one who enjoins justice and follows a straight path? (Verses 75–76)

The first example is taken from their own lives. They had slaves who owned nothing and who had no power over anything. They would never put the slave who has no independent will on the same level as his master who enjoys considerable power. How then can they justify their equation of the Master and Owner of all with any of His creation, when they all serve Him?

The second example depicts a dumb, dull and weak person who understands nothing and can do no good, and another who is eloquent, able, encouraging fairness, hard working for every good cause. No reasonable person would equate the two. How is it, then, that dumb idols of stone are equated with God Almighty, who enjoins only what is reasonable and guides to the path of truth?

With these two examples we come to the end of this passage which started with God's order that people must not worship two deities. It ends with amazement at the attitude of those who attribute Godhead to other deities. God has replaced Joseph's trials with his new position of power, and also with the promise of better things to come in the life to come. All this reward is for faith, righteousness and perseverance in the face of difficulty.

4

Denying the Undeniable

To God belongs the hidden secrets of the heavens and the earth. The advent of the Last Hour will be accomplished in a twinkling of an eye, or closer still. God has power over all things. (77)

وَلِلَّهِ غَيْبُ ٱلسَّمَٰوَٰتِ وَٱلۡأَرۡضِ وَمَآ أَمۡرُ ٱلسَّاعَةِ إِلَّا كَلَمۡحِ ٱلۡبَصَرِ أَوۡ هُوَ أَقۡرَبُ إِنَّ ٱللَّهَ عَلَىٰ كُلِّ شَيۡءٍ قَدِيرٌ ۝

God has brought you forth from your mothers' wombs devoid of all knowledge, but He has given you hearing, and sight, and minds, so that you may be grateful. (78)

وَٱللَّهُ أَخۡرَجَكُم مِّنۢ بُطُونِ أُمَّهَٰتِكُمۡ لَا تَعۡلَمُونَ شَيۡئًا وَجَعَلَ لَكُمُ ٱلسَّمۡعَ وَٱلۡأَبۡصَٰرَ وَٱلۡأَفۡـِٔدَةَ لَعَلَّكُمۡ تَشۡكُرُونَ ۝

Do they not see the birds and how they are enabled to fly in mid-air? None but God holds them aloft. In this there are signs for people who will believe. (79)

أَلَمۡ يَرَوۡاْ إِلَى ٱلطَّيۡرِ مُسَخَّرَٰتٍ فِي جَوِّ ٱلسَّمَآءِ مَا يُمۡسِكُهُنَّ إِلَّا ٱللَّهُ إِنَّ فِي ذَٰلِكَ لَأٓيَٰتٍ لِّقَوۡمٍ يُؤۡمِنُونَ ۝

And God has made your homes as places of rest, and has given you dwellings out of the skins of animals, which are easy for you to handle when you travel and when you camp. Out of their wool, fur and hair, He has given you furnishings and articles of convenience for temporary use. (80)

وَٱللَّهُ جَعَلَ لَكُم مِّنْ بُيُوتِكُمْ سَكَنًا وَجَعَلَ لَكُم مِّن جُلُودِ ٱلْأَنْعَـٰمِ بُيُوتًا تَسْتَخِفُّونَهَا يَوْمَ ظَعْنِكُمْ وَيَوْمَ إِقَامَتِكُمْ وَمِنْ أَصْوَافِهَا وَأَوْبَارِهَا وَأَشْعَارِهَا أَثَـٰثًا وَمَتَـٰعًا إِلَىٰ حِينٍ ﴿٨٠﴾

And God has made for you, out of the many things He has created, shelter and shade, and has given you places of refuge in the mountains, and has furnished you with garments to protect you from the heat and other garments to protect you from your [mutual] violence. Thus does He perfect His favours to you, so that you may submit to Him. (81)

وَٱللَّهُ جَعَلَ لَكُم مِّمَّا خَلَقَ ظِلَـٰلًا وَجَعَلَ لَكُم مِّنَ ٱلْجِبَالِ أَكْنَـٰنًا وَجَعَلَ لَكُمْ سَرَٰبِيلَ تَقِيكُمُ ٱلْحَرَّ وَسَرَٰبِيلَ تَقِيكُم بَأْسَكُمْ كَذَٰلِكَ يُتِمُّ نِعْمَتَهُ عَلَيْكُمْ لَعَلَّكُمْ تُسْلِمُونَ ﴿٨١﴾

But if they turn away [from you, remember that] your only duty is to deliver [your message] clearly. (82)

فَإِن تَوَلَّوْا فَإِنَّمَا عَلَيْكَ ٱلْبَلَـٰغُ ٱلْمُبِينُ ﴿٨٢﴾

They are certainly aware of God's favours, but they nevertheless refuse to acknowledge them. Most of them are unbelievers. (83)

يَعْرِفُونَ نِعْمَتَ ٱللَّهِ ثُمَّ يُنكِرُونَهَا وَأَكْثَرُهُمُ ٱلْكَـٰفِرُونَ ﴿٨٣﴾

One day We will raise up a witness from every community, but then the unbelievers will not be allowed to make pleas, nor will they be allowed to make amends. (84)

وَيَوْمَ نَبْعَثُ مِن كُلِّ أُمَّةٍ شَهِيدًا ثُمَّ لَا يُؤْذَنُ لِلَّذِينَ كَفَرُوا۟ وَلَا هُمْ يُسْتَعْتَبُونَ ۝

And when the wrongdoers actually see the suffering [that awaits them], it will in no way be mitigated for them, nor will they be granted respite. (85)

وَإِذَا رَءَا الَّذِينَ ظَلَمُوا۟ الْعَذَابَ فَلَا يُخَفَّفُ عَنْهُمْ وَلَا هُمْ يُنظَرُونَ ۝

And when those who associate partners with God will see their [alleged] partners, they will say: 'Our Lord, these are our partners whom we used to invoke instead of You.' But they will throw their word back at them, saying: 'You are indeed liars.' (86)

وَإِذَا رَءَا الَّذِينَ أَشْرَكُوا۟ شُرَكَاءَهُمْ قَالُوا۟ رَبَّنَا هَٰؤُلَاءِ شُرَكَاؤُنَا الَّذِينَ كُنَّا نَدْعُوا۟ مِن دُونِكَ فَأَلْقَوْا۟ إِلَيْهِمُ الْقَوْلَ إِنَّكُمْ لَكَاذِبُونَ ۝

On that day, they shall proffer submission to God; and all their inventions will have forsaken them. (87)

وَأَلْقَوْا۟ إِلَى اللَّهِ يَوْمَئِذٍ السَّلَمَ وَضَلَّ عَنْهُم مَّا كَانُوا۟ يَفْتَرُونَ ۝

Upon those who disbelieve and debar others from the path of God We will heap suffering upon suffering in punishment for all the corruption they wrought. (88)

الَّذِينَ كَفَرُوا۟ وَصَدُّوا۟ عَن سَبِيلِ اللَّهِ زِدْنَاهُمْ عَذَابًا فَوْقَ الْعَذَابِ بِمَا كَانُوا۟ يُفْسِدُونَ ۝

One day We will raise up within every nation a witness from among themselves to testify against them. And We will bring you, [Prophet] as a witness against these [i.e. your people]. We have bestowed from on high upon you the book to make everything clear, and to provide guidance and grace, and to give good news to those who submit themselves to God. (89)

وَيَوْمَ نَبْعَثُ فِى كُلِّ أُمَّةٍ شَهِيدًا عَلَيْهِم مِّنْ أَنفُسِهِمْ وَجِئْنَا بِكَ شَهِيدًا عَلَىٰ هَـٰٓؤُلَاءِ وَنَزَّلْنَا عَلَيْكَ ٱلْكِتَـٰبَ تِبْيَـٰنًا لِّكُلِّ شَىْءٍ وَهُدًى وَرَحْمَةً وَبُشْرَىٰ لِلْمُسْلِمِينَ ﴿٨٩﴾

Overview

In this passage the *sūrah* continues its discussion of the aspects confirming the truth of God's oneness, such as the great variety of creation, the perfection of God's blessings and His absolute knowledge of all things. However, in this passage, prominence is given to the question of resurrection. The Last Hour, which is a Qur'ānic expression denoting the gathering and reckoning on the Day of Judgement, is one of the secrets which God keeps to Himself. The passage refers to the different hidden secrets of God's creation in the heavens and the earth, in human beings and across the wide universe. One of these relates to the Last Hour, whose timing is known to God alone. He controls it with ease: *"The advent of the Last Hour will be accomplished in a twinkling of an eye, or closer still."* (Verse 77) Another secret relates to what is created in the wombs of females. It is God alone who lets the foetus come out of the womb, with no knowledge whatsoever of the world it comes into. It is He also who gives human beings the blessings of hearing, seeing and thinking. These are favours which deserve gratitude. The *sūrah* also refers to the birds and how they are given the ability to fly. Needless to say, they are held aloft in mid-air by none other than God.

This is followed by a reference to some material blessings given to mankind. These are relevant to the aforementioned secrets. They include the blessings of abode, rest, shade and shelter in built up homes and temporary dwellings made of animal skin. The latter have the advantage of being easy to carry and re-erect when people are on the move. Reference is also made to furniture and other articles made of animal wool, fur and hair, and to places of shelter and garments that protect people from the heat of the sun and the might of the enemy. God reminds people of His blessings and how He has perfected them, so that they may fulfil their duty: "*Thus does He perfect His favours to you, so that you may submit to Him.*" (Verse 81)

This is followed by details relating to resurrection, juxtaposed against pagans and the idols they worship. God's messengers bear witness against such unbelievers, while the Prophet Muḥammad (peace be upon him) is witness against his own people.

In the Twinkling of an Eye

To God belongs the hidden secrets of the heavens and the earth. The advent of the Last Hour will be accomplished in a twinkling of an eye, or closer still. God has power over all things. (Verse 77)

Resurrection is an essential question of faith that has attracted much controversy in all periods and communities. Every one of God's messengers had to deal with it. Yet it is part of the realm of what is known to God alone: "*To God belongs the hidden secrets of the heavens and the earth.*" People stand before the thick curtains of *ghayb*, or God's hidden knowledge, aware of their inability and inadequacy. They may have great knowledge of their world, and may be able to discover much of the treasures of the earth and its resources and potentials, but even the greatest human scientists stand helpless when it comes to the knowledge of the immediate and distant future. He simply does not know what will happen the next moment, and whether, when he has taken the next breath in, he will be able to breathe out. A human being may entertain high hopes, stretching in different directions, yet his destiny remains behind the curtain of God's own knowledge. He himself has no means of knowing when his time will come. Yet it may come the next moment and he will be among the dead. It is in fact an aspect of God's grace bestowed on human beings that they do not know anything of what will take place beyond the present moment. Their lack of knowledge gives them hope and urges them to continue to work and produce. Whatever they manage will be taken over and completed by those who succeed them, until every individual of the next generation faces, in his or her turn, their destiny.

The Last Hour is part of the knowledge kept hidden from man. If people knew in advance when their time was to come, life would cease to function, or, at least, would be seriously disrupted. It would certainly not follow the line set out for it. The irony is that people count hours, days, months and years moving all the time towards their pre-destined appointment when they will depart from this life.

"*The advent of the Last Hour will be accomplished in a twinkling of an eye, or closer still.*" (Verse 77) It is close at hand, but according to a calculation different from that of human beings. To bring it on, in full preparation, does not take much time. It is merely the twinkling of an eye and it is there, ready for all mankind: "*God has power over all things.*" (Verse 77) To resurrect such countless numbers of God's creation, gather them all together, reckon their deeds, assign the reward for each of them, is all easy for God whose will is accomplished in no time. Whenever He wills something, He only says to it, 'Be', and it is instantly accomplished. If this seems difficult, it only looks so to the eyes of those who see, measure and count by human standards and criteria. Hence they are grossly mistaken.

To make things easier for people to understand, the Qur'ān gives a simple example from human life. People can in no way accomplish it themselves, and they cannot formulate a clear idea of how it happens. Yet it takes place at every moment of the day and night: "*God has brought you forth from your mothers' wombs devoid of all knowledge, but He has given you hearing, and sight, and minds, so that you may be grateful.*" (Verse 78)

This is something close to us, yet it is so far away. We may see the different stages a foetus goes through, but we do not know how these are accomplished, because it is part of the secret of life which is known to God alone. The knowledge man claims and boasts of, and which he wants to use in order to test the reality of the Last Hour and the secrets of God's hidden knowledge, is something acquired: "*God has brought you forth from your mothers' wombs devoid of all knowledge.*" (Verse 78) Even the most advanced scientist is born devoid of knowledge. Whatever he subsequently learns is given to him as a blessing from God, within the limits He has set for mankind, and contingent upon what is needed for life on this planet: "*He has given you hearing, and sight, and minds.*" (Verse 78) It should be mentioned here that the Arabic word, *af'idah*, rendered in the translation as 'minds', originally denotes, 'hearts'. The Qur'ān, however, uses it in reference to all human faculties of perception, which are generally referred to as constituting the human mind and intellect. The Arabic term also includes the power of inspiration, the nature and working of which are unknown to us. The Qur'ān reminds us here that God has given people all these faculties, "*so that you may be grateful.*" (Verse 78) When we appreciate the value of these blessings God has given us and His other blessings, we will certainly be grateful to Him. The first step in showing our gratitude is to believe in God, the Sovereign, the Supreme, who alone deserves to be worshipped.

God's Hidden Secrets

Among the wonders that testify to God's limitless power and His control of everything in the universe is one that we see every day without giving it much thought. This is the ability of birds to fly: "*Do they not see the birds and how they are enabled to fly in mid-air? None but God holds them aloft. In this there are signs for people who will believe.*" (Verse 79) Because it is so familiar to us to see birds flying in mid-air, we do not pay attention to the fascinating wonder their flying involves. Our minds do not give it much thought unless we are fully alerted to it, contemplating it with the eye of a talented poet seeking to capture every detail and nuance. The verse makes it clear that as the birds fly, "*none but God holds them aloft.*" He does so through His laws of nature, which make the birds able to fly and make the atmosphere around us amenable for their flight. It is His laws that keep the birds in mid-air, floating safely, without fear that they may fall: "*In this there are signs for people who will believe.*" (Verse 79)

A believer's heart is one which appreciates the wonders of creation, looks at them with awe and expresses his feelings with worship and glorification of God, the Creator of all things. Believers who are talented in expressing their thoughts and feelings write masterpieces of every type in describing the wonders of God's creation. They also describe their own feelings and how they are touched when they look at different creatures. No poet can rival their work if his heart is not kindled by the light of faith.

The *sūrah* takes us another step in reviewing some manifestations of God's power and His blessings which He bestows on man. It takes us now into the dwellings of the Arabs at the time, looking at their home comforts and furnishings:

> *And God has made your homes as places of rest, and has given you dwellings out of the skins of animals, which are easy for you to handle when you travel and when you camp. Out of their wool, fur and hair, He has given you furnishings and articles of convenience for temporary use. And God has made for you, out of the many things He has created, shelter and shade, and has given you places of refuge in the mountains, and has furnished you with garments to protect you from the heat and other garments to protect you from your [mutual] violence. Thus does He perfect His favours to you, so that you may submit to Him.* (Verses 80–81)

The ease, comfort and reassurance one has at home are certainly a blessing from God but it is something best appreciated only by those who are homeless. They are mentioned here shortly after speaking about what the Qur'ān describes as *ghayb*, or what lies beyond the reach of human perception. In fact, the connotations of home comforts are not far removed from those of *ghayb*, because in both we sense that there is a reality that is kept hidden. Hence, a reminder of the comforts we find in our own homes should alert us to the value of this great blessing.

We may add a word here about the Islamic view of the home in the light of its description in the Qur'ān as a 'place of rest'. This is an expression that is inferior in its connotations to the Arabic term used in the Qur'ān, namely *sakan*. Yet it gives us an idea that Islam wants one's habitat to be a place of rest, comfort and reassurance. In the home one should feel at ease, safe and secure in one's environment and with those who share it. It is certainly not a place for contention, quarrel and conflict.

Islam guarantees the safety and sanctity of the home in order to ensure the security and peace of those who live in it. None is allowed to enter a home unless he first seeks, and obtains, permission to do so. No one forces his way in, without justification, armed with the force of authority. No one watches those living inside, or spies on them, for any reason, to disturb their peace and undermine their security. To do so constitutes a breach of the sanctity which Islam assigns to the home.

As the atmosphere in this passage is one of homes, shelter and garments, the *sūrah* refers to some fitting aspects of the creation of animals, thereby providing harmony between the two constituents of the scene. It tells people that God *"has given you dwellings out of the skins of animals, which are easy for you to handle when you travel and when you camp. Out of their wool, fur and hair, He has given you furnishings and articles of convenience for temporary use."* (Verse 80) We see how the verse highlights what is taken from animals to satisfy human needs. With furnishings, the *sūrah* mentions, 'articles of convenience,' which in Arabic usage denotes cushions, mattresses and blankets. All these are meant to add to people's comfort and enjoyment.

In this atmosphere of peace and security the language used in the following verse flows easily to speak about shade, places of shelter in the mountains, and the garments people use to protect themselves against climatic conditions as also against opponents in war. *"God has made for you, out of the many things He has created, shelter and shade, and has given you places of refuge in the mountains, and has furnished you with garments to protect you from the heat and other garments to protect you from your [mutual] violence."* (Verse 81) When we have proper shelter, we feel safe, and when we seek security in the mountains, we are also able to relax. Again the garments mentioned in the *sūrah*, providing two types of protection, give us a feeling of comfort and protection. All these feelings are akin to that of the comfort of one's own home. Hence, the comment that follows at the end of the verse reminds people of their need to submit to God, their Lord: "*Thus does He perfect His favours to you, so that you may submit to Him.*" (Verse 81) Such submission gives us a greater feeling of safety and security.

God reminds people of all this making it clear to them that they should submit to their Lord who has created all these. However, people turn away and take no heed. They should know that God's Messenger is responsible only for delivering God's message to them and he certainly fulfilled his mission. It is up to them whether they deny the truth which stares them in the face: "*But if they turn away [from you, remember that] your only duty is to deliver [your message] clearly. They are certainly aware of God's favours, but they nevertheless refuse to acknowledge them. Most of them are unbelievers.*" (Verses 82–83) They are certainly aware of God's favours, but they nevertheless refuse to acknowledge them. Most of them are unbelievers.

A Witness against Every Community

As the Last Hour when the Day of Judgement arrives is mentioned at the beginning of this passage, we are given here an idea of what awaits the unbelievers when it comes.

> One day We will raise up a witness from every community, but then the unbelievers will not be allowed to make pleas, nor will they be allowed to make amends. And when the wrongdoers actually see the suffering [that awaits them], it will in no way be mitigated for them, nor will they be granted respite. And when those who associate partners with God will see their [alleged] partners, they will say: 'Our Lord, these are our partners whom we used to invoke instead of You.' But they will throw their word back at them, saying: 'You are indeed liars.' On that day, they shall proffer submission to God; and all their inventions will have forsaken them. Upon those who disbelieve and debar others from the path of God We will heap suffering upon suffering in punishment for all the corruption they wrought. (Verses 84–88)

The scene begins with the prophets being called as witnesses, giving their accounts of the treatment they received from their peoples when they conveyed God's messages to them. The unbelievers will be standing there, not permitted to speak or make any plea or argument. They will not be allowed to make amends in order to satisfy their Lord, for it is too late to do so. It is a time for reckoning and the determination of fates. *"And when the wrongdoers actually see the suffering [that awaits them], it will in no way be mitigated for them, nor will they be granted respite."* (Verse 85)

Their silence however is broken when they see gathered with them those so-called 'partners' which they used to allege to have a share in God's divinity, and to worship them instead of God or alongside Him. They point to them, crying out: *"Our Lord, these are our partners whom we used to invoke instead of You."* (Verse 86) Their statement begins with an acknowledgement of God's position. They address Him as "Our Lord!" What is more is that they no longer describe the false deities they used to worship as God's partners. They refer to them as 'our partners'. Those very partners are frightened by such a description for it constitutes a serious accusation. Hence, they refute it, asserting most emphatically that those who worshipped them are liars. *"But they will throw their word back at them, saying: 'You are indeed liars.'"* (Verse 86) They turn to God in full submission. *"On that day, they shall proffer submission to God."* (Verse 87) Thus the unbelievers will discover that none of their inventions will be of any avail to them in their very difficult situation: *"All their inventions will have forsaken them."* (Verse 87)

The scene concludes with an emphatic statement asserting that those who tried their best to turn others from the path of faith will have their punishment increased: *"Upon those who disbelieve and debar others from the path of God We will heap suffering upon suffering in punishment for all the corruption they wrought."* (Verse 88) Disbelief in God is corruption, and turning others from God's path is also corruption. These people are guilty of both offences. Hence it is only right that their punishment should be increased.

This applies to all people and communities. The *sūrah* then singles out a special situation involving the Prophet with his own people:

"*One day We will raise up within every nation a witness from among themselves to testify against them. And We will bring you, [Prophet] as a witness against these [i.e. your people]. We have bestowed from on high upon you the book to make everything clear, and to provide guidance and grace, and to give good news to those who submit themselves to God.*" (Verse 89) What a gloomy and fraught scene is chosen as the background: that of a pagan people looking on when the false deities they used to worship declare that they are liars, and those very deities declare their own submission to God, totally disowning their former worshippers.

Against this background, the Prophet's position is clearly stated. He will be the witness against his own people. This timely piece of detail adds power to the whole scene: "*And We will bring you, [Prophet] as a witness against these [i.e. your people].*" (Verse 89) The verse mentions then that the revelations given to the Prophet "*makes everything clear,*" leaving no excuse for anyone to justify turning away from them. The revelation of the Qur'ān also provides "*guidance and grace and gives good news to those who submit themselves to God.*" (Verse 89) This shows clearly that whoever wishes to follow right guidance and receive God's mercy should declare his submission to God before the arrival of that awesome and fearful day. For when it comes, no one will be given leave to justify his position or to make amends for past deeds. Thus we see that the scenes of the Day of Judgement given in the Qur'ān serve a definite purpose endorsing the message given in the section where they occur.

5

Absolute Justice

God enjoins justice, kindness [to all], and generosity to one's kindred; and He forbids all that is shameful, all reprehensible conduct and aggression. He admonishes you so that you may take heed. (90)

إِنَّ ٱللَّهَ يَأْمُرُ بِٱلْعَدْلِ وَٱلْإِحْسَٰنِ وَإِيتَآئِ ذِى ٱلْقُرْبَىٰ وَيَنْهَىٰ عَنِ ٱلْفَحْشَآءِ وَٱلْمُنكَرِ وَٱلْبَغْىِ يَعِظُكُمْ لَعَلَّكُمْ تَذَكَّرُونَ ﴿٩٠﴾

Fulfil your covenant with God whenever you make a pledge. Do not break your oaths after you have confirmed them, and have made God your surety. God certainly knows all that you do. (91)

وَأَوْفُوا۟ بِعَهْدِ ٱللَّهِ إِذَا عَٰهَدتُّمْ وَلَا تَنقُضُوا۟ ٱلْأَيْمَٰنَ بَعْدَ تَوْكِيدِهَا وَقَدْ جَعَلْتُمُ ٱللَّهَ عَلَيْكُمْ كَفِيلًا إِنَّ ٱللَّهَ يَعْلَمُ مَا تَفْعَلُونَ ﴿٩١﴾

Be not like her who untwists the yarn which she has firmly spun, using your oaths as a means to deceive one another, simply because a particular community may be more powerful than another. By this, God puts you to the test. On the Day of Resurrection He will make clear to you all that on which you now differ. (92)

وَلَا تَكُونُوا۟ كَٱلَّتِى نَقَضَتْ غَزْلَهَا مِنۢ بَعْدِ قُوَّةٍ أَنكَٰثًا تَتَّخِذُونَ أَيْمَٰنَكُمْ دَخَلًۢا بَيْنَكُمْ أَن تَكُونَ أُمَّةٌ هِىَ أَرْبَىٰ مِنْ أُمَّةٍ إِنَّمَا يَبْلُوكُمُ ٱللَّهُ بِهِۦ وَلَيُبَيِّنَنَّ لَكُمْ يَوْمَ ٱلْقِيَٰمَةِ مَا كُنتُمْ فِيهِ تَخْتَلِفُونَ ﴿٩٢﴾

Had God so willed, He would have surely made you all one single community. But He lets go astray him that wills [to go astray] and guides aright him that wills [to be guided]. You shall certainly be called to account for all that you do. (93)

وَلَوْ شَآءَ ٱللَّهُ لَجَعَلَكُمْ أُمَّةً وَٰحِدَةً وَلَٰكِن يُضِلُّ مَن يَشَآءُ وَيَهْدِى مَن يَشَآءُ وَلَتُسْـَٔلُنَّ عَمَّا كُنتُمْ تَعْمَلُونَ ۝

Do not use your oaths as a means to deceive one another, lest your foot should slip after it has been firm, and lest you should be made to suffer the evil [consequences] of your having debarred others from the path of God, with tremendous suffering awaiting you. (94)

وَلَا تَتَّخِذُوٓاْ أَيْمَٰنَكُمْ دَخَلًۢا بَيْنَكُمْ فَتَزِلَّ قَدَمٌۢ بَعْدَ ثُبُوتِهَا وَتَذُوقُواْ ٱلسُّوٓءَ بِمَا صَدَدتُّمْ عَن سَبِيلِ ٱللَّهِ وَلَكُمْ عَذَابٌ عَظِيمٌ ۝

Do not barter away your covenant with God for a trifling price. Surely, that which is with God is far better for you, if you but knew it. (95)

وَلَا تَشْتَرُواْ بِعَهْدِ ٱللَّهِ ثَمَنًا قَلِيلًا إِنَّمَا عِندَ ٱللَّهِ هُوَ خَيْرٌ لَّكُمْ إِن كُنتُمْ تَعْلَمُونَ ۝

Whatever you have is certain to come to an end, but that which is with God is everlasting. We will certainly grant those who are patient in adversity their reward according to the best that they ever did. (96)

مَا عِندَكُمْ يَنفَدُ وَمَا عِندَ ٱللَّهِ بَاقٍ وَلَنَجْزِيَنَّ ٱلَّذِينَ صَبَرُوٓاْ أَجْرَهُم بِأَحْسَنِ مَا كَانُواْ يَعْمَلُونَ ۝

Whoever does righteous deeds, whether man or woman, and is a believer, We shall most certainly give a good life. And We shall indeed reward these according to the best that they ever did. (97)

مَنْ عَمِلَ صَلِحًا مِّن ذَكَرٍ أَوْ أُنثَىٰ وَهُوَ مُؤْمِنٌ فَلَنُحْيِيَنَّهُۥ حَيَوٰةً طَيِّبَةً وَلَنَجْزِيَنَّهُمْ أَجْرَهُم بِأَحْسَنِ مَا كَانُوا۟ يَعْمَلُونَ ۞

Whenever you read the Qur'ān, seek refuge with God from Satan, the accursed. (98)

فَإِذَا قَرَأْتَ ٱلْقُرْءَانَ فَٱسْتَعِذْ بِٱللَّهِ مِنَ ٱلشَّيْطَٰنِ ٱلرَّجِيمِ ۞

He certainly has no power over those who believe and place their trust in their Lord. (99)

إِنَّهُۥ لَيْسَ لَهُۥ سُلْطَٰنٌ عَلَى ٱلَّذِينَ ءَامَنُوا۟ وَعَلَىٰ رَبِّهِمْ يَتَوَكَّلُونَ ۞

He has power only over those who are willing to follow him, and thus ascribe to him a share in God's divinity. (100)

إِنَّمَا سُلْطَٰنُهُۥ عَلَى ٱلَّذِينَ يَتَوَلَّوْنَهُۥ وَٱلَّذِينَ هُم بِهِۦ مُشْرِكُونَ ۞

When We replace one verse by another – and God knows best what He reveals – they say: 'You are but a fabricator.' Indeed most of them have no knowledge. (101)

وَإِذَا بَدَّلْنَآ ءَايَةً مَّكَانَ ءَايَةٍ وَٱللَّهُ أَعْلَمُ بِمَا يُنَزِّلُ قَالُوٓا۟ إِنَّمَآ أَنتَ مُفْتَرٍ بَلْ أَكْثَرُهُمْ لَا يَعْلَمُونَ ۞

Say: 'The Holy Spirit has brought it down from your Lord in truth, so as to strengthen the believers, and to provide guidance and good news to those who surrender themselves to God.' (102)

قُلْ نَزَّلَهُۥ رُوحُ ٱلْقُدُسِ مِن رَّبِّكَ بِٱلْحَقِّ لِيُثَبِّتَ ٱلَّذِينَ ءَامَنُوا۟ وَهُدًى وَبُشْرَىٰ لِلْمُسْلِمِينَ ۞

We know full well that they say:
'It is but a man that teaches him
[all] this.' But the man to whom
they so maliciously allude speaks
a foreign tongue, while this is
Arabic speech, pure and clear.
(103)

وَلَقَدْ نَعْلَمُ أَنَّهُمْ يَقُولُونَ إِنَّمَا
يُعَلِّمُهُ بَشَرٌ لِّسَانُ ٱلَّذِى
يُلْحِدُونَ إِلَيْهِ أَعْجَمِىٌّ وَهَٰذَا
لِسَانٌ عَرَبِىٌّ مُّبِينٌ ۝

Those who do not believe in
God's revelations shall not be
granted guidance by God.
Grievous suffering awaits them.
(104)

إِنَّ ٱلَّذِينَ لَا يُؤْمِنُونَ بِـَٔايَٰتِ ٱللَّهِ
لَا يَهْدِيهِمُ ٱللَّهُ وَلَهُمْ عَذَابٌ أَلِيمٌ ۝

It is only those who do not
believe in God's revelations that
invent falsehood. It is they indeed
who are liars. (105)

إِنَّمَا يَفْتَرِى ٱلْكَذِبَ ٱلَّذِينَ
لَا يُؤْمِنُونَ بِـَٔايَٰتِ ٱللَّهِ وَأُوْلَٰٓئِكَ
هُمُ ٱلْكَٰذِبُونَ ۝

As for anyone who denies God
after having accepted the faith –
and this certainly does not apply
to one who does it under duress,
while his heart remains true to his
faith, but applies to him who
willingly opens his heart to
unbelief – upon all such falls
God's wrath, and theirs will be a
tremendous suffering. (106)

مَن كَفَرَ بِٱللَّهِ مِنۢ بَعْدِ إِيمَٰنِهِۦٓ
إِلَّا مَنْ أُكْرِهَ وَقَلْبُهُۥ مُطْمَئِنٌّ
بِٱلْإِيمَٰنِ وَلَٰكِن مَّن شَرَحَ
بِٱلْكُفْرِ صَدْرًا فَعَلَيْهِمْ غَضَبٌ مِّنَ
ٱللَّهِ وَلَهُمْ عَذَابٌ عَظِيمٌ ۝

This is because they love the life
of this world better than the life
to come. God does not bestow
His guidance on those who reject
the truth. (107)

ذَٰلِكَ بِأَنَّهُمُ ٱسْتَحَبُّوا۟ ٱلْحَيَوٰةَ
ٱلدُّنْيَا عَلَى ٱلْءَاخِرَةِ وَأَنَّ ٱللَّهَ
لَا يَهْدِى ٱلْقَوْمَ ٱلْكَٰفِرِينَ ۝

Such are those whose hearts and ears and eyes are sealed by God; such are the heedless. (108)

أُوْلَٰٓئِكَ ٱلَّذِينَ طَبَعَ ٱللَّهُ عَلَىٰ قُلُوبِهِمْ وَسَمْعِهِمْ وَأَبْصَٰرِهِمْ وَأُوْلَٰٓئِكَ هُمُ ٱلْغَٰفِلُونَ ۝

Without doubt, in the life to come they will be the losers. (109)

لَا جَرَمَ أَنَّهُمْ فِي ٱلْءَاخِرَةِ هُمُ ٱلْخَٰسِرُونَ ۝

But then, your Lord [grants forgiveness] to those who forsake their homes after enduring trials and persecution, and strive hard [in God's cause] and remain patient in adversity. After all this, your Lord is certainly Much-Forgiving, Most Merciful. (110)

ثُمَّ إِنَّ رَبَّكَ لِلَّذِينَ هَاجَرُوا۟ مِنۢ بَعْدِ مَا فُتِنُوا۟ ثُمَّ جَٰهَدُوا۟ وَصَبَرُوٓا۟ إِنَّ رَبَّكَ مِنۢ بَعْدِهَا لَغَفُورٌ رَّحِيمٌ ۝

One day every soul will come pleading for itself. Every soul will be repaid in full for all its actions, and none shall be wronged. (111)

يَوْمَ تَأْتِى كُلُّ نَفْسٍ تُجَٰدِلُ عَن نَّفْسِهَا وَتُوَفَّىٰ كُلُّ نَفْسٍ مَّا عَمِلَتْ وَهُمْ لَا يُظْلَمُونَ ۝

Overview

The previous passage ended with a verse that included the following statement: "*We have bestowed from on high upon you the book to make everything clear, and to provide guidance and grace, and to give good news to those who submit themselves to God.*" (Verse 89) This new passage begins with a clarification giving some glimpses of what the Qur'ān contains of clear guidance, grace and the good news it brings. The passage also includes orders to maintain justice and to act with kindness, particularly to relatives, and to steer away from indecency, evil and transgression, and to remain true to one's pledges and promises. It forbids going back on oaths once they have been made. All these are essential practices that we must maintain, as the Qur'ān impresses upon us.

The passage also states that those who violate pledges or swear solemn oaths to deceive others will endure tremendous suffering. It also brings good news for those who persevere in the face of adversity. These will certainly be rewarded in accordance with their best actions.

It outlines some of the good manners which must be maintained when reading the Qur'ān, such as seeking refuge with God against Satan, so that he does not come near the place where the Qur'ān is being read. It mentions some of the fabrications the pagans used to repeat about the Qur'ān. Some plainly accused the Prophet of inventing it, while others claimed that a foreigner taught it to the Prophet. The passage concludes by stating the punishment for those who disbelieve after having accepted the faith, and the position of those who are compelled to declare their rejection of the faith while their hearts are full of the certainty of its truth. It tells us about the reward of those who are subjected to oppression on account of their faith, and who strive and fight hard, always remaining patient in adversity. All this serves as clarification, guidance, mercy and good news, as the last verse of the previous passage mentions.

An Order Combining All Goodness

God enjoins justice, kindness [to all], and generosity to one's kindred; and He forbids all that is shameful, all reprehensible conduct and aggression. He admonishes you so that you may take heed. (Verse 90)

This book, the Qur'ān, has been revealed in order to bring a nation into existence, and to regulate a community; to establish a different world and initiate a new social order. It represents a world message for the whole of mankind, which does not allow any special allegiance to tribe, nation or race. Faith is the only bond that unites a community and a nation. It puts forward the principles that ensure unity within the community, security and reassurance for individuals, groups, nations and states, as well as complete trust that governs all transactions, pledges and promises.

It requires that justice should be established and maintained, because justice ensures a solid and constant basis for all transactions and deals between individuals and communities; a basis subject to no prejudice, preference or favouritism; a basis influenced by no family relationship, wealth or strength; a basis that ensures equal treatment for all and subjects all to the same standards and laws.

Along with justice, the Qur'ān urges kindness, which relaxes the strictness of absolute justice. It lays the door open for anyone who wishes to win the heart of an opponent to forgo part of what is rightfully his. This means that the chance is available to all to go beyond strict justice, which is both a right and a duty, to show kindness in order to allow wounds to heal or to win favour.

Kindness has an even broader sense. Every good action is a kindness. The command enjoining kindness includes every type of action and transaction. It thus covers every aspect of life, including a person's relationship with his Lord, family, community and with the rest of mankind.

Perhaps we should add here that some commentators on the Qur'ān say that 'justice' is the obligatory part, while 'kindness' is voluntary, but highly encouraged, particularly in so far as matters of worship are concerned. They say that this verse is part of the revelations received by the Prophet in Makkah, when the legal provisions had not as yet been outlined. But the way the verse is phrased uses both justice and kindness in their broadest sense. Moreover, from a purely ethical point of view, both are generally applicable principles, not mere legal provisions.

One aspect of kindness is 'generosity to one's kindred', but it is specially highlighted here in order to emphasize its importance. From the Islamic point of view, this is not based on narrow family loyalty, but on the Islamic principle of common solidarity which moves from the smaller, local circle to the larger, social context. The principle is central to the implementation of the Islamic social system.

The verse proceeds to outline three prohibitions in contrast to the three orders with which it begins, stating that God *"forbids all that is shameful, all reprehensible conduct and aggression."* (Verse 90) Under shameful conduct everything that goes beyond the limits of propriety is included, but the term is often used to denote dishonourable assault and indecency. Thus it combines both aggression and transgression. Hence it has become synonymous with shamefulness.

'Reprehensible conduct' refers to any action of which pure, undistorted human nature disapproves. Islam also disapproves of any such conduct because it is the religion of pure human nature. Human nature can however become distorted, but Islamic law remains constant, pointing to what human nature is like before distortion creeps in.

'Aggression' in this context denotes injustice as well as any excess that goes beyond what is right and fair. No community can survive when it is based on the spread of shameful, reprehensible conduct and aggression. No community can hope to flourish if it does not stamp out shameful conduct, reprehensible actions and aggression. Hence human nature is bound to rebel against these whenever they are allowed to spread in society.

Human nature will not allow such destructive forces to remain in full play without staging a rebellion. This is inevitable even though such forces may be exceedingly powerful, functioning under the protection of tyrant rulers. In fact the history of humanity is full of such rebellions aiming to purge humanity of such parasites, in the same way that the human body mobilizes its defences to expel any alien organism. The very fact that human nature rebels against them proves that they are alien to proper human life. While God enjoins justice and kindness, He forbids shameful, reprehensible conduct and aggression. This is in perfect accord with what pure human nature desires. It strengthens human nature and supports its resistance to such alien forces. Hence the final comment in the verse tells us that God *"admonishes you so that you may take heed."* (Verse 90) The admonition serves to awaken human conscience and support an undistorted human nature.

Using Oaths for Deceit

Fulfil your covenant with God whenever you make a pledge. Do not break your oaths after you have confirmed them, and have made God your surety. God certainly knows all that you do. (Verse 91)

Fulfilment of God's covenant includes the pledge Muslims give to the Prophet (peace be upon him) when they accept the Islamic faith, as well as every pledge or promise that involves something permissible or encouraged. The fulfilment of promises and pledges ensures that trust is maintained in human transactions. Without such trust human society, and humanity generally, cannot have a solid foundation. The verse makes sure that those who make a pledge or a covenant are ashamed to break their oaths after having confirmed them, making God the surety for their fulfilment, and appealing to Him as their witness. This is followed by an implicit warning: "*God certainly knows all that you do.*" (Verse 91)

Islam takes a very strict view on the question of fulfilling covenants, allowing no breach or violation under any circumstances. This is important because it constitutes the basis of trust in any community. Without strict fulfilment of covenants, the whole structure of the community collapses. The treatment of this point in the *sūrah* does not stop at merely stating an order to fulfil all covenants and pledges and a prohibition of their violation. It goes further than that, showing the violation of covenants in a very bad light. It also dismisses every excuse people make to justify their going back on covenants: "*Be not like her who untwists the yarn which she has firmly spun, using your oaths as a means to deceive one another, simply because a particular group may be more powerful than another. By this, God puts you to the test. On the Day of Resurrection He will make clear to you all that on which you now differ.*" (Verse 92)

A person who goes back on his pledges is shown like a stupid, imbecile woman who has no resolve. She spins her yarn and then breaks it leaving it in loose thread. Every little detail given in the example suggests shame and ignominy. The whole picture is meant to give a completely repulsive impression. No honourable person would compromise himself to look so idiotic as the woman who spends her life doing what is of no use and no value whatsoever.

Some people tried to justify going back on the covenants they had made with the Prophet Muḥammad (peace be upon him) by saying that he and his companions were but a weak group, while the Quraysh enjoyed strength of numbers and position. The *sūrah* makes it clear that this is no justification for making their oaths a means of deception, showing themselves ready to go back on them whenever it suited them:

"using your oaths as a means to deceive one another, simply because a particular community may be more powerful than another." This is a clear order not to contemplate breaking pledges in order to gain favour with a community that may appear to be more powerful.

The Qur'ānic statement includes cases when a breach of a covenant is justified on the basis of what we call today, 'national interests'. A certain country may abrogate a treaty it has signed with another, or with a group of countries, only because a stronger nation or group of nations happen to be on the other side. 'National interest' is used to justify such violation of binding covenants and treaties. Islam does not approve of such justification. It makes its firm stand that covenants must be honoured; and oaths must never be made in deception. At the same time Islam does not approve of any pledge, treaty or covenant that is not based on righteousness and God-consciousness. Islam is very clear on this. No pledge or cooperation in injustice, transgression, disobedience to God, usurpation of other people's rights or exploitation of other communities and countries is admissible in Islam. Such is the foundation on which the Muslim community and the Islamic state were built. Hence, security, trust as also sound and healthy relationships on individual and international levels were enjoyed by the whole world at the time when Islam assumed the leadership.

This Qur'ānic statement warns against seeking such an excuse. It warns that when a situation like the one described in the verse prevails, and one community appears to be far more powerful than another, it serves as a trial to Muslims. God wishes to test their resolve to honour their covenants so that they may prove their unwillingness to break a covenant when they have made God their witness to it. *"By this, God puts you to the test."* (Verse 92) As for differences that may exist between nations and communities, these are left to God to resolve on the appointed day: *"On the Day of Resurrection He will make clear to you all that on which you now differ."* (Verse 92) This statement serves to reassure the Muslim community as it resolves to honour its pledges to, and treaties with, communities that do not share its faith.

Had God so willed, He would have surely made you all one single community. But He lets go astray him that wills [to go astray] and guides aright him that wills [to be guided]. You shall certainly be called to account for all that you do. (Verse 93)

It is God's will that people should be created with different aptitudes and susceptibilities. He could have created them with the same aptitude, but He has so willed that each individual is so unlike any other. He has set into operation rules and laws which ensure that people can follow His guidance or choose to go astray. These fulfil His will in relation to mankind. Within these laws, everyone is responsible for the actions he or she takes. Bearing this in mind, it follows that differences of faith and beliefs cannot be used as an excuse to violate treaties and covenants. These differences have their reasons which are subject to God's will. Covenants are to be honoured regardless of differences in faith.

Do we need to comment on such clean and straightforward dealings, or such religious tolerance? The fact is that throughout history, such cleanliness and honest dealing were only experienced under Islam, when the Muslim community was truly guided by the Qur'ān.

Ideals Made Practical

The *sūrah* places even greater emphasis on the fulfilment of pledges and the prohibition of resorting to oaths in order to deceive others, lulling them into a false sense of security in order to make transitory gain. It warns that the only result of such deception is to weaken the basis of social life and undermine bonds, commitments and beliefs. It warns against God's severe punishment in the hereafter. At the same time, it holds the promise of a much better reward which more than compensates for any trivial gain they may have had to sacrifice in honouring their pledges. It reminds them that what they have in this life is transitory, certain to come to an end, while that which God holds is inexhaustible, everlasting.

Do not use your oaths as a means to deceive one another, lest your foot should slip after it has been firm, and lest you should be made to suffer the evil [consequences] of your having debarred others from the path of God, with tremendous suffering awaiting you. Do not barter away your covenant with God for a trifling price. Surely, that which is with God is far better for you, if you but knew it. Whatever you have is certain to come to an end, but that which is with God is everlasting. We will certainly grant those who are patient in adversity their reward according to the best that they ever did. (Verses 94–96)

When oaths are sworn only to deceive other people, the result is the weakening of faith in one's own conscience and giving to others a distorted image of it. Someone who swears in order to deceive others cannot have firm belief, and cannot walk firmly along its path. At the same time, he presents a bad image of his professed faith to those who trust him only to find themselves deceived. In this way, he sets a very bad example of believers, in effect turning others away from God's faith.

In fact whole communities accepted the faith of Islam when they realized how faithful to their trust the Muslims were. The unhesitating fulfilment by the Muslims of their promises, their true oaths and clean, straightforward dealings motivated other communities to learn more about Islam and believe in it. Thus the resulting gain was far greater than the temporary loss that appeared to be incurred by fulfilment of pledges.

The Qur'ān and the *Sunnah* of the Prophet have left a very strong impression on Muslims in relation to their promises and treaties. This has remained the distinctive characteristic of their dealings with others both at individual and international levels. It is reported that a truce was made between Mu'āwiyah, the fifth Caliph, and the Byzantine Emperor. When the truce was approaching its end, Mu'āwiyah marched towards Byzantium. He was very close to the border when the truce expired, and he began military activity. 'Umar ibn 'Utbah, a Companion of the Prophet in his army said to him: "Mu'āwiyah! God be glorified. Honour your pledges and never violate them. I have heard God's Messenger [peace be upon him] saying: 'Whoever has a treaty with other people must not break his commitment until the term has lapsed.' Mu'āwiyah ordered his army to retreat and marched home." Examples in history of Muslims honouring treaties, even though their immediate interests would have been better served by abrogating them, are numerous.

The Qur'ān was able to make such a distinctly strong impression on Muslims through repeated warnings against violation of covenants, promises of reward for honouring them, and by making the covenant a bond with God. It shows the benefit that may result from such violation of commitment to be paltry, while God rewards generously those who are true to their word: "*Do not barter away your covenant with God for a trifling price. Surely, that which is with God is far better for you, if you but knew it.*" (Verse 95) The verse reminds us that what human beings may have is transitory, even though it may be all the property of one person. On the other hand, what is with God remains for ever: "*Whatever you have is certain to come to an end, but that which is with God is everlasting.*" (Verse 96) Thus their determination to fulfil their commitments, even though they may be burdensome, is immensely strengthened. Those who persevere in the face of difficulty are promised generous reward: "*We will certainly grant those who are patient in adversity their reward according to the best that they ever did.*" (Verse 96) The promise implies that their failings are overlooked, so that their reward takes into account only the best of their actions.

Equal Reward for Equal Sexes

The next verse lays down a general rule about action and reward: "*Whoever does righteous deeds, whether man or woman, and is a believer, We shall most certainly give a good life. And We shall indeed reward these according to the best that they ever did.*" (Verse 97) The first item in this rule is that the two sexes, male and female, are equal with regard to their actions and the reward they receive for them. They enjoy the same relationship with God and the same standing in His regard. Hence, He rewards them equally, applying one measure to both of them. Although the term, 'whoever', with which the verse opens, includes both men and women, the Qur'ānic statement emphasizes this by stating it very clearly: "*Whoever does righteous deeds, whether man or woman.*" This equality is stressed emphatically in the same *sūrah* that gives us an image of how Arab *jāhiliyyah* society looked upon women.

93

It tells us how society looked down upon women, and the extent of the depression a father felt when he was given the news of the birth of a girl, leading him to hide away from his friends and acquaintances, because of the shame he felt.

Another aspect of this general rule is that good action must have a strong foundation, which must be faith. Without it, good action cannot be cemented into a well built structure. It remains haphazard, and it soon becomes like ashes blown in every direction by a strong wind. Faith provides the axis around which all bonds turn. It gives good action a motive and an aim. Thus it gives goodness a strong foundation so that it is not swayed by fleeting desires.

The rule also establishes that when good action is coupled with faith, it is rewarded by a goodly life in this world. It need not be a life of affluence and riches. It may be a goodly life with or without plenty of money. There are many things in life, other than money, which provide a goodly feeling and happiness. A strong bond with God and a feeling of trust in Him and His abounding grace make life happy indeed. Life may also be blessed with good health, a peaceful and blessed living, love and compassion. It may have the rejoice generated by good action and its effects on oneself and society. Money is only one aspect, and little of it is sufficient when one looks up to what is more blessed and longer lasting.

This general rule also makes clear that a goodly life in this world will not reduce in any way one's good reward in the life to come. Indeed the reward is based on the best actions believers do in this world. This implies, as we have stated earlier, that God will forgive them their sins. This is indeed the best reward to which human beings may aspire.

Attitude to Qur'ānic Recitation

The *sūrah* then speaks about the Qur'ān and the values to be observed when reciting it. It also mentions some of the false assertions the unbelievers used to make about it. *"Whenever you read the Qur'ān, seek refuge with God from Satan, the accursed. He certainly has no power over those who believe and place their trust in their Lord. He has power only over those who are willing to follow him, and thus ascribe to him a share in God's divinity.*" (Verses 98–100) Seeking God's refuge against Satan prepares the atmosphere such that it is more congenial for the recitation of God's book. It gives a sense of purity that strengthens the reader's bond with God, so that he is free from any other preoccupation, that is with any aspect of the world of evil that Satan represents.

This is all generated by seeking refuge with God from Satan and his schemes. Yet it is made clear that Satan "*has no power over those who believe and place their trust in their Lord.*" (Verse 99) Those who appeal to God alone and purge their hearts of any loyalty to any other bond are free of Satan's power. Much as he may whisper to them, their bond with God protects them from toeing his line. They may slip and commit errors, but they do not submit to Satan. They will always purge their hearts of Satan's influence and turn to God in repentance. "*He has power only over those who are willing to follow him, and thus ascribe to him a share in God's divinity.*" (Verse 100) It is such people who make Satan their patron, who allow their desires to dictate their actions under Satan's influence that are subject to his power. Indeed some of them make Satan their Lord. Indeed some have even worshipped Satan, or a similar deity of evil. However, following Satan's footsteps is a kind of associating him as a partner with God.

The Nature of False Fabrication

The *sūrah* also mentions some of the falsehoods the unbelievers circulated about the Qur'ān:

> *When We replace one verse by another – and God knows best what He reveals – they say: 'You are but a fabricator.' Indeed most of them have no knowledge. Say: 'The Holy Spirit has brought it down from your Lord in truth, so as to strengthen the believers, and to provide guidance and good news to those who surrender themselves to God.' We know full well that they say: 'It is but a man that teaches him [all] this.' But the man to whom they so maliciously allude speaks a foreign tongue, while this is Arabic speech, pure and clear. Those who do not believe in God's revelations shall not be*

granted guidance by God. Grievous suffering awaits them. It is only those who do not believe in God's revelations that invent falsehood. It is they indeed who are liars. (Verses 101–105)

The unbelievers do not understand the role of God's book and the fact that it has been revealed to establish a global human society and create a community to lead it along its way. They do not realize that it is the final message to come from on high to mankind. They are oblivious of the essential truth that God, who has created man, knows best which concepts, principles and legislation are best suited for humanity. When He abrogates a verse that has completed its purpose, He puts another in its place which is more suitable for the stage the new community has reached, and better suited for the long future, the duration of which is known only to Him. This is certainly His prerogative. The verses of this book may be likened to a medicine which is given in small doses to a patient until he is cured. Then he is advised to resume a normal diet which helps to protect his health.

But the unbelievers understand nothing of all this. Hence it is not surprising that they did not appreciate the purpose behind the abrogation of one verse by another and accused the Prophet of being a fabricator when he was indeed the most honest and truthful person they had ever known. Hence the verse comments: *"Indeed most of them have no knowledge."* (Verse 101)

The *sūrah* then states the truth of the revelation of the Qur'ān: *"Say: The Holy Spirit has brought it down from your Lord in truth."* (Verse 102) It could not be a fabrication when it was brought down by the Holy Spirit, the Angel Gabriel (peace be upon him). He has brought it *'from your Lord'*, not from you, and this is done *'in truth'*, which means that no falsehood can ever be attached to it. The purpose of its revelation is *'to strengthen the believers,'* who maintain the bond between God and their hearts. These realize that it has come from God to spell out the truth and make it clear for all mankind. It has another purpose as well, which is *'to provide guidance and good news to those who surrender themselves to God.'* (Verse 102) They are strengthened by the fact that they are guided along the right path, as also given the happy news of achieving victory and establishing their power.

We know full well that they say: 'It is but a man that teaches him [all] this.' But the man to whom they so maliciously allude speaks a foreign tongue, while this is Arabic speech, pure and clear. (Verse 103)

This was yet another falsehood the unbelievers tried to assert. They claimed that the Qur'ān was taught to the Prophet by a man whom they named. We have different reports about the particular person they mentioned. One report points to a foreign servant attached to one clan or another of the Quraysh who used to sell goods near al-Ṣafā. The Prophet might have sat with him and spoke to him at times. But the man spoke a foreign language. His knowledge of Arabic was sufficient only to conduct necessary business transactions.

Another report by Ibn Isḥāq in his biography of the Prophet suggests that the Prophet used to sit at al-Marwah with a Christian servant named Sabī ʿah, although some people called him Jabr. He was a slave owned by a man from al-Ḥaḍramī clan. Ibn Kathīr, the historian, and other scholars like ʿIkrimah and Qatādah mention that the man's name was Yaʿīsh.

Another scholar and historian, al-Ṭabarī, reports on the authority of Ibn ʿAbbās, the Prophet's cousin, that the Prophet used to teach a slave called Balʿām who spoke a foreign language. The unbelievers used to see the Prophet leaving his place. So they came up with their ridiculous fabrication, saying that Balʿām taught the Prophet.

God answers all these fabrications with a simple, clear statement that ends all argument: "*The man to whom they so maliciously allude speaks a foreign tongue, while this is Arabic speech, pure and clear.*" (Verse 103) It is difficult to imagine that they were serious when they made such ludicrous claims. It was all most likely a part of their evil scheming which they knew to be absolutely false. They were fully aware of the merits of the Qur'ān and its literary excellence. How could they claim that a man speaking a foreign tongue could have taught it to Muḥammad. If such a man could have produced such a masterpiece, why would he not claim it for himself, without teaching it to another?

Today, with humanity having made such huge advancements, and human talent having produced such great books and masterpieces, social orders and legislation, anyone who appreciates literature, social systems and legal codes is bound to acknowledge that the Qur'ān could not have been authored by a human being.

Even the atheists of Communist Russia who wished to criticize Islam in the Conference of Orientalists held in 1954 managed no better than to claim that the Qur'ān could not have been the work of one man. It must have been the collective work of a large community. Moreover, they claimed, it could not have been written totally in Arabia. Some parts of it must have been written in other parts of the world! They felt that no individual had the talent to produce this book, and nor had one nation the knowledge embodied in it. They could not admit to the force of sound logic and attribute the Qur'ān to its true Author, God, the Lord of all the worlds. They denied God's existence. How could they acknowledge revelation and prophethood?

This is the view of some specialist scholars in the twentieth century. Compared with it, the Makkan unbelievers' claim that a foreign slave who spoke little Arabic taught it to Muḥammad appears at its most ludicrous.

The Qur'ān states the reason behind such false assertions: "*Those who do not believe in God's revelations shall not be granted guidance by God. Grievous suffering awaits them.*" (Verse 104) Those who refuse to believe in the signs given by God will not be guided to the truth concerning this divine revelation. Indeed God does not guide them to the truth concerning anything. This is the natural consequence of their unbelief and deliberate rejection of the message God's signs impart to them. Hence, '*grievous suffering awaits them,*' after they have been in continuous error.

The *sūrah* then makes it clear that false claims against God could not be made by Muḥammad, whose honesty was exemplary. Such falsehood could only be asserted by people like them refusing to believe in God: "*It is only those who do not believe in God's revelations that invent falsehood. It is they indeed who are liars.*" (Verse 105) Lying is a cardinal sin which no believer perpetrates. The Prophet himself made it clear that a true believer could at times commit some sinful action, but a true believer would never deliberately tell a lie.

Rejecting the Faith after Accepting it

The *sūrah* outlines here the rulings concerning anyone who disavows faith after having accepted it:

> *As for anyone who denies God after having accepted the faith – and this certainly does not apply to one who does it under duress, while his heart remains true to his faith, but applies to him who willingly opens his heart to unbelief – upon all such falls God's wrath, and theirs will be a tremendous suffering. This is because they love the life of this world better than the life to come. God does not bestow His guidance on those who reject the truth. Such are those whose hearts and ears and eyes are sealed by God; such are the heedless. Without doubt, in the life to come they will be the losers.* (Verses 106–109)

The early Muslims in Makkah were subjected to such brutal oppression as could only be endured by those who had made up their minds to sacrifice their lives in pursuit of a higher destiny in the life to come. Such people endure all the atrocities the unbelievers perpetrate against them, rather than revert to pagan faith.

The *sūrah* paints in ghastly colours the crime of the person who reverts to unbelief after having known the true faith, declared his acceptance of it and experienced its blessings. Such a person only reverts to unbelief because he prefers the comforts and pleasures of this world to the happiness of the life to come. Hence such people are threatened with God's wrath and tremendous suffering, in addition to being deprived of God's guidance. They are described as heedless, as having sealed their hearts, ears and eyes, and as being certain losers in the life to come. The important point here is that faith must never be subject to bargaining or to a balance of profit and loss. When a person's heart and mind submit to faith, they do not admit any worldly influence. This world has its values and considerations, while faith has its own. The two sets cannot overlap or have anything in common. Faith must not be treated in a trifling way. It is not a bargain that you make one day and reverse the next. It is far more precious. Hence the crime is painted in such ghastly colours and the punishment is seen to be extremely stern.

The only exception from such condemnation is the one who professes, under utter duress, to have rejected the faith only to save himself from certain death, while his heart remains full of faith, certain that it is the truth. It is reported that this ruling was revealed in connection with 'Ammār ibn Yāsir. Al-Ṭabarī reports on the authority of Muḥammad, 'Ammār's son, that "the unbelievers in Makkah tortured his father, 'Ammār ibn Yāsir, continuously until he gave in to some of their demands. He then reported this to the Prophet who asked him: 'How do you feel deep at heart?' He said: 'My heart is full of faith, entertaining no doubt whatsoever.' The Prophet said to him: 'If they try again, do likewise.' This was a concession, and it applies to anyone in similar circumstances."[1]

Yet many believers refused to satisfy their torturers, preferring to die rather than give in, even only verbally, to their demands. This was the stance taken by 'Ammār's own parents. His mother, Sumayyah, was so resolute in her resistance that she was stabbed with a spear in her vagina and died a martyr. His father also was tortured to death without giving in. Similarly did Bilāl, who was singled out for a special treatment. The unbelievers laid him down on the burning sands in the summer heat of Arabia and put on his chest a large rock and dragged him along, ordering him to reject his faith, but he refused and declared: "He is only One God." He then said to them: "Had I known anything that would give you more displeasure, I would have said it."

Another example is that of Ḥabīb ibn Zayd al-Anṣārī, when Musaylamah, the liar who claimed to be a messenger of God asked him: "Do you believe that Muḥammad is God's Messenger?" Ḥabīb said: "Yes, indeed." Musaylamah asked him: "Do you believe that I, too, am God's messenger?" Ḥabīb said: "I hear nothing." Musaylamah then ordered that Ḥabīb be dismembered. He kept asking him and he kept giving the same replies until he died under such torture.

'Abdullāh ibn Ḥudhāfah of the Sahm clan of the Quraysh was a companion of the Prophet who was once taken captive by the Byzantines. He was taken to their ruler who offered him a share in his kingdom and that he would give him his own daughter as a wife if he

1. Abū Ja'far Muḥammad Ibn Jarīr al-Ṭabarī, *Jāmi' al-Bāyan 'An Ta'wīl Āy al-Qur'ān*. Dār al-Fikr, Beirut, 1984, Vol. 8, Part 14, p. 182.

would embrace Christianity. 'Abdullāh said: "If you were to give me all your kingdom and all the wealth and property of all Arabs in return for disowning the faith of Muhammad, (peace be upon him), I would not accept for even a blink of an eye." The Byzantine ruler said: "If you refuse, then I will kill you." 'Abdullāh said: "Do what you like." The ruler then ordered that he should be crucified. Soldiers then shot at him with arrows piercing his legs and arms, but he refused to convert to Christianity despite all this.

The ruler then ordered that he should be brought down from the cross. A large pan made of copper was put over a great fire until it was boiling fiercely. Another Muslim captive was then thrown into the pan and soon his bones were visible. 'Abdullāh was then told to convert to Christianity, threatened that he would suffer the same fate if he did not. He refused, and the ruler ordered that he should be thrown into the pan. As he was being lifted, the ruler noticed that his eyes were tearful. He ordered that he should be brought down. He then spoke to him only to be astonished by 'Abdullāh's explanation of his crying. 'Abdullāh said: "I only cried because I have one soul, and I am subjected to this torture for my faith. I wish I had as many souls as the number of hairs on my body and each one of them was subjected to the same fate."

Another report suggests that the Byzantine ruler then imprisoned 'Abdullāh ibn Hudhāfah for several days without food or water. He then sent him wine and pork. 'Abdullāh touched nothing of this. He was then taken to the ruler who asked him why he did not eat or drink. 'Abdullāh said: "In my condition, [i.e. a case of starvation approaching death] it is lawful for me to eat and drink the otherwise forbidden things you sent me. But I will not give you the pleasure of feeling that you have broken my resolve." The ruler secretly admired 'Abdullāh for his great resistance under pressure. He said to him: "Kiss my head and I will set you free." 'Abdullāh said: "I will do so if you will also set free all the other Muslim captives you hold." The ruler agreed and 'Abdullāh kissed his head. The ruler was true to his promise and set them all free. 'Abdullāh took them all to Madinah and reported what happened to the Caliph, 'Umar ibn al-Khaṭṭāb who said: "It is the duty of every Muslim to kiss 'Abdullāh ibn Hudhāfah's head. I will be the first to do so." He then stood up and kissed 'Abdullāh's head.

This shows that faith is a matter of grave importance. There can be no compromise about it. To uphold it may require paying a heavy price. But, to a Muslim, faith is far more valuable than any price. It is so also in God's view. It is a trust honoured only by one who is prepared to sacrifice his life for it.[2] Indeed the life of this world and all the comforts it may provide is of little consequence compared with faith.

> *But then, your Lord [grants forgiveness] to those who forsake their homes after enduring trials and persecution, and strive hard [in God's cause] and remain patient in adversity. After all this, your Lord is certainly Much-Forgiving, Most Merciful. One day every soul will come pleading for itself. Every soul will be repaid in full for all its actions, and none shall be wronged.* (Verses 110–111)

The reference here is to some believers who were among the weaker elements of Arabian society. They were subjected to great pressure and had to renounce their faith. However, they subsequently migrated and joined the believers when they had a chance to do so. They strove hard for the cause of Islam, enduring much hardship along the way. The verse gives them the good news of God's forgiveness and an abundance of His grace: *"After all this, your Lord is Much-Forgiving, Most Merciful."* (Verse 110)

This will take place on a day when every soul will be preoccupied with its own affairs. It has no time for anyone else. The statement, *"every soul will come pleading for itself,"* gives us a sense of the seriousness of the whole matter. Everyone will be trying hard to save themselves from the suffering that awaits the wrongdoers. But pleading will be of no avail, for it is the time of reckoning and reward. Hence: *"Every soul will be repaid in full for all its actions, and none shall be wronged."* (Verse 111)

---

2. The author himself honoured this trust when he refused to succumb to all the pressure and torture he was subjected to. He sacrificed his life when he was executed for no crime other than holding his views. This was in the summer of 1966, in the reign of Nasser, the Egyptian dictator. – Editor's note.

6

Advocacy by Example

God cites the case of a town living in security and ease. Its sustenance comes to it in abundance from all quarters. Yet it was ungrateful for God's favours. Therefore, God caused it to experience the misery of hunger and fear for what its people used to do. (112)

وَضَرَبَ ٱللَّهُ مَثَلًا قَرْيَةً كَانَتْ ءَامِنَةً مُّطْمَئِنَّةً يَأْتِيهَا رِزْقُهَا رَغَدًا مِّن كُلِّ مَكَانٍ فَكَفَرَتْ بِأَنْعُمِ ٱللَّهِ فَأَذَاقَهَا ٱللَّهُ لِبَاسَ ٱلْجُوعِ وَٱلْخَوْفِ بِمَا كَانُوا۟ يَصْنَعُونَ ﴿١١٢﴾

There had come to them a messenger from among themselves, but they denied him. Therefore suffering overwhelmed them as they were wrongdoers. (113)

وَلَقَدْ جَآءَهُمْ رَسُولٌ مِّنْهُمْ فَكَذَّبُوهُ فَأَخَذَهُمُ ٱلْعَذَابُ وَهُمْ ظَـٰلِمُونَ ﴿١١٣﴾

So eat of all the lawful and good things God has provided for you, and be grateful to God for His favours, if it is truly Him that you worship. (114)

فَكُلُوا۟ مِمَّا رَزَقَكُمُ ٱللَّهُ حَلَـٰلًا طَيِّبًا وَٱشْكُرُوا۟ نِعْمَتَ ٱللَّهِ إِن كُنتُمْ إِيَّاهُ تَعْبُدُونَ ﴿١١٤﴾

He has forbidden you only carrion, blood, the flesh of swine and anything over which any name other than God's has been invoked. But if anyone is driven to it by necessity, neither desiring it nor exceeding his immediate need, then God is Much-Forgiving, Merciful. (115)

إِنَّمَا حَرَّمَ عَلَيْكُمُ ٱلْمَيْتَةَ وَٱلدَّمَ وَلَحْمَ ٱلْخِنزِيرِ وَمَآ أُهِلَّ لِغَيْرِ ٱللَّهِ بِهِۦ فَمَنِ ٱضْطُرَّ غَيْرَ بَاغٍ وَلَا عَادٍ فَإِنَّ ٱللَّهَ غَفُورٌ رَّحِيمٌ ﴿١١٥﴾

Do not say – for any false thing you may utter with your tongues – that 'This is lawful and this is forbidden', so as to attribute your lying inventions to God. Indeed those who attribute their lying inventions to God will never be successful. (116)

وَلَا تَقُولُوا۟ لِمَا تَصِفُ أَلْسِنَتُكُمُ ٱلْكَذِبَ هَـٰذَا حَلَـٰلٌ وَهَـٰذَا حَرَامٌ لِّتَفْتَرُوا۟ عَلَى ٱللَّهِ ٱلْكَذِبَ إِنَّ ٱلَّذِينَ يَفْتَرُونَ عَلَى ٱللَّهِ ٱلْكَذِبَ لَا يُفْلِحُونَ ﴿١١٦﴾

Brief is their enjoyment [of this life], and grievous suffering awaits them [in the life to come]. (117)

مَتَـٰعٌ قَلِيلٌ وَلَهُمْ عَذَابٌ أَلِيمٌ ﴿١١٧﴾

To the Jews We have made unlawful such things as We have mentioned to you earlier. We did them no wrong, but they were the ones who persistently wronged themselves. (118)

وَعَلَى ٱلَّذِينَ هَادُوا۟ حَرَّمْنَا مَا قَصَصْنَا عَلَيْكَ مِن قَبْلُ وَمَا ظَلَمْنَـٰهُمْ وَلَـٰكِن كَانُوٓا۟ أَنفُسَهُمْ يَظْلِمُونَ ﴿١١٨﴾

But indeed your Lord [grants forgiveness] to those who do evil out of ignorance, and then repent and mend their ways. After all this, your Lord is certainly Much-Forgiving, Merciful. (119)

ثُمَّ إِنَّ رَبَّكَ لِلَّذِينَ عَمِلُوا السُّوٓءَ بِجَهَـٰلَةٍ ثُمَّ تَابُوا۟ مِنۢ بَعْدِ ذَٰلِكَ وَأَصْلَحُوٓا۟ إِنَّ رَبَّكَ مِنۢ بَعْدِهَا لَغَفُورٌ رَّحِيمٌ ۝

In truth Abraham was a model, devoutly obedient to God, and true in faith. He was not one of those who associated partners with God. (120)

إِنَّ إِبْرَٰهِيمَ كَانَ أُمَّةً قَانِتًا لِّلَّهِ حَنِيفًا وَلَمْ يَكُ مِنَ الْمُشْرِكِينَ ۝

He showed his gratitude for the blessings bestowed by Him who had chosen him and guided him to a straight path. (121)

شَاكِرًا لِّأَنْعُمِهِ ٱجْتَبَٰهُ وَهَدَىٰهُ إِلَىٰ صِرَٰطٍ مُّسْتَقِيمٍ ۝

We bestowed on him good in this world; and truly, in the life to come he will be among the righteous. (122)

وَءَاتَيْنَٰهُ فِى ٱلدُّنْيَا حَسَنَةً وَإِنَّهُۥ فِى ٱلْأَخِرَةِ لَمِنَ ٱلصَّٰلِحِينَ ۝

And now We have inspired you with [this message]: 'Follow the creed of Abraham, who was true in faith, and who was not one of those who associated partners with God.' (123)

ثُمَّ أَوْحَيْنَآ إِلَيْكَ أَنِ ٱتَّبِعْ مِلَّةَ إِبْرَٰهِيمَ حَنِيفًا وَمَا كَانَ مِنَ ٱلْمُشْرِكِينَ ۝

105

[The observance of] the Sabbath was ordained only to those who differed about him. Your Lord will judge between them on the Day of Resurrection with regard to all that on which they dispute. (124)

إِنَّمَا جُعِلَ ٱلسَّبْتُ عَلَى ٱلَّذِينَ ٱخْتَلَفُوا۟ فِيهِ وَإِنَّ رَبَّكَ لَيَحْكُمُ بَيْنَهُمْ يَوْمَ ٱلْقِيَٰمَةِ فِيمَا كَانُوا۟ فِيهِ يَخْتَلِفُونَ ﴿١٢٤﴾

Call people to the path of your Lord with wisdom and goodly exhortation, and argue with them in the most kindly manner. Your Lord knows best who strays from His path and who are rightly guided. (125)

ٱدْعُ إِلَىٰ سَبِيلِ رَبِّكَ بِٱلْحِكْمَةِ وَٱلْمَوْعِظَةِ ٱلْحَسَنَةِ وَجَٰدِلْهُم بِٱلَّتِى هِىَ أَحْسَنُ إِنَّ رَبَّكَ هُوَ أَعْلَمُ بِمَن ضَلَّ عَن سَبِيلِهِ وَهُوَ أَعْلَمُ بِٱلْمُهْتَدِينَ ﴿١٢٥﴾

If you should punish, then let your punishment be commensurate with the wrong done to you. But to endure patiently is far better for those who are patient in adversity. (126)

وَإِنْ عَاقَبْتُمْ فَعَاقِبُوا۟ بِمِثْلِ مَا عُوقِبْتُم بِهِ وَلَئِن صَبَرْتُمْ لَهُوَ خَيْرٌ لِّلصَّٰبِرِينَ ﴿١٢٦﴾

Endure, then, with patience, remembering always that it is only God who helps you to be patient; and do not grieve over them, nor be distressed by their intrigues. (127)

وَٱصْبِرْ وَمَا صَبْرُكَ إِلَّا بِٱللَّهِ وَلَا تَحْزَنْ عَلَيْهِمْ وَلَا تَكُ فِى ضَيْقٍ مِّمَّا يَمْكُرُونَ ﴿١٢٧﴾

God is indeed with those who remain God-fearing and those who do good. (128)

إِنَّ ٱللَّهَ مَعَ ٱلَّذِينَ ٱتَّقَوا۟ وَّٱلَّذِينَ هُم مُّحْسِنُونَ ﴿١٢٨﴾

Overview

Earlier in the *sūrah* God gave two examples to drive home to people an important principle of faith. Now He gives another to portray the situation of Makkah and its pagan people who denied the blessings God had bestowed on them. The example serves to make clear what destiny awaits them if they persist in their attitude. The example highlights the blessings of abundant provisions, peace and security given to the city before mentioning the good and wholesome things they prohibit themselves on the basis of their pagan myths. In fact God has made these lawful to mankind. He has clearly outlined what He has forbidden, and it does not include the matters they prohibit themselves. This is an act of ingratitude to God, giving no thanks to Him for His blessings. By adopting this attitude they lay themselves open to God's severe punishment.

As it outlines the foul things God has forbidden to Muslims, the *sūrah* mentions the wholesome things God had forbidden to the Jews because of their wrongdoing. These were not forbidden to their forefathers at the time of Abraham who was a devout servant of God. These were indeed permissible to him and his offspring. Some were later forbidden to the Jews as a sort of punishment for their subsequent disobedience. Those who then mended their ways could receive God's forgiveness and mercy.

Then God revealed a new message to Muḥammad as the final version of His faith. Thus all wholesome things were made lawful again. The same applies to the restrictions of the Sabbath, the day on which the Jews are forbidden fishing and hunting. The Sabbath applies to its own people who disagreed over it. Some of them obeyed the orders and refrained from doing what God had forbidden, while others transgressed and incurred God's punishment. They were sent to a depth far below that of human beings.

At this point the *sūrah* comes to its close with an order given to God's Messenger to call on people to follow God's guidance. He should make his call with wisdom and goodly admonition, and with argument that is kindly. He is also told to maintain the laws of justice, replying to any aggression with similar measure, knowing that patience and

107

forbearance are even better. The final outcome is indeed in favour of the God-fearing because God is with them, showing them the way to success, supporting and taking good care of them.

An Example to Avoid

God cites the case of a town living in security and ease. Its sustenance comes to it in abundance from all quarters. Yet it was ungrateful for God's favours. Therefore, God caused it to experience the misery of hunger and fear for what its people used to do. There had come to them a messenger from among themselves, but they denied him. Therefore suffering overwhelmed them as they were wrongdoers. (Verses 112–113)

This case is very similar to that of Makkah where God's sacred house was built. It was made a consecrated city where everyone could feel secure. No one was threatened, even though he might be guilty of murder. All enjoyed the security of being in the neighbourhood of God's Inviolable House. People all around were threatened by all manner of dangers, while the people of Makkah enjoyed peace and security. Their provisions came to them easily from all over the world, carried by pilgrims or trade caravans which travelled in peace. Yet they lived in a barren valley with no cultivation or vegetation. Nevertheless, ever since the days of Abraham, they enjoyed a life of prosperity in addition to their security.

Then a Messenger came to them: a man from among them whom they knew to always tell the truth and to be exemplary in his honesty. They could find nothing wrong with his character. It was God who sent him as His Messenger, bringing mercy to them and to all mankind, preaching the same faith as that of Abraham, who built the Inviolable House of worship which ensured their security and prosperity. But they were quick to reject his message, levelling at him all sorts of false accusations, and subjecting him and his followers to persecution.

The example cited here by God is practically identical with their own situation: "*God cites the case of a town living in security and ease. Its sustenance comes to it in abundance from all quarters. Yet it was ungrateful for God's favours.*" (Verse 112) The result of these people's attitude is placed before their very eyes. They denied the messenger God sent them, *"Therefore, God caused it to experience the misery of hunger and fear for what its people used to do."* (Verse 112) The inevitable result was that *"suffering overwhelmed them as they were wrongdoers."* (Verse 113)

The Arabic text brings this image to life by enhancing the effects of the hunger and fear, making them a garment to be worn, but then they are also made to 'taste' or 'experience' these to generate a more profound effect than that of the image of contact between skin and garment. The text highlights the response of different senses to enhance the effect of experiencing hunger and fear and how this affects the unbelievers. The *sūrah* does this so that they may take heed and endeavour to spare themselves the same destiny which is inevitable if they persist in their wrongdoing.

In virtue of this example which highlights the blessings and the provisions given to them, and by contrast, the risks of restriction and deprivation, they are ordered to eat of the good things God has made lawful to them and to show their gratitude to Him. This is how to maintain the path of true faith, submitting totally to God alone and associating no partners with Him. It is when partners are associated with God that wholesome things are made forbidden in the name of such false deities: *"So eat of all the lawful and good things God has provided for you, and be grateful to God for His favours, if it is truly Him that you worship."* (Verse 114)

The Lawful and the Forbidden

Now the *sūrah* defines what is forbidden, listing the prohibitions in detail. The list does not include what the Arabs forbade themselves, giving these special names such as *baḥīrah, sā'ibah, waṣīlah* and *ḥām.*

We note the exclusivity in the way the prohibitions are listed: *"He has forbidden you only carrion, blood, the flesh of swine and anything over which any name other than God's has been invoked."* (Verse 115) These are forbidden either because they are physically harmful, as in the case of dead animals, blood and pig meat, or because they are outrageous to faith or to mental well-being as when invoking a creature's name at the time of slaughter. *"But if anyone is driven to it by necessity,*

109

neither desiring it nor exceeding his immediate need, then God is Much-Forgiving, Merciful." (Verse 115) This faith of Islam is made easy, involving no affliction. If someone fears to die or becomes ill as a result of hunger and thirst, he may eat something of these forbidden items. We mentioned earlier the differences among scholars as to how much one may eat in such cases. The important thing is that one must neither transgress the principle of prohibition, nor exceed the limits of necessity that override the prohibition in order to permit what is normally restricted.

These are the limits of what God has prohibited or left lawful in relation to food. These limits must not be trespassed on the basis of pagan myths. No one can make a false claim describing as prohibited what God has permitted. Permissibility and prohibition are made by order from God, because they are part of legislation, which is the prerogative of God alone. Anyone who claims legislative authority for himself, on any basis other than God's orders, is an inventor of untruth. Those who invent anything without God's authority will never prosper:

> *Do not say – for any false thing you may utter with your tongues – that 'This is lawful and this is forbidden', so as to attribute your lying inventions to God. Indeed those who attribute their lying inventions to God will never be successful. Brief is their enjoyment [of this life], and grievous suffering awaits them [in the life to come].* (Verses 116–117)

This is an express order that they must not describe anything as lawful or unlawful without appropriate warrant. When they say that something is lawful and another prohibited, without a reliable statement in support, they are stating a naked lie, which they falsely attribute to God. The *sūrah* makes it clear that those who invent falsehood and attribute it to God will have nothing but brief enjoyment in this life. Beyond this, they will be made to experience grievous suffering.

Yet some people have the audacity to enact legislation of their own, relying on no valid text to serve as the basis of what they legislate. What is most amazing is that they still expect to prosper in this life and in the life to come as well.

Beyond this, God has made certain prohibitions applicable to the Jews. These were stated earlier in *Sūrah* 6, Cattle: " *To those who followed the Jewish faith did We forbid all animals that have claws; and We forbade them the fat of both oxen and sheep, except that which is in their backs and entrails and what is mixed with their bones.* " (6: 146) But this was a punishment to the Jews in particular. It does not apply to Muslims. Now this *sūrah* states: " *To the Jews We have made unlawful such things as We have mentioned to you earlier. We did them no wrong, but they were the ones who persistently wronged themselves. But indeed your Lord [grants forgiveness] to those who do evil out of ignorance, and then repent and mend their ways. After all this, your Lord is certainly Much-Forgiving, Merciful.* " (Verses 118–119)

The Jews deserved that these wholesome things be made forbidden because of their transgression and disobedience of God. It was they who thus wronged themselves, while God did them no wrong. However, a person who does wrong in ignorance, without persistently disobeying God until his death, and who follows his repentance with doing good will surely enjoy God's forgiveness. God will bestow His mercy on him. The statement here is general, so as to include the Jews who repented and anyone else who, in future, repents after committing a wrong. This applies right to the Day of Judgement.

The *sūrah* then mentions Abraham and states the truth about his faith. His mention is relevant to the prohibitions made specially applicable to the Jews. It is also relevant to the claims of the pagan Arabs of the Quraysh that they followed Abraham's faith, particularly in what they prohibited for themselves, consecrating it to their false deities. The *sūrah* makes it clear that the message of the Prophet Muḥammad is directly related to Abraham's faith:

In truth Abraham was a model, devoutly obedient to God, and true in faith. He was not one of those who associated partners with God. He showed his gratitude for the blessings bestowed by Him who had chosen him and guided him to a straight path. We bestowed on him good in this world; and truly, in the life to come he will be among the righteous. And now We have inspired you with [this message]: 'Follow the creed of Abraham, who was true in faith,

and who was not one of those who associated partners with God.'
[The observance of] the Sabbath was ordained only to those who
differed about him. Your Lord will judge between them on the
Day of Resurrection with regard to all that on which they dispute.
(Verses 120–124)

The Qur'ān describes Abraham as the perfect follower of God's
guidance, obedient to his Lord, grateful to Him. The Arabic term
describing him here, *ummah*, means a 'nation' or a 'leader'. Thus the
verse may be taken to mean that Abraham was equal to a whole nation
in his faith and true obedience. Or it may be understood to mean that
he was a leader to be followed in all goodly matters. In commentaries
on the Qur'ān, both meanings are mentioned. In fact they are not that
far apart. A leader who encourages his followers to do what is good
leads a whole nation and receives his own reward and a reward similar
to that given to all those whom he guides. This means that he is, in his
goodness and reward, like a whole nation. Abraham is also described
as being *'devoutly obedient to God'*, always seeking to be pure in his
devotion, *'and true in faith'* which means that he always sought the
truth and abided by it. Since he never associated partners with God,
those who do so must not claim any relationship with him, because
there is no such affinity.

Abraham also showed his gratitude, by word and deed, *'for the
blessings bestowed by Him'*. He was totally unlike those pagans who
denied God's blessings verbally and showed their ingratitude by deed.
They even claimed that what they enjoyed of God's sustenance was
given to them by the false deities they associated with Him. Hence
God chose Abraham and *'guided him to a straight path.'* This is the
path of faith based on God's absolute oneness.

This is the truth about Abraham whom both the Jews and the Arab
unbelievers claimed to follow. *"And now We have inspired you with
[this message]: 'Follow the creed of Abraham, who was true in faith, and
who was not one of those who associated partners with God.'"* (Verse
123) This means a re-establishment of the faith based on God's oneness,
followed by Abraham and reiterated in the new message revealed to
Muḥammad.

The restrictions of the Sabbath apply to the Jews only, who differ on its details. It was neither a part of the faith of Abraham nor sanctioned in the faith of Muḥammad who followed Abraham's footsteps. "*[The observance of] the Sabbath was ordained only to those who differed about him.*" (Verse 124) Their case is left to God who knows the truth about all matters: "*Your Lord will judge between them on the Day of Resurrection with regard to all that on which they dispute.*" (Verse 124)

The Best Method of Advocacy

The *sūrah* has thus clarified what similarities may appear between the faith based on believing in God's oneness as outlined by Abraham and perfected by Islam, God's final message to mankind, and the deviant beliefs to which the Jews or the pagan Arabs adhered. All this is part of what the Qur'ān has been revealed to set right. The Prophet is told to continue his efforts, calling on people to follow the divine faith, but utilizing wisdom and good exhortation, and delivering his argument in a kindly manner. If his opponents go on the offensive and act aggressively, the penalty should be of the same type as the aggression, or the Prophet may choose the better way of forgiveness and patience in adversity, despite being able to exact punishment. This is sure to bring him a better outcome. He need not grieve however over those who reject God's guidance, nor should he be afflicted by their scheming against him and his followers.

> *Call people to the path of your Lord with wisdom and goodly exhortation, and argue with them in the most kindly manner. Your Lord knows best who strays from His path and who are rightly guided. If you should punish, then let your punishment be commensurate with the wrong done to you. But to endure patiently is far better for those who are patient in adversity. Endure, then, with patience, remembering always that it is only God who helps you to be patient; and do not grieve over them, nor be distressed by their intrigues. God is indeed with those who remain God-fearing and those who do good.* (Verses 125–128)

Such are the basic rules of Islamic advocacy and such are its appropriate methods. The proper approach is being shown here to the Prophet and to all who succeed him in advocating the Islamic faith. The advocate must make it clear that he simply calls on people to follow the path outlined by God. He is not calling for any personal or national cause. He is simply discharging his duty towards his Lord. He claims no credit for himself, nor does he have a favour to curry with the message itself or with those who respond to his call and follow divine guidance. He receives his reward from God alone.

Advocacy must be undertaken with wisdom. The advocate of the divine message must take into consideration the situation and circumstances of the people whom he addresses in order to determine what he tells them on each occasion. He must not make things appear difficult to them, nor should he burden them with a long list of duties before they are so prepared. He must also consider how he should address them, and how to diversify his method of address in accordance with different circumstances. He must not let his enthusiasm carry the day so as to overlook the prerequisites of wisdom.

Together with wisdom goes goodly exhortation which addresses hearts gently, seeking to kindle good feeling and response. No unnecessary reproach or remonstration should be thrown at them. An advocate of Islam does not publicize genuine mistakes which people commit with good intention. Kindly exhortation often attracts people to follow God's guidance, achieving good results that cannot be achieved through reproach or rebuke.

The third element in this proper approach to Islamic advocacy is to argue 'in the most kindly manner'. This means that there should be no personal criticism or humiliation of an opponent. It is important in such an argument to make the other party realize that, as advocates of the cause of faith, we have no vain desire to win an argument or to boast about having an irrefutable case. Our aim must always be clear, namely, to arrive at the truth. Human beings have their pride, and they will not concede any point unless the argument is carried on in a kindly manner. No one likes to be defeated in argument. People often confuse their own prestige with the value of their opinion, considering that they are humiliated when they have to admit that their view is mistaken. It is only when argument is carried out kindly that people's sensitivity can be tempered, as they realize that their own dignity is preserved. They then recognize that an advocate of Islam seeks only the truth and has no desire to press home personal advantage.

In order to help advocates of Islam restrain themselves and not allow themselves to be carried away by enthusiasm, the *sūrah* mentions that it is God who truly knows those who follow His guidance and those who are in error. Hence there is no need to press an argument beyond what is reasonable. Issues should be stated clearly and matters should then be left to God: *"Your Lord knows best who strays from His path and who are rightly guided."* (Verse 125)

This is the proper method of advocacy as long as it remains within the realm of verbal address and stating a point. Should the advocates of Islam suffer aggression, then the whole situation changes. Aggression is an action that must be repelled with similar force in order to preserve the dignity of the truth and to ensure that falsehood does not triumph. Response to aggression, however, must not exceed the limits of repelling it. Islam is the faith of justice and moderation, peace and reconciliation. It repels any aggression launched against it or its followers, without committing any aggression against others: *"If you should punish, then let your punishment be commensurate with the wrong done to you."* (Verse 126)

This is indeed part of the method of advocacy. To repel aggression within the limits of justice preserves the dignity of the Islamic message so that it suffers no humiliation. A humiliated message has no appeal for anyone. Indeed no one will accept that humiliation be suffered by a divine message. God does not permit His message to suffer humiliation without repelling it. Those who believe in God do not sit idle in the face of persecution and humiliation. They are entrusted with the task of establishing the truth in human life, maintaining justice between people, and leading mankind to the right path. How are they to fulfil their tasks when they do not reply to aggression or respond to unjust punishment?

Yet at the same time that the rule of equal punishment is established, the Qur'ān calls on believers to endure with fortitude and to forgive. This applies in situations when the believers are able to repel aggression and to eradicate evil. In such cases, forgiveness and patience are more effective and of greater value to the Islamic message. Their own personal position or prestige is of secondary importance when the interests of the message are better served by forgiveness and endurance. However, should such forgiveness compromise the position of the message and lead to its humiliation, then the first rule of equal retaliation is preferable.

Since endurance requires resisting one's feelings and impulses, restraining one's emotions and maintaining control over natural reactions, the Qur'ān relates it to faith and earning God's pleasure. It also assures the believers that it brings them good: "*But to endure patiently is far better for those who are patient in adversity. Endure, then, with patience, remembering always that it is only God who helps you to be patient.*" (Verses 126–127) It is God who gives a believer the strength to be patient in adversity and to control his instinctive reactions. Seeking God's pleasure is the one thing that restrains the impulse to retaliate and punish.

The Qur'ān encourages the Prophet, and every advocate of Islam as well, not to grieve when they see people turning their backs on God's guidance. They have their duty to fulfil. Guiding people aright or leaving them to go astray are matters determined by God, in accordance with His laws of nature which control people's souls and their striving to follow guidance or to turn away from it. "*Do not grieve over them, nor be distressed by their intrigues.*" (Verse 127) The Prophet should not be distressed when he sees such people scheme against him. God will protect him against their scheming and intrigue. He will never let them have the upper hand when he conveys his message, seeking no personal gain for himself. He may have to endure harm, but that is only to test his patience. He may feel that victory is slow in coming, but that is only to test his trust in God's support. The ultimate outcome is known in advance: "*God is indeed with those who remain God-fearing and those who do good.*" (Verse 128) He who has God on his side need not worry about anyone's scheming or intrigue.

Such is the constitution that any advocacy of God's message should follow. It is the only way to ensure victory as promised by God. This is what God tells us, and God always tells the truth.

SŪRAH 17

Al-Isrā'
(The Night Journey)

Prologue

This *sūrah*, *Al-Isrā'*, or The Night Journey, was revealed whilst the Prophet lived in Makkah. It begins with glorifying God and ends with praising Him. It includes a number of themes, most of which directly relate to the issue of faith, but some tackle certain aspects of individual and social behaviour and its moral basis of faith. It also includes stories about the Children of Israel relevant to the Aqṣā Mosque, the Prophet's terrestrial destination on his night journey, as well as some aspects of the story of Adam and Satan, and the honour God has granted to mankind.

However, the most prominent element in the *sūrah* and its central point is the Prophet himself (peace be upon him). It examines the attitude adopted by the people of Makkah to him, as well as the message he preached, embodied in the Qur'ān, and the guidance it provides and how the unbelievers received it. This leads to a discussion about the nature of the message and the role of God's messengers. It points to the distinction of the Prophet's message by virtue of it having no physical, preternatural phenomenon to support it. It has been God's will that when such a phenomenon, or miracle, was formerly given in support of a divine message, those who continued to deny the message

117

were shortly destroyed in consequence. It also states the principle of individual responsibility in matters of faith, guidance and error, and collective responsibility in matters of social behaviour. However all such responsibility applies after God has made His message clear to mankind through prophets and messengers whose task is to advise, warn and give sound counsel, and also to make everything clear: "*Most clearly have We spelled out everything.*" (Verse 12)

The *sūrah* repeatedly praises God and glorifies Him and mentions the need to praise and thank Him for all the blessings He bestows on His servants. It begins with glorifying Him: "*Limitless in His glory is He who transported His servant by night from the Sacred Mosque [in Makkah] to the Aqṣā Mosque [in Jerusalem]…*" (Verse 1) Soon afterwards, the Children of Israel are commanded to believe in God's oneness and are reminded that they belong to the offspring of Noah who was '*a truly grateful servant of Ours.*' (Verse 3) When the unbelievers' claims about their false deities are mentioned, the *sūrah* comments: "*Limitless is He in His glory and sublimely exalted is He above everything they may say [about Him]. The seven heavens extol His limitless glory, as does the earth, and all who dwell in them. Indeed every single thing extols His glory and praise, but you cannot understand their praises. He is indeed Forbearing, Much Forgiving.*" (Verses 43–44) The *sūrah* quotes some of the people of earlier divine religions who say when the Qur'ān is recited to them: "*Limitless in His glory is our Lord! Truly has the promise of our Lord been fulfilled.*" (Verse 108) The last verse in the *sūrah* states: "*And say, 'All praise is due to God who has never begotten a son; who has no partner in His dominion; who needs none to support Him against any difficulty.' And extol His greatness.*" (Verse 111)

Thus the *sūrah* revolves around one axis although it tackles several subjects. Its first part mentions the night journey: "*Limitless in His glory is He who transported His servant by night from the Sacred Mosque [in Makkah] to the Aqṣā Mosque [in Jerusalem] – the environs of which We have blessed.*" (Verse 1) It also specifies the purpose of this journey: "*so that We might show him some of Our signs.*" (Verse 1) In connection with the mosque in Jerusalem the *sūrah* mentions the book revealed to Moses and what God determined in it for the Children of Israel, speaking about two episodes of destruction and diaspora because of their injustice and corruption. They are warned about a third and a fourth time if they revert to the same ways. It then states that this last divine revelation, the Qur'ān, guides to the path that is straightest, while man is often driven by uncontrollable reactions. It also states the rule of individual responsibility with regard to following divine guidance or straying away from it, and collective responsibility with regard to behaviour and practice.

The second part speaks about the truth of God's oneness, considering it the basis upon which the whole social set up should be built, including the values of work and behaviour. This central issue of faith should be the pivot around which all human life turns.

The third part speaks of pagan superstitions which attribute daughters and partners to God. It also mentions resurrection and how the unbelievers could never imagine it would take place. It shows how they received Qur'ānic revelations and the fabrications they reiterated about the Prophet (peace be upon him). It commands the believers to say something better, unlike the falsehood of unbelievers.

In the fourth part the *sūrah* explains the reason for not giving the Prophet physical miracles or preternatural phenomena. When such miracles were given to earlier communities and they continued to deny the message of truth, the law God has set in such cases applied to them and they were destroyed. It refers to the unbelievers' attitude to the warnings based on the vision God showed to the Prophet, and their persistence in their erring ways. In this connection a part of the story of *Iblīs*, or Satan, is mentioned and his declaration that he would remain for ever man's determined foe. This part of the story appears to be an exposition of the reasons for the unbelievers going astray. It comments on this by warning mankind against incurring God's punishment, coupled with a reminder of God's grace and the honour He has given to mankind. It tells them about what awaits God's obedient servants, contrasting it with what awaits the disobedient on the day when every community is summoned by calling their leaders or guides. "*Those who are given their records in their right hands will read their records. None shall be wronged by as much as a hair's breadth. But whoever is blind in this world will be even more blind in the life to come, and still further astray from the path of truth.*" (Verses 71–72)

The final part of the *sūrah* speaks about the unbelievers' schemes against the Prophet (peace be upon him), and their attempts to lure him away from at least part of what was revealed to him. It mentions their attempt to expel him from Makkah. When he actually left, he did so carrying out God's orders. Had they forcibly expelled him, they would have been destroyed, as happened to communities which in former times expelled their prophets or killed them. God commands the Prophet in the *sūrah* to carry on with his mission, reciting the Qur'ān and attending to his prayers, appealing to God to enable him to enter and leave in a true and sincere manner, and to declare that the truth has come to light and falsehood is certain to wither away. The *sūrah* states that this Qur'ān is a source of cure and guidance to believers. Man's knowledge, however, remains inadequate. "*You, [mankind], have been granted but little knowledge.*" (Verse 85)

The *sūrah* continues to speak about the Qur'ān and its challenge to all mankind. Yet the unbelievers required physical miracles, and asked for angels to be sent down in support of the Prophet's message. They suggested that the Prophet should have a house of adornments, or a garden with date and vine trees, through which rivers run, or that he should cause a spring of water to gush forth for them, or that he himself should climb up to heaven and bring them a written letter to read. All these demands were dictated by intransigence, not by the desire to have proof to ensure conviction. The *sūrah* replies that all this is beyond the limits of the role of God's Messenger and the nature of his message. It leaves matters in this regard to God. It derides such demands and those who make them, telling them that had they had control over the treasures of God's grace, which is always abundant, never exhausted, they would still fear to give it away. It was sufficient for them to realize that everything in the universe glorifies God. They should have remembered that the miracles given to Moses did not lead the ones determined to oppose him to change their minds and follow him. Hence, God inflicted His punishment on them.

The *sūrah* concludes with a short discourse about the truth inherent in the Qur'ān. It was revealed in passages, so that the Prophet could read it to people over a long time, as would befit different occasions and circumstances. People would then be influenced by its practical approach to living conditions. It was received by people of sound knowledge with humility. They were so influenced by it to the extent that they wept and prostrated themselves to God. The *sūrah* then concludes with praising God who has never taken to Himself a son or a partner, just as it began with glorifying Him.

A Unique Experience

The story of the night journey by the Prophet from the Sacred Mosque in Makkah to the Aqṣā Mosque in Jerusalem, and then his ascension from there to the highest heaven and the world of which we know nothing, is mentioned in several reports. It has been the subject of much controversy, which continues even today. There are various reports about the place from which the Prophet's night journey started. Some suggest that it was the mosque itself, which fits with the phraseology of the verse. One report quotes the Prophet as saying: "As I was in the mosque, at Ḥijr Ismāʿīl, half asleep, Gabriel came to me with al-Burāq..." It is also reported that his journey began from the house of his cousin Umm Hānī. This report is acceptable on the basis that the term, 'the Sacred Mosque', includes the whole Ḥaram area, which surrounds the mosque. Ibn ʿAbbās is reported to have said, "The whole of the Ḥaram area is a mosque."

It is also reported that he was sleeping in Umm Hānī's house when he was taken on his journey and returned home before the night was over. He related the event to his cousin and told her: "I saw the prophets and led them in prayer." As he was about to leave to go to the mosque, she stopped him, saying: "I fear that people will not believe you if you tell them what you have just told me." The Prophet made clear his intention to tell them, 'even though they would not believe me.'

When the Prophet sat in the mosque, Abū Jahl, the arch-enemy of Islam, went to him and asked him whether he had any news. The Prophet told him of his night journey. Abū Jahl called on people to gather and listen to the strange news the Prophet had to tell them. As the Prophet did so, some of them started clapping as a gesture of rejecting what they heard while others put their hands on their heads in disbelief. Some who had earlier accepted Islam now turned away declaring that they were no longer Muslims. Some went to Abū Bakr, the Prophet's closest Companion, to find out what his reaction would be. When they assured him that Muḥammad actually claimed to have made the return journey to Jerusalem overnight, Abū Bakr said: "If he has actually said this, he is telling the truth." When they expressed their amazement that he would believe such a singular story, Abū Bakr said: "What is so surprising? I do believe him when he says something even more incomprehensible. He says he receives revelations from on high and I believe him." Abū Bakr was then given the title *Ṣiddīq*, which denotes 'a true and firm believer'.

Some of them had been to Jerusalem and so asked the Prophet to describe it to them. Its picture was raised before his eyes and he described it to them in detail. They said that his description was accurate. They then asked him to tell them about their trade caravan and when it would arrive. He told them the number of its camels and its condition at the time. He further told them that it would arrive at sunrise on a particular day, headed by a white camel. On the day appointed by the Prophet, they went out to make sure the caravan arrived. When the sun began to rise, they said: Here is the sun rising. Then they looked and said: And here is the caravan headed by a white camel, just like Muḥammad said. Yet still they refused to believe.

On the same night, the Prophet ascended from Jerusalem to heaven. Disagreement among scholars touches on the point of whether or not the Prophet went on this night journey when he was awake or if it was a dream-like journey. It is reported that 'Ā'ishah, his wife, said: "By God, the Prophet's body was never missing, but it was his soul which ascended." Al-Ḥasan is reported to have said that it was all in a dream he saw. Other reports make it clear that it was a journey he took, body and soul, and that his bed was still warm when he came back.

The weightier view, on the basis of all the reports we have, is that the Prophet left his bed in his cousin's home and went to the Ka'bah. When he was at Ḥijr Ismā'īl, half awake, he was taken on his journey to Jerusalem and from there he ascended to heaven, before returning to his bed which was still warm.

Having clarified this, we do not see much point in the long arguments people have engaged in over the past, and still do, concerning the nature of this event which certainly took place. Whether it was a physical or spiritual trip, or a vision he saw while awake or asleep, does not make much difference. It does not alter much of the nature of this event to say that it was an act of unveiling that enabled the Prophet to see remote places and worlds in a brief moment. Those who understand even a little of the nature of God's power and the nature of prophethood will find nothing strange in this event. To God's power and ability, all matters, which appear easy or difficult by our human standards and according to what is familiar to us, are the same. What is familiar to us in our world is not to be taken as the criterion for making a judgement in relation to God's ability. The nature of prophethood is a link with God, which may not be compared to anything familiar in human life. That a remote place or world be shown to the Prophet, or that the Prophet visited such a place by means that we know or do not know about, are no more strange or miraculous than for him to receive God's message. Indeed Abū Bakr put the matter in its proper perspective when he told the people of Makkah that he believed the Prophet in what was even more incomprehensible: the revelations he received from on high.

The Quraysh had ample hard evidence of the truth of this journey when they asked the Prophet to tell them about their trade caravan, and their subsequent verification of every point of detail he mentioned. But they were bound to meet his story with total disbelief at first. The point to be noted here is that the Prophet did not listen to his cousin, Umm Hānī, when she tried to persuade him not to tell them about his journey for fear of their reaction to what would sound totally impossible. The Prophet's trust in the truth of his message and the reality of his journey was such that he went out and told them, paying little heed to how they would receive his news. His mission was to convey to them his message complete, and he was not one to evade his duty. Some of those who had believed in the new faith turned back. Unbelievers found in his story material for ridicule and doubt about everything he said. But none of this made him hesitate to declare the truth as he saw and believed it. In this the Prophet teaches a lesson to the advocates of Islam across all generations: they must declare the truth plainly in all situations. They should not fear what reaction this brings about. They must not try to tailor their faith so as to fit in with what people like to hear.

We also note that the Prophet did not try to describe the event as a miracle or a supernatural happening that would make people believe in his message. In fact they were always asking him for a miracle to prove his claims. Now they had the miraculous event and they knew it to be true when they verified the details the Prophet identified. Islam does not rely on miraculous events to present itself to people. Instead it relies only on the nature of its message and its direct appeal to human nature when it is purged of all corrupting influences. When the Prophet spoke out about his journey, he did not seek to make it proof confirming the truth of his message. He only stated a true event, purely and simply because it was true.

I

God's Infinite Power

Al-Isrā' (The Night Journey)

In the Name of God, the Merciful, the Beneficent

Limitless in His glory is He who transported His servant by night from the Sacred Mosque [in Makkah] to the Aqṣā Mosque [in Jerusalem] – the environs of which We have blessed – so that We might show him some of Our signs. Indeed He alone is the One who hears all and sees all. (1)

We gave Moses the book and made it a [source of] guidance for the Children of Israel, saying: 'Do not take anyone for a guardian other than Me. (2)

You are the descendants of those whom We carried [in the ark] with Noah. He was a truly grateful servant of Ours.' (3)

We made it clear to the Children of Israel in the book: 'Twice will you spread corruption on earth and will indeed become grossly overbearing.' (4)

وَقَضَيْنَآ إِلَىٰ بَنِيٓ إِسْرَٰٓءِيلَ فِى ٱلْكِتَٰبِ لَتُفْسِدُنَّ فِى ٱلْأَرْضِ مَرَّتَيْنِ وَلَتَعْلُنَّ عُلُوًّا كَبِيرًا ٤

When the prediction of the first of these came true, We sent against you some of Our servants of great might who wrought havoc throughout the land. Thus [Our] warning came to be fulfilled. (5)

فَإِذَا جَآءَ وَعْدُ أُولَىٰهُمَا بَعَثْنَا عَلَيْكُمْ عِبَادًا لَّنَآ أُوْلِى بَأْسٍ شَدِيدٍ فَجَاسُواْ خِلَٰلَ ٱلدِّيَارِ وَكَانَ وَعْدًا مَّفْعُولًا ٥

Then We let you prevail against them once more, and We gave you wealth and offspring, and made you more numerous [than ever. (6)

ثُمَّ رَدَدْنَا لَكُمُ ٱلْكَرَّةَ عَلَيْهِمْ وَأَمْدَدْنَٰكُم بِأَمْوَٰلٍ وَبَنِينَ وَجَعَلْنَٰكُمْ أَكْثَرَ نَفِيرًا ٦

And We said:] 'If you do good, you will be but doing good to yourselves; and if you do evil, it will be also against yourselves.' And when the second prediction came true, [We allowed your enemies] to disgrace you utterly, and to enter the Mosque just like [their predecessors] had entered it the first time, and to visit with destruction all that fell into their power. (7)

إِنْ أَحْسَنتُمْ أَحْسَنتُمْ لِأَنفُسِكُمْ وَإِنْ أَسَأْتُمْ فَلَهَا فَإِذَا جَآءَ وَعْدُ ٱلْأَخِرَةِ لِيَسُـُٔواْ وُجُوهَكُمْ وَلِيَدْخُلُواْ ٱلْمَسْجِدَ كَمَا دَخَلُوهُ أَوَّلَ مَرَّةٍ وَلِيُتَبِّرُواْ مَا عَلَوْاْ تَتْبِيرًا ٧

126

It may be that your Lord will have mercy on you; but if you revert [to your old ways], We shall revert [to punishing you]. Indeed We have made hell a place of confinement for the unbelievers. (8)

عَسَىٰ رَبُّكُمْ أَن يَرْحَمَكُمْ وَإِنْ عُدتُّمْ عُدْنَا ۚ وَجَعَلْنَا جَهَنَّمَ لِلْكَٰفِرِينَ حَصِيرًا ۝

Surely this Qur'ān shows the way to that which is most upright. It gives the believers who do good deeds the happy news that theirs will be a rich reward; (9)

إِنَّ هَٰذَا ٱلْقُرْءَانَ يَهْدِى لِلَّتِى هِىَ أَقْوَمُ وَيُبَشِّرُ ٱلْمُؤْمِنِينَ ٱلَّذِينَ يَعْمَلُونَ ٱلصَّٰلِحَٰتِ أَنَّ لَهُمْ أَجْرًا كَبِيرًا ۝

and [declares] that We have prepared a grievous suffering for those who do not believe in the life to come. (10)

وَأَنَّ ٱلَّذِينَ لَا يُؤْمِنُونَ بِٱلْءَاخِرَةِ أَعْتَدْنَا لَهُمْ عَذَابًا أَلِيمًا ۝

Yet man prays for evil as eagerly as he prays for good. Truly man is ever hasty. (11)

وَيَدْعُ ٱلْإِنسَٰنُ بِٱلشَّرِّ دُعَاءَهُ بِٱلْخَيْرِ ۖ وَكَانَ ٱلْإِنسَٰنُ عَجُولًا ۝

We have made the night and the day as two [of Our] signs. Then We have effaced the sign of the night while the sign of the day We have left enlightened, so that you may seek bounty from your Lord, and you may learn to compute the years and be able to reckon. Most clearly have We spelled out everything. (12)

وَجَعَلْنَا ٱلَّيْلَ وَٱلنَّهَارَ ءَايَتَيْنِ ۖ فَمَحَوْنَا ءَايَةَ ٱلَّيْلِ وَجَعَلْنَا ءَايَةَ ٱلنَّهَارِ مُبْصِرَةً لِّتَبْتَغُوا۟ فَضْلًا مِّن رَّبِّكُمْ وَلِتَعْلَمُوا۟ عَدَدَ ٱلسِّنِينَ وَٱلْحِسَابَ ۚ وَكُلَّ شَىْءٍ فَصَّلْنَٰهُ تَفْصِيلًا ۝

Every human being's action have We tied around his own neck. On the Day of Resurrection We shall produce for him a record which he will find wide open. (13)

وَكُلَّ إِنسَنٍ أَلْزَمْنَهُ طَٰٓئِرَهُۥ فِى عُنُقِهِۦ وَنُخْرِجُ لَهُۥ يَوْمَ ٱلْقِيَمَةِ كِتَٰبًا يَلْقَىٰهُ مَنشُورًا ۝

[And We will say:] 'Read this your record! Sufficient it is for you today that your own soul should make out your account.' (14)

ٱقْرَأْ كِتَٰبَكَ كَفَىٰ بِنَفْسِكَ ٱلْيَوْمَ عَلَيْكَ حَسِيبًا ۝

Whoever chooses to follow guidance does so for his own good, and whoever goes astray does so to his own loss. No soul shall be made to bear the burden of another. We would never inflict punishment [on anyone] until We have sent a Messenger [to give warning]. (15)

مَّنِ ٱهْتَدَىٰ فَإِنَّمَا يَهْتَدِى لِنَفْسِهِۦ وَمَن ضَلَّ فَإِنَّمَا يَضِلُّ عَلَيْهَا وَلَا تَزِرُ وَازِرَةٌ وِزْرَ أُخْرَىٰ وَمَا كُنَّا مُعَذِّبِينَ حَتَّىٰ نَبْعَثَ رَسُولًا ۝

When it is Our will to destroy a community, We convey Our command to those of its people who live a life of affluence. If they persist in sin, judgement is irrevocably passed, and We utterly destroy them. (16)

وَإِذَآ أَرَدْنَآ أَن نُّهْلِكَ قَرْيَةً أَمَرْنَا مُتْرَفِيهَا فَفَسَقُوا۟ فِيهَا فَحَقَّ عَلَيْهَا ٱلْقَوْلُ فَدَمَّرْنَٰهَا تَدْمِيرًا ۝

Many generations have We destroyed since Noah's time. Suffice it that your Lord is well aware of His servants' sins, and observes them all. (17)

وَكَمْ أَهْلَكْنَا مِنَ ٱلْقُرُونِ مِنۢ بَعْدِ نُوحٍ وَكَفَىٰ بِرَبِّكَ بِذُنُوبِ عِبَادِهِۦ خَبِيرًۢا بَصِيرًا ۝

As for those who care only for [the pleasures of] this fleeting life, We readily grant of it whatever We may please to whomever We will. In the end We consign any such person to hell, where he will burn disgraced and rejected. (18)

مَّن كَانَ يُرِيدُ ٱلْعَاجِلَةَ عَجَّلْنَا لَهُۥ فِيهَا مَا نَشَآءُ لِمَن نُّرِيدُ ثُمَّ جَعَلْنَا لَهُۥ جَهَنَّمَ يَصْلَىٰهَا مَذْمُومًا مَّدْحُورًا ﴿١٨﴾

But those who care only for the life to come, strive for it as it should be striven for, and are true believers, are indeed the ones who will have their endeavours well rewarded. (19)

وَمَنْ أَرَادَ ٱلْأَخِرَةَ وَسَعَىٰ لَهَا سَعْيَهَا وَهُوَ مُؤْمِنٌ فَأُوْلَـٰئِكَ كَانَ سَعْيُهُم مَّشْكُورًا ﴿١٩﴾

On all – these as well as those – do We bestow the bounty of your Lord. Indeed your Lord's bounty is not denied [to anyone]. (20)

كُلًّا نُّمِدُّ هَـٰٓؤُلَآءِ وَهَـٰٓؤُلَآءِ مِنْ عَطَآءِ رَبِّكَ وَمَا كَانَ عَطَآءُ رَبِّكَ مَحْظُورًا ﴿٢٠﴾

See how We have bestowed more bounty on some than on others. But the life to come will be higher in rank and greater in merit. (21)

ٱنظُرْ كَيْفَ فَضَّلْنَا بَعْضَهُمْ عَلَىٰ بَعْضٍ وَلَلْأَخِرَةُ أَكْبَرُ دَرَجَـٰتٍ وَأَكْبَرُ تَفْضِيلًا ﴿٢١﴾

A Unique Journey

The *sūrah* begins with glorifying God, the most fitting action to confirm the bond between God and His servants in the atmosphere of compassion and friendliness imparted by the mention of the night journey:

Limitless in His glory is He who transported His servant by night from the Sacred Mosque [in Makkah] to the Aqṣā Mosque [in Jerusalem] – the environs of which We have blessed – so that We might show him some of Our signs. Indeed He alone is the One who hears all and sees all. (Verse 1)

The *sūrah* emphasizes the position of man as God's servant: "*He who transported His servant by night…*" The emphasis here is needed in the context of the Prophet's ascension to heaven where no human being had gone before. It is important in this context that the status of man's servitude to God should always be remembered. There must be no confusion of status similar to that which happened in the case of Jesus on account of his birth, his being raised to heaven at the end of his life on earth, and the powers which were given to him during life. All these caused some people to confuse his status and to claim that he had a divine nature. In its simplicity and purity, Islam insists that no similarity could ever exist between God and any creature.

The Arabic text of this opening verse uses the verb, *asrā*, which denotes 'travelling during the night'. It is sufficient then to use this verb to denote the time of the action. Yet the verse adds the phrase, *laylan*, or 'by night', to give an added sense of the still night and the ease of travel. The journey from the Sacred Mosque to the Aqṣā Mosque was one chosen by God, the Compassionate who knows everything. It provided a link between all monotheistic faiths from the time of Abraham and Ishmael to the time of the last Prophet, Muḥammad (peace be upon them all). It also established a link between the holy places in all these religions. It seems that this unusual journey served as an announcement that the last Messenger was the heir to the heritage of all former messengers. His message staked a claim to all these holy places. Thus it becomes a journey that goes beyond the scope of time and place.

The opening verse describes the Aqṣā Mosque as one with blessed environs. This description shows the blessings surrounding the mosque and flowing in abundance. This impression could not have been given with a direct description such as 'the mosque which we have blessed.' This is another example of the refined use of language characteristic of the Qur'ān.

The Prophet's night journey was a telling sign, and it was accompanied by others, as the opening verse says in stating its purpose, "*so that We might show him some of Our signs.*" Covering the distance between the Sacred Mosque in Makkah and the Aqṣā Mosque in

Jerusalem, in a very short period that did not allow the Prophet's bed to become cold, is a sign of God's power, whatever the means used to accomplish it. It opens our minds to new horizons in the universe and reveals latent potentials within mankind. It shows that those human beings chosen by God to be the bearers of His message have the latent ability to receive whatever greater powers God wishes to give them. It is God who has honoured man, giving him a favoured position among His creation, and endowed him with such potentials. "*He alone is the One who hears all and sees all.*" (Verse 1) He indeed hears and sees all that is beyond the reach of our hearing and seeing faculties.

It is especially impressive that the opening verse of this *sūrah* starts with glorifying God, "*Limitless in His glory is He who transported His servant by night*". After defining the purpose of this journey, it finishes with highlighting two of God's attributes, perfect hearing and seeing that encompass all things. This quick movement across purposes reflects the finest points of the expression used. The glorification is addressed to God Himself, and the statement about the purpose of the night journey comes from Him, while the description of God's powers is made in the form of an indisputable statement. All these forms are combined in one verse so as to give their different imports.

The Promise to the Israelites

The night journey is a remarkable sign which God wished to demonstrate. It is an amazing journey by human standards. The Aqṣā Mosque in Jerusalem, which was the destination of the first part of this journey, is at the heart of the Holy Land which God assigned to the Children of Israel before He caused them to be driven out of it. Thus it is appropriate to relate in the passage that follows the history of Moses and his people, the Israelites:

We gave Moses the book and made it a [source of] guidance for the Children of Israel, saying: 'Do not take anyone for a guardian other than Me. You are the descendants of those whom We carried [in the ark] with Noah. He was a truly grateful servant of Ours.' We made it clear to the Children of Israel in the book: 'Twice will you spread corruption on earth and will indeed become grossly overbearing.'

When the prediction of the first of these came true, We sent against you some of Our servants of great might who wrought havoc throughout the land. Thus [Our] warning came to be fulfilled. Then We let you prevail against them once more, and We gave you wealth and offspring, and made you more numerous [than ever. And We said:] 'If you do good, you will be but doing good to yourselves; and if you do evil, it will be also against yourselves.' And when the second prediction came true, [We allowed your enemies] to disgrace you utterly, and to enter the Mosque just like [their predecessors] had entered it the first time, and to visit with destruction all that fell into their power. It may be that your Lord will have mercy on you; but if you revert [to your old ways], We shall revert [to punishing you]. Indeed We have made hell a place of confinement for the unbelievers. (Verses 2–8)

This episode in the Children of Israel's history is mentioned only in this *sūrah* in the Qur'ān. It refers to the fate of the Jews which led to the collapse of their state. It reveals the direct relationship between the spread of corruption and loose morality in a nation and its decline and destruction. This comes in fulfilment of a law of nature God has set in operation, and which the *sūrah* refers to. The law states that the corruption and immorality of the affluent in any community is the cause of its destruction by God.

The story begins here by mentioning Moses' revealed book, the Torah, and the warnings it gives to the Israelites. It reminds them of their great ancestor, Noah, God's obedient and truly grateful servant, and also of their ancestors who were carried with him in the ark. It should be remembered that only the believers were allowed on the ark: *"We gave Moses the book and made it a [source of] guidance for the Children of Israel, saying: Do not take anyone for a guardian other than Me. You are the descendants of those whom We carried [in the ark] with Noah. He was a truly grateful servant of Ours."* (Verses 2–3)

Both the warning and the reminder are confirmation of the promise that the *sūrah* soon mentions. The promise makes it clear that God will not inflict punishment on any community unless He sends them first a messenger to warn and remind them. It makes clear the primary purpose of giving the book to Moses. It serves as a source of guidance and warns them: "*Do not take anyone for a guardian other than Me.*" They must rely on none other than God and turn to Him only for guidance. This is the essence of faith. Anyone who seeks a guardian other than God is misguided and devoid of true faith.

The *surah* makes its address to them in the name of their ancestors who were carried in the ark with Noah. These were the best of mankind at the time of the first messenger on earth. Pointing out this relationship in this address serves to remind them of God's grace when He saved their forefathers with His truly grateful servant, Noah. Thus it establishes an age-long bond of faith. That Noah is described here as God's servant is intended to emphasize this point and also to highlight the essential quality of God's chosen messengers, which is their servitude to Him. In the first verse Muḥammad is described as 'God's servant'. This follows the Qur'ānic method of maintaining an air of harmony and coherence throughout each *surah*.

In the book which God gave Moses to serve as a source of guidance to the Israelites, He issued them with a warning that they would be doomed to destruction should they spread corruption on earth. The destruction was visited on them twice because its causes were repeated. This is followed by a warning of further episodes of destruction should they revert to their old ways of spreading corruption. This leads to the inevitable operation of God's laws of nature that never fail: "*We made it clear to the Children of Israel in the book: 'Twice will you spread corruption on earth and will indeed become grossly overbearing.'*" (Verse 4)

This judgement is merely information given to them by God, spelling out what they will do and what will happen to them as a result. It is based on God's knowledge of their fate. It is not an act of predestination that they cannot escape, or that forces their hands so as to behave in a certain way. God does not compel anyone to be corrupt or to spread corruption. "*Say: never does God enjoin what is indecent.*" (7: 28) It is the nature of God's knowledge that makes Him aware of what will happen in the future in the same way as He is aware of what is happening now. What is yet to happen, and is totally unknown to all human beings, is, to God, the same as what has already happened.

Same Action, Same Penalty

In the book He gave to Moses, the Torah, God warned the Children of Israel that they would spread corruption on earth twice and that they would gain power and be the masters in the Holy Land. Every time they held power and used it corruptly or spread corruption, God sent some of His servants against them who overpowered and destroyed them, abusing their rights: "*When the prediction of the first of these came true, We sent against you some of Our servants of great might who wrought havoc throughout the land. Thus [Our] warning came to be fulfilled.*" (Verse 5)

This was the first time: they gained power in the Holy Land and they established their strong state. But then they resorted to tyranny and corruption. As a result, God brought them face to face with some of His servants who combined great might with strong determination. They overran those who had erred and spread corruption, completely subjugating them. Thus the warning came to pass, as is always the case with God's promises.

After the Children of Israel were vanquished and suffered humiliation, they turned back to their Lord, mended their ways and applied the lessons they had learnt. In the meantime, their conquerors were blinded by victory and travelled along the same road of tyranny and corruption. As a result, the tables were turned. The vanquished were victorious again: "*Then We let you prevail against them once more, and We gave you wealth and offspring, and made you more numerous than ever.*" (Verse 6) History thus repeated itself.

Before the *sūrah* continues its account of the true prophesy and warning, it states a basic rule of action and reward: "*If you do good, you will be but doing good to yourselves; and if you do evil, it will be also against yourselves.*" (Verse 7) This is a never changing rule with effects that transcend this life into the next. It makes everything a human being does, with all its results and consequences, totally his own. Thus, reward is the natural fruit of action. Hence it is determined by the nature of the action done. This is to say that a human being is responsible for himself. It is he who chooses to do good or evil, and he alone who will receive the reward or bear the consequences of what he does. He has only himself to blame when the result of his action leads him to suffer punishment.

Having established the rule, the *sūrah* goes on to complete the telling of true prophesy: "*When the second prediction came true, [We allowed your enemies] to disgrace you utterly, and to enter the Mosque just like [their predecessors] had entered it the first time, and to visit with destruction all that fell into their power.*" (Verse 7)

The *sūrah* does not include in its text any account of how the Israelites spread corruption again after they regained power. Its mention of the first occasion is sufficient: "*Twice will you spread corruption on earth.*" (Verse 4) But it tells us of what God inflicted on them the second time: "*When the second prediction came true, [We allowed your enemies] to disgrace you utterly.*" (Verse 7) This is a vivid description of the widespread destruction that causes acute humiliation, visible even on their faces. Or the disgrace was physically painted on their faces, coupled with what they felt when they saw their sanctities desecrated. And they "*enter[ed] the Mosque just like [their predecessors] had entered it the first time.*" (Verse 7) They wrought total destruction, leaving nothing in place.

The warning was fulfilled. God sent enemies against the Jews who overpowered them, destroyed their kingdom and left them in their great diaspora. The Qur'ān does not specify the nationality of those God sent against the Jews, because such information adds nothing to the lesson to be drawn, or to the effect of the law God has made applicable to all communities.

The *sūrah* comments on this true warning and prophesy by saying that this destruction may be a way leading to God's mercy if the right lesson is drawn and acted upon: "*It may be that your Lord will have mercy on you.*" (Verse 8) But if the Jews revert to spreading corruption on earth, then the law will inevitably operate and the punishment will again be inflicted: "*But if you revert [to your old ways], We shall revert [to punishing you].*" (Verse 8) They certainly did revert to their corrupt ways and God sent the Muslims against them who drove them out of Arabia. They did this again with the same results, until He caused them to be humiliated during the twentieth century. We see now how they have again reverted to tyranny and corruption in the state of Israel which uses very cruel tactics against the Arabs, the owners of the land. God is certain to send His servants against them who will make them suffer much for their corruption in fulfilment of His firm warning and in accordance with His law which never fails. We need only wait and see this take place.

The *sūrah* concludes this episode by defining the destiny the unbelievers will suffer in the hereafter. It is the same destiny as will be suffered by those who spread corruption: "*Indeed We have made hell a place of confinement for the unbelievers.*" (Verse 8) They will be surrounded, unable to escape. Furthermore, it is large enough to contain them all.

Guidance in All Fields

The *sūrah* now speaks about the Qur'ān, making it clear that it is a book of true and full guidance:

> *Surely this Qur'ān shows the way to that which is most upright. It gives the believers who do good deeds the happy news that theirs will be a rich reward; and [declares] that We have prepared a grievous suffering for those who do not believe in the life to come.* (Verses 9–10)

"*Surely this Qur'ān shows the way to that which is most upright.*" This is a general statement applicable to all those who are guided by the Qur'ān and the goals to which it guides. Thus, the guidance is given to communities and generations that are not restricted by time or place. And the superiority of its guidance applies to all that they may attain when they follow any method or approach. It is also superior to every good thing to which people may be guided at any time or place.

The Qur'ān guides to that which is 'most upright' in relation to man's inner feelings and thoughts, outlining a clear faith, free of complication and ambiguity. Its guidance frees the human spirit of the burden of myth and superstition, and releases human energy so that it is constructive, bringing benefit, providing a harmonious link between the laws that govern the universe and those governing human nature.

The Qur'ān also ensures harmony between man's outward and inward existence, feelings and behaviour, faith and action. In all this it shows the way to what is 'most upright', linking all these aspects to the true and unseverable bond that exists between man and God. This enables man to look up to a higher horizon while he is still on earth. Thus what man does in his daily life becomes an act of worship, provided that he does so seeking God's acceptance. This is true even when the action itself provides him with pure enjoyment of what is available in this life.

In the field of worship also, the Qur'ān establishes a perfect balance between duties and abilities. This ensures that duties are not seen as too hard so as to constitute a heavy burden, or induce despair of ever fulfilling one's obligations. Maintaining this balance ensures that a person neither takes matters too lightly or complacently on the one hand, nor exceeds the limits of what is reasonable and perfectly bearable on the other. Thus we can say without fear of contradiction that in worship, the Qur'ān shows the way to that which is most upright.

The same applies to human interaction whether between individuals and couples, governments and peoples, or states and races. Relations between all these groups are established on a firm basis, influenced neither by personal prejudice and interest, nor by feelings of love and hatred. This firm foundation in human relations is chosen by God, the Creator who knows His creation and what is certain to promote goodness in their lives. The Qur'ān shows the way which gives the best course of action in the fields of politics and finance, as well as in those of social and international relations.

The Qur'ān also endorses all divine religions, establishing a firm link between them, honouring all that is sacred in them, and protecting all that they hold in reverence. This ensures that humanity, with all its divine faiths live in peace. In this again the Qur'ān provides its perfect guidance. This is all summed up in the verse which says: *"Surely this Qur'ān shows the way to that which is most upright."* (Verse 9)

"It gives the believers who do good deeds the happy news that theirs will be a rich reward; and [declares] that We have prepared a grievous

suffering for those who do not believe in the life to come." (Verses 9–10) This is the basic rule laid down by the Qur'ān in respect of action and reward. The Islamic structure is built on the two pillars of faith and good action. Faith that is not confirmed by action is hollow, unfulfilled, while action that is not based on faith lacks firm roots. It is when both are combined that life maintains its most upright course, and with them both together guidance shown in the Qur'ān takes its proper effect.

Man's Hasty Characteristic

Those who do not follow the guidance of the Qur'ān are left to their own devices. But man is hasty, unaware of what benefits him and what causes him harm, impulsive, unable to control his reactions even when they bring about evil consequences: "*Yet man prays for evil as eagerly as he prays for good. Truly man is ever hasty.*" (Verse 11) He does not know the ultimate results. He may do something that is evil and precipitate its results unaware that these only bring about immense harm to himself; or he may be aware of such results but is unable to control himself. This is a long, long way away from the assured, calm and consistent guidance given in the Qur'ān. The two ways of Qur'ānic guidance and human desire are too widely divergent.

So far the *sūrah* has pointed to some of the signs God gave to His messengers, such as the Prophet's night journey, Noah's ark, Moses' book, and, above all, the Qur'ān. Now the *sūrah* mentions some of God's universal signs and relates these to people's actions, efforts and earnings on the one hand and their fruits and reward on the other. We thus see that the laws that govern action and reward are closely linked to the laws governing the whole universe. Both are based on perfect rules that never fail. They are as accurate as the system that ensures that day and night succeed each other. They are operated by the Creator who has made them two of His signs:

We have made the night and the day as two [of Our] signs. Then We have effaced the sign of the night while the sign of the day We have left enlightened, so that you may seek bounty from your Lord, and you may learn to compute the years and be able to reckon. Most clearly have We spelled out everything. (Verse 12)

The universal law that governs the succession of day and night is linked to numerous aspects of human life. It is linked with people's efforts in earning their living, and their knowledge of time and calculation. It also relates to the good and evil man may earn in life and what reward he may achieve in the end for either his good or bad actions. Indeed the consequences of following guidance or error relate to it, as is the individual nature of responsibility which means that no one will have to answer for anyone else. The same universal law is linked to God's promise that He will not inflict punishment on anyone until He has sent His messengers. This link further applies to the law which governs the destruction of communities only after the affluent among them have been guilty of immense transgression. The law further relates to the diverse destinies of those who seek the pleasures of this world and those who prefer the good reward of the hereafter, and what God grants to both in this life and in the life to come. All these aspects follow a well set system and certain immutable laws besides. Nothing takes place haphazardly.

"*We have made the night and the day as two [of Our] signs. Then We have effaced the sign of the night while the sign of the day We have left enlightened, so that you may seek bounty from your Lord, and you may learn to compute the years and be able to reckon. Most clearly have We spelled out everything.*" (Verse 12) The night and the day are two major universal signs which confirm the accuracy of the law governing the universe which operates all the time, suffering neither a failure nor a temporary need for repairs. So what is meant here by '*effacing the sign of the night*', when we see that this sign remains operative as much as the sign of the day? It seems to me, and God knows best, that the reference here is to the darkness of the night which hides everything and during which movement slows down. The darkness gives the impression that the night is effaced when compared with the day, its light and the bustling activity that takes place under its light. It is as though the day is able to see things by its light and reveals everything for us to behold.

The effacing of the night and the full visibility of the day have a clearly specified purpose: "*so that you may seek bounty from your Lord, and you may learn to compute the years and be able to reckon.*" This makes things very clear: the night is for rest and recuperation, and the day for work, earning one's living and activity. The succession of the day and night enables people to compute the years and determine the seasons and set times for different transactions. "*Most clearly have We spelled out everything.*" There is nothing in the universe that has been left to chance. The accuracy that is manifested in the succession of day and night confirms the elaborate and faultless design of everything God has created.

Personal Responsibility

The law of action and reward is directly linked to the meticulous law of the universe:

> *Every human being's action have We tied around his own neck. On the Day of Resurrection We shall produce for him a record which he will find wide open. [And We will say:] 'Read this your record! Sufficient it is for you today that your own soul should make out your account.'* (Verses 13–14)

The Arabic phraseology of this verse provides a highly graphic description which uses the word, 'bird', in place of 'action', as used in the translated text. Thus we have here a metaphor referring to what flies of a person's actions and becomes tied around his neck, so that it never parts from him. Thus does the Qur'ān in graphically describing things in order to emphasize its point. A person's actions do not leave him, and he cannot disown them. The same applies to the wide open record of all his actions. Thus whatever he has done in life is laid bare. He cannot hide, ignore or disown it. Both descriptions, of the bird denoting action and the record thrown open, produce a very strong effect that adds to the fears experienced on that very difficult day when nothing remains hidden. Everyone is told to read their own records because, "*Sufficient it is for you today that your own soul should make out your account.*" (Verse 14)

Again the same accurate universal law is linked to the rules governing action and reward: "*Whoever chooses to follow guidance does so for his own good, and whoever goes astray does so to his own loss. No soul shall be made to bear the burden of another.*" (Verse 15) It is all individual responsibility. When one follows guidance, one reaps the fruits, and when one chooses error, one bears the consequences. None will bear or lighten the burden of another. Everyone will be questioned about their own actions and will have the reward for what they have done in this life. Close friends will be of no help to each other.

Yet as a sign of God's grace, He does not leave man's guidance dependent only on the signs that are available in the universe. Nor does He leave him to the covenant God has made with human nature before a person is born. He has sent messengers to warn and remind: "*We would never inflict punishment [on anyone] until We have sent a messenger [to give warning].*" (Verse 15) This is certainly an aspect of God's grace which gives everyone ample opportunity to follow His guidance. Only when they have been properly warned and still persist in error does He punish them, if He so wills.

Affluence Leading to Destruction

The same consistent and universal law that governs the succession of day and night also applies to the destruction of any community: "*When it is Our will to destroy a community, We convey Our command to those of its people who live a life of affluence. If they persist in sin, judgement is irrevocably passed, and We utterly destroy them.*" (Verse 16)

The affluent who enjoy wealth, servants, luxuries, comfort and power are prone to carelessness and decadence in their lives. They thus lead a life of corruption, transgress all limits, trample over values, desecrate sanctities and defile other people's honour. Unless they are taken to task for their misdeeds, they will spread corruption and indecency throughout their community. They will debase the sound values and principles which every community needs to observe in order to survive. Thus their corruption will lead to the loss of strength, vigour and means of survival by the whole community. It then becomes lifeless, and is soon overtaken by destruction.

141

The verse here restates this law which God has set in operation. When God determines that a certain community is to be destroyed, this is only the natural outcome of its pursuit of ways and practices that lead to destruction. The affluent become too numerous and no one takes any action to curb their transgressions. They spread corruption, and bit by bit the whole community becomes corrupt. Consequently, it is liable to the effects of the law God has set in operation, condemning such communities to destruction. Indeed the community in question is responsible for the destruction it suffers, because it did not take the necessary action to stop such foul practices. Had it done so, it would have spared itself destruction. It would not have had corrupt people to lead it astray until it has faced the dire results.

God has willed that human life should run according to set laws which never fail or change. A cause has its effect, and the effect takes place as a result of the operation of God's will that has set this law in operation. God does not approve of indecency or transgression. However, the presence of those who are exceedingly rich in a community is indicative that its fabric has become loose and that it has set itself on the way to decline. This will seal its fate, because it has set itself open to the operation of this law when it allowed those who are excessively rich to lead their corrupt life.

The mention of God's will in the verse, *"When it is Our will to destroy a community, We convey Our command to those of its people who live a life of affluence,"* does not mean a commanding will which initiates the cause. It is a will that brings the effect when the cause takes place. Thus the effect becomes inevitable as a result of the operation of God's laws of nature. Similarly, the 'command' in the same statement does not refer to a directive requiring them to indulge in sin. It simply refers to the natural result which comes about in consequence of those people leading such a life. Hence, the verse states that: *"If they persist in sin, judgement is irrevocably passed, and We utterly destroy them."* (Verse 16)

This statement highlights the responsibility of every community, as it makes clear that this law has remained operative since Noah's time: *"Many generations have We destroyed since Noah's time. Suffice it that your Lord is well aware of His servants' sins, and observes them all."* (Verse 17)

Choices and Rewards

Someone who wishes to lead a life based solely on this world, looking up to nothing beyond this earth and its pleasures, will have whatever God has assigned to him of these. In the life to come, hell will be waiting for him because he will have deserved it. This is because those who do not aspire to anything beyond this world are keen to immerse themselves in its carnal pleasures. This however inevitably leads them to hell: *"As for those who care only for [the pleasures of] this fleeting life, We readily grant of it whatever We may please to whomever We will. In the end We consign any such person to hell, where he will burn disgraced and rejected."* (Verse 18) He is disgraced by his actions, rejected, suffering severe punishment.

On the other side is a totally different picture: *"But those who care only for the life to come, strive for it as it should be striven for, and are true believers, are indeed the ones who will have their endeavours well rewarded."* (Verse 19) Someone who desires the rich reward of the life to come must pursue his goal diligently. He should fulfil the duties God requires of him. Moreover, he must have faith which serves as the basis of his pursuit for the life to come. Faith is not a matter that people attain through idle wishes, but it is rather an idea that is firmly held as a belief, and clearly endorsed by action. Pursuit of the hereafter does not deprive anyone of the wholesome pleasures of this life. It simply opens up wider horizons before us. Thus, enjoyment and pleasure are not the driving goal. There is no harm in seeking pleasure, provided however that one is not captivated or enslaved by it.

A life that seeks nothing more than the pleasures of this world is fitting only for worms, reptiles, insects, cattle and wild beasts. It is only the life that pursues the rewards of the hereafter that is fitting for man who has been the recipient of honour bestowed on him by God. It is God who has created man and fashioned him, planting in his soul a secret that motivates him to look up to higher horizons even when his feet are solidly planted on earth.

No Limits to God's Grace

Yet both groups receive God's bounty which is open to all and restricted to none. Both those who seek only this world's pleasures and enjoy them to the full and those who pursue the reward of the life to come partake of God's bounty which God grants to all: *"On all – these as well as those – do We bestow the bounty of your Lord. Indeed your Lord's bounty is not denied [to anyone]."* (Verse 20) This bounty bestowed by God differs widely, in accordance with people's means, aims and actions. They differ despite the fact that the scope on earth is very limited and its expanse so narrow. How then will they differ when they are in the other place, where the scope is limitless? How can we compare the expanses of the two worlds, when, in God's sight, this world and all that it contains counts for less that the span of a mosquito's wings, as stated by the Prophet?

"See how We have bestowed more bounty on some than on others. But the life to come will be higher in rank and greater in merit." (Verse 21) If one seeks to have the higher prize and the greater grace, then one should aim for the hereafter. For there lies the limitless expanse and scope whose boundaries are known only to God. It is for this prize that people should compete, not for the petty comforts of this world.

2

A Code Based on Justice

Do not set up any deity side by side with God, lest you find yourself disgraced, forsaken. (22)

لَّا تَجْعَلْ مَعَ اللَّهِ إِلَٰهًا ءَاخَرَ فَتَقْعُدَ مَذْمُومًا مَّخْذُولًا ۝

Your Lord has ordained that you shall worship none but Him, and that you must be kind to your parents. Should one of them, or both, attain to old age in your care, never say 'Ugh' to them or chide them, but always speak gently and kindly to them, (23)

وَقَضَىٰ رَبُّكَ أَلَّا تَعْبُدُوٓا۟ إِلَّآ إِيَّاهُ وَبِالْوَٰلِدَيْنِ إِحْسَٰنًا إِمَّا يَبْلُغَنَّ عِندَكَ ٱلْكِبَرَ أَحَدُهُمَآ أَوْ كِلَاهُمَا فَلَا تَقُل لَّهُمَآ أُفٍّ وَلَا تَنْهَرْهُمَا وَقُل لَّهُمَا قَوْلًا كَرِيمًا ۝

and spread over them humbly the wings of your tenderness, and say, 'My Lord, bestow on them Your grace, even as they reared and nurtured me when I was a child.' (24)

وَٱخْفِضْ لَهُمَا جَنَاحَ ٱلذُّلِّ مِنَ ٱلرَّحْمَةِ وَقُل رَّبِّ ٱرْحَمْهُمَا كَمَا رَبَّيَانِى صَغِيرًا ۝

Your Lord knows best what is in your hearts. If you are righteous, He is certainly most forgiving to those who turn repeatedly to Him [seeking His mercy]. (25)

رَّبُّكُمْ أَعْلَمُ بِمَا فِى نُفُوسِكُمْ إِن تَكُونُوا۟ صَٰلِحِينَ فَإِنَّهُۥ كَانَ لِلْأَوَّٰبِينَ غَفُورًا ۝

Give to the near of kin their due, and also to the needy and the traveller in need. Do not squander your substance wastefully, (26)

وَءَاتِ ذَا ٱلْقُرْبَىٰ حَقَّهُۥ وَٱلْمِسْكِينَ وَٱبْنَ ٱلسَّبِيلِ وَلَا تُبَذِّرْ تَبْذِيرًا ﴿٢٦﴾

for the wasteful squanderers are Satan's brothers, and Satan has always been ungrateful to his Lord. (27)

إِنَّ ٱلْمُبَذِّرِينَ كَانُوٓا۟ إِخْوَٰنَ ٱلشَّيَٰطِينِ وَكَانَ ٱلشَّيْطَٰنُ لِرَبِّهِۦ كَفُورًا ﴿٢٧﴾

But if you must turn aside from them in pursuit of an act of kindness you hope to receive from your Lord, then at least speak to them kindly. (28)

وَإِمَّا تُعْرِضَنَّ عَنْهُمُ ٱبْتِغَآءَ رَحْمَةٍ مِّن رَّبِّكَ تَرْجُوهَا فَقُل لَّهُمْ قَوْلًا مَّيْسُورًا ﴿٢٨﴾

Do not be miserly, allowing your hand to remain shackled to your neck, nor stretch it out fully to the utmost limit, lest you find yourself being blamed or reduced to destitution. (29)

وَلَا تَجْعَلْ يَدَكَ مَغْلُولَةً إِلَىٰ عُنُقِكَ وَلَا تَبْسُطْهَا كُلَّ ٱلْبَسْطِ فَتَقْعُدَ مَلُومًا مَّحْسُورًا ﴿٢٩﴾

Your Lord gives in abundance, or in scant measure, to whom He wills. He is indeed fully aware of all His servants, and sees them all. (30)

إِنَّ رَبَّكَ يَبْسُطُ ٱلرِّزْقَ لِمَن يَشَآءُ وَيَقْدِرُ إِنَّهُۥ كَانَ بِعِبَادِهِۦ خَبِيرًۢا بَصِيرًا ﴿٣٠﴾

Do not kill your children for fear of want. It is We who shall provide for them and for you. To kill them is indeed a great sin. (31)

وَلَا تَقْتُلُوٓا۟ أَوْلَٰدَكُمْ خَشْيَةَ إِمْلَٰقٍ نَّحْنُ نَرْزُقُهُمْ وَإِيَّاكُمْ إِنَّ قَتْلَهُمْ كَانَ خِطْـًٔا كَبِيرًا ﴿٣١﴾

Do not come near adultery. It is indeed an abomination and an evil way. (32)

Do not kill anyone, for God has forbidden killing, except in [the pursuit of] justice. If anyone is slain wrongfully, We have given his heir authority [to seek just retribution]. He [i.e. the heir] must not exceed the bounds of equity in [retributive] killing. He is given help. (33)

Do not come near the property of an orphan before he comes of age, except with the best of intentions. Be true to all your promises, for you will be called to account for all that you promise. (34)

And give full measure whenever you measure, and weigh with accurate scales. That is fair, and best in the end. (35)

Do not pursue that of which you have no knowledge. Man's ears, eyes and heart shall all be called to account. (36)

Do not walk on earth with an air of self-conceit; for you cannot rend the earth asunder, nor can you rival the mountains in height. (37)

وَلَا تَقْرَبُوا۟ ٱلزِّنَىٰٓ ۖ إِنَّهُۥ كَانَ فَٰحِشَةً وَسَآءَ سَبِيلًا ﴿٣٢﴾

وَلَا تَقْتُلُوا۟ ٱلنَّفْسَ ٱلَّتِى حَرَّمَ ٱللَّهُ إِلَّا بِٱلْحَقِّ ۗ وَمَن قُتِلَ مَظْلُومًا فَقَدْ جَعَلْنَا لِوَلِيِّهِۦ سُلْطَٰنًا فَلَا يُسْرِف فِّى ٱلْقَتْلِ ۖ إِنَّهُۥ كَانَ مَنصُورًا ﴿٣٣﴾

وَلَا تَقْرَبُوا۟ مَالَ ٱلْيَتِيمِ إِلَّا بِٱلَّتِى هِىَ أَحْسَنُ حَتَّىٰ يَبْلُغَ أَشُدَّهُۥ ۚ وَأَوْفُوا۟ بِٱلْعَهْدِ ۖ إِنَّ ٱلْعَهْدَ كَانَ مَسْـُٔولًا ﴿٣٤﴾

وَأَوْفُوا۟ ٱلْكَيْلَ إِذَا كِلْتُمْ وَزِنُوا۟ بِٱلْقِسْطَاسِ ٱلْمُسْتَقِيمِ ۚ ذَٰلِكَ خَيْرٌ وَأَحْسَنُ تَأْوِيلًا ﴿٣٥﴾

وَلَا تَقْفُ مَا لَيْسَ لَكَ بِهِۦ عِلْمٌ ۚ إِنَّ ٱلسَّمْعَ وَٱلْبَصَرَ وَٱلْفُؤَادَ كُلُّ أُو۟لَٰٓئِكَ كَانَ عَنْهُ مَسْـُٔولًا ﴿٣٦﴾

وَلَا تَمْشِ فِى ٱلْأَرْضِ مَرَحًا ۖ إِنَّكَ لَن تَخْرِقَ ٱلْأَرْضَ وَلَن تَبْلُغَ ٱلْجِبَالَ طُولًا ﴿٣٧﴾

| All this is evil; odious in your Lord's sight. (38) | كُلُّ ذَٰلِكَ كَانَ سَيِّئُهُۥ عِندَ رَبِّكَ مَكۡرُوهًا ۝ |
| These [injunctions] are but a part of the wisdom with which your Lord has inspired you. Do not set up any deity alongside God, lest you should be cast into hell, blamed and rejected. (39) | ذَٰلِكَ مِمَّآ أَوۡحَىٰٓ إِلَيۡكَ رَبُّكَ مِنَ ٱلۡحِكۡمَةِ وَلَا تَجۡعَلۡ مَعَ ٱللَّهِ إِلَٰهًا ءَاخَرَ فَتُلۡقَىٰ فِي جَهَنَّمَ مَلُومًا مَّدۡحُورًا ۝ |

Overview

1-21

In the preceding passage, which comprises the first 21 verses of the *sūrah*, the rules of action and reward, guidance and error, earnings and reckoning are linked to the great universal law that governs the succession of night and day. In the current passage, the rules for

22-39

behaviour, manners, individual and social duties are linked to belief in God's oneness. Indeed this belief provides the essential tie to which all other ties are linked, within the family, community and humanity as a whole.

In the previous passage we learnt that the Qur'ān "*shows the way to that which is most upright.*" We have also been told that God has most clearly '*spelled out everything.*' In this new passage, the *sūrah* gives us an outline of the commandments and prohibitions which demarcate the way to the most upright standards. They spell out in detail some rules of behaviour, telling us of permissible or prohibited practices.

This new passage begins with a commandment that prohibits the association of partners with God. It declares God's clear order that worship must be addressed to Him alone. This is followed by an outline of duties and obligations, such as maintaining kindness to one's parents, being generous without extravagance to relatives, the needy and travellers in need. It also prohibits killing one's offspring, adultery and murder under any circumstances. Further commandments make it clear that believers must take good care of orphans, ensuring that whatever property they have is well looked after, and that they must

fulfil their pledges and promises. They should also conduct their transactions in fairness, giving due weight and measure, and they must endeavour to establish and maintain the truth. They are commanded not to behave arrogantly in any situation. The passage concludes with a warning against associating partners with God. Thus all the commandments and prohibitions are given between the opening and ending of the passage, clearly attached to the basic belief in God's oneness which provides the firm foundation of human life as indeed all life.

Kindness to Parents

"*Do not set up any deity side by side with God, lest you find yourself disgraced, forsaken.*" (Verse 22) This is a commandment forbidding the association of partners with God and a warning against the results it brings about. Although it is a general order, it is nonetheless addressed to each individual so that everyone feels it is personally issued to them. Believing is a personal matter for which every individual is responsible for themselves. The outcome that awaits anyone who deviates from the path of believing in God's oneness is such that they find themselves 'disgraced' by the foul deed, 'forsaken', without support. Whoever is deprived of God's support is forsaken, no matter how numerous his supporters are. The Arabic description, *fataq'uda madhmūman makhdhūlā*, is especially graphic: in place of '*lest you find yourself*', read, 'lest you sit'. This aptly describes the person who finds such disgrace too shameful that it weighs heavily on him and he sits down forsaken, weak, unable to stand and powerless. The description also suggests that this state is permanent because 'sitting down in disgrace' suggests there is no action to change the situation.

"*Your Lord has ordained that you shall worship none but Him.*" (Verse 23) This order to offer all worship to God alone follows the one prohibiting the association of partners with God. It takes the form of a decisive ruling to be implemented without fail, by all mankind. The term, *qaḍā*, used in the Arabic text and translated as 'ordained', signifies a final verdict imparting additional emphasis to an already emphatic order that also uses the construction of a negation and exception: "*You shall worship none but Him."* The mode is one of total emphasis and stress. When this basic ruling is well established, individual and community duties are outlined. These rely on a firm belief in the One God. Hence, motives and goals behind actions and practices work towards the same end.

The most important bond next to that of faith is the family. Hence the *sūrah* links kindness to parents with the worship of God, in order to emphasize its importance in God's sight:

> *And that you must be kind to your parents. Should one of them, or both, attain to old age in your care, never say 'Ugh' to them or chide them, but always speak gently and kindly to them, and spread over them humbly the wings of your tenderness, and say, 'My Lord, bestow on them Your grace, even as they reared and nurtured me when I was a child.'* (Verses 23–24)

With inspirational expression that is full of tenderness the Qur'ān enhances our feelings of compassion towards our parents. As life goes on, its momentum carries the living and focuses our attention on what lies ahead, on our own children, the new generation. Rarely are we motivated to look back and attend to the former generation of parents, who represent a life that is already on the decline. Hence, as sons and daughters we need a strong charge of conscience so that we will look back and take care of our mothers and fathers.

Parents are naturally motivated to look after their children, sacrificing everything in the process, even when the sacrifice includes them personally. An early green shoot absorbs every particle of nutrition in its seed to leave it as dust, and a chic eats up everything in the egg, leaving only the shell. Similarly, children take up all their parents' vigour, health, effort and attention, leaving them in the weakness of old age, yet happy to have given their children everything they could give. But children soon forget all this and move ahead, caring more for their spouses and own offspring. This is the natural course of life.

Thus parents do not need any encouragement to be kind to their children. It is the children who need to be reminded of their duty towards the generation that has become dry, in need of tender care, after having spent most of its vitality in bringing up their young. Hence, the divine command to take good care of parents comes in the form of a ruling from God, following immediately after the command to worship God alone.

The *sūrah* then imparts an air of tenderness to the whole atmosphere. It engenders memories of childhood, of compassion, love and tender care: "*Should one of them, or both, attain to old age in your care...,*" (Verse 23) Old age commands veneration, and the weakness of the elderly imparts certain feelings. Use of the phrase, '*in your care*', describes an elderly person weakened by advancing years needing shelter and care. Hence, sons and daughters are told: "*Never say 'Ugh' to them or chide them.*" (Verse 23) This is the first step in taking care of one's parents and being kindly to them. Sons and daughters must never use words which suggest their being vexed or bothered by their parents, or say anything that betrays disrespect. On the contrary, they must "*always speak gently and kindly to them.*" (Verse 23) This is a higher and more positive step. What sons and daughters say to their parents must always be coupled with genuine respect.

"*And spread over them humbly the wings of your tenderness.*" (Verse 24) At this point the Qur'ān uses very tender words to touch our hearts and consciences. Mercy and compassion are so heightened that they border on humility, making the son and daughter too respectful to look their parents straight in the face, but willing to obey them. It is as if such tenderness spreads wings over one's parents. This is followed by a prayer: "*My Lord, bestow on them Your grace, even as they reared and nurtured me when I was a child.*" (Verse 24)

The prayer recalls the care and love, exercised by parents for vulnerable children. Yet now it is the parents themselves who are similarly weak and in need of tender, loving care. Hence, the address to God to bestow His grace on them. Indeed His grace is far greater, and His care is much more wide-ranging. He is better able to reward them for their kindness, while their children can never repay them for it. A *ḥadīth* mentions that "a man was carrying his mother while he was doing the *ṭawāf* [i.e. the obligatory walk around the Kaʿbah] during pilgrimage. He asked the Prophet whether he had discharged his duty towards her. The Prophet said, 'No, not even for a single deep sigh.'"

151

This *ḥadīth* speaks of a mother so weakened she was no longer able to walk in order to fulfil her religious duty of *ṭawāf*. Her son carried her so that she could fulfil that duty, just like a mother carries her child when it is very young. However, that is far from fulfilling a mother's claim against her children, which is constituted by the constant care she took of them, with every breath of her life.

Since all feelings, actions and reactions are related to faith in the context of the *sūrah*, it adds a final comment, referring all matters to God who knows people's intentions and what lies behind words and actions: "*Your Lord knows best what is in your hearts. If you are righteous, He is certainly Most Forgiving to those who turn repeatedly to Him [seeking His mercy].*" (Verse 25)

Coming as it does immediately before a range of orders, duties and standards, this verse serves as a guideline for everything we say or do. It also leaves the door open for anyone who makes a mistake or falls short of expectations to declare his repentance and seek forgiveness. When a person's heart is set on the right track, the door to forgiveness remains open. The verse mentions in particular those who turn back to God every time they slip or make a mistake.

Kindness to All

The *sūrah* proceeds to include all relatives and the need to be kindly to them, adding also the needy and travellers who may find themselves in difficulty. It expands on family relations so as to include all human bonds in their broadest sense:

> Give to the near of kin their due, and also to the needy and the traveller in need. Do not squander your substance wastefully, for the wasteful squanderers are Satan's brothers, and Satan has always been ungrateful to his Lord. But if you must turn aside from them in pursuit of an act of kindness you hope to receive from your Lord, then at least speak to them kindly. (Verses 26–28)

The Qur'ān makes it clear that the near of kin, the needy and stranded travellers have a right against us which may only be discharged by financial assistance. This does not come as a favour which one person does to another; it is rather a duty imposed by God and associated with worshipping Him alone. When we fulfil this duty we are only discharging our responsibility, and cultivating a close relationship between ourselves and those to whom we give. The giver has no favour against the recipient, because he is only fulfilling a duty towards God.

The Qur'ān speaks strongly against squandering, which is defined as spending one's money in the wrong way. Mujāhid says that if one spends all one's money for rightful purposes, one is not a squanderer, but if one spends a small amount in the wrong way, then one is. Thus, it is not the amount which one spends, but the purpose for which one spends it. Hence, squanderers are indeed Satan's brothers because they spend their money for evil purposes, and to finance their disobedience of God. This makes them Satan's cronies. It must be remembered that "*Satan has always been ungrateful to his Lord.*" (Verse 27) Both Satan and those who squander do not fulfil their duty of appreciating God's favours, which means that they should use it only in purposes that earn God's pleasure, doing His bidding and refraining from anything He has forbidden.

When a person does not have the means to do his duty by relatives, the needy and stranded travellers, and he finds it embarrassing to meet them face to face, he should turn to God praying to Him to give him good provisions and to provide for those in need. At the same time, he should promise the needy that he will give to them whenever his means improve. At the same time, he should speak to them kindly. He must not be bored with them, nor should he remain silent and so embarrass them. A kind word serves a good purpose and opens up hope: "*But if you must turn aside from them in pursuit of an act of kindness you hope to receive from your Lord, then at least speak to them kindly.*" (Verse 28)

Within the context of prohibiting the squandering of money, the Qur'ān orders moderation in all spending: "*Do not be miserly, allowing your hand to remain shackled to your neck, nor stretch it out fully to the utmost limit, lest you find yourself being blamed or reduced to destitution.*" (Verse 29) Striking a proper balance is the Islamic rule. To move to either extreme leads to imbalance. The verse employs subtle imagery to enhance the intended meaning. It paints miserliness as a hand tied up to one's neck, while a spendthrift is shown as one with hands stretched out completely, unable to hold on to anything. The end of miserliness and the end of squander is drawn as a person sitting down, facing blame, powerless. It implies a position of weakness like that which makes an animal refuse to move. This applies to the miserly person whose miserliness weakens him to the point of inaction, and to the spendthrift who finds himself deprived of all power. Both are blamed in the end, one for stinginess, the other for squandering. The best attitude is a middle of the road one, tilting neither towards a tight fist nor towards careless extravagance.

The order to seek a middle course is followed with a comment stating that the provider for all is God, and it is He who may give abundant provisions or may give only in a tight measure. Yet the One who gives to all is the One who orders a middle course: "*Your Lord gives in abundance, or in scant measure, to whom He wills. He is indeed fully aware of all His servants, and sees them all.*" (Verse 30) Whichever way He gives to any one of His servants is determined on the basis of His wisdom. He commands all to follow a course of moderation, prohibiting both extremes of miserliness and careless extravagance on the basis of His perfect knowledge of what is most suitable for all His servants at all times. It is He who has revealed the Qur'ān to always guide along the straight path.

Setting Values Right

As the Qur'ān makes this statement clear, it follows it with reference to the fact that some people in pre-Islamic days used to kill their daughters for fear of want and poverty. It then adds a clear order prohibiting the killing of children for any such reason. Since God is the One who determines the means people have, there is no connection, then, between poverty and the number or sex of the children they have. The matter is fully in God's hands. When people purge their thoughts of the false notion of any direct relationship between poverty and having children, and when they adopt the correct concept in this regard, there is no reason for that ghastly crime which flies in the face of human nature and the right to life: "*Do not kill your children for fear*

154

of want. It is We who shall provide for them and for you. To kill them is indeed a great sin." (Verse 31)

When people adopt false beliefs, these beliefs affect their everyday lives. The effect is not confined to the adoption of wrong notions or the offering of worship rituals. On the other hand, purging faith from any false notion does have a positive effect on feelings, behaviour and social life generally. The fact that people in pre-Islamic Arabia used to bury their daughters alive provides a clear case of how far religious beliefs can affect human life so as to establish such horrendous crime as an acceptable social norm. It testifies to the fact that life is affected by the sort of beliefs people adopt. Indeed faith cannot remain isolated from human life.

A word should be said here about the meticulous care the Qur'ānic style reflects in its usage. In this particular verse we note that the provision for offspring is mentioned before provision for parents. In *Sūrah* 6, Cattle or *al-An'ām*, it is provision for parents which comes first: *"We provide for you and for them."* (6: 151) The usage in both cases is related to the different emphasis they have. Here the verse is translated as: *"Do not kill your children for fear of want. It is We who shall provide for them and for you. To kill them is indeed a great sin."* (Verse 31) The verse in *Sūrah* 6 reads as follows: *"Do not kill your children because of your poverty: We provide for you and for them."* (6: 151) It is clear that this *sūrah* is referring to the killing of children from fear that their presence will lead to poverty. Hence, providing for children is mentioned first. In *Sūrah* 6, the children are killed because of their parents' actual poverty. Hence, the provision for parents is mentioned first. Thus every little Qur'ānic detail, even putting something first on one occasion and second on another is for a definite reason.

Adultery Outlawed

The prohibition of killing children is followed by a prohibition against adultery:[1] *"Do not come near adultery. It is indeed an*

---

1. The Arabic word *zinā*, translated here as 'adultery', refers to sexual intercourse outside wedlock, regardless of whether the man or the woman is married. Thus, it includes fornication. – Editor's note.

abomination and an evil way." (Verse 32) There is a definite link between the killing of children and adultery. We find that the prohibition of adultery here intervenes between the prohibition of killing one's children and that of killing oneself. This takes into account the link to which we are here referring.

Adultery represents killing in various ways. It is a killing because it wastes life matter as it puts it in the wrong place. It is often followed by a desire to get rid of its natural consequences through abortion or infanticide. If the child is spared and allowed to live, it is abandoned to a life of misery and deprivation, which is a killing in a different form. Moreover, it is a killing of the community because family relations are thus lost, and blood ties are confused. People will have little trust that the children they bring up are their own. Thus community relations become weakened and the spirit of the community more or less dies.

Adultery may also be described as a killing of the community for a different reason. The ease which it provides for the fulfilment of sexual desires makes marriage a redundant institution, and the family an unnecessary responsibility. We must not forget that the family provides the proper home where the young should be reared, and where sound human nature is consolidated. It is the home where sound upbringing can be ensured for boys and girls alike.

Throughout history, every community that allowed immorality to spread saw its own decline brought about. Some people may feel that this is not true, looking at the fact that Europe and the United States continue to enjoy power despite the fact that immorality is widespread there. Yet the results of such loose morality are now apparent in older nations, such as France. As for new nations like the US, it may take some time yet before such effects are visible. The case is like that of a young man who gives rein to his desire. The effects may not manifest themselves when he is young, but as he grows older, his decline is rapid.

The Qur'ān even warns against 'coming near' to adultery, in order to give stronger emphasis that it is something to guard against. Since adultery is committed to satisfy a strong desire, steering away from it is safer. When adultery is made easy, resisting it becomes that much harder. Hence Islam takes appropriate preventive measures. It dislikes the mixing of the two sexes where it is unnecessary, forbids that a man stay with a woman in a closed place, and prohibits the indecent appearance of women when they go out or attend social functions. It encourages marriage and recommends fasting for those who cannot marry. It disapproves of all types of barriers that prevent people from getting married such as exorbitant dowries. It makes it clear that no one should ever fear poverty as a result of having children, and encourages its followers to provide help to those who wish to marry in order to preserve their chastity. It also prescribes very severe punishments for the crimes of adultery and false accusations of adultery against others, without providing proper evidence to support the same. Such measures are taken in order to prevent the Muslim community from throwing itself on the slippery road to decline.

A Peaceful Community

The *surah* follows this with a prohibition of killing anyone, except for a valid reason: *"Do not kill anyone, for God has forbidden killing, except in [the pursuit of] justice. If anyone is slain wrongfully, We have given his heir authority [to seek just retribution]. He [i.e. the heir] must not exceed the bounds of equity in [retributive] killing. He is given help."* (Verse 33)

Islam is a religion which preserves life and ensures peace. Hence it considers the killing of any human being to be a crime of the highest order, ranking next to associating partners with God. It is God who gives life. Hence, no one can take life away except by God's permission and within the limits which He has allowed. Every human life has a sanctity which cannot be violated. The limits which God has allowed for the infliction of capital punishment are very clear. They are not subject to any influence by prejudice or personal view. A highly authentic *hadīth* related by al-Bukhārī and Muslim quotes the Prophet as saying: "No Muslim person who bears witness that there is no deity other than God and that Muḥammad is God's Messenger may be killed except for one of three reasons: a life for a life, a married adulterer and a rebel who renounces his faith and abandons his community."

The first of these three legitimate ways to inflict capital punishment ensures fair retribution. It allows the killing of one person in order to

157

guarantee life for many others. God tells us that "*There is life for you, men of understanding, in this law of just retribution, so that you may remain God-fearing.*" (2: 179) Human life is thus preserved by stopping those who are intent on assaulting and killing others for no reason. When someone intent on killing another realizes that just retribution will make him pay for his ghastly crime with his own life, he will stop short of killing. Again there is life for the community as the law of just retribution stops the relatives of the victim from vengeance killing, which often goes beyond just killing the offender. When vengeance killing is allowed free reign it leads to the killing of innocent people as the family feud ensues. On the contrary, just retribution gives security to all, making sure that no one other than the offender is threatened. Thus, everyone goes about his life in peace and security.

The second reason for executing an offender is to prevent the spread of immorality which threatens the life of the community, as we have already explained.

The third justification seeks to repel spiritual corruption which leads to chaos within the Muslim community, threatens its peace and security and destroys the system God has chosen for it. The one who rebels, renouncing his faith and abandoning his community condemns himself by his own action. He adopted Islam by choice, under no compulsion, and became a member of the community, aware of its secrets. Hence, when he abandoned it, his action constituted a threat to it. Had he remained a non-Muslim, no one would have compelled him to adopt Islam. Indeed Islam would have ensured that he remained safe and secure if he belonged to another divine religion, or that he was protected and given safe conduct to reach his own community if he was a pagan. This represents complete fairness with those who belong to any faith other than Islam.

"*Do not kill anyone, for God has forbidden killing, except in [the pursuit of] justice.*" (Verse 33) These are the only three reasons which justify capital punishment in Islamic law. Otherwise any killing is considered wrongful, bringing other provisions of Islamic law into operation: "*If anyone is slain wrongfully, We have given his heir authority [to seek just retribution]. He [i.e. the heir] must not exceed the bounds of equity in [retributive] killing. He is given help.*" (Verse 33) Thus wrongful killing gives the victim's heir, or his next of kin, an authority to seek the implementation of the law of just retribution. It is up to the next of kin to demand that the killer pays with his life for his crime, or to spare his life in return for the payment of blood money, or to forgive the offender altogether, demanding no compensation. This authority over the killer is given to the victim's next of kin because he is in possession of the killer's blood, as it were.

In return for this authority, Islam prohibits the victim's relatives from going too far in exercising their authority. This may take the form of exceeding their limits, killing others in addition to the actual killer of their relative. This is the way vengeance killing works in non-Islamic communities where the killer's close relatives may be murdered in revenge. They may be free of all guilt, but they are killed simply because they are relatives of the first killer. Another aspect of exceeding one's limits is to disfigure the killer when his life is taken in just retribution. The victim's next of kin may insist on the killer being executed, but he has no justification to resort to disfigurement, which is totally prohibited in Islam.

"He [i.e. the heir] must not exceed the bounds of equity in [retributive] killing. He is given help." (Verse 33) That help is given in the fact that God's law judges in his favour and the ruling authorities ensure that justice is done. Hence, he is required to remain within the confines of justice so that he receives the help he needs in order to obtain what rightfully belongs to him.

Giving the next of kin of a murder victim authority to exact just retribution, and assuring him of the help of the law and the authorities, constitutes a fair response to the demands of human nature. Relatives may be highly agitated, and even blinded by their desire for revenge. In their anger they may lash out against the innocent. But when they realize that God has given them authority to exact just retribution, and that they may demand that the killer should pay with his life for his crime, and that the ruler is required to help them achieve justice, they may well be pacified. This makes it easier for them to stop at the proper legal limits in this case. They are assured of justice.

It is inappropriate to require people to go beyond their nature so as to stifle their burning desire for revenge. Islam acknowledges this fact and meets the demands of human nature in a way which ensures safety for the individual and the community. It does not try to impose forgiveness and reconciliation by force. Indeed it urges such forgiveness and clearly makes it the better option, assigning rich reward for forgiveness but only after it states legal rights. Thus the relatives of a murdered person may seek punishment of the killer, or they may pardon him. That they have the option is more likely to encourage them to forgive. To try to force forgiveness could be counterproductive. It could even make them more violent in seeking retribution.

Perfect Honesty

Having completed its instructions concerning the sanctity of people's honour and life, the *surah* tackles the question of orphans' property and the requirement of fulfilling one's promises and pledges towards them:

> Do not come near the property of an orphan before he comes of age, except with the best of intentions. Be true to all your promises, for you will be called to account for all that you promise. (Verse 34)

Islam makes it clear that a Muslim's life, honour and property are to be protected and preserved. The Prophet says: "Everything that belongs to a Muslim is forbidden to be taken away by another: his blood, honour and property." [Related by al-Bukhārī, Muslim, Mālik and Abū Dāwūd and al-Tirmidhī] The *surah*, however, makes a special case concerning the property of an orphan, ensuring its full protection. It forbids the mere coming near it except for what is best for the orphan. That is because an orphan is too weak to manage his property or defend it against assault. Hence, the Muslim community is required to take proper care of the orphan and his property until he comes of age and is able to take care of his own affairs.

An important point to be noted in connection with all these instructions is that matters which an individual needs to implement in person, as an individual, are phrased in the singular form. By contrast, the instructions that are addressed to the Muslim community are given in the plural. Thus we see that orders to be kind to parents, to be charitable to relatives, the needy and stranded travellers, and to refrain from extravagance, maintain a middle way between being tight-fisted and spendthrift, to ascertain the truth in every situation and refrain from showing arrogance and conceit, are all given in the singular form. This is due to the fact that responsibility in these areas is shouldered by the individual. On the other hand, the plural form is used to express the instructions prohibiting the killing of children, adultery, and homicide, and those concerning the protection of an orphan's property, honouring promises and pledges, and giving fair weight and measure, because these concern the community as a whole.

Here we see that the order not to come near the property of an orphan, except with the best of intentions, is given in the plural in order to make the whole community responsible for the protection of orphans and their property. It is then a collective responsibility.

Looking after an orphan's property is an act of trust which constitutes a pledge by the whole community. Hence, it is followed with an order to honour all promises and pledges: *"Be true to all your promises, for you will be called to account for all that you promise."* (Verse 34) God will certainly question people about their promises and will hold to account anyone who is in breach of any trust or pledge. Islam attaches great importance to the fulfilment of promises and pledges and to being true to one's trust because this is the essence of honesty and integrity, both personal and social. In fact, fulfilment of promises and honouring trust is mentioned in various ways and forms in the Qur'ān and *ḥadīth*, both with regard to pledges given to people or to God, by the individual, community or state, ruler or ruled. In practice, Islam has set an example for such fulfilment which humanity has never seen except under Islamic rule.

Just Weight and Measure

The code of conduct the *sūrah* outlines also speaks about fairness in commercial dealings:

And give full measure whenever you measure, and weigh with accurate scales. That is fair, and best in the end. (Verse 35)

The relevance of fulfilling promises and giving fair and full measure and weight is readily apparent, both in meaning and expression. This makes the progress from one to the other easy and smooth. To be fair in transactions and to give full weight and measure are actions which mark honest dealing and good faith. Thus internal dealings within the community are set on the right footing which promotes trust and honesty, and ensures blessings all round: "*That is fair, and best in the end.*" (Verse 35) It is good in this life as it maintains fairness, and better in the hereafter as it ensures good reward.

The Prophet (peace be upon him) said: "Anyone who is able to secure unlawful gain yet abandons this for no reason other than fearing God will certainly receive from God what is better than such gain here in this life, before they receive their reward in the life to come."

Giving in to greed and stinginess in weight and measure betrays meanness and dishonesty which destroys trust within the community. It leads to poor trading, and a lack of blessings and trust in the community. This is bound to have repercussions on individuals who find themselves losers after they had thought to gain through selling people short. Whatever gain they may make is superficial and short-lived. Stagnation of trade, which is a by-product of such stinting, is certain to show its effects on individuals.

This is a fact, recognized by far-sighted business people. They maintain honesty as a business principle not because of any ethical, moral or religious motive, but because they see from practical experience that it delivers much better gain. Thus one person may be fair in business and give full weight and measure for practical and trade reasons while another does the same as part of implementing his religious convictions. The difference between the two is that the latter gets all the benefits received by the former in addition to maintaining a clear conscience and looking towards higher horizons. He benefits by a much broader vision of life. This clearly shows that Islam fulfils the objectives of practical life while building its wider concepts and happier environment.

Accountability for All Actions

A basic characteristic of the Islamic faith is that it is straightforward, clear and transparent. Nothing is permitted on the basis of suspicion, myth or unsubstantiated impression:

> *Do not pursue that of which you have no knowledge. Man's ears, eyes and heart shall all be called to account.* (Verse 36)

These few words establish a complete method for the human mind and heart, incorporating the scientific approach that humanity has begun to apply only recently. It adds, however, honesty and fear of God. This is an advantage Islam adds over cold rational approaches that are devoid of spirituality.

Making certain of every report, action or situation before passing a judgement concerning it is the essence of the Qur'ānic approach. When hearts and minds faithfully follow this approach, there remains no room for superstition in matters of faith, or for suspicion in legal affairs. What is more is that there is no room for theoretical assumptions or superficial conclusions in science and research.

Scientific integrity which, in modern times, people unreservedly praise is no more than the conscientious integrity which the Qur'ān establishes as a requirement to be accounted for. The Qur'ān makes everyone responsible and accountable for their hearing, seeing and feelings in front of God who has given them their ears, eyes and hearts. This is the integrity and honesty of senses, heart and mind. Man is accountable for all these and the organs themselves will be questioned about their actions on the Day of Judgement. When we consider the magnitude of this responsibility, we are overwhelmed because it applies to every word we say and every judgement we make.

"*Do not pursue that of which you have no knowledge.*" (Verse 36) Certain knowledge must be the only basis for judgement or conviction. Whatever is not certain must never constitute such a basis. In an authentic *ḥadīth*, the Prophet is quoted as saying: "Refrain from assumption, for assumption is the basis of the worst lies." Another *ḥadīth* related by Abū Dāwūd quotes the Prophet as saying: "It is indeed a bad practice for a man to always begin his statements with, 'it is

163

claimed.'" In another *ḥadīth* the Prophet said: "The worst falsehood is that a man makes his eyes see what they have not seen."

Thus we see how Qur'ānic verses and *aḥādīth* combine to establish such a complete and integrated system which requires the mind to make certain of its grounds for any judgement it makes. But Islam does not stop at this. It also requires the heart to make sure of its basis for whatever thoughts or feelings it entertains. Thus people must ascertain every detail, circumstance and factor before making any judgement or arriving at any conclusion. This is a practical fulfilment of the Qur'ānic statement made earlier in this *sūrah*: "*Surely this Qur'ān shows the way to that which is most upright.*" (Verse 9)

These orders and instructions that are closely linked to the faith based on God's oneness are concluded with an order prohibiting conceit and arrogance: "*Do not walk on earth with an air of self-conceit; for you cannot rend the earth asunder, nor can you rival the mountains in height.*" (Verse 37) When man is devoid of belief in God, the Creator who has power over all creation, he may feel himself too powerful or admirable on account of his wealth, power or beauty. If only he remembers that whatever blessing he enjoys is granted to him by God and that he is powerless in front of God, he will see how misplaced his conceit is and so refrain from such arrogance.

The Qur'ān puts the conceited and arrogant face to face with their humbleness and powerlessness: "*You cannot rend the earth asunder, nor can you rival the mountains in height.*" (Verse 37) Physically man is small and insignificant, particularly when compared to giant creation. But he is strong when he relies on God's power, honourable with His honour, and noble with His spirit which God has breathed into him. God has given man all this so that he always remembers and remains conscious of Him.

Such humility which the Qur'ān calls upon people to adopt, decrying at the same time all types of conceit, is a mark of maintaining proper relations with God and one's fellow human beings, and a proper personal and social attitude. No one abandons such good manners except the petty and the conceited. Such people are disliked by God because they overlook His favours which they enjoy, and are hated by human beings for their arrogance. The Prophet is reported to have said: "Whoever maintains humility for God's sake, God will elevate him. Thus he looks humbly at himself but people look at him with respect. By contrast, God humiliates an arrogant person so as he rates himself highly while people look down upon him. Indeed he may be more disliked by people than a dog or a pig."[2]

As we have seen, these instructions are mainly concerned with prohibiting evil action and improper behaviour. Their outline concludes with declaring God's disapproval of them: "*All this is evil; odious in your Lord's sight.*" (Verse 38) This serves as a summary and reminder that commandments are issued by God alone. The reason for prohibition is God's dislike of such evil. No mention is made here of good matters which Islam orders to be practised or maintained. It is the prohibitions that are outlined in this code of conduct which the *sūrah* gives in detail.

This outline of the Islamic code of conduct is brought to an end by showing its details again linked to faith in God's oneness, which was also stated at the outset of this passage. This is coupled with a warning against associating partners with God. Furthermore, we are told that this code is only a part of the wisdom to which the Qur'ān guides people: "*These [injunctions] are but a part of the wisdom with which your Lord has inspired you. Do not set up any deity alongside God, lest you should be cast into hell, blamed and rejected.*" (Verse 39)

Thus the ending is akin to the opening, with both emphasizing the basis on which Islam builds its structure for human life, namely, the concept of God's oneness. For it is to God that all worship should be addressed.

---

2. This *ḥadīth* is cited by Ibn Kathīr in his commentary on the Qur'ān.

3

God: The One and Glorious

Has your Lord distinguished you by [giving you] sons and taken for Himself daughters from among the angels? That which you utter is indeed an enormity. (40)

أَفَأَصْفَىٰكُمْ رَبُّكُم بِالْبَنِينَ وَاتَّخَذَ مِنَ الْمَلَٰٓئِكَةِ إِنَٰثًا إِنَّكُمْ لَتَقُولُونَ قَوْلًا عَظِيمًا ﴿٤٠﴾

We have certainly explained things in various ways in this Qur'ān, so that they may take it to heart, but it only increases their aversion. (41)

وَلَقَدْ صَرَّفْنَا فِى هَٰذَا الْقُرْءَانِ لِيَذَّكَّرُوا۟ وَمَا يَزِيدُهُمْ إِلَّا نُفُورًا ﴿٤١﴾

Say: 'If there were other deities alongside Him, as some people assert, they would have to seek a way to the Lord of the Throne.' (42)

قُل لَّوْ كَانَ مَعَهُۥٓ ءَالِهَةٌ كَمَا يَقُولُونَ إِذًا لَّابْتَغَوْا۟ إِلَىٰ ذِى الْعَرْشِ سَبِيلًا ﴿٤٢﴾

Limitless is He in His glory and sublimely exalted is He above everything they may say [about Him]. (43)

سُبْحَٰنَهُۥ وَتَعَٰلَىٰ عَمَّا يَقُولُونَ عُلُوًّا كَبِيرًا ﴿٤٣﴾

The seven heavens extol His limitless glory, as does the earth, and all who dwell in them. Indeed every single thing extols His glory and praise, but you cannot understand their praises. He is indeed Forbearing, Much Forgiving. (44)

تُسَبِّحُ لَهُ ٱلسَّمَٰوَٰتُ ٱلسَّبْعُ وَٱلْأَرْضُ وَمَن فِيهِنَّ ۚ وَإِن مِّن شَيْءٍ إِلَّا يُسَبِّحُ بِحَمْدِهِۦ وَلَٰكِن لَّا تَفْقَهُونَ تَسْبِيحَهُمْ ۗ إِنَّهُۥ كَانَ حَلِيمًا غَفُورًا ﴿٤٤﴾

When you read the Qur'ān, We place an invisible barrier between you and those who do not believe in the life to come. (45)

وَإِذَا قَرَأْتَ ٱلْقُرْءَانَ جَعَلْنَا بَيْنَكَ وَبَيْنَ ٱلَّذِينَ لَا يُؤْمِنُونَ بِٱلْءَاخِرَةِ حِجَابًا مَّسْتُورًا ﴿٤٥﴾

We cast a veil over their hearts which makes them unable to grasp its meaning, and their ears We make deaf. And so, when you mention your Lord in the Qur'ān as the One and only God, they turn their backs in aversion. (46)

وَجَعَلْنَا عَلَىٰ قُلُوبِهِمْ أَكِنَّةً أَن يَفْقَهُوهُ وَفِيٓ ءَاذَانِهِمْ وَقْرًا ۚ وَإِذَا ذَكَرْتَ رَبَّكَ فِي ٱلْقُرْءَانِ وَحْدَهُۥ وَلَّوْا۟ عَلَىٰٓ أَدْبَٰرِهِمْ نُفُورًا ﴿٤٦﴾

We are fully aware of what they are listening for when they listen to you, and what they say when they speak to each other in private. The wrongdoers say: 'The man you follow is certainly bewitched.' (47)

نَّحْنُ أَعْلَمُ بِمَا يَسْتَمِعُونَ بِهِۦٓ إِذْ يَسْتَمِعُونَ إِلَيْكَ وَإِذْ هُمْ نَجْوَىٰٓ إِذْ يَقُولُ ٱلظَّٰلِمُونَ إِن تَتَّبِعُونَ إِلَّا رَجُلًا مَّسْحُورًا ﴿٤٧﴾

See to what they liken you. They have certainly gone astray and are unable to find a way back [to the truth]. (48)

ٱنظُرْ كَيْفَ ضَرَبُوا۟ لَكَ ٱلْأَمْثَٰلَ فَضَلُّوا۟ فَلَا يَسْتَطِيعُونَ سَبِيلًا ﴿٤٨﴾

They say: 'When we are bones and dust, shall we be raised to life again as a new creation?' (49)

وَقَالُوٓاْ أَءِذَا كُنَّا عِظَٰمًا وَرُفَٰتًا أَءِنَّا لَمَبْعُوثُونَ خَلْقًا جَدِيدًا ﴿٤٩﴾

Say: 'Be you stones or iron, (50)

قُلْ كُونُواْ حِجَارَةً أَوْ حَدِيدًا ﴿٥٠﴾

or some other form of creation which, to your minds, appears even harder [to bring to life].' They will say: 'Who is it that will bring us back [to life]?' Say: 'He who created you the first time.' Thereupon they shake their heads [in disbelief] and ask: 'When will this be?' Say: 'It may very well be near at hand. (51)

أَوْ خَلْقًا مِّمَّا يَكْبُرُ فِي صُدُورِكُمْ فَسَيَقُولُونَ مَن يُعِيدُنَا قُلِ ٱلَّذِي فَطَرَكُمْ أَوَّلَ مَرَّةٍ فَسَيُنْغِضُونَ إِلَيْكَ رُءُوسَهُمْ وَيَقُولُونَ مَتَىٰ هُوَ قُلْ عَسَىٰٓ أَن يَكُونَ قَرِيبًا ﴿٥١﴾

On that day He will call you, and you will answer by praising Him, thinking that you stayed on earth but a very short while.' (52)

يَوْمَ يَدْعُوكُمْ فَتَسْتَجِيبُونَ بِحَمْدِهِ وَتَظُنُّونَ إِن لَّبِثْتُمْ إِلَّا قَلِيلًا ﴿٥٢﴾

Tell My servants that they should always say that which is best. Satan tries to sow discord between them. Satan is indeed man's open foe. (53)

وَقُل لِّعِبَادِي يَقُولُواْ ٱلَّتِي هِيَ أَحْسَنُ إِنَّ ٱلشَّيْطَٰنَ يَنزَغُ بَيْنَهُمْ إِنَّ ٱلشَّيْطَٰنَ كَانَ لِلْإِنسَٰنِ عَدُوًّا مُّبِينًا ﴿٥٣﴾

Your Lord is fully aware of what you are. If He so wills, He will bestow His grace on you; and if He so wills, He will inflict punishment on you. We have not sent you, Prophet, to be their guardian. (54)

رَّبُّكُمْ أَعْلَمُ بِكُمْ إِن يَشَأْ يَرْحَمْكُمْ أَوْ إِن يَشَأْ يُعَذِّبْكُمْ وَمَآ أَرْسَلْنَٰكَ عَلَيْهِمْ وَكِيلًا ﴿٥٤﴾

Your Lord is fully aware of all beings that are in the heavens and earth. Indeed We have exalted some of the Prophets above others, just as We gave the Psalms to David. (55)

وَرَبُّكَ أَعْلَمُ بِمَن فِي ٱلسَّمَٰوَٰتِ وَٱلْأَرْضِ وَلَقَدْ فَضَّلْنَا بَعْضَ ٱلنَّبِيِّنَ عَلَىٰ بَعْضٍ وَءَاتَيْنَا دَاوُۥدَ زَبُورًا ۝

Say: 'Call on those whom you claim [to be gods] besides Him, but they have no power to remove any affliction from you, nor can they shift it.' (56)

قُلِ ٱدْعُوا۟ ٱلَّذِينَ زَعَمْتُم مِّن دُونِهِۦ فَلَا يَمْلِكُونَ كَشْفَ ٱلضُّرِّ عَنكُمْ وَلَا تَحْوِيلًا ۝

Those whom they invoke strive to obtain their Lord's favour, vying with each other to be near Him. They hope for His grace and dread His punishment. Indeed your Lord's punishment is something to beware of. (57)

أُو۟لَٰٓئِكَ ٱلَّذِينَ يَدْعُونَ يَبْتَغُونَ إِلَىٰ رَبِّهِمُ ٱلْوَسِيلَةَ أَيُّهُمْ أَقْرَبُ وَيَرْجُونَ رَحْمَتَهُۥ وَيَخَافُونَ عَذَابَهُۥٓ إِنَّ عَذَابَ رَبِّكَ كَانَ مَحْذُورًا ۝

Overview

The second passage of this *sūrah*, discussed in Chapter 2, starts and finishes with a strong emphasis on God's oneness and the prohibition of associating any partners with Him. Within its two ends, it contains a number of orders, prohibitions and values that are all based on the central principle of God's oneness. The present passage begins and ends with the denunciation of the very concept of assigning a son or a partner to God, explaining its absurdity. It states that the whole universe functions on the basis of believing in God as one, having no partners: "*Indeed every single thing extols His glory and praise.*" (Verse 44) It stresses the fact that all shall return to God in the life to come, and that God knows everything about all creatures in the heavens and earth.

He is the One who controls the destinies of all His creatures, and no one has any say about it: *"If He so wills, He will bestow His grace on you; and if He so wills, He will inflict punishment on you."* (Verse 54)

As the passage goes on, we see the fallacy of all beliefs based on associating partners with God, and we watch how they collapse. We also see that God is the One who controls everything in this universe, this life and the life to come, what is visible to us and what we do not see. We realize that it all addresses its praises, sincere and devoted to God alone. In such praises all creatures and living things take part.

All Glorify Him

Has your Lord distinguished you by [giving you] sons and taken for Himself daughters from among the angels? That which you utter is indeed an enormity. (Verse 40)

This question implies a sarcastic response to what the unbelievers used to do, as they described the angels as God's daughters. God is indeed too exalted to take to Himself a son or a wife, and He is too sublime to have any partner or associate. The verse also ridicules the assigning of daughters to God, when the Arabs considered girls to be of lesser status than boys. They indeed killed their daughters for fear of poverty or shame. Nevertheless they considered angels to be female and made them God's daughters. When it is God who gives life and gives everyone their sons and daughters, how come He favours them with the better sons and takes to Himself the inferior daughters!

This is stated merely for argument's sake, so as to make apparent the hollowness and fallacy of their claims. The whole issue is too bizarre to merit any discussion: *"That which you utter is indeed an enormity."* (Verse 40) It is enormously odd, impudent, false and outlandish.

"We have certainly explained things in various ways in this Qur'ān, so that they may take it to heart, but it only increases their aversion." (Verse 41) The Qur'ān preaches the faith of God's oneness, presenting it in a variety of ways, styles and methods, so that people may 'take warning'. Indeed accepting the faith based on God's oneness does not require

more than a reminder and a reference to uncorrupted human nature. It only needs to reflect on the various signs presented in the universe. But they only grow in their aversion to this faith whenever they listen to the Qur'ān. They show that they are averse to the faith the Qur'ān preaches, and averse to the Qur'ān itself, lest it clearly show the fallacy of their erroneous beliefs based on myth and superstition.

Here also the *sūrah* goes part of the way with them to make its argument about their alleged deities. It states that had such deities existed, they themselves would have tried to get closer to God and believe in Him: "*Say: 'If there were other deities alongside Him, as some people assert, they would have to seek a way to the Lord of the Throne.'*" (Verse 42) As linguists tell us, the construction of the sentence means that the whole supposition is false. There are no deities alongside God. What they claim to be their gods are no more than some of His creatures, be they stars, human beings, animals, plants and trees or other inanimate objects. All these turn to God, submitting themselves to His will, in accordance with the law of nature. They find their way to God through their obedience to His will and His laws: "*They would have to seek a way to the Lord of the Throne.*" (Verse 42)

Mention of the Throne here indicates God's clear exaltation above all creatures, including those they claim to be deities alongside Him. They are below His Throne, which means that they cannot be 'with Him'. This is followed by a clear statement glorifying God: "*Limitless is He in His glory and sublimely exalted is He above everything they may say [about Him].*" (Verse 43)

The *sūrah* then portrays the whole universe, with all creatures living in it, under God's Throne. They all turn to God glorifying Him: "*The seven heavens extol His limitless glory, as does the earth, and all who dwell in them. Indeed every single thing extols His glory and praise, but you cannot understand their praises. He is indeed Forbearing, Much Forgiving.*" (Verse 44) Every single particle in this vast universe shares in this glorification. Indeed it comes alive as it praises God and glorifies Him. The scene shows the whole universe full of life and activity, sharing in a single action, addressing God in His exalted nature in a glorification that implies submission to His will and acknowledgement of His authority over everything.

Deaf Ears, Sealed Hearts

It is a powerful and majestic scene in which we see every stone, large and small, every seed and leaf, every flower and fruit, every little shoot and every tree, every insect and reptile, every animal and human being, every creature that walks the earth, swims in the water or floats in the air, in short, all creatures in the whole universe glorifying God and turning to Him in submission. We are filled with awe as we sense that everything that comes within our vision or stays beyond it comes alive. Whenever we stretch our hands out to touch something, and whenever we put our feet to step over something, we feel that it is alive, glorifying God.

"Indeed every single thing extols His glory and praise," in its own way and language. *"But you [human beings] cannot understand their praises."* (Verse 44) Human beings are limited by their own constitution which has a clay origin. This debars them from understanding the praises of other creatures. Had they listened with their hearts, directing them to appreciate the subtle laws that operate in the universe and make everything, large or small, turn to the Creator of all, they would have appreciated something of that praise. When human souls are purified and when they hearken to every animate and inanimate object as it addresses its glorification to God alone, they are better prepared to be in contact with the Supreme Society. They are better able to understand the secrets of the universe than those who limit themselves to the material world.

"He is indeed Forbearing, Much Forgiving." (Verse 44) These attributes of God are mentioned here because of what seems clear of people's failing in their duties towards Him. Compared with this great show of submission to God in the whole universe, human beings seem to be in a singular position. Some associate partners with God, while others allege that He has daughters, and still others remain oblivious of their duty to praise and glorify Him. In fact human beings should have been the first among all creatures to acknowledge God, declare their submission to Him and extol His praises. Had it not been for God's forbearance and forgiveness, He would have hastened their punishment. But He allows them time, reminds and admonishes them because '*He is indeed Forbearing, Much Forgiving.*'

The leaders of the Quraysh, the Prophet's own tribesmen who rejected his call, tried hard to prevent their hearts and souls from responding positively to the truth of the Qur'ān. As a result, God raised an invisible curtain between them and the Prophet, and placed coverings on their hearts preventing them from understanding it. Their ears were in a state similar to deafness, which meant that they could not understand its message.

> When you read the Qur'ān, We place an invisible barrier between you and those who do not believe in the life to come. We cast a veil over their hearts which makes them unable to grasp its meaning, and their ears We make deaf. And so, when you mention your Lord in the Qur'ān as the One and only God, they turn their backs in aversion. We are fully aware of what they are listening for when they listen to you, and what they say when they speak to each other in private. The wrongdoers say: 'The man you follow is certainly bewitched.' See to what they liken you. They have certainly gone astray and are unable to find a way back [to the truth]. (Verses 45–48)

One report states that the elders of the Quraysh issued a general order telling everyone not to listen to the Qur'ān when they heard it being recited by Muslims. But the Qur'ān had its attraction even to the most outspoken enemies of Islam. Protected by the cover of darkness, three of those elders, Abū Jahl, Abū Sufyān and al-Akhnas ibn Sharīq sat just outside the Prophet's house, listening to the Qur'ān being recited from inside. Every one of them was on his own, thinking that no one would know about his action. As the day began to break, each took his way home, so that no one would find out. Soon, the three of them met. There was only one reason for their presence there at that particular time. Therefore they counselled each other against such action: "Should some of your followers see you," one of them said, "you would stir doubts in their minds."

The following night they did the same, and once again they met at the break of day. Again they counselled each other against their 'irresponsible' action. Nevertheless, the third night each of them went to sit outside the Prophet's home and listen to the Qur'ān. When they met in the morning, they were ashamed of themselves. One suggested that they should each give their word of honour not to return. This they did before going home.

Later that morning al-Akhnas ibn Sharīq went to see Abū Sufyān at his home. He asked him what he thought about what he had heard Muḥammad reciting. Abū Sufyān said: "I heard things which I know and recognize to be true, but I also heard things whose nature I cannot understand." Al-Akhnas said that he felt the same. He then left and went to Abū Jahl's home to put the same question to him. Abū Jahl's answer was totally different. For once, he was candid and honest with himself and his interlocutor: "I will tell you about what I heard! We have competed with the clan of 'Abd Manāf for honours: they fed the poor, and we did the same; they provided generous support to those who needed it and we did the same. When we were together on the same level, like two racehorses running neck and neck, they said that one of their number was a Prophet receiving revelations from on high! When can we attain such an honour? By God, we shall never believe in him."

It is abundantly clear then that these three elders were touched by the Qur'ān, their souls attracted to its message, but they deliberately sealed their hearts to it. As a result, God placed between them and His Messenger a secret seal that could not be seen with the human eye, yet it is felt by the heart. Its effect was to ensure that they would not benefit by the presence of God's Messenger among them and would not be guided by the Qur'ān he recited. Thus, they would speak to each other about the beauty and the truth of the Qur'ān but would pledge not to listen to it again. They might feel its power again and go out to listen to it anew, but they would remain determined to oppose it, and pledge a word of honour to stop listening to the Qur'ān and its message that addresses both mind and heart. They felt that the message of God's oneness, which is the central message of the Qur'ān, threatened their interests, privileges and pride: "*And so, when you mention your Lord in the Qur'ān as the One and only God, they turn their backs in aversion.*" (Verse 46)

They were averse to the very principle of God's oneness because they felt that it threatened their social position based on the myths that prevailed in those dark ages. In fact, the elders of the Quraysh were too intelligent not to realize the hollow nature of their beliefs as compared with the profound faith of Islam. They could easily appreciate the superb nature of the Qur'ān. Indeed their very nature motivated them to listen to it, but their pride caused them to take a hostile attitude to it. Thus they even fabricated allegations against the Prophet to justify their opposition: *"The wrongdoers say: 'The man you follow is certainly bewitched.'"* (Verse 47)

Their very words carried an implicit recognition of the nature of the Qur'ān. They realized deep inside that the Qur'ān was far too superior to be the word of a human being. They felt that its superiority transcended the realm of human beings. They also felt that it penetrated their own feelings. Hence, they alleged that it was the word of a sorcerer. Thus they claimed that Muḥammad was not speaking for himself, but by the power of magic. Had they been fair to him and to themselves, they would have acknowledged its divine nature. Indeed no human being and no other creature could have produced anything like the Qur'ān.

"See to what they liken you. They have certainly gone astray and are unable to find a way back [to the truth]." (Verse 48) They likened the Prophet to those who are bewitched when he was nothing like them. He was simply a Messenger chosen by God. As they made this analogy, they went astray. They could find no way ahead. They could not even justify their suspicions.

Bringing the Dead Back to Life

Such was what they said about the Qur'ān and the Messenger who recited it. They also denied resurrection and the life to come:

They say: 'When we are bones and dust, shall we be raised to life again as a new creation?' Say: 'Be you stones or iron, or some other form of creation which, to your minds, appears even harder [to bring to life].' They will say: 'Who is it that will bring us back [to life]?' Say: 'He who created you the first time.' Thereupon they shake their heads [in disbelief] and ask: 'When will this be?' Say: 'It may very well be near at hand. On that day He will call you, and you will answer by praising Him, thinking that you stayed on earth but a very short while.' (Verses 49–52)

The concept of resurrection was the subject of a long controversy between the Prophet and the unbelievers. The Qur'ān relates much of this argument. Yet the whole issue is very clear and simple for anyone who contemplates the nature of life and death, resurrection and the gathering of all creation. The Qur'ān explains it in full on various occasions. Yet people could not take it in its simple and clear nature. They could not imagine how a person could be brought back to life after the body had decomposed: *"They say: 'When we are bones and dust, shall we be raised to life again as a new creation?'"* (Verse 49)

They simply did not reflect on the fact that there was a time when they were not alive, yet they were brought to life. Nor did they appreciate that the second origination is simpler than the first. They did not fully understand that, as far as God is concerned, nothing can be described as 'easier' or 'more difficult'. Nor did they appreciate that the method of creation is the same in all cases. It is just that God issues His command for any creature to 'Be', and it comes into existence immediately. It is immaterial whether people consider something to be easy or difficult. When God wants it to happen, it will, without fail.

The reply comes in the form of an instruction to the Prophet to say to them: *"Be you stones or iron, or some other form of creation which, to your minds, appears even harder [to bring to life]."* (Verses 50–51) The bones and dust may still have some traces or memory of life, but iron and stones seem even further away from life. Hence they are told to be stones or iron or any other form that cannot ever be associated with life. Even if they are made of material that is least imagined to have life, God will bring them alive. They naturally cannot make themselves stones or iron or some other form of creation. This is given only by way of a challenge and reproach. Stones and iron have no feelings and cannot be inspired or influenced. This sounds as an implicit reference to their hardened nature.

"They will say: 'Who is it that will bring us back [to life]?'" (Verse 51) Who is it that brings bones and dust, or even more lifeless objects, back to life? *"Say: 'He who created you the first time.'"* (Verse 51) The answer puts the whole question into its proper perspective, which is both simple and direct. The One who originated them the first time is able to bring them back to life. Yet this reply is ignored: *"Thereupon*

they shake their heads [in disbelief]." (Verse 51) They simply shake their heads in disapproval, or even in ridicule. They try to make this sound too far fetched by asking: *"When will this be?"* (Verse 51) The Prophet is told to reply: *"It may very well be near at hand."* (Verse 51) The Prophet does not know its exact timing, but it may very well be nearer than they think. They should fear then lest it happen when they are engaged in such opposition and ridicule.

The *sūrah* then paints a speedy image of what happens when that event takes place, as it will indeed do: *"On that day He will call you, and you will answer by praising Him, thinking that you stayed on earth but a very short while."* (Verse 52) The image shows those people who were bent on denying the resurrection rising up to respond to the call that brings them back to life. As they do, they praise God in clear terms. They have nothing else to say apart from praising God. This is a strange response from those who were dogged in their denial of resurrection and the Day of Judgement altogether. They simply rise, saying nothing except: "Praised be God, praised be God." Thus this whole life is shown to be very brief, like a flickering light: *"You will answer by praising Him, thinking that you stayed on earth but a very short while."* (Verse 52)

Describing this life in this way is sure to belittle its importance in the minds of those to whom this address is made. It is a very short life. Nothing of its effects is of a lasting nature. It is no more than a brief moment that has passed, accompanied by a brief enjoyment.

Man's Open Enemy

After it has described their attitude of ridiculing God's promise and the Prophet's message, the *sūrah* turns away from those who deny the life to come and resurrection. It has something to say about the believers, instructing the Prophet to direct them to say only what is best. They should always be in the habit of saying a good word: *"Tell My servants that they should always say that which is best. Satan tries to sow discord between them. Satan is indeed man's open foe."* (Verse 53)

"Tell My servants that they should always say that which is best." It is a general order that applies in all situations and positions. They should choose the best to say. In this way they will be able to spoil Satan's

attempts to undermine the bond of mutual love that exists between them. Indeed he always tries to sow the seeds of discord between them, helped by an impolite word said by one person, followed by a similarly rude answer by another. Thus the atmosphere of love and brotherhood is spoilt, only to be replaced by an air of alienation, estrangement and even hostility. A good word always helps to clear the air and heal grievances.

"*Satan is indeed man's open foe.*" (Verse 53) He tries to build on every slip of a person's tongue to spread an air of alienation between brothers. Good words simply foil his attempts and protect the bond of brotherhood among all believers.

The *sūrah* then returns to those unbelievers who responded to the call to rise on the Day of Judgement. All destiny is in God's hands: He may forgive or punish. They will have to face God's judgement. The Prophet is no more than a Messenger. He is not their protector against God's will: "*Your Lord is fully aware of what you are. If He so wills, He will bestow His grace on you; and if He so wills, He will inflict punishment on you. We have not sent you, Prophet, to be their guardian. Your Lord is fully aware of all beings that are in the heavens and earth.*" (Verses 54–55) God's knowledge is absolute. Whatever He may determine of punishment or forgiveness is based on His knowledge. The Prophet's mission is completed when he has conveyed his message. God's knowledge encompasses all that is in heaven and earth, including the angels, prophets, human beings and *jinn*, as well as other creatures which are known only to God.

Competition to Be Closer to God

It is on the basis of this knowledge that He has exalted some prophets over others as He states here: "*Indeed We have exalted some of the prophets above others.*" (Verse 55) God alone knows the reasons behind this preference. As for the practical aspects of such exaltation and preference, these were discussed in commenting on verse 253 of *Sūrah* 2, which also mentions this exaltation.[3]

---

3. Volume I, pp. 395–403.

"*Just as We gave the Psalms to David.*" (Verse 55) This is one example of what God may give to one of His prophets, and one of the aspects of exaltation. The fact is that revelation and scripture are more lasting than supernatural events that may be witnessed by only a handful of people.

This passage, which begins with a definitive negation of the concept of God having a son or partner before calling on people to turn to God alone in all situations, concludes with a challenge to those who associate partners with God. The challenge is simply that they should call on those partners to remove any harm that befalls them, should God decide to punish them, or that they should divert His punishment to others: "*Say: 'Call on those whom you claim [to be gods] besides Him, but they have no power to remove any affliction from you, nor can they shift it.'*" (Verse 56) No one can remove hardship or change its nature or recipient except God Himself. He alone is in control of the destinies of all creation.

The *sūrah* tells them that those whom they claim to be deities, be they angels, *jinn* or human, are no more than forms of God's creation. They all try to find their way to God's pleasure, competing in this pursuit, fearing His punishment, which truly deserves to be feared: "*Those whom they invoke strive to obtain their Lord's favour, vying with each other to be near Him. They hope for His grace and dread His punishment. Indeed your Lord's punishment is something to beware of.*" (Verse 57)

Some of them claimed that Ezra was the son of God, while others attributed this position to Jesus Christ and worshipped him. Others claimed that the angels were God's daughters and worshipped them. Still others associated other creatures with God. To all of them the Qur'ān says: even the closest to God of all those you invoke try hard to approach their Lord, the One God, and worship Him alone hoping to receive His grace and fearing His punishment. Indeed His punishment is severe and it should be feared. Thus, it behoves you well to turn to God, as do those you claim to be deities.

The passage, then, ends on the same note on which it began, illustrating the hollow nature of polytheistic beliefs and showing clearly that God is the only Lord in the universe. Human beings should turn to Him alone with their appeals and worship.

4

Honour Granted to Mankind

There is no community but We shall destroy or severely punish before the Day of Resurrection. That is laid down in Our decree. (58)

وَإِن مِّن قَرْيَةٍ إِلَّا نَحْنُ مُهْلِكُوهَا قَبْلَ يَوْمِ الْقِيَامَةِ أَوْ مُعَذِّبُوهَا عَذَابًا شَدِيدًا كَانَ ذَٰلِكَ فِي الْكِتَابِ مَسْطُورًا ۝

Nothing hinders Us from sending miraculous signs except that the people of former times treated them as false. To the Thamūd We gave the she-camel as a sign to open their eyes, but they did wrong in respect of her. We never send signs for any purpose other than to give warning. (59)

وَمَا مَنَعَنَا أَن نُّرْسِلَ بِالْآيَاتِ إِلَّا أَن كَذَّبَ بِهَا الْأَوَّلُونَ وَآتَيْنَا ثَمُودَ النَّاقَةَ مُبْصِرَةً فَظَلَمُوا بِهَا وَمَا نُرْسِلُ بِالْآيَاتِ إِلَّا تَخْوِيفًا ۝

We said to you that your Lord encompasses all mankind. We have made the vision which We have shown you, as also the tree cursed in this Qur'ān, only a trial for people. We seek to put fear in their hearts, but it only increases their gross transgression. (60)

وَإِذْ قُلْنَا لَكَ إِنَّ رَبَّكَ أَحَاطَ بِالنَّاسِ وَمَا جَعَلْنَا الرُّؤْيَا الَّتِي أَرَيْنَاكَ إِلَّا فِتْنَةً لِّلنَّاسِ وَالشَّجَرَةَ الْمَلْعُونَةَ فِي الْقُرْآنِ وَنُخَوِّفُهُمْ فَمَا يَزِيدُهُمْ إِلَّا طُغْيَانًا كَبِيرًا ۝

When We said to the angels, 'Prostrate yourselves before Adam,' they all prostrated themselves; but not so *Iblīs*. He said, 'Am I to bow down before one whom You have created out of clay?' (61)

وَإِذْ قُلْنَا لِلْمَلَـٰٓئِكَةِ ٱسْجُدُواْ لِـَٔادَمَ فَسَجَدُوٓاْ إِلَّآ إِبْلِيسَ قَالَ ءَأَسْجُدُ لِمَنْ خَلَقْتَ طِينًا ۝

And he added: 'You see this being whom You have exalted above me! Indeed, if You will give me respite until the Day of Resurrection, I shall bring his descendants, all but a few, under my sway.' (62)

قَالَ أَرَءَيْتَكَ هَـٰذَا ٱلَّذِى كَرَّمْتَ عَلَىَّ لَئِنْ أَخَّرْتَنِ إِلَىٰ يَوْمِ ٱلْقِيَـٰمَةِ لَأَحْتَنِكَنَّ ذُرِّيَّتَهُۥٓ إِلَّا قَلِيلًا ۝

[God] said: 'Begone! As for those of them who follow you, hell will be the recompense of you all, a most ample recompense. (63)

قَالَ ٱذْهَبْ فَمَن تَبِعَكَ مِنْهُمْ فَإِنَّ جَهَنَّمَ جَزَآؤُكُمْ جَزَآءً مَّوْفُورًا ۝

Entice with your voice such of them as you can. Muster against them all your cavalry and your infantry, and share with them wealth and offspring, and promise them [what you will] – indeed, whatever Satan promises them is nothing but a means of deception. (64)

وَٱسْتَفْزِزْ مَنِ ٱسْتَطَعْتَ مِنْهُم بِصَوْتِكَ وَأَجْلِبْ عَلَيْهِم بِخَيْلِكَ وَرَجِلِكَ وَشَارِكْهُمْ فِى ٱلْأَمْوَٰلِ وَٱلْأَوْلَـٰدِ وَعِدْهُمْ وَمَا يَعِدُهُمُ ٱلشَّيْطَـٰنُ إِلَّا غُرُورًا ۝

But over My servants you shall have no power. Your Lord is sufficient as a Guardian.' (65)

إِنَّ عِبَادِى لَيْسَ لَكَ عَلَيْهِمْ سُلْطَـٰنٌ وَكَفَىٰ بِرَبِّكَ وَكِيلًا ۝

Your Lord is He who makes ships go smoothly through the sea, so that you may go about in quest of His bounty. He is indeed Most Merciful to you. (66)

رَّبُّكُمُ ٱلَّذِى يُزْجِى لَكُمُ ٱلْفُلْكَ فِى ٱلْبَحْرِ لِتَبْتَغُوا۟ مِن فَضْلِهِۦٓ إِنَّهُۥ كَانَ بِكُمْ رَحِيمًا ۝

And when you are in distress at sea, all those you may call upon to help you will forsake you, except Him. Yet when He has brought you safe to dry land, you turn away. Indeed, bereft of all gratitude is man! (67)

وَإِذَا مَسَّكُمُ ٱلضُّرُّ فِى ٱلْبَحْرِ ضَلَّ مَن تَدْعُونَ إِلَّآ إِيَّاهُ فَلَمَّا نَجَّىٰكُمْ إِلَى ٱلْبَرِّ أَعْرَضْتُمْ وَكَانَ ٱلْإِنسَٰنُ كَفُورًا ۝

Can you feel so sure that He will not let a tract of the land cave in beneath you, or let loose against you a deadly stormwind? You will not find then anyone to protect you. (68)

أَفَأَمِنتُمْ أَن يَخْسِفَ بِكُمْ جَانِبَ ٱلْبَرِّ أَوْ يُرْسِلَ عَلَيْكُمْ حَاصِبًا ثُمَّ لَا تَجِدُوا۟ لَكُمْ وَكِيلًا ۝

Or can you feel so sure that He will not let you go back to sea again, and then let loose against you a violent tempest to drown you for your ingratitude? You shall not find then anyone to help you against Us. (69)

أَمْ أَمِنتُمْ أَن يُعِيدَكُمْ فِيهِ تَارَةً أُخْرَىٰ فَيُرْسِلَ عَلَيْكُمْ قَاصِفًا مِّنَ ٱلرِّيحِ فَيُغْرِقَكُم بِمَا كَفَرْتُمْ ثُمَّ لَا تَجِدُوا۟ لَكُمْ عَلَيْنَا بِهِۦ تَبِيعًا ۝

We have indeed honoured the children of Adam, and borne them over land and sea, and provided for them sustenance out of the good things of life, and favoured them far above many of Our creatures. (70)

وَلَقَدْ كَرَّمْنَا بَنِىٓ ءَادَمَ وَحَمَلْنَٰهُمْ فِى ٱلْبَرِّ وَٱلْبَحْرِ وَرَزَقْنَٰهُم مِّنَ ٱلطَّيِّبَٰتِ وَفَضَّلْنَٰهُمْ عَلَىٰ كَثِيرٍ مِّمَّنْ خَلَقْنَا تَفْضِيلًا ۝

One day We shall summon every community by their leaders. Those who are given their records in their right hands will read their records. None shall be wronged by as much as a hair's breadth. (71)

يَوْمَ نَدْعُواْ كُلَّ أُنَاسٍ بِإِمَٰمِهِمْ فَمَنْ أُوتِىَ كِتَٰبَهُۥ بِيَمِينِهِۦ فَأُوْلَٰٓئِكَ يَقْرَءُونَ كِتَٰبَهُمْ وَلَا يُظْلَمُونَ فَتِيلًا ٧١

But whoever is blind in this world will be even more blind in the life to come, and still further astray from the path of truth. (72)

وَمَن كَانَ فِى هَٰذِهِۦٓ أَعْمَىٰ فَهُوَ فِى ٱلْأَخِرَةِ أَعْمَىٰ وَأَضَلُّ سَبِيلًا ٧٢

Overview

The passage discussed in Chapter 3 concluded with a statement making clear that God alone is the One who determines the destiny of all His creatures. He bestows His grace on them or punishes them as He pleases. The deities they worship beside Him have no power to remove harm from them or to shift it to others. They are powerless.

The present passage speaks about the ultimate destiny of all mankind, as it is determined by God's justice. All cities and communities will suffer death before the Day of Judgement, although some may suffer a doom of some sort should they incur something that deserves God's punishment. Thus, every living creature will have come to its life's end, either by natural death or by destruction.

Within the context of the destruction suffered by some communities, the *surah* mentions the miracles accomplished at the hands of earlier messengers ahead of such destruction. This was the case prior to the message of the Prophet Muḥammad (peace be upon him). Such miracles and supernatural events were excluded with the advent of this final message. The law that applied to earlier communities meant that they suffered inevitable doom and destruction when they denied the truth after having received such miracles. But complete destruction was, by God's grace, not to be visited on the Muslim community. Therefore, the Prophet Muḥammad was not given any material miracle. Such miracles were given to strike the fear of God into the hearts of earlier communities.

God also held people's hands away from the Prophet, meaning that they could not kill him. He showed him some of His true signs on his night journey, which was a form of test for people. It was not meant as a supernatural event as those shown to earlier communities. All people are warned against being made to eat of the cursed tree, which the Prophet saw with his own eyes, coming out of the heart of hell, but such warnings only hardened them in their transgression. This demonstrates that had they been shown any miracles, these would only have further hardened their deviant stance.

At this point in the *surah* reference is made to the story of Adam and Satan, and God's permission to the latter to try to seduce human beings away from the right path, except for the God-fearing among them. Thus the *surah* explains the true reasons which lead people away from the truth into unbelief. They are unwilling to reflect on the signs pointing to the truth. Our emotions are touched here however as the *surah* mentions God's blessings bestowed on people, while they continue to deny God and His grace except when they find themselves in desperate situations. When they are in heavy seas, they appeal to God to save them. When they are safe on land, they turn away. Yet God is able to smite them on land and sea alike. Indeed God has honoured human beings and favoured them with grace that He does not bestow on other creatures, but people neither reflect nor show gratitude.

The passage concludes with a scene from the Day of Judgement, when people will have the reward for their deeds. None will be saved unless his actions in this life ensure his safety.

Clear Warnings, Increased Transgression

There is no community but We shall destroy or severely punish before the Day of Resurrection. That is laid down in Our decree. (Verse 58)

185

God has determined that the Day of Judgement will take place when the face of the earth is devoid of all life. Every living thing will have died before that promised day falls due. God has also determined that some communities will be made to suffer punishment for the sins they commit. This is part of God's knowledge which admits no uncertainty. God knows the future in the same way as He knows the present. Indeed what has taken place in the past and what will take place in the future are equally known to God.

Miraculous events took place in the past in order to endorse the messages preached by God's messengers, and to warn people against rejecting them. Such rejection ensured that the whole community was punished. Yet only those whose hearts and minds were receptive to the message of the truth declared their belief. Those with hardened hearts denied God's messages and the miraculous events that took place during their time. Hence the final message was not accompanied by any such preternatural event: "*Nothing hinders Us from sending miraculous signs except that the people of former times treated them as false. To the Thamūd We gave the she-camel as a sign to open their eyes, but they did wrong in respect of her. We never send signs for any purpose other than to give warning.*" (Verse 59)

Islam has one miracle to prove its truth. That is the Qur'ān. It is a book that maps a whole system of life, addressing both the mind and heart and meeting all the needs of human nature. It remains open to all generations to read and to believe in. It is valid for all time. A physical miracle is given to one generation, and its effects are limited to those who witness it. Yet the majority of those who witnessed such physical miracles did not believe in them. The example given here is that of the Thamūd who were given the miracle they sought. It came in the shape of a she-camel. Yet they transgressed and slaughtered the she-camel. Hence, God's warning came to pass and they were destroyed as a result of their denials that continued even after this clear, miraculous sign had been given them. All such signs were given by way of warning. They heralded the inevitable punishment, a punishment that was bound to be inflicted should rejection of the message continue.

Past history being such, it was necessary that the final message should not be accompanied by any physical miracle. This message is not meant for one generation; it is addressed to all future generations. It is a message that addresses the human mind with all its receptive faculties. It respects man's intellect and power of understanding.

The preternatural events that took place at the time of the Prophet, or happened to him, such as that of his night journey, were not meant as proof of his message. These were given as a test for his people.

We said to you that your Lord encompasses all mankind. We have made the vision which We have shown you, as also the tree cursed in this Qur'ān, only a trial for people. We seek to put fear in their hearts, but it only increases their gross transgression. (Verse 60)

Some of those who believed in the message preached by the Prophet Muḥammad (peace be upon him) reverted to unbelief after he told them about his night journey. Others, however, became firmer than ever in their belief. Hence, it is true that what God showed His Messenger on that night was meant as 'a trial for men', so that they would reaffirm their faith. The Prophet is reminded that God encompasses all mankind. This was given to him as a promise from God, assuring him of ultimate victory. In the meantime, God would protect him against any evil scheme they might devise against him. He would come to no harm at their hands.

The Prophet told his people of God's promise and what he had seen in his true vision. This included the tree of *zaqqūm* which grows in hell. It is a tree which God cites as a warning to unbelievers. However, they continued to deny the message and whatever the Prophet said. Abū Jahl, the arch-enemy of Islam even ridiculed the tree, playing on the sense given by its name. He asked for dates and butter and mixed them together and ate them. He said to those around: "Come and eat. This is the only *zaqqūm* we know."

Of what use could any miraculous event be with such people, had it constituted proof of the Prophet's message, as was the case with some messengers before him? The whole event of his night journey and the warning about the tree of hell only caused them to become more insolent and to transgress even further.

God had not pre-determined to destroy them. Hence, He did not give them a physical miracle. It was His will to destroy those who continued to reject the truth of His message after they had been given miraculous evidence confirming it. The Arabs of the Quraysh were given more time. They were not subjected to the same fate that befell the peoples of Noah, Hūd, Ṣāliḥ, Lot and Shuʿayb. Some of those who rejected the message of the Qur'ān at first subsequently changed their mind, believed in Islam and were among its true servants. Others who died as unbelievers were the fathers of good believers. The Qur'ān – the miracle of Islam – continued to be a book open to future generations just like it was open to the generation of the Prophet's Companions. People who did not see the Prophet or his companions came to believe in it when they read it or heard it being read. It remains open to all future generations, a guide for many who are not yet born. Some future believers in the Qur'ān may be even stronger in faith and better servants of Islam than many in past generations.

An Ever-Raging Battle

The vision the Prophet was shown included a complete world that he had not known before. The verse that refers to this vision also mentions the accursed tree which provides the food eaten in hell by those who follow Satan. The *sūrah* follows this with an image in which we see the devil threatening to seduce human beings.

When We said to the angels, 'Prostrate yourselves before Adam,' they all prostrated themselves; but not so Iblīs. He said, 'Am I to bow down before one whom You have created out of clay?' And he added: 'You see this being whom You have exalted above me! Indeed, if You will give me respite until the Day of Resurrection, I shall bring his descendants, all but a few, under my sway.' [God] said: 'Begone! As for those of them who follow you, hell will be the recompense of you all, a most ample recompense. Entice with your voice such of them as you can. Muster against them all your cavalry and your infantry, and share with them wealth and offspring, and promise them [what you will] – indeed, whatever Satan promises them is nothing but a means of deception. But over My servants you shall have no power. Your Lord is sufficient as a Guardian.' (Verses 61–65)

Thus the real reason behind the attitude of those who go astray is revealed. This serves as a warning to mankind to be careful, lest they go astray. They see here *Iblīs*, their enemy and the enemy of Adam, the father of all mankind, threatening to tempt them away from the truth. It is a determined effort on his part to lead them astray: *"When We said to the angels, 'Prostrate yourselves before Adam,' they all prostrated themselves; but not so Iblīs. He said, 'Am I to bow down before one whom You have created out of clay?'"* (Verse 61)

Here we see the envy that eats at *Iblīs'* heart. He states that Adam was created of clay, but omits the fact that God breathed of His soul in that clay. *Iblīs* further speaks contemptuously of Adam's weakness and his susceptibility to err. He says to God in an arrogant manner, *"You see this being whom You have exalted above me!"* (Verse 62) You have given this weak creature a position of honour. Yet, *"if You will give me respite until the Day of Resurrection, I shall bring his descendants, all but a few, under my sway."* (Verse 62) I will have power over them, and I will be able to direct their course and subject them to my power.

Iblīs here overlooks the fact that man is equally susceptible to goodness and following divine guidance as he is to evil and error. He chooses not to see man when he is elevated by God's guidance, able to resist temptation and evil. He is unaware of this great, distinctive characteristic that places man above all creatures that follow a single route, having no element of choice. Indeed man's position of distinction lies in his free-will and the exercise of his power of choice.

It is God's will that the advocate of evil, Satan, should have his respite to try to tempt mankind away from divine guidance. Hence, God says to him: *"Begone! As for those of them who follow you, hell will be the recompense of you all, a most ample recompense."* (Verse 63) Go and do your utmost. If you try to tempt them, they have been given reason and will. They can follow you or reject your advances. Now anyone who follows you, preferring error to My guidance, ignoring the signs I have placed in the world around him, deserves the fate that he is bound to suffer in hell. Indeed, both Satan and his followers will have the same end: *"Hell will be the recompense of you all, a most ample recompense."* (Verse 63)

"*Entice with your voice such of them as you can. Muster against them all your cavalry and your infantry.*" (Verse 64) This description seeks to magnify the means employed by Satan to encompass people and impose his power over their hearts and minds. We are looking here at a battle in which loud voices are heard, and horses and soldiers employed. A loud outcry irritates opponents and brings them out of their fortifications. They may thus fall into a trap, or find themselves facing a surprise attack.

"*And share with them wealth and offspring.*" (Verse 64) This partnership is seen in certain false beliefs. The pagans used to assign a portion of their property to their false gods, or in effect to Satan himself, and they would also assign some of their offspring as a dedication to their deities. These were indeed dedicated to Satan by virtue of their being offered to idols. The same partnership is seen in every kind of illegitimate earning, and any money spent illegally, to buy what is forbidden. It is also manifested in every child born in sin. The statement describes a partnership between Satan and his followers that includes wealth and offspring, the two main elements in this life.

Iblīs is given leave to employ all his devices, including tempting promises: "*And promise them [what you will] – indeed, whatever Satan promises them is nothing but a means of deception.*" (Verse 64) Such promises include Satan's assertions to man that he will escape God's punishment and the promise of acquiring wealth or power through easy or dirty means.

Perhaps the most tempting promise Satan makes is that of God's forgiveness of sins. It is the point which Satan uses to attack those who will not respond to his temptation of open defiance of God's orders. With such people he employs a softer attitude trying to paint sin as very tempting, and promising people that they will be forgiven by God whose mercy is greater than all sin.

While Satan has been given leave to try to seduce those who will listen to his promises, some people will not respond to him and he has no power over them. These have immunity against all his devices and can easily resist his power: "*But over My servants you shall have no power. Your Lord is sufficient as a Guardian.*" (Verse 65) When man's heart is kept alive by his bond with God, and when man addresses his worship purely to God, he maintains the bond that will never be severed. His soul is brightened with the sublime light of heaven. Over the hearts and souls of such people Satan has no power. "*Your Lord is sufficient as a Guardian.*" (Verse 65) He protects them and renders Satan's scheming futile.

Ever since that day, Satan has been trying hard to make his word come true. He enslaves those who yield to his temptation, but those who address worship purely to God, the Most Merciful, are immune from his scheming.

Aspects of God's Favours

Satan tries to inflict only evil on mankind, yet there are those who listen to his temptations and do his bidding, turning their backs on God's guidance. God is always merciful to them, provides them with help, support and guidance, facilitates their living, saves them from harm, removes their distress and responds to them when they pray to Him to lift their suffering and hardship. Yet despite all this, they turn away, denying Him and the message He has sent them:

> *Your Lord is He who makes ships go smoothly through the sea, so that you may go about in quest of His bounty. He is indeed most merciful to you. And when you are in distress at sea, all those you may call upon to help you will forsake you, except Him. Yet when He has brought you safe to dry land, you turn away. Indeed, bereft of all gratitude is man!* (Verses 66–67)

The *surah* portrays this scene of distress at sea by way of an example of hard times. At sea, people realize much more quickly and keenly that they cannot do without God's help. Any boat or ship they use is no more than a little spot of wood or metal on the surface of an endless great sea. It is subject to the winds and currents that travel in different directions. They cling to life over this little spot, their vessel, which needs God's care more than anything else.

It is an inspiring image, the effects of which come more readily to anyone who has experienced it. People remember how, in their fear and apprehension, their hearts turn only to God, no matter how large their vessel is. At times when the wind is very strong and in high seas, even huge liners, designed to cross the oceans with ease and comfort, look vulnerable, like a feather blown away by the wind.

The Qur'ān touches people's hearts as it shows them that it is God's hand that allows their ships to travel smoothly over the sea, so that they may seek God's bounty. God is indeed Most Merciful to man. It is God's grace that man's heart seeks most in such a situation of helplessness. The *surah* then shows them the other extreme. After a smooth phase in their journey, they experience great turbulence in high seas. Enormous waves seem to carry their vessel and throw it around in every direction. They realize then that they have no real support and no saviour except God. They turn to Him in a sincere prayer, addressed to Him alone: "*And when you are in distress at sea, all those you may call upon to help you will forsake you, except Him.*" (Verse 67)

But man remains the same. When the hardship is over and he feels himself steady, moving easily on dry land, the experience he suffered disappears gradually from his mind, and as a result he forgets God. He then allows his desire to get the better of him and overshadow the beckoning of his uncorrupted nature: "*Yet when He has brought you safe to dry land, you turn away. Indeed, bereft of all gratitude is man!*" (Verse 67) This applies to all people except those who maintain their strong bond with God. Their hearts continue to have the light of right guidance.

At this point the *surah* makes a direct and emotional address to people's consciences, depicting the danger they left at sea as though it were chasing them on land, or engulfing them again when they return to sea. It wants them to feel that safety and security can only be ascertained with God's protection. It cannot be guaranteed at sea or on land, with easy waves and moderate wind, or with a comfortable home or fortified shelter:

> Can you feel so sure that He will not let a tract of the land cave in beneath you, or let loose against you a deadly stormwind? You will not find then anyone to protect you. Or can you feel so sure that He will not let you go back to sea again, and then let loose against you

a violent tempest to drown you for your ingratitude? You shall not find then anyone to help you against Us. (Verses 68–69)

Human beings are subject to God's will at every place and time, on land and at sea. How can they feel secure against His will? How can they feel secure that they will not be overwhelmed by an earthquake or volcanic eruption, or by any other natural phenomenon? All such phenomena operate by God's will. He may send a volcanic explosion that overwhelms them with lava, rocks, mud and water. Thus they may be destroyed before they can receive any help from anyone. Or He may let them return to sea and then send a violent tempest or hurricane which overturns ships and destroys vessels. They will thus be drowned as a result of their rejection of the truth. There will be none to seek compensation for their drowning.

How can they feel secure against any such event? Yet people easily overlook the stark facts that look them in the face. They easily reject God and deny Him, and this gives them a false sense of security. Yet when they experience hardship, they turn to Him alone. When He has saved them and removed their hardship, they forget Him, as though it were the last hardship they will ever experience.

A Special Honour for Man

God has honoured mankind, favouring the human race over many of His creatures. He honoured man when He created him in this particular fashion, giving him a nature that combines the characteristics of clay, from which he was made, and the spirit that was breathed into him. Thus he combines elements of heaven and earth in his constitution. God has also honoured man by placing in his nature such faculties that make him able to take charge of the earth, able to be active and make changes in it. Thus human beings initiate and produce new things, combine things together and analyse complex matters in order to elevate life to the highest standard attainable.

God has also honoured man by making natural forces on earth subservient to his will and endeavour, and by making other natural forces operating in the universe helpful to him. A further aspect of the honour God has given man is seen in the reception given him when he was first created. It was a reception in which the angels prostrated themselves in a gesture of respect, because God Himself declared that man is to be honoured. Then there comes the additional honour when God states in His book, sent down from on high and which He guaranteed to remain intact for the rest of time, that man is given a position of honour.

> *We have indeed honoured the children of Adam, and borne them over land and sea, and provided for them sustenance out of the good things of life, and favoured them far above many of Our creatures.* (Verse 70)

"*And borne them over land and sea.*" This is accomplished by making natural laws fit with human nature and its abilities. Had these laws been at odds with human nature, life would have been impossible to sustain on earth. Indeed man is weak when his strength is measured against the natural forces that operate on land and sea, but man is given the ability to live on earth and to make use of its resources and treasures. This is all an aspect of God's grace.

"*And provided for them sustenance out of the good things of life.*" (Verse 70) Man tends to forget that whatever sustenance is given to him is indeed granted by God, because its different aspects become familiar to him. He only remembers the different forms of sustenance he is given when he loses access to them. It is then that he realizes the value of what he was given. But man's memory is short. He soon forgets again all God's blessings. He forgets what role the sun, air, and water play in sustaining human life. He forgets how important health is to him, and how he is given mobility, senses and reason, in addition to different types of food and drink. Indeed he is placed in charge of a complete world which includes countless blessings.

"*And favoured them far above many of Our creatures.*" (Verse 70) Indeed God has favoured human beings by giving them mastery of this wide planet. Furthermore, He placed in their nature such abilities that make them unique among God's creatures.

One aspect of God's favour is to make human beings responsible for themselves, accountable for their actions. This is the first quality which distinguishes mankind and makes them worthy of their exalted position on earth: freedom of choice and individual responsibility. It is only fair that people should receive the results of their work and get their reward in the life to come, when everyone's record is considered:

One day We shall summon every community by their leaders. Those who are given their records in their right hands will read their records. None shall be wronged by as much as a hair's breadth. But whoever is blind in this world will be even more blind in the life to come, and still further astray from the path of truth. (Verses 71–72)

This is a scene showing all creatures gathered together. Every group is called by the doctrine it followed in this life, or the messenger in whom it believed, or the leader it followed in this first life. It is called to be handed the record of its actions and the result that determines its reward in the life to come. Whoever is given his record in his right hand will be full of joy, reading through his record and looking carefully at its details. Such people are given their reward in full. Nothing is denied them, even though it may be no larger than a hair's breadth. On the other hand, a person who chooses in this life to remain blind to all indications of guidance will be also blind to the way of goodness in the life to come. They will be even far more astray. The outcome they will suffer is well known. However, the *surah* portrays them in this overcrowded scene as blind, moving aimlessly, lacking a guide to lead them. They are left like this without a final abode mentioned for them. This is because the blindness and strayness in that difficult situation is a destiny to be avoided at all costs.

5

Why People Reject the Divine Message

They endeavour to tempt you away from that which We have revealed to you, hoping that you would invent something else in Our name, in which case they would have made you their trusted friend. (73)

وَإِن كَادُواْ لَيَفْتِنُونَكَ عَنِ ٱلَّذِىٓ أَوْحَيْنَآ إِلَيْكَ لِتَفْتَرِىَ عَلَيْنَا غَيْرَهُۥ وَإِذًا لَّٱتَّخَذُوكَ خَلِيلًا ﴿٧٣﴾

Indeed, had We not given you strength, you might have inclined to them a little. (74)

وَلَوْلَآ أَن ثَبَّتْنَٰكَ لَقَدْ كِدتَّ تَرْكَنُ إِلَيْهِمْ شَيْـًٔا قَلِيلًا ﴿٧٤﴾

And in that case We would have made you taste a double punishment in life and a double punishment after death, and you would have none to support you against Us. (75)

إِذًا لَّأَذَقْنَٰكَ ضِعْفَ ٱلْحَيَوٰةِ وَضِعْفَ ٱلْمَمَاتِ ثُمَّ لَاتَجِدُ لَكَ عَلَيْنَا نَصِيرًا ﴿٧٥﴾

And they endeavour to scare you off the land with a view to driving you away. But, then, after you have gone, they will not remain there except for a short while. (76)

وَإِن كَادُواْ لَيَسْتَفِزُّونَكَ مِنَ ٱلْأَرْضِ لِيُخْرِجُوكَ مِنْهَا وَإِذًا لَّايَلْبَثُونَ خِلَٰفَكَ إِلَّا قَلِيلًا ﴿٧٦﴾

197

Such was the way with all Our messengers whom We sent before you. No change shall you find in Our ways. (77)

سُنَّةَ مَن قَدْ أَرْسَلْنَا قَبْلَكَ مِن رُّسُلِنَا وَلَا تَجِدُ لِسُنَّتِنَا تَحْوِيلًا ٧٧

Keep up prayer when the sun is on its decline, in the darkness of the night, and recite the Qur'ān at dawn, for the recitation of the Qur'ān at dawn is indeed witnessed. (78)

أَقِمِ ٱلصَّلَوٰةَ لِدُلُوكِ ٱلشَّمْسِ إِلَىٰ غَسَقِ ٱلَّيْلِ وَقُرْءَانَ ٱلْفَجْرِ إِنَّ قُرْءَانَ ٱلْفَجْرِ كَانَ مَشْهُودًا ٧٨

At night, rise from your sleep to recite it in prayer, as an additional offering from you. Your Lord may thus raise you to an honourable station. (79)

وَمِنَ ٱلَّيْلِ فَتَهَجَّدْ بِهِ نَافِلَةً لَّكَ عَسَىٰ أَن يَبْعَثَكَ رَبُّكَ مَقَامًا مَّحْمُودًا ٧٩

Say, 'My Lord, cause me to enter in a true and sincere manner and to leave in a true and sincere manner, and grant me, by Your grace, sustaining strength.' (80)

وَقُل رَّبِّ أَدْخِلْنِي مُدْخَلَ صِدْقٍ وَأَخْرِجْنِي مُخْرَجَ صِدْقٍ وَٱجْعَل لِّي مِن لَّدُنكَ سُلْطَٰنًا نَّصِيرًا ٨٠

And say, 'The truth has now come about while falsehood has withered away. For falsehood is always bound to wither away.' (81)

وَقُلْ جَآءَ ٱلْحَقُّ وَزَهَقَ ٱلْبَٰطِلُ إِنَّ ٱلْبَٰطِلَ كَانَ زَهُوقًا ٨١

We bestow of the Qur'ān from on high what serves as a healing and a blessing to true believers, while it only adds to the ruin of the evildoers. (82)

وَنُنَزِّلُ مِنَ ٱلْقُرْءَانِ مَا هُوَ شِفَآءٌ وَرَحْمَةٌ لِّلْمُؤْمِنِينَ وَلَا يَزِيدُ ٱلظَّٰلِمِينَ إِلَّا خَسَارًا ٨٢

Yet when We bestow Our blessings on man, he turns his back and draws arrogantly aside, and when he is afflicted by evil he gives himself up to despair. (83)

وَإِذَآ أَنْعَمْنَا عَلَى ٱلْإِنسَٰنِ أَعْرَضَ وَنَـَٔا بِجَانِبِهِۦ وَإِذَا مَسَّهُ ٱلشَّرُّ كَانَ يَـُٔوسًا ٨٣

Say, 'Everyone acts according to his own disposition. Your Lord is fully aware as to who has chosen the best path.' (84)

قُلْ كُلٌّ يَعْمَلُ عَلَىٰ شَاكِلَتِهِۦ فَرَبُّكُمْ أَعْلَمُ بِمَنْ هُوَ أَهْدَىٰ سَبِيلًا ٨٤

They question you about the spirit. Say, 'The [knowledge of the nature of the] spirit belongs to my Lord alone. You, [mankind], have been granted but little knowledge.' (85)

وَيَسْـَٔلُونَكَ عَنِ ٱلرُّوحِ قُلِ ٱلرُّوحُ مِنْ أَمْرِ رَبِّي وَمَآ أُوتِيتُم مِّنَ ٱلْعِلْمِ إِلَّا قَلِيلًا ٨٥

Had We so willed, We would have taken away that which We have revealed to you. In that case, you would not find anyone to plead with Us on your behalf, (86)

وَلَئِن شِئْنَا لَنَذْهَبَنَّ بِٱلَّذِىٓ أَوْحَيْنَآ إِلَيْكَ ثُمَّ لَا تَجِدُ لَكَ بِهِۦ عَلَيْنَا وَكِيلًا ٨٦

except through the grace of your Lord. His favour towards you has been great indeed. (87)

إِلَّا رَحْمَةً مِّن رَّبِّكَ إِنَّ فَضْلَهُۥ كَانَ عَلَيْكَ كَبِيرًا ٨٧

Say, 'If all mankind and the *jinn* were to gather together for the purpose of producing the like of this Qur'ān, they would not produce anything like it, even though they helped one another as best they could.' (88)

قُل لَّئِنِ ٱجْتَمَعَتِ ٱلْإِنسُ وَٱلْجِنُّ عَلَىٰٓ أَن يَأْتُوا۟ بِمِثْلِ هَٰذَا ٱلْقُرْءَانِ لَا يَأْتُونَ بِمِثْلِهِۦ وَلَوْ كَانَ بَعْضُهُمْ لِبَعْضٍ ظَهِيرًا ٨٨

Indeed We have explained to mankind, in this Qur'ān, every kind of lesson. Yet most people refuse to accept anything other than unbelief. (89)

وَلَقَدْ صَرَّفْنَا لِلنَّاسِ فِي هَٰذَا ٱلْقُرْءَانِ مِن كُلِّ مَثَلٍ فَأَبَىٰٓ أَكْثَرُ ٱلنَّاسِ إِلَّا كُفُورًا ﴿٨٩﴾

They say: 'We shall not believe in you till you cause a spring to gush forth for us from the earth, (90)

وَقَالُوا۟ لَن نُّؤْمِنَ لَكَ حَتَّىٰ تَفْجُرَ لَنَا مِنَ ٱلْأَرْضِ يَنۢبُوعًا ﴿٩٠﴾

or you have a garden of date-palms and vines, and you cause rivers to flow through it, (91)

أَوْ تَكُونَ لَكَ جَنَّةٌ مِّن نَّخِيلٍ وَعِنَبٍ فَتُفَجِّرَ ٱلْأَنْهَٰرَ خِلَٰلَهَا تَفْجِيرًا ﴿٩١﴾

or you cause the sky to fall upon us in pieces, as you have threatened, or you bring God and the angels face to face before us, (92)

أَوْ تُسْقِطَ ٱلسَّمَآءَ كَمَا زَعَمْتَ عَلَيْنَا كِسَفًا أَوْ تَأْتِىَ بِٱللَّهِ وَٱلْمَلَٰٓئِكَةِ قَبِيلًا ﴿٩٢﴾

or you have a house of gold, or you ascend to heaven. Indeed we shall not believe in your ascent to heaven until you bring us a book for us to read.' Say, 'Limitless in His glory is my Lord. Surely I am only a man and a Messenger.' (93)

أَوْ يَكُونَ لَكَ بَيْتٌ مِّن زُخْرُفٍ أَوْ تَرْقَىٰ فِي ٱلسَّمَآءِ وَلَن نُّؤْمِنَ لِرُقِيِّكَ حَتَّىٰ تُنَزِّلَ عَلَيْنَا كِتَٰبًا نَّقْرَؤُهُۥ قُلْ سُبْحَانَ رَبِّى هَلْ كُنتُ إِلَّا بَشَرًا رَّسُولًا ﴿٩٣﴾

Nothing has ever prevented people from believing, whenever guidance came to them except that they would say: 'Can it be that God has sent a human being as His messenger?' (94)

وَمَا مَنَعَ ٱلنَّاسَ أَن يُؤْمِنُوٓا۟ إِذْ جَآءَهُمُ ٱلْهُدَىٰٓ إِلَّآ أَن قَالُوٓا۟ أَبَعَثَ ٱللَّهُ بَشَرًا رَّسُولًا ﴿٩٤﴾

Say, 'Had there been angels walking about on earth as their natural abode, We would have sent them an angel messenger from heaven.' (95)

قُل لَّوۡ كَانَ فِى ٱلۡأَرۡضِ مَلَـٰٓئِكَةٌ يَمۡشُونَ مُطۡمَئِنِّينَ لَنَزَّلۡنَا عَلَيۡهِم مِّنَ ٱلسَّمَآءِ مَلَكًا رَّسُولًا ﴿٩٥﴾

Say, 'Sufficient is God for a witness between me and you. He is indeed fully aware of His servants, and He sees all things.' (96)

قُلۡ كَفَىٰ بِٱللَّهِ شَهِيدًۢا بَيۡنِى وَبَيۡنَكُمۡ إِنَّهُۥ كَانَ بِعِبَادِهِۦ خَبِيرًۢا بَصِيرًا ﴿٩٦﴾

He whom God guides is indeed rightly guided; whereas for those whom He leaves to go astray you cannot find anyone to protect them from Him. On the Day of Resurrection We shall gather them together, prone upon their faces, blind, dumb and deaf. Hell shall be their abode. Every time it abates We will increase for them its blazing flame. (97)

وَمَن يَهۡدِ ٱللَّهُ فَهُوَ ٱلۡمُهۡتَدِ وَمَن يُضۡلِلۡ فَلَن تَجِدَ لَهُمۡ أَوۡلِيَآءَ مِن دُونِهِۦ وَنَحۡشُرُهُمۡ يَوۡمَ ٱلۡقِيَـٰمَةِ عَلَىٰ وُجُوهِهِمۡ عُمۡيًا وَبُكۡمًا وَصُمًّا مَّأۡوَىٰهُمۡ جَهَنَّمُ كُلَّمَا خَبَتۡ زِدۡنَـٰهُمۡ سَعِيرًا ﴿٩٧﴾

That is their reward for having disbelieved in Our revelations and said, 'When we are bones and dust, shall we be raised to life again as a new creation?' (98)

ذَٰلِكَ جَزَآؤُهُم بِأَنَّهُمۡ كَفَرُواْ بِـَٔايَـٰتِنَا وَقَالُوٓاْ أَءِذَا كُنَّا عِظَـٰمًا وَرُفَـٰتًا أَءِنَّا لَمَبۡعُوثُونَ خَلۡقًا جَدِيدًا ﴿٩٨﴾

Do they not see that God, who has created the heavens and the earth, has power to create their like? He has beyond any doubt set a term for their resurrection. But the evildoers refuse to accept anything other than disbelief. (99)

أَوَلَمۡ يَرَوۡاْ أَنَّ ٱللَّهَ ٱلَّذِى خَلَقَ ٱلسَّمَـٰوَٰتِ وَٱلۡأَرۡضَ قَادِرٌ عَلَىٰٓ أَن يَخۡلُقَ مِثۡلَهُمۡ وَجَعَلَ لَهُمۡ أَجَلًا لَّا رَيۡبَ فِيهِ فَأَبَى ٱلظَّـٰلِمُونَ إِلَّا كُفُورًا ﴿٩٩﴾

Say, 'Had you possessed the treasures of my Lord's mercy, you would have been tight-fisted for fear of spending them. For man has always been niggardly.' (100)

قُل لَّوۡ أَنتُمۡ تَمۡلِكُونَ خَزَآئِنَ رَحۡمَةِ رَبِّيٓ إِذًا لَّأَمۡسَكۡتُمۡ خَشۡيَةَ ٱلۡإِنفَاقِ وَكَانَ ٱلۡإِنسَٰنُ قَتُورًا ﴿١٠٠﴾

To Moses We gave nine clear signs. Ask the Children of Israel [about what happened]. When he came to them, Pharaoh said to him, 'Indeed, Moses, I think that you are bewitched.' (101)

وَلَقَدۡ ءَاتَيۡنَا مُوسَىٰ تِسۡعَ ءَايَٰتِۭ بَيِّنَٰتٖ فَسۡـَٔلۡ بَنِيٓ إِسۡرَٰٓءِيلَ إِذۡ جَآءَهُمۡ فَقَالَ لَهُۥ فِرۡعَوۡنُ إِنِّي لَأَظُنُّكَ يَٰمُوسَىٰ مَسۡحُورًا ﴿١٠١﴾

[Moses] said, 'You know full well that none other than the Lord of the heavens and the earth has revealed these eye-opening signs. Indeed, Pharaoh, I think that you are utterly lost.' (102)

قَالَ لَقَدۡ عَلِمۡتَ مَآ أَنزَلَ هَٰٓؤُلَآءِ إِلَّا رَبُّ ٱلسَّمَٰوَٰتِ وَٱلۡأَرۡضِ بَصَآئِرَ وَإِنِّي لَأَظُنُّكَ يَٰفِرۡعَوۡنُ مَثۡبُورًا ﴿١٠٢﴾

So he resolved to wipe them off the face of the earth, but We caused him and all those who were with him to drown. (103)

فَأَرَادَ أَن يَسۡتَفِزَّهُم مِّنَ ٱلۡأَرۡضِ فَأَغۡرَقۡنَٰهُ وَمَن مَّعَهُۥ جَمِيعًا ﴿١٠٣﴾

Then We said to the Children of Israel, 'Dwell in the land. When the promise of the Last Day shall come to pass, We will bring you all together.' (104)

وَقُلۡنَا مِنۢ بَعۡدِهِۦ لِبَنِيٓ إِسۡرَٰٓءِيلَ ٱسۡكُنُواْ ٱلۡأَرۡضَ فَإِذَا جَآءَ وَعۡدُ ٱلۡأَخِرَةِ جِئۡنَا بِكُمۡ لَفِيفًا ﴿١٠٤﴾

We have bestowed [this Qur'ān] from on high in truth, and in truth has it come down. We have sent you only as a herald of good news and a warner. (105)

وَبِٱلْحَقِّ أَنزَلْنَٰهُ وَبِٱلْحَقِّ نَزَلَ وَمَآ أَرْسَلْنَٰكَ إِلَّا مُبَشِّرًا وَنَذِيرًا ﴿١٠٥﴾

We have divided the Qur'ān into parts so that you may recite it to people with deliberation. We have indeed bestowed it from on high step by step. (106)

وَقُرْءَانًا فَرَقْنَٰهُ لِتَقْرَأَهُۥ عَلَى ٱلنَّاسِ عَلَىٰ مُكْثٍ وَنَزَّلْنَٰهُ تَنزِيلًا ﴿١٠٦﴾

Say, 'You may believe in it or you may not.' Those who were given knowledge before it was revealed fall down on their faces in humble prostration when it is recited to them, (107)

قُلْ ءَامِنُوا۟ بِهِۦٓ أَوْ لَا تُؤْمِنُوٓا۟ إِنَّ ٱلَّذِينَ أُوتُوا۟ ٱلْعِلْمَ مِن قَبْلِهِۦٓ إِذَا يُتْلَىٰ عَلَيْهِمْ يَخِرُّونَ لِلْأَذْقَانِ سُجَّدًا ﴿١٠٧﴾

and say, 'Limitless in His glory is our Lord. Truly has the promise of our Lord been fulfilled.' (108)

وَيَقُولُونَ سُبْحَٰنَ رَبِّنَآ إِن كَانَ وَعْدُ رَبِّنَا لَمَفْعُولًا ﴿١٠٨﴾

And upon their faces they fall down, weeping, and it increases their humility. (109)

وَيَخِرُّونَ لِلْأَذْقَانِ يَبْكُونَ وَيَزِيدُهُمْ خُشُوعًا ۩ ﴿١٠٩﴾

Say, 'Call upon God or call upon the Most Merciful. By whichever name you invoke Him, His are the most gracious names.' Do not raise your voice too loud in prayer, nor say it in too low a voice, but follow a middle course in between. (110)

قُلِ ٱدْعُوا۟ ٱللَّهَ أَوِ ٱدْعُوا۟ ٱلرَّحْمَٰنَ أَيًّا مَّا تَدْعُوا۟ فَلَهُ ٱلْأَسْمَآءُ ٱلْحُسْنَىٰ وَلَا تَجْهَرْ بِصَلَاتِكَ وَلَا تُخَافِتْ بِهَا وَٱبْتَغِ بَيْنَ ذَٰلِكَ سَبِيلًا ﴿١١٠﴾

And say, 'All praise is due to God who has never begotten a son; who has no partner in His dominion; who needs none to support Him against any difficulty.' And extol His greatness. (111)

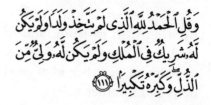

Overview

This final passage of the *sūrah* centres around its main theme, the personality of the Prophet (peace be upon him) and the attitude of his community to him after he was given his message. It also speaks about the Qur'ān and its distinctive characteristics. It begins with a reference to the attempts by the unbelievers to turn the Prophet away from some of the revelations God sent down to him. It mentions their effort to banish him from Makkah and the protection he was given by God so that he would not yield to their temptation or respond to their provocation. God guaranteed his protection because He had already decided that the people of Makkah would not be annihilated like earlier communities who rejected His messengers. He chose instead to give them respite and allowed them to have their term in this world. Had they ousted the Prophet from their community and banished him from their city, severe punishment would have been inflicted on them, in accordance with God's law that inflicts immediate punishment on any community that ousts the messenger sent to them.

The Prophet is commanded to stick to his way, offering his prayers to God alone, reciting the Qur'ān revealed to him and supplicating that God may help him to be true and sincere in all situations and events, and give him clear support. He is also commanded to declare that the truth has come to be established and that falsehood is certain to be vanquished. It is this support granted by God that serves as his best equipment. It protects him against all designs and ensures his ultimate victory.

This is followed by a clear statement on the effect of the Qur'ān: it is a cure and an aspect of grace for those who believe in it, and a means of punishment and suffering for those who deny it. They suffer on its account in this life and they suffer punishment in the life to come because of denying its truth.

Within the context of grace and punishment, the *surah* describes man's reaction to both. When he is enjoying God's blessings and grace, man is arrogant, turning away from God's guidance. When he is afflicted with suffering, he is in utter despair. This is followed with an implicit threat, requiring every human being to work in accordance with their own nature until they receive their fair reward in the life to come.

The *surah* also makes it clear that human knowledge is scanty. This comes in connection with the question the unbelievers put about the spirit, all knowledge of which God has chosen to keep to Himself. It is not for any human being to get to know it. Sure knowledge is that which God has given to His Messenger as part of His grace. If God so wills, He is able to withdraw that grace and no one will ever be able to bring it back to mankind. However, He bestows His grace on His Messenger as He is Merciful, Compassionate.

The *surah* mentions that the Qur'ān, which is a miraculous book, the like of which cannot be produced by human beings or *jinn*, even though they may mobilize all their resources in a single effort, was not sufficient for the unbelievers in Makkah as evidence of God's message. Although God included in it a whole variety of evidence to the truth of its message and made this suitable for human reason and hearts, with all their different leanings, still the unbelievers saw it as inadequate. They naïvely demanded material evidence of a miraculous nature, such as springs gushing from the earth, or a richly decorated home for the Prophet. Their arrogance went even further, demanding things that are beyond the ability of human beings, such as that God's Messenger should rise up into the sky in front of their eyes and bring them a book to read, or that he should cause some matter to fall from the sky and destroy them. They even demanded that God should come to them in person, accompanied by a delegation of angels!

At this point the *surah* portrays a scene showing the fate that awaits them in the life to come. This is certain to be their lot as a result of their arrogance and denial of the truth of the Day of Judgement when people will be resurrected after they have become bones and dust.

The *sūrah* ridicules their arrogant demands. Had they been the guardians of God's grace, they would have succumbed to the miserly characteristics of human beings. They would have been in fear lest God's grace should be exhausted, when God's treasures of mercy are indeed inexhaustible. Yet they stop at nothing in their demands.

In connection with their demands for material miracles, the *sūrah* reminds them of the miracles which were given to Moses, yet Pharaoh and his people denied those which God gave them. As a result, God destroyed them according to His law of destroying those who persist in their denial of the truth after clear evidence has been given to them.

The Qur'ān remains as the true miracle that shines for all time. It was revealed in parts and portions, in accordance with the needs of the community it was educating and equipping for its great task. Those who believe in the truth among earlier communities recognize the truth contained in the Qur'ān and submit to it. They believe in it and submit to its authority.

The *sūrah* concludes with a directive to the Prophet (peace be upon him) to worship none but God, and to glorify and praise Him alone. Thus the *sūrah* ends as it began, calling on believers to glorify God, the only deity in the universe.

Vain Endeavours

They endeavour to tempt you away from that which We have revealed to you, hoping that you would invent something else in Our name, in which case they would have made you their trusted friend. Indeed, had We not given you strength, you might have inclined to them a little. And in that case We would have made you taste a double punishment in life and a double punishment after death, and you would have none to support you against Us. And they endeavour to scare you off the land with a view to driving you away. But, then, after you have gone, they will not remain there except for a short while. Such was the way with all Our messengers whom We sent before you. No change you shall find in Our ways. (Verses 73–77)

The *sūrah* refers to the unbelievers' attempts to dissuade the Prophet from fulfilling the task entrusted to him. Firstly, they tried to make him turn his back on what God revealed to him so as to invent some other matter and attribute it falsely to God. They did this even though he was known for his honesty and truthfulness. They also offered to worship God in return for a compromise that ensured that the Prophet would stop denouncing their deities as false. Some of them tried to persuade him to make their land as sacred as the Ka'bah which God had sanctified. Their nobility also tried to get him to allocate a special meeting place, to which no poor person would be admitted.

Reference to these attempts is made in general terms so that it leads to a reminder of the grace God bestowed on His Messenger as He strengthened him in his faith and protected him from the unbelievers' temptations. Without God's support, he might have responded to them, and they would have made of him an intimate friend. But then he would have left himself open to God's severe punishment. Indeed his would be a double punishment in this life and in the life to come, without any to support him against God.

Such efforts are always made by people in power in dealing with the advocates of God's message. They always tempt them into deviation even if just a little, from the clear and solid line of the message, seeking to persuade them to accept compromise in return for seeming substantial gain. Some may fall for such temptation, because they do not realize the seriousness of the matter. After all, they are not being asked to abandon their call altogether, only to make some minor amendments in order to arrive at a compromise. Satan always endeavours to persuade the advocates of God's message in this way, arguing that it is better for the achievement of their goals to make such compromises so that the rulers are won over to the faith.

However, a small deviation at the beginning leads to a total turning away at the end. An advocate of God's message who agrees to abandon even a small part of it at the outset cannot maintain his ground and refuse to abandon more. Indeed his willingness to retreat further is greater with every backward step he takes, losing more and more ground.

The point at issue here is the principle of faith, and belief in the whole message. A person who gives up even a minute part of it cannot be a true believer in the message itself. To a true believer, every aspect of the message, and every small detail is true like the rest. We cannot judge between its parts, dividing them into essential and optional. There is nothing in God's message that can be left out or suspended. It is a complete and whole entity, which loses all its characteristics when any of its parts are lost, in the same way as a chemical compound loses all its qualities when any of its components is missing.

People in power always try to ensnare advocates of the divine message. Should the latter give up a small part, they lose their dignity and high standing. Their adversaries also realize that more bargaining and a higher price will induce them to give up the whole message.

Indeed seeking a compromise, by making even small concessions, to win over people in power represents a spiritual defeat for advocates of the divine message. This is so because they now rely on rulers and people in power for support when they should rely on God alone. When defeat creeps into people's minds, it can never turn into victory.

Bearing this in mind, we can appreciate the fact that God directs His Messenger to the fact that He has granted him a great favour by strengthening his resolve to stick to what He has revealed to him and protected him from the unbelievers' temptations. God also favoured him with protection against inclining to the unbelievers even in a small way. For had he so inclined, God would have inflicted on him a double punishment both in this life and in the life to come, and would have left him without help and support.

When the unbelievers of the Quraysh found it impossible to persuade the Prophet to compromise, they tried to turn him out of their land, i.e. Makkah. But God directed him to leave of his own accord and migrate to Madinah. God always knew that He would not exterminate the Quraysh. Yet had they driven the Prophet out of their city by force, that would have been their fate: *"And they endeavour to scare you off the land with a view to driving you away. But, then, after you have gone, they will not remain there except for a short while."* (Verse

76) This is the way God has set to operate in this life: *"Such was the way with all Our messengers whom We sent before you. No change shall you find in Our ways."* (Verse 77)

God has made this way a law which does not fail. Driving a messenger of God out of his land is a great offence which incurs severe punishment. God operates certain laws in this universe, which are not altered for individual cases. This universe is not subject to coincidences that influence its existence; it is subject to constant laws. Since God, in His infinite wisdom, chose not to exterminate the Quraysh, as He did with earlier communities, He did not give His Messenger, the Prophet Muḥammad, miraculous proofs, and did not allow that he be driven away. Instead, He inspired him to leave voluntarily. God's laws remained in operation, without alteration or modification.

The Truth Will Triumph

At this point in the *sūrah*, the Prophet is directed to remain in contact with his Lord, seeking His support and following His directives, proclaiming the fact that the truth is certain to triumph, while falsehood will inevitably wither away.

> *Keep up prayer when the sun is on its decline, in the darkness of the night, and recite the Qur'ān at dawn, for the recitation of the Qur'ān at dawn is indeed witnessed. At night, rise from your sleep to recite it in prayer, as an additional offering from you. Your Lord may thus raise you to an honourable station. Say, 'My Lord, cause me to enter in a true and sincere manner and to leave in a true and sincere manner, and grant me, by Your grace, sustaining strength.' And say, 'The truth has now come about while falsehood has withered away. For falsehood is always bound to wither away. We bestow of the Qur'ān from on high what serves as a healing and a blessing to true believers, while it only adds to the ruin of the evildoers.* (Verses 78–82)

This directive applies to the Prophet in particular. It does not relate to the obligatory prayers which have their own timings, outlined in several authentic *aḥādīth* and numerous reports of the Prophet's practical *Sunnah*. Some scholars suggest that the reference here to the sun's decline means its beginning to move down from its zenith, while they take the reference to the 'darkness of the night' to mean the beginning of the night, and the 'recitation at dawn' to mean the obligatory prayer at dawn. They thus suggest that the Qur'ānic statement here groups together the times of all five obligatory prayers, *Zuhr*, *'Aṣr*, *Maghrib* and *'Ishā'*, [when the sun is on its decline to the darkness of the night], and then *Fajr* at dawn. They consider that only recitation of the Qur'ān in prayer at night is obligatory on the Prophet as a bonus. For our part, we feel that the first view is more accurate, considering all else that these two verses mention as being applicable to the Prophet only. As for the timing of daily prayers, these are properly outlined in the *Sunnah*, both verbally and practically.

"*Keep up prayer when the sun is on its decline, in the darkness of the night.*" (Verse 78) This is an instruction to the Prophet to offer prayer at the time between the sun starting to set and the night creeping in to spread its darkness. He is also ordered to "*recite the Qur'ān at dawn, for the recitation of the Qur'ān at dawn is indeed witnessed.*" (Verse 78) These two periods when the day and night succeed each other in a continuous cycle have their special significance. Both times mark a change as the light dwindles to give way to the enveloping darkness, and then as the darkness is removed to allow the light to spread. Both times have their effect, softening hearts and inviting people to contemplate how the laws of nature operate without fail. Needless to say, the Qur'ān and prayer also have their effects on people's hearts, particularly at dawn with its calm serenity, and approaching light, leading to another lively day.

"*At night, rise from your sleep to recite it in prayer, as an additional offering from you.*" (Verse 79) The instruction here is to the Prophet to rise after having had some sleep in the early part of the night. The Qur'ān is recited in night worship because it is the hard core of prayer and its most important part. "*Your Lord may thus raise you to an honourable station.*" (Verse 79) This is achieved through a constant link with God, manifested by prayer and recitation of the Qur'ān in night worship. Such a position is only achievable in this way. If God's Messenger (peace be upon him), in his particular status, is instructed to maintain prayer and rise from his sleep at night to worship and recite the Qur'ān, so that he attains the honourable station that is allowed him, certainly other people need to follow suit so that they also may attain the good positions to which they aspire. This is the only way for them to travel. The equipment they need as they go along is thus outlined for them.

"Say: My Lord, cause me to enter in a true and sincere manner and to leave in a true and sincere manner, and grant me, by Your grace, sustaining strength." (Verse 80) This is a supplication that God has taught to His Messenger so that his followers learn how to pray to God. It is a supplication for true and sincere entrance and exit. This implies a true and sincere journey, from start to finish and along the way. Truth and sincerity have their own connotations here in reference to the attempts made by the unbelievers to persuade the Prophet to invent something different from the Qur'ān. Moreover, truth and sincerity add an air of steadfastness, reassurance and total dedication. *"And grant me, by Your grace, sustaining power."* (Verse 80) This is a supplication for strength that would enable the Prophet to look down on all earthly powers and all that the unbelievers could muster. The expression, *'by Your grace,'* implies closeness to God and contact with Him, as well as seeking His help and support.

A true advocate of faith derives strength only from God, and acquires a position commanding respect only through God's power. Such an advocate seeks no shelter or support from a ruler or a person of influence unless he first turns to God for help and protection. The divine message may touch the hearts of people in power, or those occupying positions of influence, and they then become its soldiers and servants. This ensures success for them in this life and in the life to come. But the message itself will not prosper if it ranks itself among the servants and soldiers of rulers. It is God's message and, as such, it commands a position higher than that of any ruler.

"And say, 'The truth has now come about while falsehood has withered away. For falsehood is always bound to wither away." (Verse 81) With irrefutable authority derived from God Himself it is proclaimed that truth has come to be established with its overpowering might, while falsehood is totally defeated. For it is in the nature of truth to triumph

211

and establish itself with vigour, while it is in the nature of falsehood to
wither away and be vanquished.

"*For falsehood is always bound to wither away.*" (Verse 81) This is a
basic truth that is stated here with emphasis. It may appear sometimes
that falsehood is equipped with power and influence, but this is all
hollow. Falsehood will always try to assume an air of strength, because
it has no real strength at its command. It knows that it has to visually
deceive, giving the appearance of large size and physical power. But in
reality, it is fragile, easy to destroy. It is no more than the flames of
dried straw that float into the air only to subside in no time at all. By
contrast, live coal burns slowly and steadily to give sustained warmth
and long lasting heat. Falsehood is like the scum that floats at the
surface. It soon disappears while the real water stays.

Indeed falsehood ends in utter loss because it does not carry within
itself the elements necessary for survival. It derives its life, which, by
nature, is of short duration, from external elements and unnatural
support. Should such elements and support weaken or become loose,
it will collapse. Truth, by contrast, derives its power of survival from
within itself. It may have to face determined opposition, particularly
by those in ruling positions, but its inherent strength and reassurance
guarantee its eventual triumph. How could it be otherwise when
truth comes from the Eternal One who has made truth an attribute
of His own?

"*For falsehood is always bound to wither away.*" (Verse 81) Falsehood
may have all the might of Satan and those tyrannical forces which
command power behind it, but God's promise will definitely come
true and His power is far superior. Every believer who is firm of
faith is certain to experience the truth of this promise. "*Who is more
true to his promise than God?*" (9: 111) "*Whose word could be truer
than God's?*" (4: 87)

The Qur'ānic Cure

"*We bestow of the Qur'ān from on high what serves as a healing and a
blessing to true believers.*" (Verse 82) There is certainly a cure and a
blessing for those whose hearts are full of faith. Such hearts brighten

up and become ready to receive what the Qur'ān imparts of grace, reassurance and security. There is in the Qur'ān a healing power that cures obsession, anxiety and hesitation. It establishes a bond between the believer's heart and God. This bond imparts inner peace to the believer as he experiences a feeling of security in God's protection. He is happy and satisfied with what he receives from God and contented with his lot in life. Anxiety, hesitation and obsession are all terrible to experience. As the Qur'ān dispels all these, it is indeed a blessing for true believers.

In the Qur'ān we have a cure from carnal desires, greed, envy and evil thoughts. All these cause sickness of the heart and mind, leading to debility and utter ruin. As the Qur'ān cures these, it is a tool of grace bestowed by God on those who truly believe in Him.

The Qur'ān also provides a cure from deviant thoughts and feelings. It protects the mind from going far astray, while allowing it complete freedom within its fruitful pursuits. It stops the mind from wasting its energy over what is devoid of use. It lays down for it a sound approach that ensures good and useful results. The same principle applies to the human body, ensuring that its resources are utilized for what is useful and fruitful, steering human beings away from the suppression of natural desires or indulgence without restraint. Thus it ensures a healthy body. In this again we see that the Qur'ān is a means of God's grace that is bestowed on believers.

There is also in the Qur'ān a cure for social ailments that weaken the structure of society and destroy its peace and security. Under the social system established by the Qur'ān society enjoys perfect justice in peace and security. This is again a further aspect of grace bestowed through the Qur'ān.

However, the Qur'ān *"only adds to the ruin of the evildoers."* (Verse 82) They make no use of the cure it provides or the blessings it brings about. They look with dismay at the believers as they feel proud to be among the followers of the Qur'ān. In their stubborn arrogance, the evildoers persist with their corrupt and unjust methods. Yet in this life, they are defeated by the followers of the Qur'ān, which makes them losers. In the life to come, they suffer for their arrogant disbelief and tyranny, and thus they lose again. Hence the Qur'ān adds to their ruin.

When man is left to his own devices, without the cure and blessing of the Qur'ān, and without consistent restraint of his whims and desires, he moves between two extremes: when he enjoys good fortune, he is arrogant and ungrateful, and when he experiences hardship he is given to despair. *"Yet when We bestow Our blessings on man, he turns his back and draws arrogantly aside, and when he is afflicted by evil he gives himself up to despair."* (Verse 83)

Blessings and good fortune lead to arrogance unless one remembers where they come from and give thanks to God who bestowed them. On the other hand, when someone is afflicted by difficulty and hardship, he is easily lost in despair unless he trusts to God and hopes to receive His grace. It is when one truly relies on God that one feels that hardship will give way to what is better. This makes it clear that faith ensures God's grace in situations of ease and difficulty alike.

The *sūrah* then states that everyone and every camp acts according to the path it follows. The final verdict on methods and actions is left to God alone: *"Say: Everyone acts according to his own disposition. Your Lord is fully aware as to who has chosen the best path."* (Verse 84) In this statement we have an implicit warning as to the results of approaches and deeds. Hence, everyone needs to heed the warnings and strive to follow the path of divine guidance which is available to all.

Man's Scanty Knowledge

At this point the *sūrah* mentions how some unbelievers questioned the Prophet about the spirit and its nature. The consistent approach of the Qur'ān, which is indeed the best approach, is to answer people when they ask about matters that they need to know about and to give them answers that their faculties can understand and learn. It does not waste the intellectual faculties God has given them in pursuits that are of no use to them. Nor does it carry them over domains which they cannot comprehend. Hence, when they asked about the spirit and its nature, the Prophet was instructed to tell them that such knowledge belonged to God alone. None other than Him has such knowledge. *"They question you about the spirit. Say, 'The [knowledge of the nature of the] spirit belongs to my Lord alone. You, [mankind], have been granted but little knowledge.'"* (Verse 85)

Such an answer does not present a barrier preventing the proper working of the human intellect. It simply directs such intellect to concentrate its efforts within the limits of its power and the domain where it can profitably function. It is worthless to roam endlessly in a maze. Similarly, it is pointless to spend one's mental energies pursuing what we are not equipped to comprehend. The spirit is one such pursuit. It belongs to the realm that lies beyond the reach of human perception. It is a secret God has kept to Himself. He has breathed spirit into man and some other creatures whose nature is unknown to us. Compared to God's absolute knowledge, human knowledge is limited. The secrets of existence are too great to be understood by man's finite reason. It is not man's role to manage all the affairs of the universe, and as such, his powers are not limitless. Instead he has been given such powers as are sufficient for him to control his own world and to fulfil his mission of building the earth and bringing it to the best standard possible within the limits of his faculties and knowledge.

Man has been able to achieve high standards with his inventive powers. However, he looks helplessly at the spirit, unable to fathom its secrets, or to comprehend its nature. He does not know how the spirit comes to us and how it departs, where it comes from and to where it eventually goes. He knows nothing of the spirit except the information God has given us in the revelations He has bestowed from on high. This information provides knowledge that is certain, beyond doubt. It comes from the One who knows everything. Had it been His will, He would have deprived mankind of such knowledge, taking away what He revealed to His Messenger. But He does not do so as an act of grace: *"Had We so willed, We would have taken away that which We have revealed to you. In that case, you would not find anyone to plead with Us on your behalf, except through the grace of your Lord. His favour towards you has been great indeed."* (Verses 86–87)

God reminds His Messenger of this act of grace. It is undeniable grace that God has chosen to bestow revelations on His Messenger, and to keep them intact. This is a great favour granted to mankind,

215

since the Qur'ān gives them guidance and blessings, one generation after another.

Just as the spirit is one of the secrets that God keeps to Himself, the Qur'ān is God's book that human beings cannot emulate. Indeed, neither human beings nor *jinn*, representing the visible and invisible types of creation, can produce anything similar to the Qur'ān, even if they were to muster all their powers in a single effort to achieve this task: "*Say: If all mankind and the* jinn *were to gather together for the purpose of producing the like of this Qur'ān, they would not produce anything like it, even though they helped one another as best they could.*" (Verse 88)

The Qur'ān is not mere words and expressions that humans and *jinn* may try to emulate. It is but one of God's works, the like of which no creature can produce. It is just like the spirit whose nature is known only to God. Creatures cannot fathom its complete secret, even though they may understand some of its aspects, features and merits.

The Qur'ān is indeed a complete and perfect way of life. It provides a method that takes into account all the laws of nature that affect the human soul in all its situations, as well as those affecting human communities in all conditions and stages of development. It provides solutions that apply to a single human being, and others for a closely knit community, providing legislation and rules that suit human nature and its complex bonds, feelings and directions. Its solutions are perfectly coherent and fully consistent. They lose sight of nothing that is relevant, or any possible option. Nor do they ignore any of the conflicting circumstances that may affect the life of the individual or the community. This is only possible because these laws and legislation are made by God who is fully aware of human nature in all its conditions and its complexities.

Man-made systems, on the other hand, betray man's limitations and reflect his circumstances. They cannot allow for all eventualities at the same time. They may treat an individual or social aspect with something that could easily lead to a situation requiring some other treatment. The miracle of the Qur'ān is far greater than its superb construction and infallible meanings. Indeed the inability of all human beings and *jinn* to produce anything similar to it includes also their inability to produce any system that encompasses all the areas it tackles.

Only a Man and a Messenger

Indeed We have explained to mankind, in this Qur'ān, every kind of lesson. Yet most people refuse to accept anything other than disbelief. They say: 'We shall not believe in you till you cause a spring to gush forth for us from the earth, or you have a garden of date-palms and vines, and you cause rivers to flow through it, or you cause the sky to fall upon us in pieces, as you have threatened, or you bring God and the angels face to face before us, or you have a house of gold, or you ascend to heaven. Indeed we shall not believe in your ascent to heaven until you bring us a book for us to read.' Say, 'Limitless in His glory is my Lord. Surely I am only a man and a Messenger.' (Verses 89–93)

Their limited perception has failed to appreciate the inimitability of the Qur'ān. Therefore they started asking for material miracles, enlisting absurd requests that only betrayed their childish thinking. Or they spoke with impudence about God Himself. They did not benefit by the expounding of cases and examples in the Qur'ān, nor were they satisfied with the wide variety of styles and approaches the Qur'ān employed in explaining its concepts, so as to be understood by people of different standards and faculties. Hence, *"most people refuse to accept anything other than unbelief."* (Verse 89) They started to place conditions which they required to be met so that they might believe in the Prophet's message. Such conditions required him to *"cause a spring to gush forth for us from the earth."* (Verse 90) Alternatively, they told him that they would not believe in him until *"you have a garden of date-palms and vines, and you cause rivers to flow through it."* (Verse 91)

Their conditions were so irresponsible that they even demanded that the Prophet inflict on them some punishment from the sky above, mockingly stating that the sky itself should fall upon them in pieces, just as he had warned would happen on the Day of Judgement. A

217

similarly absurd condition was that he should bring God and the angels before them, so that they could support him and defend his case, like they themselves used to do in tribal arguments. Absurdity knows no limit, for they even asked him to take for himself a house of gold and similarly precious metals. They further suggested to him that he should ascend to heaven as a proof of his special position. But even if he had done so, this too would not have been enough. For he was to bring back a book with him for them to read.

The childish absurdity of all these requests and conditions is clearly apparent. They are all arbitrary suggestions and widely different in scope and nature that they cannot be placed on the same level. How could residence in a luxurious house be considered of similar value to a person's ascension to heaven? And how can the digging up of a water spring be treated as equivalent to bringing God and the angels marching in ranks before them? However, to them these are all miraculous matters, so they can be grouped together. Should Muḥammad accomplish any of these miraculous events, they would consider believing in him and his message.

They overlooked the permanent miracle of the Qur'ān when they were totally unable to produce anything similar to it in style, imagery, meaning and philosophy. Such a miracle is not physical, defying the senses. Hence they demanded to have before them a clearly physical miracle.

But producing a miracle was something that the Prophet could not accomplish. Miracles are only determined by God in His wisdom. It is not appropriate for the Prophet to request such a miracle, unless God wishes to give it to him. The Prophet's understanding and appreciation of God's wisdom prevented him from requesting such a miracle. Hence, he is commanded to say in reply to them: "*Limitless in His glory is my Lord. Surely I am only a man and a Messenger.*" (Verse 93) He confines himself to the limits of his human status and he works according to the duties outlined for him in his message. He does not suggest to God anything beyond this.

Before the Prophet Muḥammad was sent as God's Messenger and even after he began to preach his message, people wallowed under the misconception that a human being could be God's messenger. Hence they rejected God's messengers and the messages He revealed to them: *"Nothing has ever prevented people from believing, whenever guidance came to them except that they would say: 'Can it be that God has sent a human being as His messenger?'"* (Verse 94). In this way they turned away from divine guidance.

This misconception results from people's low rating of their own value and the honourable position God has given them. They thought it totally unlikely that a human being could be chosen by God to be His messenger. This betrayed a lack of understanding of the nature of the universe, the angels, and how, in their angelic form, they are unsuited to life on earth. In order for angels to live on earth, their nature must be modified which would then make it impossible for human beings to recognize them as angels.

"Say, Had there been angels walking about on earth as their natural abode, We would have sent them an angel messenger from heaven." (Verse 95) Had God willed that angels should inhabit the earth, He would have made them in the form of human beings, because it is the form that suits the laws of nature affecting the earth. He says in another verse, *"Even if We had appointed an angel as Our messenger, We would certainly have made him [appear as] a man."* (6: 9) God is certainly able to accomplish any purpose He may have. However, He has willed to set in operation laws of nature and He has made His creatures fit for life under the influence of such laws of nature which He, by His own power and choice, has made permanent and unalterable. Through the operation of His laws of nature, His purpose of creation is thus fulfilled. Yet the unbelievers understand nothing of this.

Since this is the pattern God has chosen for His creation, He instructs His Messenger to end all argument with them and leave the dispute between the two parties to God. He calls on God to be his witness, leaving them entirely to God to do with whatever He pleases. He is the One who knows everything about everyone. *"Say: Sufficient is God for a witness between me and you. He is indeed fully aware of His servants, and He sees all things."* (Verse 96) This statement carries an implicit warning. The results, however, are painted in a frightening scene of what will happen on the Day of Judgement.

Devoid of All Faculties

He whom God guides is indeed rightly guided; whereas for those whom He leaves to go astray you cannot find anyone to protect them from Him. On the Day of Resurrection We shall gather them together, prone upon their faces, blind, dumb and deaf. Hell shall be their abode. Every time it abates We will increase for them its blazing flame. That is their reward for having disbelieved in Our revelations and said, 'When we are bones and dust, shall we be raised to life again as a new creation?' Do they not see that God, who has created the heavens and the earth, has power to create their like? He has beyond any doubt set a term for their resurrection. But the evildoers refuse to accept anything other than unbelief. (Verses 97–99)

God has operated certain laws concerning His guidance and people's choice of error in preference to that guidance. He has allowed people to conduct their lives as they wish, but they remain subject to these laws and they will have to face the outcome. One of these laws is that human beings either follow God's guidance or turn away from it into error. The choice is made by man himself. Whoever deserves, on the basis of his efforts and actions, to receive God's guidance will definitely be guided aright. He is the one who will be truly guided as a result of his choice.

In the other camp we find those who deserve to be left in error because they turn away from God's revelations and blind themselves to all signs pointing the way to His guidance. Such people will have no one to protect them against God's punishment: "*You cannot find anyone to protect them from Him.*" (Verse 97) On the Day of Judgement they shall suffer humiliation and will be resurrected in a terrible situation, '*prone upon their faces*', lost as they will be '*blind, dumb and deaf.*' (Verse 97) They are thus deprived of their senses by which they might have been able to find their way through the great multitude. It is a fitting result, because it was they who chose not to use their senses in life to follow the signs of divine guidance. The final outcome is that "*Hell shall be their abode.*" It will be made to continue to burn fiercely: "*Every time it abates We will increase for them its blazing fire.*" (Verse 97)

It is certainly a horrifying end, but they have earned it through their disbelief in God's signs and revelations, and also through their denial of resurrection, the reckoning and reward: *"That is their reward, for having disbelieved in Our revelations and said, 'When we are bones and dust, shall we be raised to life again as a new creation?'"* (Verse 98)

The *sūrah* portrays the scene as though it is taking place now. It shows this life as having already come to an end and become a distant past. This follows the usual Qur'ānic method of portraying scenes of the hereafter as if they were taking place now in order to enhance their effect, so that people may take heed.

This is followed by a new argument based on what they see in real life but tend to ignore: *"Do they not see that God, who has created the heavens and the earth, has power to create their like?"* (Verse 99) Why should the concept of resurrection be difficult to accept when simple logic confirms that God who has created this majestic universe is able to create a similar one? If He is thus able to create, He is also able to bring creatures back to life after they have died. *"He has beyond any doubt set a term for their resurrection."* (Verse 99) He has allowed them a term of life and set a time for their resurrection. However, *"The evildoers refuse to accept anything other than disbelief."* (Verse 99) Hence their punishment will be fair, as they have had all signs, pointers and evidence to show them the path of guidance, but they refused to follow anything except error and unbelief.

A Threat to Exterminate the Believers

Yet those who made such suggestions and demands as related in the *sūrah* were themselves misers. Had they been in charge of God's grace, they would have held on to it, fearing to expend it. *"Say: Had you possessed the treasures of my Lord's mercy, you would have been tight-fisted for fear of spending them. For man has always been niggardly."* (Verse 100) This is an image of utter stinginess, because God's grace encompasses everything. It will never be exhausted or diminished. Yet in their miserly attitude, they would have withheld God's grace from His creation, had they been placed in charge of administering it.

Him
His Book
His Messenger

Miracles do not initiate faith in hardened hearts. Moses, for example, was given nine such clear signs, but Pharaoh and his people denied them until they suffered God's punishment. *"To Moses We gave nine clear signs. Ask the Children of Israel [about what happened]. When he came to them, Pharaoh said to him, 'Indeed, Moses, I think that you are bewitched.' [Moses] said, 'You know full well that none other than the Lord of the heavens and the earth has revealed these eye-opening signs. Indeed, Pharaoh, I think that you are utterly lost.' So he resolved to wipe them off the face of the earth, but We caused him and all those who were with him to drown. Then We said to the Children of Israel, 'Dwell in the land. When the promise of the Last Day shall come to pass, We will bring you all together.'* (Verses 101–104) This part of the history of Moses and the Children of Israel is mentioned here because it fits with the context of the *sūrah*. It started by mentioning the Aqṣā mosque in Jerusalem, and it then related a part of the history of the Israelites with Moses. This is followed by mentioning the hereafter when Pharaoh and his people will be brought forward. This also fits with the scene of the hereafter and the one showing the end of those who deny resurrection, mentioned a little earlier in the *sūrah*.

Moses' nine clear signs to which the *sūrah* refers were his hand turning white, his staff, and the tests to which Pharaoh's people were subjected, such as drought, shortage of fruit, floods, locusts, ants, frogs and blood. *"Ask the Children of Israel"* about what happened. They were witnesses to what took place between Moses and Pharaoh: *"When he came to them, Pharaoh said to him: Indeed, Moses, I think that you are bewitched."* (Verse 101) Thus the word of truth assigning divinity to God alone, and the call to abandon all injustice and tyranny cannot be uttered, according to the tyrant, except by someone bewitched, unable to realize the meaning of what he says. Indeed tyrants like Pharaoh cannot imagine that anyone in his right senses could ever adopt such an attitude or give expression to such demands.

Moses, on the other hand, realizes that his strength is based in the truth he preaches. His message stands out as a source of light. He is certain of God's support and that He will inevitably punish the tyrants: *"Moses said: You know full well that none other than the Lord of the heavens and the earth has revealed these eye-opening signs. Indeed,*

Pharaoh, I think that you are utterly lost." (Verse 102) Moses makes it clear to Pharaoh that his denial of the truth when he is fully aware that none other than God could have accomplished such clear signs will earn him a terrible punishment. These signs were clear for anyone who cared to look. They show the truth in full light, clear as the bright day. Yet Pharaoh chose to deny them all and deny God. Hence, divine justice will inflict on him a punishment that leaves him utterly ruined.

At this point, the tyrannical Pharaoh resorts to his own material force, threatening to wipe Moses and his followers off the face of the earth. Such is the method to which all tyrants resort when they are faced with the truth. But God's will is triumphant. His law of punishing the oppressors and supporting the oppressed comes into force: "*So he resolved to wipe them off the face of the earth, but We caused him and all those who were with him to drown. Then We said to the Children of Israel, 'Dwell in the land. When the promise of the Last Day shall come to pass, We will bring you all together.'*" (Verses 103–104)

Thus was the end of those who denied the clear signs which were shown to them as evidence of the truth. God gave the land to the oppressed to rule. When they are in charge, their actions will be the basis of the judgement they have to face. At the beginning of the *sūrah* we were given a clear idea of their end. Here we are only told that both they and their enemies will be gathered together on the Day of Judgement: "*When the promise of the Last Day shall come to pass, We will bring you all together.*" (Verse 104)

Method of Qur'ānic Revelations

Pharaoh's destruction by drowning was one example of material miracles worked out in past generations. The *sūrah* tells us how such miracles were received by people bent on denying the truth and how, as a result, they were doomed to suffer God's punishment. The Qur'ān, God's last message, was revealed with the truth so that it could serve as a permanent sign and basis of guidance. It was bestowed from on high in parts, so that it may be read and reflected upon at length: "*We have bestowed [this Qur'ān] from on high in truth, and in truth has it come down. We have sent you only as a herald of good news and a warner. We have divided the Qur'ān into parts so that you may recite it to people with deliberation. We have indeed bestowed it from on high step by step."* (Verses 105–106)

The Qur'ān was revealed in order to educate a community and establish for it a system and code of life. This community would then carry it to all the corners of the earth in order to educate humanity on the basis of this perfect system. Hence the Qur'ān was revealed one part at a time, according to the practical needs of that community and the circumstances attending its first formative period. Education and the moulding of a nation and a community require time as well as practical experience. Thus the Qur'ān was not revealed as a theoretical doctrine or an abstract vision to be used for academic study and polemical argument. It was revealed part by part instead so that it could be implemented gradually during this formative period. This is indeed the reason for its gradual revelation, one part or passage at a time, not a whole scripture or code given at the outset.

The first generation of believers received it in this light. They approached it as directives to be implemented in practice, be they prohibitions, recommendations or obligations. They never approached it as something for moral or intellectual debate like poetry and literature, or for amusement like legends and stories. They allowed it to influence their daily lives to the full, bringing their feelings, perceptions and behaviour in line with it, and moulding their way of life in accordance with its teachings. They discarded whatever was in conflict with it of their values, norms and practices.

'Abdullāh ibn Mas'ūd, a learned Companion of the Prophet says: "When any of us learnt ten verses of the Qur'ān, one would not try to learn more until we had fully learnt their meaning and how to put them into practice."

God revealed the Qur'ān based on the truth: *"We have bestowed [this Qur'ān] from on high in truth."* (Verse 105) And its purpose is to establish the truth on earth: *"And in truth has it come down."* (Verse 105) Thus the truth is its fabric and ultimate aim, its substance and whole concern. This is the truth as it is ingrained in the constitution of the universe, and forming the foundation of the existence of the heavens and the earth. The Qur'ān is closely linked to the constitution of the universe, always pointing to it. Indeed the truth is the ultimate goal of the Qur'ān. The Prophet gives warnings and promises of happiness on the basis of the truth which the Qur'ān expounds.

To Believe or Not to Believe

At this point the Prophet is commanded to explain the truth plainly to his people, leaving them free to make their choice to either believe in the Qur'ān or to reject it. They will have to bear the consequences of their choice. He puts in front of their eyes an example of its reception by Jewish and Christian people who were given sound knowledge before its revelation. They may feel that they will do well to follow in the footsteps of such learned people when they themselves have not been granted such knowledge:

> Say, 'You may believe in it or you may not.' Those who were given knowledge before it was revealed fall down on their faces in humble prostration when it is recited to them, and say, 'Limitless in His glory is our Lord. Truly has the promise of our Lord been fulfilled.' And upon their faces they fall down, weeping, and it increases their humility. (Verses 107–109)

This is an inspiring image showing people endowed with knowledge listening to the Qur'ān, touched by its truth and falling down on their faces in humble prostration. They cannot restrain themselves. They do not merely prostrate themselves, but fall down on their faces in complete humility. They give expression to what they feel in their hearts of God's greatness and the fulfilment of His promise: "*Limitless in His glory is our Lord. Truly has the promise of our Lord been fulfilled.*" (Verse 108) But then their feelings are further enhanced and they are deeply touched so that words are insufficient to express their feelings. Tears pour down from their eyes telling of their profound emotion: "*And upon their faces they fall down, weeping, and it increases their humility.*" (Verse 109) It is a scene of profound feelings demonstrated by people receiving the Qur'ān with open hearts, having learnt from their earlier scriptures of the truth it explains.

225

This inspiring scene is painted after the *sūrah* has given the Arabs the choice of believing in the Qur'ān or rejecting it. It is followed with a statement leaving it up to them to call on God with whatever names they choose. In their days of ignorance they declined to call God as *Raḥmān*, which means, 'Most Merciful'. Hence they are told that they may call on God with whichever one of His names they choose: "*Say: Call upon God or call upon the Most Merciful. By whichever name you invoke Him, His are the most gracious names.*" (Verse 110) Their prejudices concerning His names have no basis other than myth that they used to believe in their ignorance. They have no sound basis.

The Prophet is then instructed to recite his prayers in a middle voice. This is because the unbelievers used to ridicule him whenever they saw him praying. It is also true to say that a voice pitched in the middle is the most suited to prayer: "*Do not raise your voice too loud in prayer, nor say it in too low a voice, but follow a middle course in between.*" (Verse 110)

The *sūrah* closes in the same way as it opened, praising God and asserting His oneness, and reiterating the facts that He has neither son nor partner and is in need of no help or support from anyone. This is indeed the pivot round which the *sūrah* turns: "*And say: 'All praise is due to God who has never begotten a son; who has no partner in His dominion; who needs none to support Him against any difficulty.' And extol His greatness.*" (Verse 111)

SŪRAH 18

Al-Kahf

(The Cave)

Prologue

The most important thing to be noted about this *sūrah* is its preponderant narration of events that took place in the past. First we have the story of the sleepers in the cave, followed by that of the man with two gardens, then a reference to Adam and Satan. In the middle of the *sūrah* we see what happened between Moses and the pious man, and at the end there is an account of Dhu'l-Qarnayn. These stories form the major part of the *sūrah*, taking 71 out of its 110 verses. Most of the remaining verses comment on the stories and outline the lessons to be learnt from them. In addition, the *sūrah* also contains some scenes of the Day of Judgement, and others drawn from human life to explain an idea or emphasize a concept. In all these, we see examples of the Qur'ānic method of emphasizing its ideas through vivid imagery.

The central theme in the *sūrah*, to which all its accounts and ideas relate, is to purge faith of all alien concepts. It seeks to establish correct and accurate thought and reasoning, as also establish values that are sound according to the criterion of the Islamic faith.

Purging faith of alien concepts is determined both at the outset and conclusion. The *sūrah* opens with these verses: *"All praise is due to God who has bestowed this book from on high on His servant, and has ensured that it remains free of distortion, unerringly straight, meant to warn people of a severe punishment from Himself, and to give the believers who do good works the happy news that they shall have a goodly reward which continues to be theirs forever. Furthermore, it warns those who assert, 'God has taken to Himself a son.' No knowledge whatever have they of Him, and neither had their forefathers. Dreadful indeed is this saying that issues from their mouths. Nothing but falsehood do they utter.''* (Verses 1–5)

The *sūrah* concludes with: *"Say: I am but a human being like yourselves. It has been revealed to me that your God is the One and only God. Hence, whoever expects to meet his Lord [on Judgement Day], let him do what is right, and in the worship due to his Lord admit no one as partner."* (Verse 110) Thus the *sūrah* begins and ends with declaring God's oneness, rejecting any concept that associates partners with God, accepting revelation as true, and making a clear and absolute distinction between God and other beings.

The *sūrah* touches on this theme several times, in various ways. As it relates the history of the sleepers in the cave, those young believers are quoted as saying: *"Our Lord is the Lord of the heavens and the earth. Never shall we call upon any deity other than Him. If we did, we should indeed have uttered an enormity!"* (Verse 14) In its commentary on their story, the *sūrah* says: *"No guardian have they apart from Him; nor does He allot to anyone a share in His rule."* (Verse 26)

As it relates the story of the man with two gardens, the *sūrah* quotes the argument of the believer as he says to his friend: *"Do you deny Him who has created you out of dust, and then out of a drop of sperm, and in the end fashioned you into a man? But for my part, I believe that He is God, my Lord, and none shall I associate with my Lord."* (Verses 37–38) In the final commentary on this story, the *sūrah* includes: *"He had none to support him against God, nor was he able to save himself. For thus it is: all protection comes from God, the True One. He is the best to grant reward and the best to [determine] outcome."* (Verses 43–44)

As it draws one of the scenes of the Day of Judgement, the *sūrah* says: *"One day He will say, 'Call now on those beings whom you alleged to be My partners!' They will invoke them, but those [beings] will not respond to them; for We shall have placed an unbridgeable gulf between them."* (Verse 52) And in comment on another scene the *sūrah* says: *"Do the unbelievers think that they could take My creatures for patrons against Me? We have indeed readied hell as a dwelling place for the unbelievers."* (Verse 102)

The establishment of clear and accurate thought and reasoning is made manifest in the rejection of the claims of all those who associate partners with God, because they assert what they do not know. They have no evidence to prove what they claim. The *sūrah* also directs human beings to make their judgement only on what they know for certain. What they do not know, they should leave to God to determine. Thus at the beginning of the *sūrah* we have the verse stating: *"It warns those who assert, 'God has taken to Himself a son.' No knowledge whatever have they of Him, and neither had their forefathers."* (Verses 4–5)

The sleepers in the cave are quoted as saying: *"These people of ours have taken for worship deities other than Him, without being able to show any convincing proof of their beliefs."* (Verse 15) When they wonder how long they have been in that state of sleep, they leave the issue to God who has perfect knowledge of everything: *"They said: Your Lord knows best how long you have remained thus."* (Verse 19) The story also includes clear disapproval of those who speak about the number of the sleepers, relying only on guesswork: *"Some will say, 'They were three, the fourth of them being their dog,' while others will say, 'Five, with their dog being the sixth of them,' idly guessing at the unknown. Yet others will say, 'They were seven, the eighth of them being their dog.' Say: 'My Lord knows best how many they were. None but a few have any real knowledge of them. Hence, do not enter into argument about them, except on a matter that is clear, nor ask anyone of these people to enlighten you about them.'"* (Verse 22)

In the story of Moses and the pious man, the latter reveals to him at the end the secret behind each of his apparently wild and unreasonable actions to which Moses had objected. He says to Moses that it was all done *"by your Lord's grace. I did not do any of this of my own accord."* (Verse 82) Thus all issues and situations are attributed to God alone.

The main purpose of the *sūrah* is to make faith the basis for the evaluation of concepts, ideas, practices and values. This is shown in various places. All proper and good values are attributed to faith and good action. Any other value which does not have its basis in faith is unworthy, even though it may seem highly attractive. All that appears fascinating and beautiful in this life is meant as a test. It will all come to an end: *"We have made all that is on earth as an adornment in order to test people as to which of them are best in conduct; and, in time, We shall indeed reduce all that is on it to barren dust."* (Verses 7–8) To be under God's protection is to be in a wide and comfortable environment, even though one may have to seek refuge in a narrow and barren cave. Those young believers who abandoned their community and went to the cave are clear about their purpose: *"Now that you have withdrawn from them and all that they worship instead of God, take refuge in the cave. God may well spread His grace over you and make fitting arrangements for you in your affairs."* (Verse 16)

The *sūrah* addresses the Prophet, requiring him to persevere and be patient, associating with those who believe, paying no regard to the adornments of this world or to those who overlook their duty towards God: *"Contain yourself in patience with those who call on their Lord morning and evening, seeking His countenance. Let not your eyes pass beyond them in quest of the beauties of the life of this world. Pay no heed to any whose heart We have left to be negligent of all remembrance of Us because he had always followed his own desires, and whose case has gone beyond all bounds. Say: 'The truth [has now come] from your Lord. Let him who wills, believe in it, and let him who wills, reject it.'"* (Verses 28–29)

The story of the two gardens and their owner portrays how a believer is proud of his faith, valuing it as much higher than wealth, position or luxury. A believer states the truth clearly to his arrogant friend and reproaches him for forgetting God: *"Do you deny Him who has created you out of dust, and then out of a drop of sperm, and in the end fashioned you into a man? But for my part, I believe that He is God, my Lord, and none shall I associate with my Lord. 'If only you said as you entered your garden, "Whatever God wills [shall come to pass, for] there is no power except with God!" Although, as you see, I have less wealth and offspring than you, yet it may well be that my Lord will give me something better than your garden, just as He may let loose a calamity out of heaven upon this [your garden], so that it becomes a heap of barren dust or its water sinks deep into the ground, so that you will never be able to find it.'"* (Verses 37–41)

Once this story has been told, the *sūrah* then depicts this present life and how it is prone to rapid change. Wealth and prosperity are soon replaced by something totally different: *"Set forth to them a simile about the life of this world: [it is] like the water which We send down from the skies, and which is absorbed by the plants of the earth. In time they turn into dry stubble which the winds blow freely about. It is God alone who has power over all things."* (Verse 45) This is followed by a clear statement showing the difference between transitory values and everlasting ones: *"Wealth and children are the adornment of the life of this world: but the things that endure, good deeds, are of far greater merit in your Lord's sight, and a far better source of hope."* (Verse 46)

Dhu'l-Qarnayn is not mentioned in the *sūrah* for his being an angel, but rather because of his good deeds. When the people he found in between the two mountain passes offered him money to build a barrier to protect them against Gog and Magog, he declined because: *"That with which my Lord has established me is better"* than anything you could give me. And when the barrier has been erected, he acknowledges that it was all done by God's help, not by his own power: *"This is a mercy from my Lord. Yet when the time appointed by my Lord shall come, He will make this [rampart] level with the ground. My Lord's promise always comes true."* (Verse 98)

At the end of the *sūrah*, the fact is stated that the worst losers among all creatures are those who refuse to believe in God's revelations or in the fact of meeting Him on the Day of Judgement. Such people will have no weight and no position or status, despite the fact that they believe themselves to be doing well: *"Say: Shall we tell you who are the greatest losers in whatever they may do? It is they whose labour in this world has been misguided, and who nonetheless think that what they do is right. It is they who have chosen to disbelieve in their Lord's revelations and deny the truth that they will meet Him. Vain will be their works. No weight shall We assign to them on Resurrection Day."* (Verses 103–105)

Thus we see that the pivot round which the whole *surah* turns is that of purging faith of all false concepts, providing sound reasoning and establishing correct values on the basis of faith.

The whole *surah* concentrates on these three purposes, round after round. It begins by praising God who has revealed to His servant this book which serves to give happy news to the believers and stern warnings to those who allege that God has betaken to Himself a son. It states clearly that whatever we find on earth is made a sort of adornment only to make it a test for human beings. It will all vanish into nothing. This is followed by the story of the sleepers in the cave, which serves as a good example of making the right choice, giving preference to faith over worldly pleasures and comforts. For the sleepers seek refuge in the cave to keep their faith intact.

The second stage directs the Prophet to content himself with the company of those who appeal to their Lord morning and evening, seeking His countenance. He should abandon those who neglect to remember God. The story of the two gardens and their owner shows clearly how a believer feels his strength in his faith while the values of this world mean nothing to him.

The third stage includes several interlinked scenes of the Day of Judgement, as well as a reference to Adam and Satan. It concludes with an explanation of the rule which results in the destruction of oppressors, while treating sinners with mercy and allowing them respite until their appointed term.

The story of Moses and the pious man forms the fourth stage, while the fifth gives an account of Dhu'l-Qarnayn. Then the *surah* finishes as it began: giving happy news to the believers and more warnings to the unbelievers. It reaffirms the fact of revelation and emphasizes anew the truth of God's oneness without any partner.

I

A Distinctive System of Values

Al-Kahf (The Cave)

سُورَةُ الْكَهْفِ

In the Name of God, the Merciful, the Beneficent

بِسْمِ اللَّهِ الرَّحْمَٰنِ الرَّحِيمِ

All praise is due to God who has bestowed this book from on high on His servant, and has ensured that it remains free of distortion, (1)

ٱلْحَمْدُ لِلَّهِ ٱلَّذِىٓ أَنزَلَ عَلَىٰ عَبْدِهِ ٱلْكِتَٰبَ وَلَمْ يَجْعَل لَّهُۥ عِوَجَاۜ ۝

unerringly straight, meant to warn people of a severe punishment from Himself, and to give the believers who do good works the happy news that they shall have a goodly reward (2)

قَيِّمًا لِّيُنذِرَ بَأْسًا شَدِيدًا مِّن لَّدُنْهُ وَيُبَشِّرَ ٱلْمُؤْمِنِينَ ٱلَّذِينَ يَعْمَلُونَ ٱلصَّٰلِحَٰتِ أَنَّ لَهُمْ أَجْرًا حَسَنًا ۝

which continues to be theirs forever. (3)

مَّٰكِثِينَ فِيهِ أَبَدًا ۝

Furthermore, it warns those who assert, 'God has taken to Himself a son.' (4)

وَيُنذِرَ ٱلَّذِينَ قَالُواْ ٱتَّخَذَ ٱللَّهُ وَلَدًا ۝

No knowledge whatever have they of Him, and neither had their forefathers. Dreadful indeed is this saying that issues from their mouths. Nothing but falsehood do they utter. (5)

مَّا لَهُم بِهِۦ مِنْ عِلْمٍ وَلَا لِآبَآئِهِمْ كَبُرَتْ كَلِمَةً تَخْرُجُ مِنْ أَفْوَٰهِهِمْ إِن يَقُولُونَ إِلَّا كَذِبًا ٥

Would you, perhaps, torment yourself to death with grief over them if they will not believe in this message? (6)

فَلَعَلَّكَ بَٰخِعٌ نَّفْسَكَ عَلَىٰٓ ءَاثَٰرِهِمْ إِن لَّمْ يُؤْمِنُوا۟ بِهَٰذَا ٱلْحَدِيثِ أَسَفًا ٦

We have made all that is on earth as an adornment in order to test people as to which of them are best in conduct; (7)

إِنَّا جَعَلْنَا مَا عَلَى ٱلْأَرْضِ زِينَةً لَّهَا لِنَبْلُوَهُمْ أَيُّهُمْ أَحْسَنُ عَمَلًا ٧

and, in time, We shall indeed reduce all that is on it to barren dust. (8)

وَإِنَّا لَجَٰعِلُونَ مَا عَلَيْهَا صَعِيدًا جُرُزًا ٨

Do you think that the People of the Cave and the inscription were a wonder among Our signs? (9)

أَمْ حَسِبْتَ أَنَّ أَصْحَٰبَ ٱلْكَهْفِ وَٱلرَّقِيمِ كَانُوا۟ مِنْ ءَايَٰتِنَا عَجَبًا ٩

When those youths took refuge in the cave, they said: 'Our Lord! Bestow on us Your grace, and provide for us right guidance in our affair.' (10)

إِذْ أَوَى ٱلْفِتْيَةُ إِلَى ٱلْكَهْفِ فَقَالُوا۟ رَبَّنَآ ءَاتِنَا مِن لَّدُنكَ رَحْمَةً وَهَيِّئْ لَنَا مِنْ أَمْرِنَا رَشَدًا ١٠

So We drew a veil over their ears in the cave, for a number of years, (11)

فَضَرَبْنَا عَلَىٰٓ ءَاذَانِهِمْ فِى ٱلْكَهْفِ سِنِينَ عَدَدًا ١١

234

ثُمَّ بَعَثْنَاهُمْ لِنَعْلَمَ أَيُّ الْحِزْبَيْنِ أَحْصَىٰ لِمَا لَبِثُوٓا أَمَدًا ﴿١٢﴾

and then We awakened them so that We might mark out which of the two parties managed to calculate the time they had remained in that state. (12)

نَّحْنُ نَقُصُّ عَلَيْكَ نَبَأَهُم بِالْحَقِّ إِنَّهُمْ فِتْيَةٌ ءَامَنُوا بِرَبِّهِمْ وَزِدْنَٰهُمْ هُدًى ﴿١٣﴾

We shall relate to you their story in all truth. They were young men who believed in their Lord, so We increased them in guidance. (13)

وَرَبَطْنَا عَلَىٰ قُلُوبِهِمْ إِذْ قَامُوا فَقَالُوا رَبُّنَا رَبُّ السَّمَٰوَٰتِ وَالْأَرْضِ لَن نَّدْعُوَا۟ مِن دُونِهِۦٓ إِلَٰهًا لَّقَدْ قُلْنَآ إِذًا شَطَطًا ﴿١٤﴾

We put courage in their hearts, so that they stood up and said: 'Our Lord is the Lord of the heavens and the earth. Never shall we call upon any deity other than Him. If we did, we should indeed have uttered an enormity! (14)

هَٰٓؤُلَآءِ قَوْمُنَا اتَّخَذُوا مِن دُونِهِۦٓ ءَالِهَةً لَّوْلَا يَأْتُونَ عَلَيْهِم بِسُلْطَٰنٍ بَيِّنٍ فَمَنْ أَظْلَمُ مِمَّنِ افْتَرَىٰ عَلَى اللَّهِ كَذِبًا ﴿١٥﴾

These people of ours have taken for worship deities other than Him, without being able to show any convincing proof of their beliefs. Who does more wrong than he who invents a lie about God? (15)

وَإِذِ اعْتَزَلْتُمُوهُمْ وَمَا يَعْبُدُونَ إِلَّا اللَّهَ فَأْوُۥٓا إِلَى الْكَهْفِ يَنشُرْ لَكُمْ رَبُّكُم مِّن رَّحْمَتِهِۦ وَيُهَيِّئْ لَكُم مِّنْ أَمْرِكُم مِّرْفَقًا ﴿١٦﴾

Hence, now that you have withdrawn from them and all that they worship instead of God, take refuge in the cave. God may well spread His grace over you and make fitting arrangements for you in your affairs.' (16)

You might have seen the sun, on its rising, incline away from their cave on the right, and, on its setting, turn away from them on the left, while they lay in a space within. That was one of God's signs. He whom God guides is indeed rightly guided, but for him whom He lets go astray you can never find any protector who would point out the right way. (17)

وَتَرَى ٱلشَّمْسَ إِذَا طَلَعَت تَّزَٰوَرُ عَن كَهْفِهِمْ ذَاتَ ٱلْيَمِينِ وَإِذَا غَرَبَت تَّقْرِضُهُمْ ذَاتَ ٱلشِّمَالِ وَهُمْ فِي فَجْوَةٍ مِّنْهُ ذَٰلِكَ مِنْ ءَايَٰتِ ٱللَّهِ مَن يَهْدِ ٱللَّهُ فَهُوَ ٱلْمُهْتَدِ وَمَن يُضْلِلْ فَلَن تَجِدَ لَهُۥ وَلِيًّا مُّرْشِدًا ۝

You would have thought that they were awake, when they were certainly asleep. And We turned them over repeatedly, now to the right, now to the left; and their dog lay at the cave's entrance, with its forepaws outstretched. Had you come upon them, you would have certainly turned away from them in flight, and would surely have been filled with terror of them. (18)

وَتَحْسَبُهُمْ أَيْقَاظًا وَهُمْ رُقُودٌ وَنُقَلِّبُهُمْ ذَاتَ ٱلْيَمِينِ وَذَاتَ ٱلشِّمَالِ وَكَلْبُهُم بَٰسِطٌ ذِرَاعَيْهِ بِٱلْوَصِيدِ لَوِ ٱطَّلَعْتَ عَلَيْهِمْ لَوَلَّيْتَ مِنْهُمْ فِرَارًا وَلَمُلِئْتَ مِنْهُمْ رُعْبًا ۝

Such being their state, We awakened them; and they began to question one another. One of them asked: 'How long have you remained thus?' They answered: 'We have remained thus a day, or part of a day.' They said: 'Your Lord knows best how long you have remained thus. Let, then, one of you go with these silver coins to the town, and let him

وَكَذَٰلِكَ بَعَثْنَٰهُمْ لِيَتَسَآءَلُوا۟ بَيْنَهُمْ قَالَ قَآئِلٌ مِّنْهُمْ كَمْ لَبِثْتُمْ قَالُوا۟ لَبِثْنَا يَوْمًا أَوْ بَعْضَ يَوْمٍ قَالُوا۟ رَبُّكُمْ أَعْلَمُ بِمَا لَبِثْتُمْ فَٱبْعَثُوٓا۟ أَحَدَكُم بِوَرِقِكُمْ هَٰذِهِۦٓ إِلَى ٱلْمَدِينَةِ فَلْيَنظُرْ أَيُّهَآ أَزْكَىٰ طَعَامًا

find out what food is purest there, and bring you some of it. But let him behave with great care and by no means make anyone aware of you. (19)

For, indeed, if they should come to know of you, they might stone you to death or force you back to their faith, in which case you would never attain to any good!' (20)

In this way have We drawn people's attention to their case, so that they might know that God's promise is true and that there can be no doubt as to the Last Hour. The people disputed among themselves as to what happened to them. Some of them said: 'Erect a building in their memory. God knows their case best.' Those whose opinion prevailed in the end said: 'Indeed, we must surely raise a house of worship in their memory.' (21)

Some will say, 'They were three, the fourth of them being their dog,' while others will say, 'Five, with their dog being the sixth of them,' idly guessing at the unknown. Yet others will say, 'They were seven, the eighth of them being their dog.' Say: 'My Lord knows best how many they

فَلْيَأْتِكُم بِرِزْقٍ مِّنْهُ وَلْيَتَلَطَّفْ وَلَا يُشْعِرَنَّ بِكُمْ أَحَدًا ۝

إِنَّهُمْ إِن يَظْهَرُوا۟ عَلَيْكُمْ يَرْجُمُوكُمْ أَوْ يُعِيدُوكُمْ فِى مِلَّتِهِمْ وَلَن تُفْلِحُوٓا۟ إِذًا أَبَدًا ۝

وَكَذَٰلِكَ أَعْثَرْنَا عَلَيْهِمْ لِيَعْلَمُوٓا۟ أَنَّ وَعْدَ ٱللَّهِ حَقٌّ وَأَنَّ ٱلسَّاعَةَ لَا رَيْبَ فِيهَآ إِذْ يَتَنَازَعُونَ بَيْنَهُمْ أَمْرَهُمْ فَقَالُوا۟ ٱبْنُوا۟ عَلَيْهِم بُنْيَٰنًا رَّبُّهُمْ أَعْلَمُ بِهِمْ قَالَ ٱلَّذِينَ غَلَبُوا۟ عَلَىٰٓ أَمْرِهِمْ لَنَتَّخِذَنَّ عَلَيْهِم مَّسْجِدًا ۝

سَيَقُولُونَ ثَلَٰثَةٌ رَّابِعُهُمْ كَلْبُهُمْ وَيَقُولُونَ خَمْسَةٌ سَادِسُهُمْ كَلْبُهُمْ رَجْمًۢا بِٱلْغَيْبِ وَيَقُولُونَ سَبْعَةٌ وَثَامِنُهُمْ كَلْبُهُمْ قُل رَّبِّىٓ أَعْلَمُ بِعِدَّتِهِم مَّا يَعْلَمُهُمْ إِلَّا قَلِيلٌ فَلَا تُمَارِ فِيهِمْ

237

were. None but a few have any real knowledge of them. Hence, do not enter into argument about them, except on a matter that is clear, nor ask anyone of these people to enlighten you about them.' (22)

إِلَّا مِرَآءً ظَـٰهِرًا وَلَا تَسْتَفْتِ فِيهِم مِّنْهُمْ أَحَدًا ۝

Never say about anything, 'I shall do this tomorrow,' (23)

وَلَا تَقُولَنَّ لِشَأْىْءٍ إِنِّى فَاعِلٌ ذَٰلِكَ غَدًا ۝

without adding, 'if God so wills.' Should you forget, then call your Lord to mind and say, 'I pray that my Lord will guide me even closer than this to what is right.' (24)

إِلَّا أَن يَشَآءَ ٱللَّهُ وَٱذْكُر رَّبَّكَ إِذَا نَسِيتَ وَقُلْ عَسَىٰٓ أَن يَهْدِيَنِ رَبِّى لِأَقْرَبَ مِنْ هَٰذَا رَشَدًا ۝

So they stayed in their cave three hundred years, and [some] add nine years more. (25)

وَلَبِثُوا۟ فِى كَهْفِهِمْ ثَلَٰثَ مِا۟ئَةٍ سِنِينَ وَٱزْدَادُوا۟ تِسْعًا ۝

Say: 'God knows best how long they remained there. His alone is the knowledge of the secrets of the heavens and earth. How well does He see and hear! No guardian have they apart from Him; nor does He allot to anyone a share in His rule.' (26)

قُلِ ٱللَّهُ أَعْلَمُ بِمَا لَبِثُوا۟ لَهُۥ غَيْبُ ٱلسَّمَٰوَٰتِ وَٱلْأَرْضِ أَبْصِرْ بِهِۦ وَأَسْمِعْ مَا لَهُم مِّن دُونِهِۦ مِن وَلِىٍّ وَلَا يُشْرِكُ فِى حُكْمِهِۦٓ أَحَدًا ۝

Recite whatever has been revealed to you of your Lord's book. There is nothing that could alter His words. You can find no refuge other than with Him. (27)

وَٱتْلُ مَآ أُوحِىَ إِلَيْكَ مِن كِتَابِ رَبِّكَ لَا مُبَدِّلَ لِكَلِمَٰتِهِۦ وَلَن تَجِدَ مِن دُونِهِۦ مُلْتَحَدًا ۝

238

A Stern Warning for Outright Liars

The *surah* states its case very clearly from the outset:

All praise is due to God who has bestowed this book from on high on His servant, and has ensured that it remains free of distortion, unerringly straight, meant to warn people of a severe punishment from Himself, and to give the believers who do good works the happy news that they shall have a goodly reward which continues to be theirs forever. Furthermore, it warns those who assert, 'God has taken to Himself a son.' No knowledge whatever have they of Him, and neither had their forefathers. Dreadful indeed is this saying that issues from their mouths. Nothing but falsehood do they utter. Would you, perhaps, torment yourself to death with grief over them if they will not believe in this message? We have made all that is on earth as an adornment in order to test people as to which of them are best in conduct; and, in time, We shall indeed reduce all that is on it to barren dust. (Verses 1–8)

This opening speaks of a very straightforward and decisive position. It combines this with praising God and expressing gratitude to Him for revealing the book, i.e. the Qur'ān, to 'His servant', Muḥammad, and for making it clear, free of distortion and absolutely straight. There is nothing in it that may be described as evasive or dodgy. Its purpose is '*to warn people of a severe punishment from Himself.*' (Verse 2)

The picture is clear right at the outset. There is no ambiguity or equivocation about the Islamic faith. It is God who has bestowed the book from on high, and He is to be praised for so bestowing it. Muḥammad is God's servant, which means that everyone else is also His servant. God has no son or partner. The book itself is free of distortion and '*unerringly straight*'. The concept of the Qur'ān being straight is given first in the form of negating any possibility of distortion, and then reiterated in describing it as '*unerringly straight*'. This makes for very strong emphasis.

Such clarity is maintained as the purpose of revealing the Qur'ān is outlined. Indeed it has a dual purpose: "*To warn people of a severe punishment from Himself, and to give the believers who do good works the happy news that they shall have a goodly reward.*" (Verse 2) However, the stern warning is more strongly emphasized throughout. It begins in a general way, speaking of a severe punishment that God Himself may inflict. Then the warning is reiterated for a particular group of people: "*It warns those who assert, 'God has taken to Himself a son.'*" (Verse 4) In between the two warnings we have the happy news given to '*believers who do good works.*' This serves as a condition that ensures that faith should have practical evidence in real life. It is not confined to theoretical principles that may be endlessly discussed without effect in practice.

The *sūrah* then moves to expose their false approach by which they judge the most important issue of all, i.e. faith: "*No knowledge whatever have they of Him, and neither had their forefathers.*" (Verse 5) Theirs is a despicable attitude when they utter such an enormity without proper consideration or real knowledge: "*Dreadful indeed is this saying that issues from their mouths. Nothing but falsehood do they utter.*" (Verse 5)

The description here makes use of the sound of the words to add to the impression of horror given to the listeners. It begins with the adjective, 'dreadful', to enhance the anticipation of something totally unacceptable. This is further increased by the inversion used in the sentence. The sound and rhythm of the Arabic original is particularly significant in giving a true sense of the enormity those unbelievers utter. This is brought to its climax in the last sentence which utilizes the form of negation and limitation: "*Nothing but falsehood do they utter.*" (Verse 5)

The *sūrah* then addresses the Prophet in a way that is akin to disapproval of his being saddened by his people's attitude which denies the truth of the Qur'ān. He was pained by their rejection of God's guidance and their insistence on following the way which he knew would lead them to ruin. In a hint of disapproval, the Prophet is asked: "*Would you, perhaps, torment yourself to death with grief over them if they will not believe in this message?*" (Verse 6) Would your grief at their rejection of the truth cause you to kill yourself? These people do not deserve that you should feel any sorrow on their account. It is better that you should abandon them.

The Prophet is also reminded that God has made all the comforts and pleasures available on earth, and all riches and offspring, a sort of a test for mankind. The test will prove who of them does good in this life so as to earn its benefit as well as a happy destiny in the life to come: "*We have made all that is on earth as an adornment in order to test people as to which of them are best in conduct.*" (Verse 7)

God certainly knows the position of every one of His creatures, but he rewards everyone only on the basis of the actions a person takes. It is actual deeds that are rewarded according to their merit. The *sūrah* does not mention here those who do not do good works because the statement is clear with all that it entails.

The eventual outcome of all such adornment that is available on earth is inevitable. The earth will shed it all, and all living things on earth will die. Thus before the Day of Resurrection, the earth will be nothing more than a coarse and lifeless surface: "*In time We shall indeed reduce all that is on it to barren dust.*" (Verse 8) There is a clear element of toughness in the expression and in the scene it portrays. We are faced with an earth that has a desert-like surface with no trace of life over it.

Young Men with Clear Insight

After its brief opening, the *sūrah* speaks about the people of the cave, depicting the effect faith has on believers: giving them reassurance and inner peace. Hence, they prefer it to all material riches and pleasures. When they find it hard to live as believers within their community, they seek refuge in a cave where they receive God's care and protection and enjoy His grace.

There are countless reports that speak about the sleepers in the cave, and just as many versions of their story. However, we have no use for any of these; we will confine ourselves to what the Qur'ān tells us about them as it is the only source that provides true information. There may be other reports that have found their way into books of commentary on the Qur'ān, but we will disregard all these as they lack proof of authenticity. In this we rely on good counsel, because the *sūrah* contains an order prohibiting all argument concerning the people of the cave and reference to any source other than the Qur'ān in trying to establish the truth about them.

It is reported that the reason for the revelation of this story and that of Dhu'l-Qarnayn, related later in the *sūrah*, is that the Jews persuaded the people of Makkah to put to the Prophet questions concerning them, and also concerning the spirit. It is also said that the people of Makkah themselves asked the Jews to prepare some questions for them to test whether Muḥammad was a true Prophet. This may be partially or totally true, especially since the account giving the history of Dhu'l-Qarnayn begins with, "*They will ask you about Dhu'l-Qarnayn. Say: 'I will give you an account of him.'*" (Verse 83) But no reference is made to any question about the people of the cave. We leave this point aside and proceed to discuss the story as it is related, since it is clearly relevant to the main theme of the *sūrah*.

The structure of the story begins with a short summary before its narration in detail. It is shown in a series of scenes with some gaps left in between. Nevertheless, all omissions are clearly understood.

The story begins as follows:

> *Do you think that the people of the cave and the inscription were a wonder among Our signs? When those youths took refuge in the cave, they said: 'Our Lord! Bestow on us Your grace, and provide for us right guidance in our affair.' So We drew a veil over their ears in the cave, for a number of years, and then We awakened them so that We might mark out which of the two parties managed to calculate the time they had remained in that state. (Verses 9–12)*

This sums up the whole story showing its main lines and features. We learn from it that the people of the cave were youths, whose number is not mentioned, and that they went to the cave to isolate themselves from their community because they believed in God. We also learn that they were made to sleep in the cave for a number of years, which is not stated here, before they were aroused from their long slumber. We are told of two groups arguing about them, so they were awakened to make clear which of the two groups calculated their stay in the cave better. We are clearly told that, strange as their history is, it is not particularly marvellous among the miracles and signs given by God. Indeed there are numerous things that are much more marvellous and miraculous in the universe than the story of the cave people. Those youths are referred to in the *sūrah* as '*the people of the cave and the inscription'*. A cave is a natural chamber in a mountain or under rocky ground, while the inscription refers, most probably, to the record of their names which was, perhaps, the one hung at the entrance of the cave, where they were eventually found.

After this summary which hightens our interest in the story, the *sūrah* begins by stating that the account about to be given is the whole truth concerning their affair:

> *We shall relate to you their story in all truth. They were young men who believed in their Lord, so We increased them in guidance. We put courage in their hearts, so that they stood up and said: 'Our Lord is the Lord of the heavens and the earth. Never shall we call upon any deity other than Him. If we did, we should indeed have uttered an enormity! These people of ours have taken for worship deities other than Him, without being able to show any convincing proof of their beliefs. Who does more wrong than he who invents a lie about God? Hence, now that you have withdrawn from them and all that they worship instead of God, take refuge in the cave. God may well spread His grace over you and make fitting arrangements for you in your affairs.' (Verses 13–16)*

This is the first scene. Those believing youths were increased in guidance in order to be able to manage their affairs with their community. Along with this increased guidance, "*We put courage in their hearts,*" to make them solid in their attitude, firm in their belief in the truth, proud of the faith they had chosen.

Then we are informed that "*they stood up,*" which signifies a movement indicating resolve and firmness. "*They stood up and said: 'Our Lord is the Lord of the heavens and the earth.'*" (Verse 14) He is indeed the Creator, Lord and Sustainer of the whole universe. "*Never shall we call upon any deity other than Him.*" (Verse 14) For He is the One without partners of any sort. We make this pledge, because if we were to call upon anyone else, "*we should indeed have uttered an enormity!*" (Verse 14) We would have gone beyond all proper limits and be in total error.

They now turn to the prevailing situation among their people and express their rejection of it. They are clear that what their people do has no foundation whatsoever: "*These people of ours have taken for worship deities other than Him, without being able to show any convincing proof of their beliefs.*" (Verse 15) Indeed any faith should be founded on solid evidence of the truth. Only with such evidence can it have its say to turn people's hearts and minds to its argument. Without such proof, it is utter fabrication. What is worse is that such falsehood is asserted in relation to God Himself: "*Who does more wrong than he who invents a lie about God?*" (Verse 15)

Up to this point the attitude of the youths appears to be clear, open and straightforward. They are resolute in their adoption of the faith, betraying no hesitation whatsoever. Indeed they are shown to be very strong physically and mentally, and strong in their faith and in their rejection of the way followed by their community.

Here they are talking about two vastly different ways of life. There can be no meeting point between the two, and there can be no participation by these young believers in the life of their community. They had no choice but to flee in order to protect their faith. They are not prophets able to present to their community the true faith, calling on them to accept it. They are simply a group of young people who have been able to discern the right path out of a bleak, unbelieving environment. Should they have stood up in public to declare their faith, they might well not have been able to withstand the pressure on them to abandon it. Nor could they resort to pretence and avoidance, appearing to concur with their people while worshipping God in secret. Furthermore, it appears that, most probably, their secret was found out. Hence they had no option but to flee, seeking God's protection and support. They preferred life in the cave to all the attractions that their society offered.

Spreading Grace

That is the conclusion of their consultations and they immediately put it into effect: "*Hence, now that you have withdrawn from them and all that they worship instead of God, take refuge in the cave. God may well spread His grace over you and make fitting arrangements for you in your affairs.*" (Verse 16)

The surprise here is great indeed. These young believers who have abandoned their people and families, forsaking all the pleasures of this life and preferring instead to sleep rough in a small dark cave, begin to sense God's grace. They feel it coming, easy, comforting, abundant, limitless. It is spread over them to change the quality of their life in the cave: "*God may well spread His grace over you.*" (Verse 16) Thus, the cave becomes like a wide expanse, where God's grace is bestowed in abundance to change their whole outlook on life and bring about comfort and contentment. The solid, rocky walls of the cave are made to overlook a wide horizon, and loneliness in the cave is totally dispelled, for God has spread His grace over their young hearts and He takes care of them, arranging something for their comfort.

This is an aspect of what faith can do to a person. All appearances undergo a fundamental change. All that people may value and all their concepts with regard to life and happiness do not matter. When a human heart is full of faith, it sees a totally different world, where God's grace imparts reassurance and genuine happiness. Hence whatever turn events may take will be accepted, because the total result is comforting and fitting for one's life in this world and in the life to come: "*God may well spread His grace over you and make fitting arrangements for you in your affairs.*" (Verse 16)

With these young people proceeding to the cave, the story moves on to the next scene. Now we see them settled in the cave, overtaken by sleep:

> *You might have seen the sun, on its rising, incline away from their cave on the right, and, on its setting, turn away from them on the left, while they lay in a space within. That was one of God's signs. He whom God guides is indeed rightly guided, but for him whom He lets go astray you can never find any protector who would point out the right way. You would have thought that they were awake, when they were certainly asleep. And We turned them over repeatedly, now to the right, now to the left; and their dog lay at the cave's entrance, with its forepaws outstretched. Had you come upon them, you would have certainly turned away from them in flight, and would surely have been filled with terror of them. (Verses 17–18)*

This is a remarkable scene. Not only do we see how the young men looked and what they were doing, we have a picture full of life, with the sun rising, but deliberately moving away from their cave. The word used here, *'inclining away'*, imparts a sense of deliberate action taken for a particular purpose. Again when it is time for the sun to move in the other direction before it sets, it turns away to the left so that their cave remains unseen. All the while, they lay in a space within.

Before completing its description of the scene, the *surah* makes a familiar Qur'ānic comment which draws people's attentions to a particular aspect of faith that is relevant at that particular point: "*That was one of God's signs.*" (Verse 17) It was indeed a great sign, something highly remarkable. They were put in a cave where they could not see the sun, nor its rays. It gave them neither light nor warmth. They remained in their position, alive but motionless.

"*He whom God guides is indeed rightly guided, but for him whom He lets go astray you can never find any protector who would point out the right way.*" (Verse 17) There is a certain divine law that determines which people may receive God's guidance and which are left in error. When a person looks at God's signs and accepts what they indicate, that person finds God's guidance in accordance with His law. Hence, he is *'indeed rightly guided.'* (Verse 17) But whoever turns his back on these signs and refuses to understand the message they impart is bound, according to God's law, to go astray. Hence he is left in error and will have none to guide him.

The *surah* goes on to show the young people asleep in their cave. They are turned from one side to another in their very long slumber. Anyone looking at them would think them awake when they were fast asleep. Their dog remains at the entrance to the cave, stretching his forepaws like dogs normally do when they rest. He takes the position normally taken by a guard dog. The whole scene would fill any onlooker with terror so as to put them to flight. He would find people looking as though they were awake but in reality were asleep, unable to wake or move. This was all God's arrangement, protecting them, until the time He chose for their awakening.

The Sleepers Awake

Suddenly things change totally:

Such being their state, We awakened them; and they began to question one another. One of them asked: 'How long have you remained thus?' They answered: 'We have remained thus a day, or part of a day.' They said: 'Your Lord knows best how long you have remained thus. Let, then, one of you go with these silver coins to the town, and let him find out what food is purest there, and bring you some of it. But let him behave with great care and by no means make anyone aware of you. For, indeed, if they should come to know of you, they might stone you to death or force you back to their faith, in which case you would never attain to any good!' (Verses 19–20)

The element of surprise is always used in Qur'ānic stories in order to enhance the effect. Here the scene portrays the youths as they woke after their long slumber. They do not realize how long they have been asleep. They rub their eyes and begin to ask one another about what had happened. One turns to the others asking how long they were asleep for, just like anyone rising after having slept for many hours. He must have felt that this time his sleep was unduly long. The answer he received from his friends is indefinite: "*We have remained thus a day, or part of a day.*" (Verse 19)

But then they realize that to determine the length of their sleep is of no consequence. They leave that point aside, just like a believer should do in any matter of no specific importance. They turn to something more practical. They are hungry and have some money which they carried on them when they left home. Their discussion takes a different turn: "*They said: 'Your Lord knows best how long you have remained thus. Let, then, one of you go with these silver coins to the town, and let him find out what food is purest there, and bring you some of it.'*" (Verse 19) The most natural reaction in the circumstances! One is to go to the city to bring back the best food available for them.

They are however in an unusual position, and they have to be extra careful. They must not allow their people to find them out or discover their hiding place. For that would bring certain disaster. The people in authority in the city would stone them to death for their apostasy.

These young men worshipped God alone, associating no partners with Him, while their people were pagans. Hence they were sure to kill them or at least to torture them until they renounced their belief in God and turned back to the faith of their community. These are the only options their people would consider. Hence the young believers re-emphasize their advice to their friend who was going to the city to bring the food: *"But let him behave with great care and by no means make anyone aware of you. For, indeed, if they should come to know of you, they might stone you to death or force you back to their faith, in which case you would never attain to any good!"* (Verses 19–20) Indeed no one who turns back to unbelief in God and associates partners with Him could ever attain any good result. How could it be possible when he has incurred the greatest loss through disbelieving in God's oneness?

We are given here a panoramic view of the whole scene. The youths are apprehensive, unaware of how much time had lapsed or how many years they had remained in their cave. Indeed generations had passed by, and the city from which they departed had gone through great changes. The tyrants they feared had been removed from power. Yet the story of the young people who had fled in order to maintain their faith had been reported from one generation to another, with people differing as to their faith and what they believed in, as well as the exact timing of their escape. The awaking sleepers were totally unaware of all these events.

The *surah* however allows the curtain to fall over this scene only to raise it again showing a totally different picture, with a time lapse between the two. We understand that the present population of the city believe in God. They are so thrilled to discover the young believers through the one who was sent to fetch food. The people in the city somehow ascertain that he is one of the young men who had fled from the tyranny of the unbelievers a long time ago.

We need to stretch our imaginations somewhat to realize the magnitude of the young men's surprise as they heard from their friend what had happened during their sleep. He assures them that the city has experienced a great change since their departure. There was now nothing in the new society that they could not accept. Indeed all that they had once known in that city was now totally different. They themselves belonged to a generation that had long since gone. To the present people in the city, they were a marvel. Hence they would not be treated like ordinary human beings. They were totally unrelated to the present generation. Their relatives, friends, ties, concerns, feelings, habits and traditions had either been severed or undergone radical change. They were no more than a living memory, not real people. Therefore, God had spared them all that could result from their joining this new generation and thus caused them to die.

All this is left to our imagination. The *surah* portrays the final scene, when they are allowed to die. The people are standing outside the cave, disputing among themselves about their faith, and how to preserve their memory for future generations. It moves directly to outline the moral of this remarkable story: "*In this way have We drawn people's attention to their case, so that they might know that God's promise is true and that there can be no doubt as to the Last Hour. The people disputed among themselves as to what happened to them. Some of them said: 'Erect a building in their memory. God knows their case best.' Those whose opinion prevailed in the end said: 'Indeed, we must surely raise a house of worship in their memory.'*" (Verse 21)

The lesson here is clear. The end those young people met shows a real, tangible example of how resurrection takes place. The people in the city felt the full impact of resurrection and realized, as they could never have done otherwise, that God's promise in respect of resurrection after death will come true and that the Last Hour is certain to come. This was all seen in the awakening of those sleepers from their long sojourn in the cave.

Some people suggested that they should commemorate them: "*Erect a building in their memory.*" (Verse 21) The building thus erected would not determine their faith, as the people who discovered them did not know what faith exactly the sleepers followed: "*God knows their case best.*" (Verse 21) It is He alone who knows their faith. But the people who enjoyed authority in the city decided differently. "*Those whose opinion prevailed in the end said: 'Indeed, we must surely raise a house of worship in their memory.'*" (Verse 21) That was the way followed by Jews and Christians who erected temples over the graves of their saints and divines. Some Muslims today imitate their action in clear defiance of the Prophet's teachings. In condemning this practice, the Prophet once said: "God curses the Jews and the Christians who erect temples at the graves of their prophets and saints." [Related by Ibn Kathīr in his commentary on the Qur'ān]

How Many Were in the Cave?

Again the scene is brought to a close and another is shown with people in debate about the sleepers in the cave. This is only natural as people normally relate reports and news, adding something here and omitting something there. They may invent some details here or there, one generation after another. Thus a simple story is told in different ways as time passes. Hence, dispute about the number of youth in the cave continued for a long time:

> Some will say, 'They were three, the fourth of them being their dog,' while others will say, 'Five, with their dog being the sixth of them,' idly guessing at the unknown. Yet others will say, 'They were seven, the eighth of them being their dog.' Say: 'My Lord knows best how many they were. None but a few have any real knowledge of them. Hence, do not enter into argument about them, except on a matter that is clear, nor ask anyone of these people to enlighten you about them.' (Verse 22)

All such disputes about their number is useless. It is all the same whether they were three, five, seven or even more. Their case is left to God who knows all their details. They were also known to the few who established the facts about the whole event as it took place, or who heard its true report. There is no need, then, to go into any argument about their number, as the moral of their story may be drawn regardless. The Qur'ān directs the Prophet not to engage in any dispute over the issue and not to question any party over their case. This is consistent with the Islamic approach which spares the human mind of all useless debate. A Muslim should not pursue anything that he cannot establish through true knowledge. This event which took place a very long time ago belongs to God's knowledge which is perfect. Hence, let us leave it there.

On God We Rely

In connection with the prohibition of dispute about unknown events of the past, an order is given not to pre-judge the future or its events.

It is impossible for man to know what may happen in the future. Hence, he should not give any definite judgement of it:

> *Never say about anything, 'I shall do this tomorrow,' without adding, 'if God so wills.' Should you forget, then call your Lord to mind and say, 'I pray that my Lord will guide me even closer than this to what is right.'* (Verses 23–24)

Every action a human being does or omits to do, indeed every breath a human being takes, is subject to God's will. The curtains hiding the future are stretched in full so as to hide everything beyond the present moment. Our eyes cannot discern what is behind that curtain, and our minds are finite, no matter how advanced our knowledge may be. Hence a human being must never say that he is definitely doing something tomorrow unless he attaches his intention to God's will. This is because tomorrow belongs to the realm that lies beyond the reach of human perception. As such, it is known only to God. Hence, we do not make any assertion about it.

This does not mean that man should be fatalistic, giving no thought to the future and making no plans for it. He should not live for the present moment, cutting himself off from his past and future. No, this is not what the directive implies. Rather, what is implied is that every human being must make an allowance for what God may will in his case. He may intend to do whatever he wants, always seeking God's help, feeling that His will is in full control of everything. It may well be however that God may decide something different to what he intends. Should God help him to put into effect what he intends, then all well and good. But if God's will moves in a different direction, he should not despair or be sad. All matters belong to God at the beginning and at the end.

What this means in practice is that every person should think and plan as they wish, but they must always remember to rely on God's help and guidance. They should realize that they only have the faculties of thinking and deliberation God has given them. This should not lead to laziness or disinterestedness. On the contrary, it should give us more strength, confidence, reassurance and resolve. Should events reveal that God's will has moved in a direction different to what we planned, we should accept this with contentedness and reassurance. We submit to God's will, because it is beyond our knowledge until God makes it known.

This is the method Islam instils into the minds of its followers. Hence a Muslim does not feel alone when he plans or thinks of the future. Neither does he show any conceit or arrogance when he succeeds, nor is he overtaken by depression and despair when he fails. In all situations, he remembers God, feeling stronger for relying on Him, expressing gratitude to Him for his success, resigned for whatever God's will may determine.

"*Should you forget, then call your Lord to mind.*" (Verse 24) This is what a Muslim should do when he forgets to relate his intentions to God's will. He should remember God and renew his reliance on Him. He should also hope to remain always conscious of God, turning to Him in all situations and all future actions, always saying: "*I pray that my Lord will guide me even closer than this to what is right.*" (Verse 24) This short prayer indicates that it is not so easy to always turn to God in all affairs. Hence the prayer to try always to maintain it and improve on one's situation.

Long Was Their Sleep

With all that has been said and told, we have still not been informed of the duration of the sleepers' stay in their cave. Now we are told for certain:

> So they stayed in their cave three hundred years, and [some] add nine years more. Say: 'God knows best how long they remained there. His alone is the knowledge of the secrets of the heavens and earth. How well does He see and hear!' (Verses 25–26)

This is the truth of the length of their stay in the cave, given to us by the One who knows all secrets in the heavens and the earth. Well indeed He sees and hears. Perfect is His knowledge. His statement puts an end to the matter, leaving no room for dispute.

A final comment is added about the whole story in which we see faith in God's oneness clearly apparent in all its details: "*No guardian have they apart from Him; nor does He allot to anyone a share in His rule.*" (Verse 26) A further comment is added in the form of a directive to the Prophet to recite what God has revealed to him, as it represents the final word, and the truth that admits no falsehood whatsoever. He should seek refuge with Him, for no one can provide any shelter other than He. When the young men of the cave sought His protection, He spread His grace over them and provided them with His guidance:

> *Recite whatever has been revealed to you of your Lord's book. There is nothing that could alter His words. You shall find no refuge other than with Him.* (Verse 27)

Thus ends the story of the people of the cave. It was preceded and intermingled with directives. Indeed stories are given in the Qur'ān to add emphasis to such directives. The Qur'ān maintains perfect harmony between its directives and the way they are presented in the context of the story.

2

Faith Based on Free Choice

And contain yourself in patience with those who call on their Lord morning and evening, seeking His countenance. Let not your eyes pass beyond them in quest of the beauties of the life of this world. Pay no heed to any whose heart We have left to be negligent of all remembrance of Us because he had always followed his own desires, and whose case has gone beyond all bounds. (28)

Say: 'The truth [has now come] from your Lord. Let him who wills, believe in it, and let him who wills, reject it.' For the wrongdoers We have prepared a fire whose billowing folds will encompass them from all sides. If they beg for water, they will be given water [hot] like molten lead, which will scald their faces. Dreadful is the drink, and evil is the place to seek rest. (29)

وَٱصۡبِرۡ نَفۡسَكَ مَعَ ٱلَّذِينَ يَدۡعُونَ رَبَّهُم بِٱلۡغَدَوٰةِ وَٱلۡعَشِيِّ يُرِيدُونَ وَجۡهَهُۥ وَلَا تَعۡدُ عَيۡنَاكَ عَنۡهُمۡ تُرِيدُ زِينَةَ ٱلۡحَيَوٰةِ ٱلدُّنۡيَا وَلَا تُطِعۡ مَنۡ أَغۡفَلۡنَا قَلۡبَهُۥ عَن ذِكۡرِنَا وَٱتَّبَعَ هَوَىٰهُ وَكَانَ أَمۡرُهُۥ فُرُطٗا ﴿٢٨﴾

وَقُلِ ٱلۡحَقُّ مِن رَّبِّكُمۡ فَمَن شَآءَ فَلۡيُؤۡمِن وَمَن شَآءَ فَلۡيَكۡفُرۡ إِنَّآ أَعۡتَدۡنَا لِلظَّٰلِمِينَ نَارًا أَحَاطَ بِهِمۡ سُرَادِقُهَا وَإِن يَسۡتَغِيثُوا يُغَاثُوا بِمَآءٍ كَٱلۡمُهۡلِ يَشۡوِي ٱلۡوُجُوهَ بِئۡسَ ٱلشَّرَابُ وَسَآءَتۡ مُرۡتَفَقًا ﴿٢٩﴾

255

As for those who believe and do righteous deeds – We, for certain, do not fail to reward any who perseveres in doing good. (30)

إِنَّ ٱلَّذِينَ ءَامَنُواْ وَعَمِلُواْ ٱلصَّٰلِحَٰتِ إِنَّا لَا نُضِيعُ أَجْرَ مَنْ أَحْسَنَ عَمَلًا ۝

Theirs shall be gardens of perpetual bliss, with rivers rolling at their feet. There they will be adorned with bracelets of gold and will wear green garments of silk and brocade, and they will recline on couches. Excellent is the recompense, and comfortable is the place to rest. (31)

أُوْلَٰٓئِكَ لَهُمْ جَنَّٰتُ عَدْنٍ تَجْرِى مِن تَحْتِهِمُ ٱلْأَنْهَٰرُ يُحَلَّوْنَ فِيهَا مِنْ أَسَاوِرَ مِن ذَهَبٍ وَيَلْبَسُونَ ثِيَابًا خُضْرًا مِّن سُندُسٍ وَإِسْتَبْرَقٍ مُّتَّكِئِينَ فِيهَا عَلَى ٱلْأَرَآئِكِ نِعْمَ ٱلثَّوَابُ وَحَسُنَتْ مُرْتَفَقًا ۝

Set forth to them the case of two men, to one of whom We gave two vineyards and surrounded them with date-palms, and placed a field of grain in between. (32)

وَٱضْرِبْ لَهُم مَّثَلًا رَّجُلَيْنِ جَعَلْنَا لِأَحَدِهِمَا جَنَّتَيْنِ مِنْ أَعْنَٰبٍ وَحَفَفْنَٰهُمَا بِنَخْلٍ وَجَعَلْنَا بَيْنَهُمَا زَرْعًا ۝

Each of the two gardens yielded its produce and never failed to do so in any way. In the midst of them We caused a stream to flow. (33)

كِلْتَا ٱلْجَنَّتَيْنِ ءَاتَتْ أُكُلَهَا وَلَمْ تَظْلِم مِّنْهُ شَيْئًا وَفَجَّرْنَا خِلَٰلَهُمَا نَهَرًا ۝

And so [the man] had fruit in abundance. This man said once to his friend, in the course of a discussion between them, 'More wealth have I than you, and more power and followers.' (34)

وَكَانَ لَهُۥ ثَمَرٌ فَقَالَ لِصَٰحِبِهِۦ وَهُوَ يُحَاوِرُهُۥٓ أَنَا۠ أَكْثَرُ مِنكَ مَالًا وَأَعَزُّ نَفَرًا ۝

مال / جاه / بنون

And having thus wronged his soul, he went into his garden, saying: 'I do not think that this will ever perish! (35)

وَدَخَلَ جَنَّتَهُۥ وَهُوَ ظَالِمٌ لِّنَفْسِهِۦ قَالَ مَا أَظُنُّ أَن تَبِيدَ هَٰذِهِۦ أَبَدًا ۝

Nor do I think that the Last Hour will ever come. But even if [it does and] I am brought before my Lord, I should surely find there something better than this in exchange.' (36)

وَمَا أَظُنُّ ٱلسَّاعَةَ قَآئِمَةً وَلَئِن رُّدِدتُّ إِلَىٰ رَبِّي لَأَجِدَنَّ خَيْرًا مِّنْهَا مُنقَلَبًا ۝

His friend replied in the course of their discussion: 'Do you deny Him who has created you out of dust, and then out of a drop of sperm, and in the end fashioned you into a man? (37)

قَالَ لَهُۥ صَاحِبُهُۥ وَهُوَ يُحَاوِرُهُۥٓ أَكَفَرْتَ بِٱلَّذِي خَلَقَكَ مِن تُرَابٍ ثُمَّ مِن نُّطْفَةٍ ثُمَّ سَوَّىٰكَ رَجُلًا ۝

But for my part, I believe that He is God, my Lord, and none shall I associate with my Lord. (38)

لَّٰكِنَّا۠ هُوَ ٱللَّهُ رَبِّي وَلَآ أُشْرِكُ بِرَبِّيٓ أَحَدًا ۝

If only you said as you entered your garden, "Whatever God wills [shall come to pass, for] there is no power except with God!" Although, as you see, I have less wealth and offspring than you, (39)

وَلَوْلَآ إِذْ دَخَلْتَ جَنَّتَكَ قُلْتَ مَا شَآءَ ٱللَّهُ لَا قُوَّةَ إِلَّا بِٱللَّهِ إِن تَرَنِ أَنَا۠ أَقَلَّ مِنكَ مَالًا وَوَلَدًا ۝

yet it may well be that my Lord will give me something better than your garden, just as He may let loose a calamity out of heaven upon this [your garden], so that it becomes a heap of barren dust (40)

فَعَسَىٰ رَبِّيٓ أَن يُؤۡتِيَنِ خَيۡرًا مِّن جَنَّتِكَ وَيُرۡسِلَ عَلَيۡهَا حُسۡبَانًا مِّنَ ٱلسَّمَآءِ فَتُصۡبِحَ صَعِيدًا زَلَقًا ﴿٤٠﴾

or its water sinks deep into the ground, so that you will never be able to find it.' (41)

أَوۡ يُصۡبِحَ مَآؤُهَا غَوۡرًا فَلَن تَسۡتَطِيعَ لَهُۥ طَلَبًا ﴿٤١﴾

So his fruitful gardens were encompassed with ruin, and there he was, wringing his hands over all that he had spent on that which now lay waste, with its trellises caved in; and he could only say: 'Would that I had not associated partners with my Lord!' (42)

وَأُحِيطَ بِثَمَرِهِۦ فَأَصۡبَحَ يُقَلِّبُ كَفَّيۡهِ عَلَىٰ مَآ أَنفَقَ فِيهَا وَهِيَ خَاوِيَةٌ عَلَىٰ عُرُوشِهَا وَيَقُولُ يَٰلَيۡتَنِي لَمۡ أُشۡرِكۡ بِرَبِّيٓ أَحَدًا ﴿٤٢﴾

He had none to support him against God, nor was he able to save himself. (43)

وَلَمۡ تَكُن لَّهُۥ فِئَةٌ يَنصُرُونَهُۥ مِن دُونِ ٱللَّهِ وَمَا كَانَ مُنتَصِرًا ﴿٤٣﴾

For thus it is: all protection comes from God, the True One. He is the best to grant reward and the best to [determine] outcome. (44)

هُنَالِكَ ٱلۡوَلَٰيَةُ لِلَّهِ ٱلۡحَقِّ هُوَ خَيۡرٌ ثَوَابًا وَخَيۡرٌ عُقۡبًا ﴿٤٤﴾

Set forth to them a simile about the life of this world: [it is] like the water which We send down from the skies, and which is absorbed by the plants of the earth. In time they turn into dry stubble which the winds blow freely about. It is God alone who has power over all things. (45)

وَٱضْرِبْ لَهُم مَّثَلَ ٱلْحَيَوٰةِ ٱلدُّنْيَا كَمَآءٍ أَنزَلْنَٰهُ مِنَ ٱلسَّمَآءِ فَٱخْتَلَطَ بِهِۦ نَبَاتُ ٱلْأَرْضِ فَأَصْبَحَ هَشِيمًا تَذْرُوهُ ٱلرِّيَٰحُ وَكَانَ ٱللَّهُ عَلَىٰ كُلِّ شَىْءٍ مُّقْتَدِرًا ۝

Wealth and children are the adornment of the life of this world: but the things that endure, good deeds, are of far greater merit in your Lord's sight, and a far better source of hope. (46)

ٱلْمَالُ وَٱلْبَنُونَ زِينَةُ ٱلْحَيَوٰةِ ٱلدُّنْيَا وَٱلْبَٰقِيَٰتُ ٱلصَّٰلِحَٰتُ خَيْرٌ عِندَ رَبِّكَ ثَوَابًا وَخَيْرٌ أَمَلًا ۝

Overview

This second passage of the *surah* establishes a proper value system from a faith perspective. No real value is attached to wealth, position, influence or power, nor to indulgences and comforts. All these are transitory. Islam does not prohibit enjoyment of luxuries or comforts that are obtained in a lawful and legitimate way. But these are not the goals of human life. Whoever wants to enjoy these may do so, but he should remember that it is God who provides them. A human being must, therefore, express his gratitude to God through good work, because this is what remains in the end.

The passage starts with a directive to the Prophet to remain steadfast with those who turn to God for guidance and grace. He should abandon those who are oblivious of their Lord. An example is given of the two parties. This is given in a story involving two men, one boasts about his wealth and position, while the other maintains pure faith in God, hoping to receive from Him what is better than all material riches.

259

This is followed with an analogy showing the whole of life on earth. It appears to us short, fleeting, and having no real substance. It is just like ashes blown by the winds in all directions. The ultimate truth is that *"Wealth and children are the adornment of the life of this world: but the things that endure, good deeds, are of far greater merit in your Lord's sight, and a far better source of hope."* (Verse 46)

The Truth from Your Lord

And contain yourself in patience with those who call on their Lord morning and evening, seeking His countenance. Let not your eyes pass beyond them in quest of the beauties of the life of this world. Pay no heed to any whose heart We have left to be negligent of all remembrance of Us because he had always followed his own desires, and whose case has gone beyond all bounds. Say: 'The truth [has now come] from your Lord. Let him who wills, believe in it, and let him who wills, reject it.' (Verses 28–29)

Some reports suggest that these verses were revealed when some of the noblemen of the Quraysh demanded that the Prophet should expel his poor Companions if he were to hope that the chiefs of the Quraysh tribe would ever come to believe in his message. Thus people like Bilāl, 'Ammār, Ṣuhayb, Khabbāb and 'Abdullāh ibn Mas'ūd would have to be expelled from his companionship. Or at least the Prophet should make special arrangements, whereby he could meet the masters of the Quraysh on their own, in a place where none of the poor and the deprived were admitted. The rich, they argued, would be irritated if they had to sit in the same place with them, because their clothing smelled of perspiration.

It is also reported that the Prophet hoped dearly that these elders of the Quraysh would embrace Islam. He even contemplated making the arrangements they suggested, but before taking any steps in that direction God revealed to him the verse which starts with His command: *"Contain yourself in patience with those who call on their Lord morning and evening, seeking His countenance."* (Verse 28) Thus He sets the true values clearly and permanently. These establish a standard that never fails. When this has been accomplished and the true criterion has been put in place, then *"let him who wills, believe in it, and let him who wills, reject it."* (Verse 29) Islam will never seek to bend its values in order to please anyone and gratify his wishes. It does not borrow any value from any society implementing standards of *jāhiliyyah*. It has its own values and it will continue to implement these only.

The Prophet is thus to remain patient, and not to precipitate matters. He is to content himself with those who *"call on their Lord morning and evening, seeking His countenance."* Their aim is to win His pleasure. Hence to Him only should they appeal at all times, and in all situations. They should never change their purpose. Indeed they determinedly seek their goal which is more honourable and far superior in every way to any goal sought by people who are content with this life and seek nothing beyond its confines.

Being content and patient means that the Prophet should have for his true companions those very people the chiefs of the Quraysh wanted expelled. He is to sit with them and instruct them in their faith and its requirements. They are indeed the better set of people. It is their type that supports new messages best. A new faith or message does not rely on those who accept it only when it appears victorious, or when it gives them a position of leadership or other type of material gain. A new message is truly supported and firmly consolidated when it has adherents of sincere heart who turn to God seeking nothing other than to win His pleasure. No position of honour, pursuit of pleasure or achievement of any material gain discolours their sincerity.

"Let not your eyes pass beyond them in quest of the beauties of the life of this world." (Verse 28) Do not let your attention pass them by in order to contemplate the superficial comforts of this world, in which people compete. All this is no more than an outward beauty which remains much inferior to the high horizon to which those who *'call on their Lord morning and evening'* aspire to, because they seek only to please Him and win His acceptance.

The Prophet is further instructed: *"Pay no heed to any whose heart We have left to be negligent of all remembrance of Us because he had always followed his own desires, and whose case has gone beyond all* bounds." (Verse 28) He must not pay any attention to them when they demand that they must be separated from the poor. Had they remembered God, they would have banished from their minds any thoughts of conceit and arrogance. They would have recognized their position in front of God, who looks at all mankind in the same way and places them in the same rank. They would have felt that in faith all people are brothers. But they continue to implement standards of *jāhiliyyah*, allowing fleeting desires to dictate their attitudes. Hence, both they and their views are worth no attention, because they themselves have not paid attention to God and His commandments.

Islam places all human beings on the same level, in front of God. They do not claim a position on the basis of their wealth, lineage or social standing. All these are transient. The real criterion to distinguish people is their standing with their Lord, which is determined by their sincerity in seeking His pleasure and their dedication to His cause.

"*Pay no heed to any whose heart We have left to be negligent of all remembrance of Us.*" (Verse 28) We have left his heart alone because he directed all his attention and all his efforts to his selfish pursuits, wealth, family, pleasures and desires. Such preoccupations leave no time and no room for remembrance of God. Indeed when anyone places them at the top of his list, he does not have time for God, and in consequence, God lets him pursue these goals further and become even more removed from His remembrance. His days pass rapidly and he comes to his end in order to face what God has in store for those who wrong themselves.

"*Say: The truth [has now come] from your Lord. Let him who wills, believe in it, and let him who wills, reject it.*" (Verse 29) This is what the Prophet should proclaim in all clarity and firmness. The truth does not bend for the sake of anyone. It follows its own straight way. It is clear, solid, strong, free of all crookedness and manipulation. It is, then, each individual's own decision whether to take it up or leave it: "*Let him who wills, believe in it, and let him who wills, reject it.*" Whoever does not like the truth may banish himself from it. Anyone who does not wish to make his desires fall in line with the truth should know that no privileges are given at the expense of faith. A person who does not lower his head to God and His majesty has no place in the service of God's message.

Faith does not belong to anyone who makes concessions in it. It belongs to God who needs no one. Faith does not obtain strength if it is supported by people who do not seek it for its own sake, or who do not accept it as it is. A person who does not wish to sit with people dedicated to God's cause because he feels himself above them will have nothing to contribute to the Muslim community. Such a person is better left out.

No Rescue Available

The *sūrah* then portrays a scene of the hereafter, describing what is prepared for the unbelievers on the one hand and for the believers on the other. The unbelievers will have a fire that has been made ready to receive them: "*For the wrongdoers We have prepared a fire.*" (Verse 29) It is all made, set and brought forward. It does not require any new effort to receive them. No one is needed to kindle that fire, and it does not take any time to light or burn fiercely. God does not need anything to create whatever He wishes other than to actually will it, and it exists. The expression here uses the term, 'prepare', to indicate speed of action. Everything is put in place to take the wrongdoers and the unbelievers straight to the fire that is already prepared to receive them.

It is a fire that has huge folds that surge to encompass its inhabitants. They are securely captured there, with no hope of escape or rescue. Nor is there any chance of having a breath of cooling air, or the chance of a reduction in the suffering. Should they cry for help or to be spared the burning fire, help is given to them in the form of filthy water which is described in words which some commentators believe to mean 'molten lead', while others define it as 'boiling oil'. Should anyone's face get near it, it would certainly scald them. What will it do, then, to throats and stomachs, should the wrongdoers attempt to drink it? "*If they beg for water, they will be given water [hot] like molten lead, which will scald their faces.*" (Verse 29) It is a terrible situation that they find themselves in when they so urgently need a drink, but they only have what the Qur'ān truthfully describes as: "*Dreadful is the drink.*" (Verse 29) Moreover, the fire and its billowing folds are not the place where to seek rest: *"Evil is the place to seek rest."* (Verse 29) In this description there is an element of bitter irony. They are not in the fire to take rest, but to be burnt in punishment for their wrongdoing. But this description also serves as a contrast with the fate of the believers in heaven. The two ends are opposite extremes.

The opposite picture shows the believers who have done righteous deeds in heaven where they will permanently stay:

> *Theirs shall be gardens of perpetual bliss, with rivers rolling at their feet. There they will be adorned with bracelets of gold and will wear green garments of silk and brocade, and they will recline on couches. Excellent is the recompense, and comfortable is the place to rest.* (Verse 31)

These running waters provide all the elements of a cool atmosphere, pleasant scenery, gardens and a fresh breeze. The believers are in these gardens where they actually recline and rest, in full luxurious attire made of different types of fine silk, some of which is light, while the other is thick like velvet. They also wear bracelets of gold and enjoy other luxuries. The comment here is accurate: *"Excellent is the recompense, and comfortable is the place to rest."* (Verse 31)

These are the two widely different ends. Let everyone choose which one to have. The truth has been made absolutely clear by none other than God Himself, and the choice is open to everyone: *"The truth [has now come] from your Lord. Let him who wills, believe in it, and let him who wills, reject it."* (Verse 29) We see here a subtle reference to the attitude of the Quraysh unbelievers who demanded that the Prophet should either expel the poor from among his followers, or at least set up a different meeting place for the elders of the Quraysh, because it was beneath them to sit with the poor. They are again given the choice, either to sit with the believers, even though they are poor and smelly or they can have their resting place in the billowing folds of the fire and enjoy molten lead for refreshment. For those smelly clothes contain within them hearts that are full of faith, and minds that always remember God.

A Gulf Too Wide

This passage is followed by a story of two men and two gardens, given as an example of what is permanently valuable and what is no more than transitory. It paints two examples of human beings: the first seeks pride in the luxuries of this world, while the other is fully content with his relationship with God. Each is seen in practical life. The first who, in the Qur'ānic example, has two gardens delincates a man dazzled with riches. He feels himself powerful with what he has been given, so he forgets the Supreme Power who controls everything in people's lives, and thinks that his wealth is permanent. This gives him a feeling that his power is everlasting.

The other is a believer who derives his position and status through faith. He always remembers his Lord, realizing that the blessings he enjoys are in themselves evidence of the One who grants all such blessings. Hence, he knows that he should always praise his Lord and express his gratitude to Him for what he has been granted:

> *Set forth to them the case of two men, to one of whom We gave two vineyards and surrounded them with date-palms, and placed a field of grain in between. Each of the two gardens yielded its produce and never failed to do so in any way. In the midst of them We caused a stream to flow. And so [the man] had fruit in abundance.* (Verses 32–34)

The two gardens are full of fruit, having vineyards which are made even more splendid with a siege of date palms. In between the two gardens is a large field which the man uses to cultivate grains and other plants. A river running in between the two gardens adds much that is pleasant to the whole scene, because the running water reassures the owner of inexhaustible produce that, in turn, bring much wealth.

"*Each of the two gardens yielded its produce and never failed to do so in any way.*" (Verse 33) This is again a picture of continuing prosperity. What is worth noting here is that in the original Arabic text, negating any failure by the two gardens to yield their produce is described as 'doing no wrong or injustice' in that respect. This gives an element of contrast with their owner who does himself great wrong, by being arrogant and ungrateful to God for all the blessings he enjoys. He does not praise his Lord for what He has given him. This is an action full of conceit which means, in effect, that he is unfair to himself.

We actually see the man going into one of his gardens, gratified as he looks at it. He is full of pride, strutting like a peacock, calling for admiration. He speaks arrogantly to his friend whom he knows to be of limited means: "*This man said once to his friend, in the course of a discussion between them, 'More wealth have I than you, and more power and followers.'*" (Verse 34)

He then walks into one of the two gardens with his friend. His attitude is that of someone conceited and ungrateful. He has completely forgotten God, thinking that the two gardens will never fail to yield their produce. In the height of this conceit, he denies the Last Hour, when all are resurrected and gathered together before their Lord. Besides, should this Last Hour be true, he is certain to have a position of favour there. He has been favoured here in this life when he has been given his two gardens. So he is sure to have more favours granted to him in the hereafter.

> *And having thus wronged his soul, he went into his garden, saying: 'I do not think that this will ever perish! Nor do I think that the Last Hour will ever come. But even if [it does and] I am brought before my Lord, I should surely find there something better than this in exchange.'* (Verses 35–36)

This is plain arrogance. It makes people who have wealth, position, power and influence think that the values that dictate the way they are treated here in this life will apply in their favour in the life to come. They think they will be treated in the same way in God's Supreme Society. Their line of thinking is that since they enjoy such privileges in this life, they must then have a position of favour with the Lord of heavens.

His poor friend, who does not possess wealth, position, gardens or crops, is more confident as to the results of his nobler and better established values. He feels strong as a result of his faith, and he is certain of the support he receives from God Almighty, to whom all creatures submit. Hence, he confronts his arrogant friend with the truth showing him how conceited he is. He reminds him of how he is created from clay and from a sperm. He also directs him to the sort of attitude he should maintain towards God. He warns him against the result to which his conceit could lead him. He declares that he hopes to receive what is better than, and superior to, his friend's gardens and their fruit:

> *His friend replied in the course of their discussion: 'Do you deny Him who has created you out of dust, and then out of a drop of sperm, and in the end fashioned you into a man? But for my part, I believe that He is God, my Lord, and none shall I associate with my Lord. If only you said as you entered your garden, "Whatever God wills [shall come to pass, for] there is no power except with God!" Although, as you see, I have less wealth and offspring than you, yet it may well be that my Lord will give me something better than your garden, just as He may let loose a calamity out of heaven upon this [your garden], so that it becomes a heap of barren dust or its water sinks deep into the ground, so that you will never be able to find it.' (Verses 37–41)*

This is an example of how faith makes a believer very powerful. He does not care for wealth, might, or arrogance. He states the truth clearly, without hesitation or cowardice. There is no room for bending the truth in order to please anyone, be that a friend or someone mighty. A believer feels that he is far higher than all power and wealth. What God has for him is far superior to any riches or pleasures this life may bring. God's grace is all that he seeks, and His grace is plentiful and always available. On the other hand, God's punishment is severe and could befall the arrogant at any time.

The story then takes us suddenly from the scene of growth and prosperity to one of destruction and barrenness, from arrogance and conceit to repentance and seeking forgiveness. What the man of faith warned against has come true:

> *So his fruitful gardens were encompassed with ruin, and there he was, wringing his hands over all that he had spent on that which now lay waste, with its trellises caved in; and he could only say: 'Would that I had not associated partners with my Lord!' (Verse 42)*

The whole scene is raised before our eyes, and we see all the fruit of the gardens destroyed, as though the calamity befell it from all sides, leaving nothing untouched. The two gardens are totally destroyed with their trellises caved in. The owner realizes that he can do nothing to save any portion of his gardens or the plantation in between. He wrings his hands in sorrow, bewailing his misfortune which has left all his wealth destroyed and all his labour wasted. He is now repentant for having associated partners with God, acknowledging that He alone is the Lord of the universe. Although the man never previously mentioned the ascribing of divinity to anyone other than God, the fact that he placed a worldly value higher than the values of faith represents such association of partners with God. He now regrets his past attitude and dissociates himself from it. Alas! It is too late.

At this point the *sūrah* declares in all clarity that all protection comes from God: all power belongs to Him; all support comes from Him; His reward is the best reward; and what He stores for us is best and everlasting: "*He had none to support him against God, nor was he able to save himself. For thus it is: all protection comes from God, the True One. He is the best to grant reward and the best to [determine] outcome.*" (Verses 43–44)

Thus the curtains fall with the gardens in total destruction, and the owner wringing his hands in regret and sorrow. Beyond that, we realize that God's power and majesty overwhelm all.

Transient Pleasures

Now the *sūrah* draws another scene showing life on earth in its totality, and we realize that it is similar to those destroyed gardens. It is of a fleeting nature, lasting only a very short while and lacking solid substance: "*Set forth to them a simile about the life of this world: [it is] like the water which We send down from the skies, and which is absorbed by the plants of the earth. In time they turn into dry stubble which the winds blow freely about. It is God alone who has power over all things.*" (Verse 45)

This scene, with all its movement, is depicted rapidly so as to enhance within us the feelings of a transitory life, one which is short and ends in death. Here we see water pouring down from the skies, but it does not run or form watercourses. It is immediately absorbed by plants, but these plants do not grow, nor do they yield ripe fruit. It is all destroyed, becoming nothing more than dry stubble, blown away by the winds. The whole duration of life is thus ended within three short sentences. The original Arabic text uses all forms that indicate rapid transition from one stage to the next: the fall of water, then its absorption by plants, and then its blowing away by the wind. How short is life, and how worthless!

Having shown this scene of the present, transitory life to full effect, the *sūrah* makes a contrast between the values to which people attach great importance in this life and those which have the upper position at all times. All this is stated from the point of view of the divine faith: "*Wealth and children are the adornment of the life of this world: but the things that endure, good deeds, are of far greater merit in your Lord's sight, and a far better source of hope.*" (Verse 46)

Wealth and children are the most important things people covet in this life. Islam does not forbid enjoying these, provided that they are derived through legitimate means. Moreover, it gives them their appropriate value in relation to the everlasting life to come. They are adornments, but not criteria to evaluate people with. It is not right that people's status should be measured according to what they have of these. True value should be given to what endures, and that means all good works, including words, actions and worship.

People's hopes are normally very closely linked to wealth and children. However, the deeds that endure, i.e. good works, bring better reward and fulfil greater hopes. Hence believers should look to these for a more wholesome fulfilment of their hopes. They are bound to receive their result and reward on the Day of Reckoning.

In all this we see a consistent line, starting with the directive to the Prophet to remain patient and content "*with those who call on their Lord morning and evening, seeking His countenance.*" (Verse 28) We also see the same message imparted in the story of the two gardens and the two friends, as well as in the scene showing the value of the present life. This is all perfected with this last statement explaining the values of this life and those of the life to come. All this serves to put human values into the proper perspective.

3

Heedless of Divine Warnings

One day We shall cause the mountains to move and you will see the earth void and bare. We will gather them all together, leaving out not a single one of them. (47)

وَيَوْمَ نُسَيِّرُ ٱلْجِبَالَ وَتَرَى ٱلْأَرْضَ بَارِزَةً وَحَشَرْنَهُمْ فَلَمْ نُغَادِرْ مِنْهُمْ أَحَدًا ﴿٤٧﴾

They will be lined up before your Lord, [and He will say]: 'Now you have come to Us as We created you in the first instance, although you claimed that We would never appoint for you a time [for your resurrection]!' (48)

وَعُرِضُوا۟ عَلَىٰ رَبِّكَ صَفًّا لَّقَدْ جِئْتُمُونَا كَمَا خَلَقْنَكُمْ أَوَّلَ مَرَّةٍ بَلْ زَعَمْتُمْ أَلَّن نَّجْعَلَ لَكُم مَّوْعِدًا ﴿٤٨﴾

The record [of everyone's deeds] will be laid open; and you will see the guilty filled with dread at what it contains. They will say: 'Woe to us! What a record is this! It leaves out nothing, small or great, but takes everything into account.' They will find all that they ever wrought now facing them. Your Lord does not wrong anyone. (49)

وَوُضِعَ ٱلْكِتَبُ فَتَرَى ٱلْمُجْرِمِينَ مُشْفِقِينَ مِمَّا فِيهِ وَيَقُولُونَ يَوَيْلَتَنَا مَالِ هَذَا ٱلْكِتَبِ لَا يُغَادِرُ صَغِيرَةً وَلَا كَبِيرَةً إِلَّا أَحْصَىٰهَا وَوَجَدُوا۟ مَا عَمِلُوا۟ حَاضِرًا وَلَا يَظْلِمُ رَبُّكَ أَحَدًا ﴿٤٩﴾

271

When We said to the angels: 'Prostrate yourselves before Adam,' they all prostrated themselves. Not so *Iblīs*, who belonged to the *jinn* and he disobeyed his Lord's command. Will you, then, take him and his progeny for your masters instead of Me, when they are enemies to you? Vile is the substitute for the wrongdoers! (50)

وَإِذْ قُلْنَا لِلْمَلَٰٓئِكَةِ ٱسْجُدُواْ لِءَادَمَ فَسَجَدُوٓاْ إِلَّآ إِبْلِيسَ كَانَ مِنَ ٱلْجِنِّ فَفَسَقَ عَنْ أَمْرِ رَبِّهِۦٓ أَفَتَتَّخِذُونَهُۥ وَذُرِّيَّتَهُۥٓ أَوْلِيَآءَ مِن دُونِي وَهُمْ لَكُمْ عَدُوٌّ بِئْسَ لِلظَّٰلِمِينَ بَدَلًا ﴿٥٠﴾

I did not call them to witness at the creation of the heavens and the earth, nor at their own creation; nor do I seek aid from those who lead people astray. (51)

مَّآ أَشْهَدتُّهُمْ خَلْقَ ٱلسَّمَٰوَٰتِ وَٱلْأَرْضِ وَلَا خَلْقَ أَنفُسِهِمْ وَمَا كُنتُ مُتَّخِذَ ٱلْمُضِلِّينَ عَضُدًا ﴿٥١﴾

One day He will say, 'Call now on those beings whom you alleged to be My partners!' They will invoke them, but those [beings] will not respond to them; for We shall have placed an unbridgeable gulf between them. (52)

وَيَوْمَ يَقُولُ نَادُواْ شُرَكَآءِىَ ٱلَّذِينَ زَعَمْتُمْ فَدَعَوْهُمْ فَلَمْ يَسْتَجِيبُواْ لَهُمْ وَجَعَلْنَا بَيْنَهُم مَّوْبِقًا ﴿٥٢﴾

And when those who were lost in sin will see the fire, they will realize that they are bound to fall in it, and will find no way to escape from it. (53)

وَرَءَا ٱلْمُجْرِمُونَ ٱلنَّارَ فَظَنُّوٓاْ أَنَّهُم مُّوَاقِعُوهَا وَلَمْ يَجِدُواْ عَنْهَا مَصْرِفًا ﴿٥٣﴾

We have indeed given in this Qur'ān many facets to every kind of lesson for mankind. But man is, above all else, always given to contention. (54)

وَلَقَدْ صَرَّفْنَا فِى هَٰذَا الْقُرْءَانِ لِلنَّاسِ مِن كُلِّ مَثَلٍ وَكَانَ الْإِنسَٰنُ أَكْثَرَ شَىْءٍ جَدَلًا ۝

What is there to keep people from accepting the faith now that guidance has come to them, and from seeking forgiveness from their Lord, unless it be that they are waiting for the fate of the [sinful] people of ancient times to befall them as well, or for the suffering to be brought before their eyes? (55)

وَمَا مَنَعَ النَّاسَ أَن يُؤْمِنُوا إِذْ جَاءَهُمُ الْهُدَىٰ وَيَسْتَغْفِرُوا رَبَّهُمْ إِلَّا أَن تَأْتِيَهُمْ سُنَّةُ الْأَوَّلِينَ أَوْ يَأْتِيَهُمُ الْعَذَابُ قُبُلًا ۝

We send Our messengers only as bearers of good news and as warners. But with false arguments the unbelievers seek to confute the truth. They make My revelations and warnings a target for their mockery. (56)

وَمَا نُرْسِلُ الْمُرْسَلِينَ إِلَّا مُبَشِّرِينَ وَمُنذِرِينَ وَيُجَٰدِلُ الَّذِينَ كَفَرُوا بِالْبَٰطِلِ لِيُدْحِضُوا بِهِ الْحَقَّ وَاتَّخَذُوا ءَايَٰتِى وَمَا أُنذِرُوا هُزُوًا ۝

Who could be more wicked than one who, when reminded of his Lord's revelations, turns away from them and forgets what his own hands have done? Over their hearts We have cast veils which prevent them from grasping the truth, and into their ears, deafness. Even if you call them to the right path, they shall never be guided. (57)

وَمَنْ أَظْلَمُ مِمَّن ذُكِّرَ بِئَايَٰتِ رَبِّهِ فَأَعْرَضَ عَنْهَا وَنَسِىَ مَا قَدَّمَتْ يَدَاهُ إِنَّا جَعَلْنَا عَلَىٰ قُلُوبِهِمْ أَكِنَّةً أَن يَفْقَهُوهُ وَفِى ءَاذَانِهِمْ وَقْرًا وَإِن تَدْعُهُمْ إِلَى الْهُدَىٰ فَلَن يَهْتَدُوا إِذًا أَبَدًا ۝

Your Lord is Most Forgiving, limitless in His grace. Were He to take them now to task for whatever they do, He would indeed bring about their speedy punishment. But they have an appointed time which they cannot evade. (58)

وَرَبُّكَ ٱلْغَفُورُ ذُو ٱلرَّحْمَةِ لَوْ يُؤَاخِذُهُم بِمَا كَسَبُوا لَعَجَّلَ لَهُمُ ٱلْعَذَابَ بَل لَّهُم مَّوْعِدٌ لَّن يَجِدُوا مِن دُونِهِۦ مَوْئِلًا ٥٨

The same applied to other communities which We destroyed when they persisted in wrong-doing. For We had set a time for their destruction. (59)

وَتِلْكَ ٱلْقُرَىٰٓ أَهْلَكْنَٰهُمْ لَمَّا ظَلَمُوا وَجَعَلْنَا لِمَهْلِكِهِم مَّوْعِدًا ٥٩

Overview

The second passage of the *sūrah* ended on a note concerning the *'things that endure: good works.'* This third passage takes up the thread and talks about the day when such enduring things will have their full weight and significance. This is given against the backdrop of a whole scene from the Day of Judgement. It is followed by mention of Satan's behaviour, when he was commanded to prostrate himself before Adam, but he disobeyed his Lord. This is given by way of wondering at human beings who take Satan or *Iblīs* and his offspring for friends and protectors, when they know that these are indeed their enemies. Their behaviour is bound to end with punishment on the Day of Reckoning. The passage also refers to the partners people associate with God, showing them as totally helpless on that day.

In the Qur'ān God gives numerous examples and parables so that people will take heed and realize what they expose themselves to when they reject the faith. They had better take the necessary steps to spare themselves punishment on that day. These examples focus on the unbelievers of the past who persisted in denying the truth and rejecting the faith. Nevertheless unbelievers continue to demand that punishment should befall them or that they should be destroyed in the same way as past communities. They make false arguments to try to overcome the truth, taking God's revelations and His messengers as a source of mockery. Had it not been for God's grace, He would have hastened their punishment.

This part of the *sūrah* with its scenes of the Day of Judgement, and its reference to the destruction of past communities for their rejection of the truth is closely linked to the main theme of the *sūrah* which aims to establish the true faith, free from all distortion.

A Record to Include All Affairs

One day We shall cause the mountains to move and you will see the earth void and bare. We will gather them all together, leaving out not a single one of them. They will be lined up before your Lord, [and He will say]: 'Now you have come to Us as We created you in the first instance, although you claimed that We would never appoint for you a time [for your resurrection]!' The record [of everyone's deeds] will be laid open; and you will see the guilty filled with dread at what it contains. They will say: 'Woe to us! What a record is this! It leaves out nothing, small or great, but takes everything into account.' They will find all that they ever wrought now facing them. Your Lord does not wrong anyone. (Verses 47–49)

These verses portray an image in which nature forms an essential part. Horror is seen in its every detail as well as in people's hearts. Here we see firm mountains disappearing. What then will happen to hearts? The whole earth will appear void and barren, without hills, mountains, slopes or valleys to block anyone's view. The same applies to hearts and consciences: they will be unable to hide anything away. With all this open, level land which hides nothing, all people are brought forward: "*We will gather them all together, leaving out not a single one of them.*" (Verse 47)

Indeed not a single soul will be left out. They are all waiting for a great moment: "*They will be lined up before your Lord.*" (Verse 48) Every single one, those countless beings who walked on earth ever

275

since the day when human life began and right to the end of this world are all gathered together. They are lined up in an open space where none can hide.

The mode employed thus far is one of description. Now however the *sūrah* takes up the address mode, which adds the feeling that what we see is taking place now before our eyes. We see events unfolding, and we hear what is said. We see those who deny that day experiencing their own humiliation. Shame covers their faces: *"Now you have come to Us as We created you in the first instance, although you claimed that We would never appoint for you a time [for your resurrection]!"* (Verse 48)

This change of expression gives the scene much vividness, bringing it forward to the present so that we see it enacted. To us, the Day of Judgement is no longer something in the distant future. We almost see the shame on people's faces. We hear the majestic voice of the Almighty rebuking those people and reminding them of their position: *"Now you have come to Us as We created you in the first instance."* (Verse 48) They shamelessly persisted in their denial of such a day and their meeting with God once their life on earth had ended: *"You claimed that We would never appoint for you a time [for your resurrection]."* (Verse 48)

Having brought the scene forward to give it an added sense of reality, the *sūrah* resumes its description of what takes place there: *"The record [of everyone's deeds] will be laid open; and you will see the guilty filled with dread at what it contains."* (Verse 49) It is the record of all their deeds placed before their eyes to read and review. They realize that it is a comprehensive and accurate record, and they fear the consequences. They are embarrassed by the fact that the record includes every single thing, no matter how small or trivial. In their frustration, they exclaim: *"Woe to us! What a record is this! It leaves out nothing, small or great, but takes everything into account."* (Verse 49) This is the cry of one who is worried, fearing the worst after he has been caught red-handed, unable to evade the results or find any justification. This is because he recognizes the accuracy of the record which puts before his eyes all that he has done: *"They will find all that they ever wrought now facing them."* (Verse 49) They also realize

276

that whatever befalls them will only be fair, because *"Your Lord does not wrong anyone."* (Verse 49)

Much Too Argumentative

The guilty facing such a difficult situation are certainly aware, in this life, that Satan is their enemy. Nevertheless, they befriended him and he led them to their predicament. How strange that they should take Satan and his progeny for friends and protectors when they know them to be hostile since the first encounter between Adam and *Iblīs:* *"When We said to the angels: 'Prostrate yourselves before Adam,' they all prostrated themselves. Not so Iblīs, who belonged to the jinn and he disobeyed his Lord's command. Will you, then, take him and his progeny for your masters instead of Me, when they are enemies to you? Vile is the substitute for the wrongdoers!"* (Verse 50)

This story highlights the singularity of some people's attitude as they take Satan and his progeny for protectors and patrons in preference to God. It represents an outright disobedience of God's commands and the neglect of obligations and duties He has assigned to them.

Why do they befriend these, their enemies, when they possess neither real knowledge nor reliable strength? God has not brought them to witness His creation of the heavens and the earth, or even their own creation. Nor does He seek help or support from them: *"I did not call them to witness at the creation of the heavens and the earth, nor at their own creation; nor do I seek aid from those who lead people astray."* (Verse 51) They are no more than creatures whom God has created. They do not know what God has chosen to keep hidden from them, nor does He need their help.

It is important to reflect a little on the way the last verse ends: *"nor do I seek aid from those who lead people astray."* Is it appropriate to ask whether God seeks help from people who do not lead others astray? Sublime and great is God. He is in no need of anyone in the universe. He is the Almighty who has the power to accomplish whatever He wills. The phraseology here is intentional. It brings to the fore the myths of the unbelievers only to shoot them down. Those who seek protection from Satan and make him a partner to God only do so because they imagine that Satan has a great wealth of knowledge and overpowering might, when in fact Satan is a seducer who leads people astray. God does not like deviation or those who lead other people astray. Had He, for argument's sake, sought helpers, He would not have taken them from among the seducers who lead people into error and deviation. This is the meaning the verse and its ending aim to emphasize.

Another scene of the Day of Judgement follows, portraying the end that awaits the guilty and those to whom they ascribe a share of divinity:

> One day He will say, 'Call now on those beings whom you alleged to be My partners!' They will invoke them, but those [beings] will not respond to them; for We shall have placed an unbridgeable gulf between them. And when those who were lost in sin will see the fire, they will realize that they are bound to fall in it, and will find no way to escape from it. (Verses 52–53)

They are in a position where no claim has any value unless it is supported by irrefutable proof. The Lord who sits for judgement on that day commands them to bring their partners whom they alleged to enjoy favour with God. He tells them to call them up. Yet such people are lost. They forget that they are already witnessing the Day of Reckoning. So they call on their former partners who do not make any kind of response. They are no more than creatures of God who cannot avail themselves or anyone else of anything. They also have to face the great events that take place on the Day of Judgement. God places between such worshipped deities and those who worshipped them a gulf of doom too wide for either group to cross over. That gulf is the fire of hell: "*For We shall have placed an unbridgeable gulf between them.*" (Verse 52)

Those who are guilty will look around and fear will overwhelm them. They expect that at any moment they will fall into the fire. It is extremely hard to expect to be punished, particularly when the punishment is ready and there is no chance of escape: "*And when those who were lost in sin will see the fire, they will realize that they are bound to fall in it, and will find no way to escape from it.*" (Verse 53)

Why Reject God's Guidance?

They could certainly have escaped the fire and all punishment, had they only opened their hearts to the Qur'ān and not opposed the truth it lays down. God certainly gave them all sorts of examples, covering all situations and circumstances: "*We have indeed given in this Qur'ān many facets to every kind of lesson for mankind. But man is, above all else, always given to contention.*" (Verse 54) The *sūrah* describes man here as 'a thing'. The literal translation of the above sentence reads: "But of all things, man is the most contentious." It chooses such expression in order to encourage man to be less arrogant and to feel that he is one of God's countless creatures, although he is the worst in argument and contention, after God has given solid, irrefutable argument, clearly expounded in the Qur'ān.

The *sūrah* then documents the false arguments which the unbelievers, who represent the majority of mankind, have sought to provide:

> *What is there to keep people from accepting the faith now that guidance has come to them, and from seeking forgiveness from their Lord, unless it be that they are waiting for the fate of the [sinful] people of ancient times to befall them as well, or for the suffering to be brought before their eyes?* (Verse 55)

They have received guidance in plenty, which should have been sufficient for them to believe and follow God's orders. But they demanded for themselves the sort of suffering that befell nations of old. They made such a demand thinking that God's punishment would never overtake them, or they did so in mockery. Sometimes they modified their demands, asking for the punishment to be shown directly to them. That, they argued, would prove what the Prophets preached and then they would believe in them.

Answering such demands is not a matter for God's messengers to decide. God's rule that applied to past communities meant that when miracles were given and people continued to disbelieve, they were destroyed. To do this or to cause a scourge to overwhelm people are matters which only God determines. His messengers have a different duty, which is to bring happy news and to warn: "*We send Our messengers only as bearers of good news and as warners. But with false arguments the unbelievers seek to confute the truth. They make My revelations and warnings a target for their mockery."* (Verse 56)

The truth is clear, but the unbelievers resorted to false arguments, trying to disprove the truth. Their attitude was perverted, because even when they demanded miracles or hastened God's punishment, they still did not wish to be convinced. Essentially they were only ridiculing God's revelations and mocking His messengers.

> *Who could be more wicked than one who, when reminded of his Lord's revelations, turns away from them and forgets what his own hands have done? Over their hearts We have cast veils which prevent them from grasping the truth, and into their ears, deafness. Even if you call them to the right path, they shall never be guided.* (Verse 57)

These people who treat what God has bestowed from on high with mockery and who ridicule His warnings cannot understand the Qur'ān or comprehend its message. Hence, God places over their hearts screens which prevent them from understanding it. In their ears He causes a sort of deafness so that they cannot hear it. He has also willed that, because of their deliberate refusal and wilful turning away from His guidance, they will never be guided. For guidance to penetrate people's hearts, such hearts must be open to receive it in the first place.

"Your Lord is Most Forgiving, limitless in His grace. Were He to take them now to task for whatever they do, He would indeed bring about their speedy punishment." (Verse 58) Rather, He gives them respite and allows them time, because He is Kind and Merciful. He wishes to allow them every chance so that they can see the issues clearly. He does not hasten their punishment as they demand. However, He will not abandon them completely and leave them unpunished: *"But they have an appointed time which they cannot evade."* (Verse 58) They have a term in this life which they will fulfil. During this time a portion of their punishment will be inflicted on them. And they have a time appointed in the hereafter when whatever they have deserved will be given in full.

They have done wrong and they have been unjust. Hence they deserve punishment, or even destruction in the same way as communities of old. However, God in His mercy has determined to give them a chance for the full duration of their term on earth. That is to fulfil a purpose which He, in His wisdom, wishes to be accomplished. Therefore, He treats them differently and allows them respite until the time appointed for them, which they cannot evade:

> *The same applied to other communities which We destroyed when they persisted in wrongdoing. For We had set a time for their destruction.* (Verse 59)

They must not be deluded by the respite they are given. Their time will inevitably come. The rules God has made applicable will never fail, and He does not leave any promise unfulfilled.

4

A Special Lesson for Moses

Moses said to his servant: 'I shall journey on until I reach the point where the two seas meet, though I may march for ages.' (60)

وَإِذْ قَالَ مُوسَىٰ لِفَتَىٰهُ لَآ أَبْرَحُ حَتَّىٰٓ أَبْلُغَ مَجْمَعَ ٱلْبَحْرَيْنِ أَوْ أَمْضِىَ حُقُبًا ۝

But when they reached the junction between the two seas, they forgot their fish, and it took its way into the sea and disappeared from sight. (61)

فَلَمَّا بَلَغَا مَجْمَعَ بَيْنِهِمَا نَسِيَا حُوتَهُمَا فَٱتَّخَذَ سَبِيلَهُۥ فِى ٱلْبَحْرِ سَرَبًا ۝

And after they had marched on for some distance, Moses said to his servant: 'Bring us our midday meal; we are indeed worn out by this our journey.' (62)

فَلَمَّا جَاوَزَا قَالَ لِفَتَىٰهُ ءَاتِنَا غَدَآءَنَا لَقَدْ لَقِينَا مِن سَفَرِنَا هَٰذَا نَصَبًا ۝

Said [the servant]: 'Do you recall when we betook ourselves to that rock for rest. There I forgot the fish – and none but Satan made me thus forget it! – and it took its way into the sea. How strange!' (63)

قَالَ أَرَءَيْتَ إِذْ أَوَيْنَآ إِلَى ٱلصَّخْرَةِ فَإِنِّى نَسِيتُ ٱلْحُوتَ وَمَآ أَنسَىٰنِيهُ إِلَّا ٱلشَّيْطَٰنُ أَنْ أَذْكُرَهُۥ وَٱتَّخَذَ سَبِيلَهُۥ فِى ٱلْبَحْرِ عَجَبًا ۝

[Moses] said: 'That is [the place] we are seeking!' So they turned back, retracing their footsteps, (64)

قَالَ ذَٰلِكَ مَا كُنَّا نَبْغِ فَٱرْتَدَّا عَلَىٰٓ ءَاثَارِهِمَا قَصَصًا ﴿٦٤﴾

and found one of Our servants, on whom We had bestowed Our mercy and whom We had endowed with knowledge of Our own. (65)

فَوَجَدَا عَبْدًا مِّنْ عِبَادِنَآ ءَاتَيْنَٰهُ رَحْمَةً مِّنْ عِندِنَا وَعَلَّمْنَٰهُ مِن لَّدُنَّا عِلْمًا ﴿٦٥﴾

Moses said to him: 'May I follow you, on the understanding that you will teach me something of the wisdom you have been taught?' (66)

قَالَ لَهُۥ مُوسَىٰ هَلْ أَتَّبِعُكَ عَلَىٰٓ أَن تُعَلِّمَنِ مِمَّا عُلِّمْتَ رُشْدًا ﴿٦٦﴾

The other answered: 'You will not be able to have patience with me, (67)

قَالَ إِنَّكَ لَن تَسْتَطِيعَ مَعِيَ صَبْرًا ﴿٦٧﴾

for how can you be patient with something which you cannot fully comprehend?' (68)

وَكَيْفَ تَصْبِرُ عَلَىٰ مَا لَمْ تُحِطْ بِهِۦ خُبْرًا ﴿٦٨﴾

Moses replied: 'You will find me patient, if God so wills; and I shall not disobey you in anything.' (69)

قَالَ سَتَجِدُنِيٓ إِن شَآءَ ٱللَّهُ صَابِرًا وَلَآ أَعْصِى لَكَ أَمْرًا ﴿٦٩﴾

The other said: 'Well, then, if you are to follow me, do not question me about anything until I mention it to you myself.' (70)

قَالَ فَإِنِ ٱتَّبَعْتَنِى فَلَا تَسْـَٔلْنِى عَن شَىْءٍ حَتَّىٰٓ أُحْدِثَ لَكَ مِنْهُ ذِكْرًا ﴿٧٠﴾

And so the two went on their way, and when they embarked, [the sage] made a hole in the boat. Moses exclaimed: 'Have you made a hole in it in order to drown the people in it? Strange indeed is that which you have done!' (71)

فَٱنطَلَقَا حَتَّىٰٓ إِذَا رَكِبَا فِى ٱلسَّفِينَةِ خَرَقَهَا قَالَ أَخَرَقْتَهَا لِتُغْرِقَ أَهْلَهَا لَقَدْ جِئْتَ شَيْـًٔا إِمْرًا ﴿٧١﴾

He replied: 'Did I not say that you would not be able to have patience with me?' (72)

قَالَ أَلَمْ أَقُلْ إِنَّكَ لَن تَسْتَطِيعَ مَعِىَ صَبْرًا ﴿٧٢﴾

Moses said: 'Do not take me to task for my having forgotten, and be not hard on me on account of what I have done.' (73)

قَالَ لَا تُؤَاخِذْنِى بِمَا نَسِيتُ وَلَا تُرْهِقْنِى مِنْ أَمْرِى عُسْرًا ﴿٧٣﴾

And so the two went on until they met a certain young man. [The sage] slew him, whereupon Moses exclaimed: 'Have you killed an innocent man with no cause of just retribution for murder? Foul indeed is that which you have perpetrated!' (74)

فَٱنطَلَقَا حَتَّىٰٓ إِذَا لَقِيَا غُلَٰمًا فَقَتَلَهُ قَالَ أَقَتَلْتَ نَفْسًا زَكِيَّةً بِغَيْرِ نَفْسٍ لَقَدْ جِئْتَ شَيْـًٔا نُّكْرًا ﴿٧٤﴾

He replied: 'Did I not make it clear to you that you would not be able to have patience with me?' (75)

قَالَ أَلَمْ أَقُل لَّكَ إِنَّكَ لَن تَسْتَطِيعَ مَعِىَ صَبْرًا ﴿٧٥﴾

Moses said: 'If ever I question you again, do not keep me in your company; for then you would have had enough excuses from me.' (76)

قَالَ إِن سَأَلْتُكَ عَن شَىْءِۭ بَعْدَهَا فَلَا تُصَٰحِبْنِى قَدْ بَلَغْتَ مِن لَّدُنِّى عُذْرًا ﴿٧٦﴾

And so the two went on until they came to a town, where they asked its people for food, but they refused them all hospitality. There they found a wall on the point of falling down, and [the sage] rebuilt it. Moses said: 'Had you wished, you could have taken payment for what you did.' (77)

فَٱنطَلَقَا حَتَّىٰٓ إِذَآ أَتَيَآ أَهْلَ قَرْيَةٍ ٱسْتَطْعَمَآ أَهْلَهَا فَأَبَوْا أَن يُضَيِّفُوهُمَا فَوَجَدَا فِيهَا جِدَارًا يُرِيدُ أَن يَنقَضَّ فَأَقَامَهُۥ قَالَ لَوْ شِئْتَ لَتَّخَذْتَ عَلَيْهِ أَجْرًا ﴿٧٧﴾

[The sage] replied: 'This is the parting of ways between me and you. Now I shall explain to you the real meaning of all [those events] which you were unable to bear with patience. (78)

قَالَ هَٰذَا فِرَاقُ بَيْنِى وَبَيْنِكَ سَأُنَبِّئُكَ بِتَأْوِيلِ مَا لَمْ تَسْتَطِع عَّلَيْهِ صَبْرًا ﴿٧٨﴾

As for the boat, it belonged to some needy people who toiled upon the sea – and I desired to slightly damage it because behind them there was a king who was taking every boat by force. (79)

أَمَّا ٱلسَّفِينَةُ فَكَانَتْ لِمَسَٰكِينَ يَعْمَلُونَ فِى ٱلْبَحْرِ فَأَرَدتُّ أَنْ أَعِيبَهَا وَكَانَ وَرَآءَهُم مَّلِكٌ يَأْخُذُ كُلَّ سَفِينَةٍ غَصْبًا ﴿٧٩﴾

And as for the young man, his parents are true believers, and we feared lest he should cause them much grief by his overweening wickedness and unbelief. (80)

وَأَمَّا ٱلْغُلَٰمُ فَكَانَ أَبَوَاهُ مُؤْمِنَيْنِ فَخَشِينَآ أَن يُرْهِقَهُمَا طُغْيَٰنًا وَكُفْرًا ﴿٨٠﴾

And so we desired that their Lord grant them in his stead [a son] of greater purity than him, and closer in loving tenderness. (81)

فَأَرَدْنَا أَن يُبْدِلَهُمَا رَبُّهُمَا خَيْرًا مِّنْهُ زَكَوٰةً وَأَقْرَبَ رُحْمًا ۝

And as for the wall, it belonged to two orphan boys living in the town, and beneath it was buried a treasure belonging to them. Their father had been a righteous man. So your Lord has willed it that when they come of age they should dig up their treasure by your Lord's grace. I did not do any of this of my own accord. This is the real meaning of all [those events] which you were unable to bear with patience.' (82)

وَأَمَّا ٱلْجِدَارُ فَكَانَ لِغُلَمَيْنِ يَتِيمَيْنِ فِي ٱلْمَدِينَةِ وَكَانَ تَحْتَهُ كَنزٌ لَّهُمَا وَكَانَ أَبُوهُمَا صَلِحًا فَأَرَادَ رَبُّكَ أَن يَبْلُغَا أَشُدَّهُمَا وَيَسْتَخْرِجَا كَنزَهُمَا رَحْمَةً مِّن رَّبِّكَ وَمَا فَعَلْتُهُ عَنْ أَمْرِي ذَٰلِكَ تَأْوِيلُ مَا لَمْ تَسْطِع عَّلَيْهِ صَبْرًا ۝

Overview

This part of the *surah* begins by relating an episode in the life of the Prophet Moses which is not told or hinted at anywhere else in the Qur'ān. The *surah* does not give details of where this episode took place other than saying, *'the place where the two seas meet.'* Nor does it define the period in Moses lifetime when the events took place. Thus, we do not know whether the events related took place when Moses was still in Egypt, before he led the Israelites on their way to Palestine, or after they had left it. If the latter, was it before he led them into the Holy Land, or when they stopped, refusing to enter because they did not wish to confront its powerful inhabitants? Was it after they had begun their forty years of wandering in the land, going to and fro, in total loss?

The event involves a goodly servant of God's whom Moses meets and accompanies for a period of time. But the *surah* does not give us any details of the identity of this person. It does not mention his name or status. Was he a prophet, a messenger, a scholar, or a person favoured by God for his strong faith and complete dedication to the service of His cause?

There are many reports attributed to Ibn 'Abbās and others concerning the details of this story. One of them is related by al-Bukhārī who quotes Sa'īd ibn Jubayr, a scholar from the generation that followed the Prophet's Companions as saying: "I said to 'Abdullāh ibn 'Abbās that Nawf al-Bakkālī claims that the person who accompanied al-Khaḍir [that is the name often given to the learned man in this story] was not Moses, God's Messenger to the Children of Israel. He claims that he was a different person also named Moses. Ibn 'Abbās replied: 'That is a lie told by this enemy of God. Ubayy ibn Ka'b said to us that he heard God's Messenger saying: Moses was making a speech to the Children of Israel when he was asked which person had been endowed with most knowledge. He replied that he himself was that person. God took issue with him for not having attributed knowledge to Him, so He sent him a message saying that there was at the point where the two seas meet a person who had been given greater knowledge than he had. Moses asked his Lord to tell him how he could meet this man. God told him to take a whole fish with him, keeping it in a container. Wherever he lost his fish, he would find that person.'"

There are several reports that add details about this story. However, apart from a note on the probable location of the story, we prefer to limit ourselves to the Qur'ānic text without going into any further detail. This helps us to live 'in the shade of the Qur'ān'. We believe that the way the story is told in the Qur'ān, without defining the time or place and without mentioning names, has a definite purpose. Therefore we will look at the Qur'ānic text and study it without additions.

Where the Two Seas Meet

Moses said to his servant: I shall journey on until I reach the point where the two seas meet, though I may march for ages. (Verse 60)

Most probably, and God knows best, the place described here as the *'point where the two seas meet'* refers to the Mediterranean and the Red

Sea, and their meeting place is the area where the Bitter lakes and the Timsāh lake are found along the Suez Canal. It may also be a reference to the meeting point of the Gulf of Suez and the Gulf of 'Aqabah at the northern end of the Red Sea. This whole area witnessed the history of the Children of Israel after they left Egypt. Anyway, the Qur'ān only refers to it in passing without defining it further. There are several other reports suggesting where the area was that '*the two seas meet*', but we feel these are all unacceptable.

We understand from the general drift of the story that Moses had a definite purpose behind his journey. He declares that he will travel as far as the meeting point of the two seas, no matter how troublesome the journey may prove, or how long it takes. He expresses his determination by the words quoted in the Qur'ān: "*though I may march for ages.*" There are differences as to the exact meaning of the Arabic word, *ḥuqub*, which is given in the translation as 'ages'. Some scholars state that each such *ḥuqbah*, or age, denotes one year, while others say it denotes eighty years. Whichever meaning it may have, the expression denotes a resolve rather than duration of time.

> But when they reached the junction between the two seas, they forgot their fish, and it took its way into the sea and disappeared from sight. And after they had marched on for some distance, Moses said to his servant: 'Bring us our mid-day meal; we are indeed worn out by this our journey.' Said [the servant]: 'Do you recall when we betook ourselves to that rock for rest. There I forgot the fish – and none but Satan made me thus forget it! – and it took its way into the sea. How strange! (Verses 61–63)

Most probably, the fish was cooked. Its raising back to life and its moving straight into the sea was a sign given by God to Moses, so that he would know the place where he was to meet the man. This is indicated by the amazement expressed by the servant when he saw the fish swimming in the sea. Had the fish only dropped into the sea and settled at the bottom, there would be nothing strange in the matter. What makes this interpretation more plausible is that the whole trip was full of surprises that go beyond imagination, and this was only one of them.

Moses realized that he had gone beyond the place where he was to meet the man, which was by the rock where he and his servant had stayed for a little rest. Hence he traced his way back to it and there they met the man they sought: "*[Moses] said: 'That is [the place] we are seeking!' So they turned back, retracing their footsteps, and found one of Our servants, on whom We had bestowed Our mercy and whom We had endowed with knowledge of Our own.*" (Verses 64–65)

It also seems that this meeting was to remain Moses' secret, given to him by his Lord. His servant did not know anything about it until they met the man. Hence the following scenes in the story speak only about Moses and the pious man endowed with knowledge.

First Jolting Shock

Moses addresses the pious sage in a most polite manner. It is the sort of politeness that is worthy of a prophet. He puts his request, without making any assumptions, and he makes it clear that he seeks proper knowledge from a good servant of God:

> *Moses said to him: 'May I follow you, on the understanding that you will teach me something of the wisdom you have been taught?'* (Verse 66)

The man's knowledge however is nothing like human knowledge with its immediate causes and inevitable results. It is a part of divine knowledge that God has granted him, according to a measure He determined and for a purpose He wanted to accomplish. Moses could not be expected to be patient with the man and his actions, even though Moses was a prophet and a messenger from God. Looked at superficially, these actions may appear to have no logical justification whatsoever. They could not be understood without having access to the wisdom dictating them, and that is part of divine wisdom which people cannot begin to comprehend.

The sage understandably fears that Moses may not have the patience required to make of him a comfortable companion. He makes this clear to Moses. "*The other answered: You will not be able to have patience with me, for how can you be patient with something which you cannot fully comprehend?*" (Verses 67–68) But Moses is so eager to learn. Hence he resolves to be very patient and obedient, seeks God's help and places

God's will ahead of his own resolve: "*Moses replied: You will find me patient, if God so wills; and I shall not disobey you in anything.*" (Verse 69)

The man reiterates the difficulties ahead, stating to Moses a condition for his companionship: that he remain patient and not question the sage about any action he takes until he himself reveals its purpose: "*The other said: Well, then, if you are to follow me, do not question me about anything until I mention it to you myself.*" (Verse 70) Moses accepts the condition and the two set out together.

Soon afterwards comes the first scene from the trip: "*And so the two went on their way, and when they embarked, [the sage] made a hole in the boat.*" (Verse 71) This is certainly a strange thing to do. The boat carried both men as well as other passengers. They are all in the middle of the sea, and the sage makes a hole in the boat. On the surface, this is an action that exposes the boat and all its passengers to the risk of being drowned. Why would anyone, let alone a learned and devout person, do such an evil thing?

Confronted with such an apparently outrageous action, Moses simply forgets the conversation that he had had with the sage. A human being may accept something when it is discussed in abstract terms, but when he faces it in practice and looks at its consequences, his reaction may be totally different. Practical matters have a totally different effect. Here we see Moses, having already been warned against apparently outrageous actions and having resolved to remain patient, loses all patience when faced with a tough situation.

Moses apparently had an impulsive nature, which we detect throughout his life. Early on we see him giving an Egyptian man quarrelling with an Israelite a punch and killing him. He then repents and seeks God's forgiveness. Yet the following day he sees the same Israelite quarrelling with another Egyptian and tries to stop the latter. The details of these events are given in *Sūrah* 28.

With such an impulsive nature, Moses could not be patient when he saw his companion making a hole in the boat. He forgot all about his promise. Human nature is shown not to comprehend matters fully except through practical experience. Hence Moses says in objection: "*Have you made a hole in it in order to drown the people in it? Strange indeed is that which you have done!*" (Verse 71)

But the sage tolerates this with patience, and he gently reminds Moses of what he said earlier: *"Did I not say that you would not be able to have patience with me?"* (Verse 72) Moses now regrets his overreaction, saying that he completely forgot. He requests the man to accept his apologies and not to rebuke him. *"Do not take me to task for my having forgotten, and be not hard on me on account of what I have done."* (Verse 73) The man accepts his apologies and the two proceed further.

Patience Stretched to the Edge

There are, however, other strange events awaiting Moses which would exhaust his patience: *"And so the two went on until they met a certain young man. [The sage] slew him."* (Verse 74)

The first action exposed the boat and its passengers to certain risks. Now there is the blatant murder of a young man without provocation or justification. This was too much for Moses to tolerate patiently, despite all the promises he had given not to question anything he saw. Hence, *"Moses exclaimed: 'Have you killed an innocent man with no cause of just retribution for murder? Foul indeed is that which you have perpetrated!'"* (Verse 74)

This suggests that Moses was not unmindful of his promise. He probably remembered it, but felt unable to keep quiet when he witnessed a murder. To him, the young man was innocent. He had not perpetrated anything to justify his killing. He was perhaps even under age, so that he could not be held accountable for any misdeeds.

Once again the sage reminds Moses of the condition he has made and the promises Moses has given, referring also to what he said in the first place: *"Did I not make it clear to you that you would not be able to have patience with me?"* (Verse 75) This time, however, the sage goes further and reminds Moses that he said all this to him personally: *"Did I not make it clear to you..."* So the early warning was addressed to Moses personally, but he was not convinced. He had sought to be the man's companion accepting his conditions.

Again Moses reflects, knowing that he has broken his promises twice, forgetting it despite reminders. His regret makes him too apologetic, depriving himself of any possibility of a lengthy companionship with the sage. He gives himself only one last chance: *"Moses said: If ever I question you again, do not keep me in your company; for then you would have had enough excuses from me."* (Verse 76)

This brings us to the third and last scene: *"And so the two went on until they came to a town, where they asked its people for food, but they refused them all hospitality. There they found a wall on the point of falling down, and [the sage] rebuilt it."* (Verse 77) The two are hungry but find themselves in a town whose population are extremely inhospitable. They receive no guests and give nothing to the poor and hungry. Yet the man finds a wall there about to fall down. The Arabic text, *yrīdu an yanqaḍḍa,* is more vivid, making the wall almost like a living creature with a will that makes it want to fall. Yet this stranger occupies himself with rebuilding the wall for nothing.

Moses finds the situation full of irony. Why should such a stranger exert so much effort in rebuilding a wall in a town where they were denied even a little food and all hospitality? He should have at least demanded some money for his labours and then they could have bought some food to eat. He says: *"Had you wished, you could have taken payment for what you did."* (Verse 77)

This signalled the end of this unlikely companionship. Moses no longer had any excuse to offer: *"[The sage] replied: This is the parting of ways between me and you. Now I shall explain to you the real meaning of all [those events] which you were unable to bear with patience."* (Verse 78)

Up to this point Moses, as well as everyone following the story, have been subjected to a series of surprises with no indication as to their meaning or purpose. Our response is the same as that of Moses. We do not even know who the person was who did such singular acts. The Qur'ān does not tell us his name, in order to add to the general air of bafflement surrounding us. But what would his name add? The sage simply represents higher divine wisdom which does not attach results to their immediate causes. It aims to explain that there are objectives of which we may know nothing about. Hence, keeping his name from us fits in well with the abstract concept he represents.

Furthermore, higher forces dictate the development of the story right from the beginning. Moses is so keen to meet this man, he travels until he is totally worn out. But his servant leaves their food at the rock where they stopped to rest. But his forgetfulness is the cause of their return only to find the man at that very spot. Had they travelled on, they would have missed him. The whole atmosphere is shrouded in secrecy, just like the man's name.

All Made Clear and Simple

The secret is then revealed: *"As for the boat, it belonged to some needy people who toiled upon the sea – and I desired to slightly damage it because behind them there was a king who was taking every boat by force."* (Verse 79) This explains that the small damage the boat suffered was enough to save it for its people. Had it been seaworthy, it would certainly have been confiscated by the tyrannical king. Perpetrating some small damage to the boat saved it from the greater harm and ruinous injustice which was certain to take place without it. Hence, causing such damage was a good and kindly action.

> *And as for the young man, his parents are true believers, and we feared lest he should cause them much grief by his overweening wickedness and unbelief. And so we desired that their Lord grant them in his stead [a son] of greater purity than him, and closer in loving tenderness.* (Verses 80–81)

This young man appeared at the time to be deserving of no punishment, but God revealed his true nature to the sage. We realize now that he harboured all the seeds of wickedness and unbelief which were bound to increase as he grew up. Had he lived, he would have caused his parents, believers as they were, too much trouble. He might have led them, out of love for him, to follow him in his wickedness. Hence, God directed His goodly servant to kill the boy in order to replace him with one who would be better and more dutiful.

Had the matter been left to human knowledge, the sage could not have treated the boy except on the basis of what appeared to him. He would have had no justification in killing him, particularly since the boy appeared to be still under age, having done nothing to deserve capital punishment. It is not up to anyone, other than God Himself or one to whom God imparts knowledge from Him personally, to judge anyone on the basis of his nature. Nor is it permissible to make such knowledge the basis of any action other than that which appearances allow. But God may command what He wills, as He does in this case.

> *And as for the wall, it belonged to two orphan boys living in the town, and beneath it was buried a treasure belonging to them. Their father had been a righteous man. So your Lord has willed it that when they come of age they should dig up their treasure by your Lord's grace.* (Verse 82)

This wall which the sage laboured to rebuild, asking no wages for his labours despite the refusal of hospitality from the townspeople, had a treasure underneath. This treasure belonged to two young orphans in the town. Had the wall been left to fall down, the treasure would have become visible and the two boys would not have been able to claim it, considering their weakness. Since their father was a pious and righteous man, God allowed his children to benefit by his piety while they were weak. He willed to give them the time necessary to grow up and dig up their treasure when they were in a position to keep it.

The sage then disowns any share in this whole matter. It is God's grace that dictated all his actions. It was all by God's command who had imparted to him the necessary knowledge in such cases and others, showing him what to do in each case: "*I did not do any of this of my own accord.*" (Verse 82)

Thus the secret is made clear, and all the actions of the sage which seemed preposterous in the first instance appear to be simple and wise. Now that the curtain has been removed and the secret revealed, the man disappears totally from the scene and no further mention is made of him in this *sūrah* nor indeed throughout the rest of the Qur'ān. The story itself represents God's great wisdom, which reveals itself only when and as needed.

Within the context of the whole *sūrah*, this story about Moses and the sage is closely linked to the story of the young sleepers in the cave. Both agree that what lies beyond our human perception should be left totally to God, who will conduct it on the basis of His perfect and absolute knowledge. As for us, we know only what is told to us.

5

Accurate Historical Accounts

They will ask you about Dhu'l-Qarnayn. Say: 'I will give you an account of him.' (83)

We established his power on earth, and gave him means to achieve anything. (84)

So he followed a certain way (85)

and [marched westwards] till, when he came to the setting of the sun, it appeared to him that it was setting in dark, turbid waters; and nearby he found a certain people. 'Dhu'l-Qarnayn,' We said, 'you may either punish them or treat them with kindness.' (86)

He replied: 'The one who does wrong we shall punish. Then he will return to his Lord and be sternly punished by Him. (87)

وَيَسْـَٔلُونَكَ عَن ذِى ٱلْقَرْنَيْنِ قُلْ سَأَتْلُواْ عَلَيْكُم مِّنْهُ ذِكْرًا ۝

إِنَّا مَكَّنَّا لَهُۥ فِى ٱلْأَرْضِ وَءَاتَيْنَهُ مِن كُلِّ شَىْءٍ سَبَبًا ۝

فَأَتْبَعَ سَبَبًا ۝

حَتَّىٰٓ إِذَا بَلَغَ مَغْرِبَ ٱلشَّمْسِ وَجَدَهَا تَغْرُبُ فِى عَيْنٍ حَمِئَةٍ وَوَجَدَ عِندَهَا قَوْمًا قُلْنَا يَنذَا ٱلْقَرْنَيْنِ إِمَّآ أَن تُعَذِّبَ وَإِمَّآ أَن تَتَّخِذَ فِيهِمْ حُسْنًا ۝

قَالَ أَمَّا مَن ظَلَمَ فَسَوْفَ نُعَذِّبُهُۥ ثُمَّ يُرَدُّ إِلَىٰ رَبِّهِۦ فَيُعَذِّبُهُۥ عَذَابًا نُّكْرًا ۝

But the one who believes and does righteous deeds shall have a goodly reward, and we shall assign to him a task that is easy to fulfil.' (88)

وَأَمَّا مَنْ ءَامَنَ وَعَمِلَ صَلِحًا فَلَهُۥ جَزَآءً ٱلْحُسْنَىٰ وَسَنَقُولُ لَهُۥ مِنْ أَمْرِنَا يُسْرًا ﴿٨٨﴾

Then he followed another way (89)

ثُمَّ أَتْبَعَ سَبَبًا ﴿٨٩﴾

and [marched eastwards] till, when he came to the rising of the sun, he found that it was rising on a people for whom We had provided no coverings against it. (90)

حَتَّىٰٓ إِذَا بَلَغَ مَطْلِعَ ٱلشَّمْسِ وَجَدَهَا تَطْلُعُ عَلَىٰ قَوْمٍ لَّمْ نَجْعَل لَّهُم مِّن دُونِهَا سِتْرًا ﴿٩٠﴾

So he did; and We had full knowledge of all the means available to him. (91)

كَذَٰلِكَ وَقَدْ أَحَطْنَا بِمَا لَدَيْهِ خُبْرًا ﴿٩١﴾

Then he followed yet another way (92)

ثُمَّ أَتْبَعَ سَبَبًا ﴿٩٢﴾

and [marched on] till, when he reached a place between the two mountain-barriers he found beneath them a people who could scarcely understand a word. (93)

حَتَّىٰٓ إِذَا بَلَغَ بَيْنَ ٱلسَّدَّيْنِ وَجَدَ مِن دُونِهِمَا قَوْمًا لَّا يَكَادُونَ يَفْقَهُونَ قَوْلًا ﴿٩٣﴾

'Dhu'l-Qarnayn,' they said, 'Gog and Magog are ravaging this land. May we pay you a tribute so that you erect a barrier between us and them?' (94)

قَالُوا يَٰذَا ٱلْقَرْنَيْنِ إِنَّ يَأْجُوجَ وَمَأْجُوجَ مُفْسِدُونَ فِي ٱلْأَرْضِ فَهَلْ نَجْعَلُ لَكَ خَرْجًا عَلَىٰٓ أَن تَجْعَلَ بَيْنَنَا وَبَيْنَهُمْ سَدًّا ﴿٩٤﴾

He answered: 'That with which my Lord has established me is better [than any tribute]. Hence, do but help me with strength, and I shall erect a rampart between you and them! (95)

قَالَ مَا مَكَّنِّي فِيهِ رَبِّي خَيْرٌ فَأَعِينُونِي بِقُوَّةٍ أَجْعَلْ بَيْنَكُمْ وَبَيْنَهُمْ رَدْمًا ﴿٩٥﴾

Bring me blocks of iron!' At length, when he had filled up the gap between the two mountain-sides, he said: 'Ply your bellows!' Then, when he made [the iron glow like] fire, he said: 'Bring me molten copper which I will pour over it.' (96)

ءَاتُونِي زُبَرَ الْحَدِيدِ حَتَّى إِذَا سَاوَى بَيْنَ الصَّدَفَيْنِ قَالَ انْفُخُوا حَتَّى إِذَا جَعَلَهُ نَارًا قَالَ ءَاتُونِي أُفْرِغْ عَلَيْهِ قِطْرًا ﴿٩٦﴾

And thus their enemies were unable to scale [the rampart], nor could they dig their way through it. (97)

فَمَا اسْطَاعُوٓا أَن يَظْهَرُوهُ وَمَا اسْتَطَاعُوا لَهُ نَقْبًا ﴿٩٧﴾

He said: 'This is a mercy from my Lord. Yet when the time appointed by my Lord shall come, He will make this [rampart] level with the ground. My Lord's promise always comes true.' (98)

قَالَ هَٰذَا رَحْمَةٌ مِّن رَّبِّي فَإِذَا جَآءَ وَعْدُ رَبِّي جَعَلَهُ دَكَّآءَ وَكَانَ وَعْدُ رَبِّي حَقًّا ﴿٩٨﴾

On that day We shall leave them to surge like waves dashing against one another. The trumpet will be blown, and We shall gather them all together. (99)

وَتَرَكْنَا بَعْضَهُمْ يَوْمَئِذٍ يَمُوجُ فِي بَعْضٍ وَنُفِخَ فِي الصُّورِ فَجَمَعْنَاهُمْ جَمْعًا ﴿٩٩﴾

And We shall, on that day, present hell, all spread out, for the unbelievers, (100)

وَعَرَضْنَا جَهَنَّمَ يَوْمَئِذٍ لِّلْكَافِرِينَ عَرْضًا ۝

who have turned a blind eye to My admonition and a deaf ear to My warning. (101)

ٱلَّذِينَ كَانَتْ أَعْيُنُهُمْ فِي غِطَاءٍ عَن ذِكْرِى وَكَانُوا لَا يَسْتَطِيعُونَ سَمْعًا ۝

Do the unbelievers think that they could take My creatures for patrons against Me? We have indeed readied hell as a dwelling place for the unbelievers. (102)

أَفَحَسِبَ ٱلَّذِينَ كَفَرُوٓا أَن يَتَّخِذُوا عِبَادِى مِن دُونِىٓ أَوْلِيَآءَ إِنَّآ أَعْتَدْنَا جَهَنَّمَ لِلْكَافِرِينَ نُزُلًا ۝

Say: 'Shall we tell you who are the greatest losers in whatever they may do? (103)

قُلْ هَلْ نُنَبِّئُكُم بِٱلْأَخْسَرِينَ أَعْمَالًا ۝

It is they whose labour in this world has been misguided, and who nonetheless think that what they do is right. (104)

ٱلَّذِينَ ضَلَّ سَعْيُهُمْ فِي ٱلْحَيَوٰةِ ٱلدُّنْيَا وَهُمْ يَحْسَبُونَ أَنَّهُمْ يُحْسِنُونَ صُنْعًا ۝

It is they who have chosen to disbelieve in their Lord's revelations and deny the truth that they will meet Him. Vain will be their works. No weight shall We assign to them on Resurrection Day. (105)

أُوْلَٰٓئِكَ ٱلَّذِينَ كَفَرُوا بِـَٔايَٰتِ رَبِّهِمْ وَلِقَآئِهِۦ فَحَبِطَتْ أَعْمَٰلُهُمْ فَلَا نُقِيمُ لَهُمْ يَوْمَ ٱلْقِيَٰمَةِ وَزْنًا ۝

That will be their reward, hell, for having rejected the faith, and made My revelations and My messengers a target of their mockery.' (106)

ذَٰلِكَ جَزَآؤُهُمْ جَهَنَّمُ بِمَا كَفَرُوا وَٱتَّخَذُوٓا ءَايَٰتِى وَرُسُلِى هُزُوًا ۝

But those who have faith and do righteous deeds shall have the gardens of paradise as their dwelling place. (107)

إِنَّ ٱلَّذِينَ ءَامَنُوا۟ وَعَمِلُوا۟ ٱلصَّٰلِحَٰتِ كَانَتْ لَهُمْ جَنَّٰتُ ٱلْفِرْدَوْسِ نُزُلًا ۝

Therein they will abide, and never will they desire any change to befall them. (108)

خَٰلِدِينَ فِيهَا لَا يَبْغُونَ عَنْهَا حِوَلًا ۝

Say: 'If the sea were ink for my Lord's words, the sea would surely dry up before my Lord's words are exhausted, even though we were to add to it another sea to replenish it.' (109)

قُل لَّوْ كَانَ ٱلْبَحْرُ مِدَادًا لِّكَلِمَٰتِ رَبِّى لَنَفِدَ ٱلْبَحْرُ قَبْلَ أَن تَنفَدَ كَلِمَٰتُ رَبِّى وَلَوْ جِئْنَا بِمِثْلِهِۦ مَدَدًا ۝

Say: 'I am but a human being like yourselves. It has been revealed to me that your God is the One and only God. Hence, whoever expects to meet his Lord [on Judgement Day], let him do what is right, and in the worship due to his Lord admit no one as a partner.' (110)

قُلْ إِنَّمَآ أَنَا۠ بَشَرٌ مِّثْلُكُمْ يُوحَىٰٓ إِلَىَّ أَنَّمَآ إِلَٰهُكُمْ إِلَٰهٌ وَٰحِدٌ فَمَن كَانَ يَرْجُوا۟ لِقَآءَ رَبِّهِۦ فَلْيَعْمَلْ عَمَلًا صَٰلِحًا وَلَا يُشْرِكْ بِعِبَادَةِ رَبِّهِۦٓ أَحَدًۢا ۝

Overview

This final passage of the *sūrah* is mainly concerned with Dhu'l-Qarnayn and his three journeys, to the east, west and the central areas, as well as his erection of a strong barrier to prevent Gog and Magog from getting through. The *sūrah* tells us that after he had erected the barrier, Dhu'l-Qarnayn said: "*This is a mercy from my Lord. Yet when the time appointed by my Lord shall come, He will make this [rampart] level with the ground. My Lord's promise always comes true.*" (Verse 98)

301

The reference to the 'true promise' is followed with the blowing of the trumpet and a scene of the resurrection before the *surah* concludes with three short sections, each of which starts with the command, 'Say'. These three sections sum up all the main topics of the *surah* and follow its drift. They serve as the final strong beats of an evenly flowing tune.

The Mysterious Traveller

The story of Dhu'l-Qarnayn begins as follows: "*They will ask you about Dhu'l-Qarnayn. Say: 'I will give you an account of him.'*" (Verse 83) Speaking about the reasons that led to the revelation of this *surah*, Muḥammad ibn Isḥāq mentions a report attributed to Ibn 'Abbās, the Prophet's cousin and Companion. The report mentions that the Quraysh sent al-Naḍr ibn al-Ḥārith and 'Uqbah ibn Abī Mu'ayṭ to ask the Jewish rabbis in Madinah about Muḥammad, outlining for them their terms of reference. The Quraysh elders told the two men to describe Muḥammad in detail to the Jewish rabbis and to report to them truthfully what he advocated. "The Jews," said the Quraysh elders, "are the people of early Scriptures and they have a wealth of knowledge about prophets which is not available to us."

In Madinah, the two men from the Quraysh put their questions to the rabbis and solicited their honest opinion about Muḥammad. The rabbis told them to ask Muḥammad three questions. "If he gives you satisfactory answers, then he is a prophet and messenger of God. If he has no answer to give, then he is fabricating whatever he says. You may do what you like with him. Ask him about a group of young people about whom there was a strange story in ancient times, and let him tell you what happened to them. Ask him also about a man who travelled all over the place and went to the far east and far west. The third question you should ask him is to tell you about the spirit."

Al-Naḍr and 'Uqbah travelled back to Makkah and told their tribesmen that they had brought the answer to their problem with Muḥammad. When they told them of the advice of the Jewish rabbis, they went to the Prophet and put the three questions to him. The Prophet told them that he would answer them the following day. Apparently he did not qualify the promise by saying, 'God willing'. as he should have done and as Muslims should always do. As a result nothing was revealed to him for fifteen days, nor did the angel Gabriel meet him during this period. The people of Makkah began to spread a fresh propaganda campaign, saying: 'Muḥammad has promised to give us an answer on the morrow, and now it has been fifteen days since we asked him, without him giving us any reply to our questions.'

The Prophet was very sad at this delay in revelation and he was much distressed by what the people of Makkah said about him. Then the angel Gabriel came down revealing this *sūrah*, The Cave, which tells him in its early verses not to grieve too much for his people if they refuse to listen to him. It then proceeds to answer the questions put to him, relating the stories of the young men and the traveller of old times. He also gave the Prophet the answer to the third question about the spirit, which occurs in *Sūrah* 17, The Night Journey.

Another report by Ibn 'Abbās tells of the reason for the revelation of the verse giving the reply to the question about the spirit. This mentions that the Jews themselves put the question to the Prophet: "Tell us about the spirit, and how the spirit inside the body can be tortured, when the spirit belongs to God?" As nothing about the spirit had been revealed to him, he could not answer them. Gabriel then came down to him with the verse stating: *"Say: The [knowledge of the nature of the] spirit belongs to my Lord alone. You [mankind] have been granted but little knowledge."* (17: 85)

Since there are several reports about the immediate reason behind the revelation of this *sūrah*, we prefer not to go into these, limiting our discussion to the Qur'ānic text, which provides us with true and accurate information. On the basis of this text we realize that a question was asked about Dhu'l-Qarnayn, but we do not know for certain who put the question. Knowing the questioner will not add anything about the import of the story. We will now discuss the text.

The Qur'ānic text does not mention anything about the personality of Dhu'l-Qarnayn or where and when he lived. This is typical of Qur'ānic stories. The intention is not to provide historical accounts, but to learn the lessons that may be derived from the stories mentioned. In most cases, these lessons can be drawn without the need to define time and place.

Documented history refers to a king called Iskandar, or Alexander Dhu'l-Qarnayn. It is also certain that the person to whom the Qur'ān refers by the name Dhu'l-Qarnayn is not the Greek king, Alexander, for he was a pagan worshipping idols, while the Qur'ān speaks about someone who believed in God's oneness and in resurrection and the life to come.[1] In his book, *Al-Āthār Al-Bāqiyah 'an al-Qurūn Al-Khāliyah*, al-Bīrūnī mentions that Dhu'l-Qarnayn, about whom the Qur'ān gives us this account, was a king of Ḥimyar in Yemen. This is based on the fact that his name begins with 'Dhu', which is typical of Ḥimyarī kings. His actual name was Abū Bakr ibn Afrīqish. He travelled at the head of his army along the southern Mediterranean coast, passing through Tunisia and Morocco and building the town of Afriqiya. Thus the whole continent was named after him. He was nicknamed Dhu'l-Qarnayn because he reached as far as the two furthest points in relation to the sun.

This view may be correct, but we have no means of verifying it. It is not possible to undertake research based on documented history with the aim of establishing the real personality of Dhu'l-Qarnayn of whose history the Qur'ān gives us a glimpse. The same applies to most historical accounts given in the Qur'ān, such as those concerning the people of the prophets Noah and Hūd, or the Thamūd, etc. History itself is only a recent addition, compared to the length of human life on earth. Great events took place in the periods preceding what history reports, and these remain unknown to historians. Hence, we cannot refer to them for answers.

Had the Torah remained intact, without distortion or addition, it would have been a reliable source of information concerning some of these events. But the Torah has been mixed with legends that have, without doubt, no foundation. It has been infused with reports that have, most certainly, been added to the original text revealed by God. Hence, the Torah cannot be treated as a reliable source for the historical

---

1. It may appear that Sayyid Quṭb is doing what he says he will not do, discussing the identity of the central figure of the story and the locations mentioned, but in fact he is only illustrating why history could not be referred to in search for more details of the Qur'ānic accounts. His discussion of the probable locations remains very close to the Qur'ānic statements. The footnote speaking about the wall near Tirmidh simply mentions a probability without any attempt to evaluate it. – Editor's note.

accounts it contains. Thus, the only source left for us is the Qur'ān, since God has guaranteed its preservation in its original form and its protection against any distortion. It is indeed the only source for its historical accounts.

Needless to say, it is wrong to try to evaluate the Qur'ān with reference to history. There are two obvious reasons for this. The first is the fact that history is a recent creation which has missed countless events in mankind's progress. The Qur'ān tells us some of these events which remain totally unknown to history and historians. Secondly, even though history may record some of these events, it remains the product of human beings. Thus, it suffers from the shortcomings of human action, such as imperfection, error, distortion, etc. In our own time, when means of communication and facilities of verification have become available in plenty, we find the same piece of news or the same incident reported in a variety of ways, each looking at it from a particular angle, and giving it a different interpretation. It is out of such heaps of confusion that historical accounts are made, regardless of what may be said about research and verification.

Hence, whatever is said about referring to history in order to evaluate the accounts given in the Qur'ān cannot be admitted on the basis of the scientific rules adopted by people, let alone by Islam which states clearly that the Qur'ān is the final arbiter. Such reference to history cannot be advocated by a believer in the Qur'ān or in scientific research. It is no more than useless polemic.

A Policy of Justice for All

Some people, then, asked God's Messenger about Dhu'l-Qarnayn, and God revealed to him what this *sūrah* contains about his history and actions. We have no source other than the Qur'ān to give us further information. Hence, we will not try to expand or elaborate, because that would not be based on any accurate information. Commentaries on the Qur'ān provide many accounts and plenty of information, but none of these has any reliable basis. Hence, they should be approached very cautiously, particularly because they include Israelite reports and other legends.

Of the history of Dhu'l-Qarnayn the Qur'ān mentions three journeys, one to the west, one to the east and the third to a place described as an area 'between two mountains'. Let us now consider this Qur'ānic account.

The story of Dhu'l-Qarnayn, as given in this *sūrah*, begins with a brief introduction of the man himself: *"We established his power on earth, and gave him means to achieve anything."* (Verse 84) God then has established his power on earth, giving him uncontested authority. He has also given him the means of government and victory, the facilities to build civilization, enjoy the blessings God has made available to mankind, and all that make human life on earth steady and prosperous.

So he followed a certain way." (Verse 85) Thus, he went along one way which was made easy for him, aiming westwards: *"When he came to the setting of the sun, it appeared to him that it was setting in dark, turbid waters; and nearby he found a certain people. 'Dhu'l-Qarnayn,' We said, 'you may either punish them or treat them with kindness.' He replied: 'The one who does wrong we shall punish. Then he will return to his Lord and be sternly punished by Him. But the one who believes and does righteous deeds shall have a goodly reward, and we shall assign to him a task that is easy to fulfil.'* (Verses 86–88)

Reaching the setting of the sun means the place where a person feels that the sun sets beyond the horizon. This varies according to geographic location. In some places we may feel that the sun sets beyond a mountain, while in others we feel that it goes down into the water, as is the case when we look at the sea or ocean. In other places still, the sun seems to set in the sand, as when we are in a desert with no hills or mountains around.

It appears from the text that Dhu'l-Qarnayn went westwards until he reached a point on the Atlantic coast which people believed to be at the end of dry land. He saw the sun setting in the sea. It is even more likely that this was at a river mouth, where there would be plenty of weeds and the area muddy. Little lakes form in such situations and may look like water springs. He saw the sun setting there, going down in a spring of murky water. But it is impossible for us to define the area, because the *sūrah* does not give us any clue. We have no other reliable source. Hence, every view other than this cannot be considered accurate because it has no reliable basis.

At this lake of turbid and murky waters, Dhu'l-Qarnayn found a community and God gave him a choic'e: "*Dhu'l-Qarnayn, We said, you may either punish them or treat them with kindness.*" (Verse 86) Now, how did God say this to Dhu'l-Qarnayn? Was it revelation, or a mere statement of the situation, resulting from the fact that God had given him power over those people, so that he could determine whatever he wished to do with them. In this case, it would be just as if it was said to him: Here they are at your command: you may choose to punish them or to follow a lenient course of action. Both are possible. There is nothing to stop us understanding the text in either way. What is important to realize is that Dhu'l-Qarnayn declared his policy in the areas that came under his rule and their population became subject to his authority.

> *He replied: 'The one who does wrong we shall punish. Then he will return to his Lord and be sternly punished by Him. But the one who believes and does righteous deeds shall have a goodly reward, and we shall assign to him a task that is easy to fulfil.'* (Verses 87–88)

This is a declaration that those who transgress the bounds of justice will be subject to their own punishment in this life. Then they will return to their Lord who is certain to inflict on them severe punishment that has no parallel in what is known in human life. On the other hand, pious and true believers will receive kindly treatment, generous reward, honour and help in all their affairs.

These are the outlines of just and good government. A true believer should receive from rulers every sort of kindly treatment and generous reward, while transgressors who are unjust to their fellow human beings should be punished severely. When those who do well in the community, pursuing a fair line of action in all their pursuits, receive a good reward for their actions, and when the unjust and oppressors receive a fair punishment and humiliation, then the whole community is motivated to follow the line of goodness. But when matters go wrong, and the unjust, oppressor and corrupt people are the ones who enjoy favour with the ruler, while those who are good and fair are persecuted, then the ruler's power becomes no more than a tool of corruption and misery for the whole community. Nothing remains fair. The whole society sinks into chaos.

After Dhu'l-Qarnayn's return from his westward journey he took his way eastward. Again we realize that his authority was well established, and that all means were made available to him:

> *Then he followed another way and [marched eastwards] till, when he came to the rising of the sun, he found that it was rising on a people for whom We had provided no coverings against it. So he did; and We had full knowledge of all the means available to him.* (Verses 89–91)

What we said about the setting of the sun is also true of its rising place. What is meant here is the point where it rises in the east as we look up beyond the horizon. Again the Qur'ān does not define the place. It simply describes it and the situation of the people Dhu'l-Qarnayn found there: *"When he came to the rising of the sun, he found that it was rising on a people for whom We had provided no coverings against it."* (Verse 90) This suggests that the land was open, unscreened from the sun by any hills or trees. Thus when the sun rose, the people were directly exposed to it. This description applies to deserts and vast plateaus. It does not specify a particular location. All that we say is that it is likely that this place was in the far east, where the sun rose over its open, flat land. It might have also been on the east coast of Africa.

Another probability is that the description, *'for whom We had provided no covering against it,'* means that those people were always in the nude and did not employ clothing. Hence, they were not screened from the sun.

Since Dhu'l-Qarnayn had announced his policy of government, the *sūrah* does not repeat it here. Nor is any further action mentioned because God is fully aware of his intention and behaviour.

It is important, however, to reflect very briefly here on an artistic touch in the image provided. The scene portrayed for us is open and clear: a blazing sun which is in no way screened from the people.

Similarly, Dhu'l-Qarnayn's conscience and intentions are open, known fully to God Almighty. This provides harmony between the natural scene and man's conscience in the inimitable style of the Qur'ān.

A Barrier against Evil Forces

Then he followed yet another way and [marched on] till, when he reached a place between the two mountain-barriers he found beneath them a people who could scarcely understand a word. 'Dhu'l-Qarnayn,' they said, 'Gog and Magog are ravaging this land. May we pay you a tribute so that you erect a barrier between us and them?' He answered: 'That with which my Lord has established me is better [than any tribute]. Hence, do but help me with strength, and I shall erect a rampart between you and them! Bring me blocks of iron!' At length, when he had filled up the gap between the two mountain-sides, he said: 'Ply your bellows!' Then, when he made [the iron glow like] fire, he said: 'Bring me molten copper which I will pour over it.' And thus their enemies were unable to scale [the rampart], nor could they dig their way through it. He said: 'This is a mercy from my Lord. Yet when the time appointed by my Lord shall come, He will make this [rampart] level with the ground. My Lord's promise always comes true.' (Verses 92–98)

Now we come to the third of Dhu'l-Qarnayn's journeys which took him to a place *'between the two mountain-barriers.'* We cannot make any definite suggestion as to the exact location of this place, nor do we have any information about the nature of these barriers. All that we can understand from the text is that he reached a place lying in between two natural or man-made barriers, separated by a gap or low passage. Down there he found some backward people, whom the Qur'ān describes as *'could scarcely understand a word.'*

These people realized that Dhu'l-Qarnayn was both powerful and able. They also discovered that he was pious and God-fearing. Hence, they offered him payment in return for erecting a barrier to stop Gog and Magog, who frequently attacked them from beyond the mountain barriers and used the passage in between, from wreaking havoc in their land. These people had exhausted all the means available to them, yet still they could not repel those evil forces. Hence they were prepared to pay for a solution to their problem utilizing Dhu'l-Qarnayn's power.

Following the policy declared by that pious ruler, which was based on resisting all evil and corruption on earth, he declined to take their money, and offered instead to erect the barrier without charge. He judged that the easiest way to do so was to close the passage between the two mountain-barriers. However, he asked the backward people to help him by employing their physical strength: *"Help me with strength, and I shall erect a rampart between you and them! Bring me blocks of iron!"* (Verses 95–96) They began to gather whatever blocks of iron were available. He put all these blocks in a heap to close the gap between the two barriers, so that the two mountain-sides became like two crusts covering a heap of iron articles in between.

"At length, when he had filled up the gap between the two mountain-sides," (Verse 96) and the heap of iron was as high as the top of the two barriers, *"he said: Ply your bellows!"* (Verse 96) They were to generate air to increase the fire which heated the iron. *"Then, when he made [the iron glow like] fire, he said: 'Bring me molten copper which I will pour over it.'"* (Verse 96) The molten copper thus filled the gaps between the iron blocks, making the new barrier impregnable.

This method has recently been used in strengthening iron by adding a percentage of copper to it, thereby reinforcing it. It is to this fact that God guided Dhu'l-Qarnayn, recording the fact in His book many centuries before it was discovered by human science.

Thus the two natural barriers joined together with the man-made one, and the gap through which Gog and Magog launched their attacks was completely sealed. Hence, *"Their enemies were unable to scale [the rampart]"* by climbing it. *"Nor could they dig their way through it,"* to resume their attacks. For the first time, those vulnerable, backward people felt secure in their land.[2]

---

2. A wall was discovered close to the city of Tirmidh in central Asia, and was mentioned by a German and a Spanish historian who passed by it early in the fifteenth century. They referred to Bāb Al-Ḥadīd, meaning 'the iron door', and which can be found between Samarqand and India. This may be the wall built by Dhu'l-Qarnayn.

Dhu'l-Qarnayn looked at the great work which he accomplished, yet experienced neither pride nor conceit. Nor was he elated by this edifice which testified to both his power and knowledge. Rather, he remembered God and thanked Him, acknowledging that it was He who guided him to what work should be done, and that his own power was granted to him by God, and that future events would take place according to His will. He also declared his belief that all mountains, walls and barriers are certain to be levelled before the Day of Judgement so that the whole earth will be flat. He said: "*This is a mercy from my Lord. Yet when the time appointed by my Lord shall come, He will make this [rampart] level with the ground. My Lord's promise always comes true.*" (Verse 98)

Thus ends this passage which relates part of the history of Dhu'l-Qarnayn, a good example of a pious ruler who is given power and secure position as well as other means and facilities. He goes with his armies east and west, but he does not tyrannize or show conceit. Nor does he consider his conquering of other people's lands a means to exploit individuals, communities and countries in order to ensure a luxurious life for himself or his people. He does not treat the vanquished people as slaves, making them the means for his self-aggrandisement. On the contrary, he spreads justice, assists the weak and backward, ensures that no aggression is launched against them, and charges nothing for his services. He utilizes the power God granted him in building proper and secure communities where everyone gets what rightfully belongs to him. He then attributes every good work he does to the grace of God, claiming no part of it for himself. Even at the height of his power, he does not forget God's power and that to Him he certainly shall return.

The Truth about Gog and Magog

Now who were Gog and Magog? Where are they now? What did they do and what will happen to them? Such questions are very difficult to answer with any degree of accuracy. Our knowledge of them is limited to what is mentioned specifically in the Qur'ān and in authentic *aḥādīth*. The Qur'ān includes here a quotation of what Dhu'l-Qarnayn says: "*Yet when the time appointed by my Lord shall come, He will make this [rampart] level with the ground. My Lord's promise always comes true.*" (Verse 98) This statement does not specify a time. God's promise to destroy the rampart may already have occurred when the Tatars swept across huge areas, destroying whole kingdoms.

Another mention of them is found in *Sūrah* 21, The Prophets, where it is stated: "*When Gog and Magog are let loose and swarm down from every corner, when the true promise draws close [to its fulfilment], staring in horror shall be the eyes of the unbelievers.*" (21: 96–97) Again this statement does not specify a time for the promised appearance of Gog and Magog. That God's promise has come near to fulfilment, in the sense that the Last Hour or the Day of Judgement is soon to come, is an accomplished fact ever since the time of the Prophet. In the Qur'ān we read: "*The Hour has drawn near, and the moon was cleft asunder.*" (54: 1) In God's reckoning, time has a totally different perspective from that of human reckoning. The time gap between the moment when the Hour becomes near and its actual occurrence may stretch to millions of years or centuries. Thus human beings may see this as a very long period of time, while, by God's standards, it may signify nothing more than a blink of an eye.

This means that the rampart built by Dhu'l-Qarnayn might have been penetrated in the period that has lapsed between the revelation of the verse stating, '*the Hour has drawn near,*' and our present day. This suggests that the conquests of the Tatars in the eastern provinces might have represented a sort of fulfilment of the warning which tells of Gog and Magog forging ahead and sweeping across the earth. An authentic *hadīth* related by Imām Aḥmad ibn Ḥanbal on the authority of Zainab bint Jaḥsh, the Prophet's wife, mentions that the Prophet woke up once, red in the face, saying: "Woe to the Arabs! A calamitous event is drawing near. The rampart of Gog and Magog has been breached today by as much as this, [rounding his thumb with his first finger]." I said, "Messenger of God! Would we be destroyed when righteous people are living among us?" He said: "Yes, if evil becomes widespread."

The Prophet's dream occurred more than thirteen and a half centuries ago. The conquests of the Tatars took place subsequently, destroying the 'Abbāsid Caliphate. It was Hülegü who destroyed it, ending the reign of al-Musta'ṣim, the last 'Abbāsid Caliph. This might have been the realization of the Prophet's dream. But true knowledge belongs to God. All that we say in this respect is by way of probability, not certainty.

Deaf and Blind

The *sūrah* follows the reference by Dhu'l-Qarnayn to God's true promise with a scene from the Day of Judgement:

On that day We shall leave them to surge like waves dashing against one another. The trumpet will be blown, and We shall gather them all together. And We shall, on that day, present hell, all spread out, for the unbelievers, who have turned a blind eye to My admonition and a deaf ear to My warning. (Verses 99–101)

This is a scene showing the movement of huge masses of people of all colours, races and geographical areas, belonging to all generations and times, after they have been resurrected and brought back to life. They move across in a chaotic way, unaware of what is around them. They push each other like waves in the sea and mix like the surf raised by the waves. Then suddenly a trumpet is blown and they are gathered according to a specific order: "*The trumpet will be blown, and We shall gather them all together.*" (Verse 99)

We see also the unbelievers who turned away from remembrance of God as though their eyes were covered and their ears deaf. Now we see them with hell brought before them and they cannot turn away from it as they used to turn away from God's guidance. On that day, the option of turning away is not within their power. The cover over their eyes has been drawn, and they now see clearly the consequence of their deliberate turning away. This is a fair recompense.

The *sūrah* provides symmetry between their turning away and their vision of hell as it is brought before them. The two actions are shown in contrast both in scene and movement.

This contrast is followed by a comment full of derision: "*Do the unbelievers think that they could take My creatures for patrons against Me? We have indeed readied hell as a dwelling place for the unbelievers.*"

313

(Verse 102) Do these unbelievers think that they can choose from among God's creatures which fully submit to Him some who could support them against God? Can these give them help or grant them protection against God's might? If such thoughts are entertained by them, then let them experience the results of such self-delusion: "*We have indeed readied hell as a dwelling place for the unbelievers.*" (Verse 102) This is an evil abode already prepared to receive them. There is no need for waiting. It is all ready to receive its unbelieving dwellers.

Deceptive Thoughts of Bad Action

The *sūrah* concludes with a few verses that bring together its many different lines of discussion in harmonious tone and rhythm. We have here three different aspects which, together, sum up the whole theme of the *sūrah*. The first of these revolves around values and standards as they are reflected in deviant societies and as they truly are. These relate to both actions and people.

> *Say: 'Shall we tell you who are the greatest losers in whatever they may do? It is they whose labour in this world has been misguided, and who nonetheless think that what they do is right. It is they who have chosen to disbelieve in their Lord's revelations and deny the truth that they will meet Him. Vain will be their works. No weight shall We assign to them on Resurrection Day.'* (Verses 103–105)

"*Shall we tell you who are the greatest losers in whatever they may do?*" (Verse 103) These are the ones whose loss cannot be exceeded by any human being in history. The answer to this question comes very quickly. "*It is they whose labour in this world has been misguided.*" (Verse 104) It did not lead them to follow any proper guidance. It did not yield any real fruit, nor did it achieve any objective. But these people "*nonetheless think that what they do is right.*" (Verse 104) This tells how misguided these people are. They have no inclination that whatever they do in this world takes them further into error and is thus completely wasted. Hence, they continue spending their whole lives in such vain pursuits.

Now the listeners are asked whether they want to know who these people are. The question heightens their curiosity, holding the attentions of everyone within hearing range. Then when everyone eagerly anticipates the information, the identity of these unrivalled losers is revealed: "*It is they who have chosen to disbelieve in their Lord's revelations and deny the truth that they will meet Him. Vain will be their works.*" (Verse 105) The linguistic sense imparted by the Arabic term, *habitat*, describing their actions as 'vain' is derived from a very special case. It is that of an animal feeding on poisonous grass. Its belly is swollen before it dies. The same is the case with the actions of those who are misguided. They grow and seem fair and rewarding, but the fact is that they come to nothing whatsoever.

"*No weight shall We assign to them on Resurrection Day.*" (Verse 105) Thus they are shown to be worthless, having no value in the scale of true standards and principles. This is their condition 'on Resurrection Day'. But they only have the requital they deserve. "*That will be their reward, hell, for having rejected the faith, and made My revelations and My messengers a target of their mockery.*" (Verse 106)

Contrast in the scene is given by showing how the believers fare and what their value score is on the true scales used on the Day of Judgement. "*But those who have faith and do righteous deeds shall have the gardens of paradise as their dwelling place. Therein they will abide, and never will they desire any change to befall them.*" (Verses 107–108) This abode in the gardens of paradise is contrasted here with the other abode in hell. The gulf between the two is colossal.

There is also here a fine reference to human nature and its appreciation of pleasure and enjoyment. This is expressed in the sentence, '*never will they desire any change to befall them.*' (Verse 108) We need to reflect a little on this statement which assures us that the believers are to dwell in paradise permanently. By nature however human beings are bored with any state that continues *ad infinitum*. When they are satisfied that the blessings they enjoy are permanent, they are no longer keen to preserve them, seeking changes instead.

This is how human nature is made, and for a definite purpose. Moreover, this is more suited to the role assigned to man in this life, placing him in charge of the earth. This role requires developing human life so as to achieve the level of perfection God in His wisdom has determined for it. Hence, He has made man a creature who loves change, discovery and movement from one stage, place or scene to another. This aspiration enables man to move on, to change things in his life, to discover new things as also reinvent his social system. In this way, man's whole life changes and develops. It continues to progress gradually until it achieves its best level of perfection.

At the same time, human nature loves what is familiar and tries to preserve customs and traditions. However, this is kept at a degree that does not obstruct progress or prevent the development of thought or new ideas. The two trends achieve a balance which ensures progress. Every time the balance is disturbed so as to impose stagnation, it is followed by a revolt which gives new momentum in the opposite direction. This may even exceed the limits of moderation. The best periods in human life are those which achieve an equilibrium between the driving force and social controls, and between motivation and restraint. Should stagnation persist, it heralds a retreat in social conditions and a slow death in the life of both individuals and the community.

Such is the nature that is more suitable for human life on earth. In heaven, which is the world of absolute perfection, there is no duty and responsibility commensurate with human nature. Should people retain their nature that fits their life on earth while living in the permanent and self-renewing bliss of heaven, they will, in time, feel exceedingly bored with it. Heaven will become like a prison and its dwellers will seek to leave it for a while, just to have a change, even though this may mean paying a visit to a place of misery. They will need such a departure from heaven to satisfy their innate and strong desire for change.

But the Creator, who knows well the nature of His creation, will change human desire so that when they are in heaven, they will not want to change or to leave. Instead, they will be keen to continue their lives there for as long as time stretches.

Preparing for a Meeting with the Lord

The second concluding element shows the limits of human knowledge when compared with God's infinite knowledge. As our imagination cannot reach the absolute, the Qur'ān gives us a simple analogy which we can easily comprehend, using its method of image drawing: "*Say: If the sea were ink for my Lord's words, the sea would surely dry up before my Lord's words are exhausted, even though we were to add to it another sea to replenish it.*" (Verse 109) The sea is the largest and richest thing known to mankind. People use ink to write down whatever they want to record. This is how they document their knowledge which they imagine to be great. Hence the Qur'ān puts forward the image of the sea with all its vast expanse, but which is now made of ink with which to write down God's words that indicate His knowledge. Even though the whole sea is used, God's words are not finished. At this point another sea of similar magnitude is brought forward, but it too is used in full while God's words are far from finished.

It is with such a clear image and movement that the concept of the infinite is placed before the finite human intellect. A universal and abstract concept remains beyond human conception until it is described in specific terms. No matter how powerful a human being's ability to understand the abstract is, he needs to relate an abstract concept to images and shapes, types and characteristics. This applies to abstract concepts of what is limited or tangible. How then can it fathom what is unlimited and intangible?

Hence, the Qur'ān gives analogies and draws on similarities in order to give people images and scenes that describe the great concepts it wants them to understand. It often uses what is tangible, and what has shape and definite characteristics and recognizable features in the same way as is employed here. In this example, the sea represents human knowledge which people imagine to be great. But huge and rich as the seas and the oceans may be, they remain limited. God's words, on the other hand, represent His infinite knowledge for which people cannot set any limit. Indeed they cannot receive or record it all, let alone comprehend it.

Conceit may creep into the human soul as people are able to make new discoveries about themselves or about the universe. They are elated with these scientific discoveries feeling that they have achieved what there is to achieve, or at least are on the way to it. But when they look at the areas which remain unknown, they realize that they have only taken a few steps into the sea which remains so vast, stretching beyond the horizon. The fact remains that man's ability to receive and record

God's knowledge is very limited indeed, because it represents a relationship of what is finite and what is infinite.

Man may gain as much knowledge as he can, and he may discover much of the secrets of the universe, but he must never arrogantly boast about his knowledge. For the utmost that he can achieve is to transform the seas and oceans into ink, yet all that ink is insufficient to record God's words.

With such a comparison that shows man's knowledge to be extremely limited in relation to God's, the final touch in the *sūrah* paints the highest and noblest degree for man, which is that of recipient of God's final message. This again is something close and finite in relation to the limitless horizon our sight cannot reach:

> *Say: I am but a human being like yourselves. It has been revealed to me that your God is the One and only God. Hence, whoever expects to meet his Lord [on Judgement Day], let him do what is right, and in the worship due to his Lord admit no one as partner.* (Verse 110)

That is the ultimate horizon of Godhead. How does the horizon of prophethood compare with it, when it is, after all, a human horizon? *"Say: I am but a human being like yourselves. It has been revealed to me..."* I am a human being who receives something from that highest level. I get my knowledge from that inexhaustible source. Yet I am a human being who does not go beyond the guidance which I receive from my Lord. I am a human being who is taught something, learns it and then teaches it to others. Whoever aspires to a position close to this height must first of all benefit by whatever he or she learns from God's Messenger. They must also utilize the only means that leads there: *"Whoever expects to meet his Lord [on Judgement Day], let him do what is right, and in the worship due to his Lord admit no one as a partner."* (Verse 110) This is the passport to that splendid meeting.

Thus ends the *sūrah* which began by mentioning revelation and the oneness of God, utilizing themes and tones that gradually grow more and more profound until they reach this final climax. It is a distinguished beat which generates all the tunes in the splendid music of faith.

SŪRAH 19

Maryam
(Mary)

Prologue

The central theme of this *sūrah* focuses on God's oneness, rejecting all concepts and ideas assigning a son or a partner to Him. It also touches on the important issue of resurrection, intertwined as it is with the concept of God's oneness. In this, the *sūrah* follows the same pattern as most, if not all, *sūrahs* revealed in Makkah.

The *sūrah* explores its theme through several stories, beginning with that of Zachariah and his son, John, and follows this with the story of Mary and the birth of Jesus. We then have a part of Abraham's story with his father, followed by brief references to other prophets: Isaac, Jacob, Moses, Aaron, Ishmael, Idrīs, Adam and Noah. These stories take up nearly two-thirds of the *sūrah*, driving home the truth of God's oneness, resurrection, the non-existence of any children or partners with God. They also clearly outline the attitudes towards the prophets of those who follow guidance and those who go astray.

The *sūrah* also includes some scenes of the Day of Judgement, some arguments against those who deny resurrection, and a reference to the fate of the unbelievers who deny God's message, both in this life and in the life to come. All this fits perfectly with the drift of the stories the *sūrah* relates and reinforces its central theme. The *sūrah* has its distinctive atmosphere which permeates through all its accounts and pervades its themes.

The *sūrah* portrays a full range of reaction and feeling within the human soul as also within the universe around it. This world which we imagine to be senseless is shown to have a soul of its own capable of sense and feeling. This adds to the general atmosphere of the *sūrah* as we see the heavens, the earth and the mountains in anger, reacting so strongly as to almost be rent asunder or levelled down. All this because *"people should ascribe a son to the Most Merciful, although it is inconceivable that the Most Merciful should take to Himself a son."* (Verses 91–92) Reactions within the human soul are shown throughout the *sūrah* from start to finish. Its main stories are full of such reactions, particularly in that of Mary and the birth of Jesus.

The *sūrah* has a distinctive ambience of compassion, contentedness and direct relation with God. It opens with an account of the grace God bestowed on Zachariah, and how he addressed God in a secret appeal: *"This is an account of the grace which your Lord bestowed on His servant Zachariah: when he called out to his Lord in the secrecy of his heart."* (Verses 2–3) The words of grace, compassion and their synonyms are frequently mentioned throughout the *sūrah*, together with God's attributes of beneficence and mercy. The happiness the believers will enjoy in the life to come is described as love: *"As for those who believe and do righteous deeds, God will certainly bestow love on them."* (Verse 96) Among the favours God bestowed on John is that he was compassionate: *"We granted him wisdom while he was still a youth, as well as, by Our grace, compassion and purity; and he was [always] righteous."* (Verses 12–13) Similarly, Jesus was, by the grace of God, dutiful to his mother, gentle and friendly in his manners: *"He has made me kind to my mother, not haughty or bereft of grace."* (Verse 32)

We indeed feel God's abounding grace extending over all human life in the vocabulary and sentence structure of the *sūrah*. We also feel that the whole universe shudders to the sound of the preposterous claims that God has partners. For the universe cannot countenance such absurdity. We recognize that the *sūrah* has a distinctive musical rhythm and tempo. Even the sound of its vocabulary and the words ending its verses impart a clear sense of ease. Where the context requires firmness, such verse-endings have a doubled, voiced sound of either the plosive or fricative variety, to enhance the impression of firmness or power.

The *sūrah* provides good examples of variations in cadence, verse-endings and rhymes according to the subject being discussed and the overall atmosphere. At the start, when the *sūrah* relates its account of the prophets Zachariah and John, the verses rhyme with the syllable, 'ya' giving a medium vowel at the end. The same rhyme is maintained throughout the story of Mary and Jesus as well as the brief accounts of other prophets that follow. When these accounts are concluded, the *sūrah* comments on the truth about Jesus, son of Mary, with the final verdict on his sonship. Here we have a different kind of verse-ending where words with a long 'ee' or 'oo' vowel are followed by a nasal 'm' or 'n' giving the impression of a settled and final matter.

When this is complete, the *sūrah* resumes its accounts of earlier prophets commencing with Abraham and his father. The earlier, easy and gentle rhyme is picked up again until the *sūrah* begins its discussion of the punishment that awaits those who reject the truth and oppose God's message and messengers. Here the cadence becomes stronger, and the rhyme changes to be a medium vowel 'a' preceded by the voiced, plosive 'd' sound. When the attitude of the unbelievers comes in for criticism and denunciation, the rhythm becomes even more powerful, reflected by a doubled 'd' sound for the rhyme. Thus the *sūrah* provides a perfect example of manipulated rhyme and rhythm such that it is in flawless harmony with the overall meaning and atmosphere. Both contribute to the general ambience of the *sūrah* as it moves with perfect ease from one subject to another.

The whole *sūrah* may be divided into three parts. The first includes the story of Zachariah and his son John, together with the story of Mary and her son Jesus, culminating in a comment that gives the final verdict on Jesus whose birth and nature were the subject of much controversy among both the Jews and Christians.

The second part includes an episode from Abraham's life story, in which he dissociated himself from the beliefs of his idolatrous community. It tells how God compensated him with offspring that brought a whole nation into being. It includes brief references to other prophets, those who followed their guidance and those who erred in succeeding generations, explaining the ultimate destiny of both groups. It ends with a declaration that Lordship in the universe is one and the Lord must be worshipped without association of partners with Him: *"He is the Lord of the heavens and the earth and all that is between them. Worship Him alone, then, and remain steadfast in His worship. Do you know any whose name is worthy to be mentioned side by side with His?"* (Verse 65)

The final part begins with the arguments advanced about resurrection, portraying some scenes from the Day of Judgement. It provides an image of the rejection of all polytheistic claims by the whole universe. It ends with a highly effective scene of the doom of earlier communities: *"How many a generation have We destroyed before their time! Can you find a single one of them [now], or hear so much as a whisper of them?"* (Verse 98)

I

God's Unbridled Will

Maryam (Mary)

In the Name of God, the Merciful, the Beneficent

Kāf. Hā. Yā. 'Ayn. Ṣād. (1)

This is an account of the grace which your Lord bestowed on His servant Zachariah: (2)

when he called out to his Lord in the secrecy of his heart, (3)

he prayed: 'My Lord! Feeble have become my bones, and my head glistens with grey hair. But never, my Lord, has my prayer to You remained unanswered. (4)

Now, I fear [what] my kinsmen [will do] after I am gone, for my wife is barren. Bestow, then, upon me, out of Your grace, a successor (5)

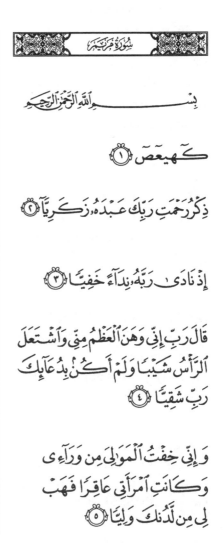

who will be my heir as well as an heir of the House of Jacob; and make him, my Lord, one with whom You are pleased.' (6)

يَرِثُنِى وَيَرِثُ مِنْ ءَالِ يَعْقُوبَ وَٱجْعَلْهُ رَبِّ رَضِيًّا ٦

'Zachariah! We bring you the happy news of [the birth of] a son whose name shall be John. Never have We given this name to anyone before him.' (7)

يَٰزَكَرِيَّآ إِنَّا نُبَشِّرُكَ بِغُلَٰمٍ ٱسْمُهُۥ يَحْيَىٰ لَمْ نَجْعَل لَّهُۥ مِن قَبْلُ سَمِيًّا ٧

[Zachariah] said: 'My Lord! How can I have a son when my wife is barren, and I am well advanced in years?' (8)

قَالَ رَبِّ أَنَّىٰ يَكُونُ لِى غُلَٰمٌ وَكَانَتِ ٱمْرَأَتِى عَاقِرًا وَقَدْ بَلَغْتُ مِنَ ٱلْكِبَرِ عِتِيًّا ٨

He said: 'Thus it is. Your Lord says, "This is easy for Me; even as I had earlier created you when you were nothing."' (9)

قَالَ كَذَٰلِكَ قَالَ رَبُّكَ هُوَ عَلَىَّ هَيِّنٌ وَقَدْ خَلَقْتُكَ مِن قَبْلُ وَلَمْ تَكُ شَيْئًا ٩

[Zachariah] said: 'My Lord! Give me a sign.' He replied: 'Your sign will be that for full three nights [and days] you will not speak to people.' (10)

قَالَ رَبِّ ٱجْعَل لِّىٓ ءَايَةً قَالَ ءَايَتُكَ أَلَّا تُكَلِّمَ ٱلنَّاسَ ثَلَٰثَ لَيَالٍ سَوِيًّا ١٠

He then came out to his people from the sanctuary and signified to them [by gesture] to extol God's limitless glory by day and by night. (11)

فَخَرَجَ عَلَىٰ قَوْمِهِۦ مِنَ ٱلْمِحْرَابِ فَأَوْحَىٰٓ إِلَيْهِمْ أَن سَبِّحُواْ بُكْرَةً وَعَشِيًّا ١١

[To his son We said]: 'John! Hold fast to the book with [all your] strength.' We granted him wisdom while he was still a youth, (12)

يَـٰيَحْيَىٰ خُذِ ٱلْكِتَـٰبَ بِقُوَّةٍ وَءَاتَيْنَـٰهُ ٱلْحُكْمَ صَبِيًّا ﴿١٢﴾

as well as, by Our grace, compassion and purity; and he was [always] righteous, (13)

وَحَنَانًا مِّن لَّدُنَّا وَزَكَوٰةً وَكَانَ تَقِيًّا ﴿١٣﴾

and kind to his parents. Never was he haughty or rebellious. (14)

وَبَرًّۢا بِوَٰلِدَيْهِ وَلَمْ يَكُن جَبَّارًا عَصِيًّا ﴿١٤﴾

So peace was upon him on the day he was born, and on the day of his death, and will be on the day when he shall be raised to life again. (15)

وَسَلَـٰمٌ عَلَيْهِ يَوْمَ وُلِدَ وَيَوْمَ يَمُوتُ وَيَوْمَ يُبْعَثُ حَيًّا ﴿١٥﴾

Relate in the book [the story of] Mary and how she withdrew from her family to a place in the east, (16)

وَٱذْكُرْ فِى ٱلْكِتَـٰبِ مَرْيَمَ إِذِ ٱنتَبَذَتْ مِنْ أَهْلِهَا مَكَانًا شَرْقِيًّا ﴿١٦﴾

where she kept herself in seclusion from them. We, then, sent to her Our angel, who appeared to her in the shape of a well-made human being. (17)

فَٱتَّخَذَتْ مِن دُونِهِمْ حِجَابًا فَأَرْسَلْنَآ إِلَيْهَا رُوحَنَا فَتَمَثَّلَ لَهَا بَشَرًا سَوِيًّا ﴿١٧﴾

She said: 'May the Most Merciful protect me from you. [Do not come near me] if you fear God.' (18)

قَالَتْ إِنِّىٓ أَعُوذُ بِٱلرَّحْمَـٰنِ مِنكَ إِن كُنتَ تَقِيًّا ﴿١٨﴾

'I am but an emissary of your Lord,' he said, '[and have come] to give you a son endowed with purity.' (19)

قَالَ إِنَّمَا أَنَا۠ رَسُولُ رَبِّكِ لِأَهَبَ لَكِ غُلَامًا زَكِيًّا ﴿١٩﴾

She said: 'How shall I have a child when no man has ever touched me and I have never been a loose woman?' (20)

قَالَتْ أَنَّىٰ يَكُونُ لِي غُلَامٌ وَلَمْ يَمْسَسْنِي بَشَرٌ وَلَمْ أَكُ بَغِيًّا ﴿٢٠﴾

He answered: 'Thus did your Lord speak: This is easy for Me. We will make him a sign for mankind and an act of grace from Us. It is a matter [We have] decreed.' (21)

قَالَ كَذَٰلِكِ قَالَ رَبُّكِ هُوَ عَلَيَّ هَيِّنٌ وَلِنَجْعَلَهُ ءَايَةً لِّلنَّاسِ وَرَحْمَةً مِّنَّا وَكَانَ أَمْرًا مَّقْضِيًّا ﴿٢١﴾

So she conceived him, and retired to a far-off place. (22)

فَحَمَلَتْهُ فَٱنتَبَذَتْ بِهِۦ مَكَانًا قَصِيًّا ﴿٢٢﴾

And the throes of childbirth drove her to the trunk of a palm-tree. [In her anguish] she cried: 'Would that I had died before this and passed into complete oblivion!' (23)

فَأَجَآءَهَا ٱلْمَخَاضُ إِلَىٰ جِذْعِ ٱلنَّخْلَةِ قَالَتْ يَٰلَيْتَنِي مِتُّ قَبْلَ هَٰذَا وَكُنتُ نَسْيًا مَّنسِيًّا ﴿٢٣﴾

But [a voice] from below called out to her: 'Do not give in to grief. Your Lord has provided a brook running beneath you. (24)

فَنَادَىٰهَا مِن تَحْتِهَآ أَلَّا تَحْزَنِي قَدْ جَعَلَ رَبُّكِ تَحْتَكِ سَرِيًّا ﴿٢٤﴾

And if you shake the trunk of the palm tree towards you, it will drop you fresh ripe dates. (25)

وَهُزِّي إِلَيْكِ بِجِذْعِ ٱلنَّخْلَةِ تُسَٰقِطْ عَلَيْكِ رُطَبًا جَنِيًّا ﴿٢٥﴾

So eat and drink and be happy. Should you see any human being, just convey this to him: "I have vowed a fast to the Most Merciful and will not speak today to any human being." (26)

فَكُلِى وَٱشْرَبِى وَقَرِّى عَيْنًا فَإِمَّا تَرَيِنَّ مِنَ ٱلْبَشَرِ أَحَدًا فَقُولِى إِنِّى نَذَرْتُ لِلرَّحْمَٰنِ صَوْمًا فَلَنْ أُكَلِّمَ ٱلْيَوْمَ إِنسِيًّا ۝

At length, she went to her people carrying the child. They said: 'Mary, you have indeed done an amazing thing! (27)

فَأَتَتْ بِهِۦ قَوْمَهَا تَحْمِلُهُۥ قَالُوٓا۟ يَٰمَرْيَمُ لَقَدْ جِئْتِ شَيْئًا فَرِيًّا ۝

Sister of Aaron, your father was not a wicked man, nor was your mother a loose woman!' (28)

يَٰٓأُخْتَ هَٰرُونَ مَا كَانَ أَبُوكِ ٱمْرَأَ سَوْءٍ وَمَا كَانَتْ أُمُّكِ بَغِيًّا ۝

But she pointed to the child. They said: 'How can we talk to a babe in the cradle?' (29)

فَأَشَارَتْ إِلَيْهِ قَالُوا۟ كَيْفَ نُكَلِّمُ مَن كَانَ فِى ٱلْمَهْدِ صَبِيًّا ۝

Whereupon he said: 'I am a servant of God. He has vouchsafed to me revelations and made me a prophet, (30)

قَالَ إِنِّى عَبْدُ ٱللَّهِ ءَاتَىٰنِىَ ٱلْكِتَٰبَ وَجَعَلَنِى نَبِيًّا ۝

and made me blessed wherever I may be. He has enjoined on me prayer and charity as long as I live. (31)

وَجَعَلَنِى مُبَارَكًا أَيْنَ مَا كُنتُ وَأَوْصَٰنِى بِٱلصَّلَوٰةِ وَٱلزَّكَوٰةِ مَا دُمْتُ حَيًّا ۝

He has made me kind to my mother, not haughty or bereft of grace. (32)

وَبَرًّۢا بِوَٰلِدَتِى وَلَمْ يَجْعَلْنِى جَبَّارًا شَقِيًّا ۝

Peace was on me on the day when I was born, and [will be on me] on the day of my death and on the day when I shall be raised to life again.' (33)

وَٱلسَّلَـٰمُ عَلَيَّ يَوْمَ وُلِدتُّ وَيَوْمَ أَمُوتُ وَيَوْمَ أُبْعَثُ حَيًّا ۝

Such was, in the words of truth, Jesus the son of Mary, about whose nature they still dispute. (34)

ذَٰلِكَ عِيسَى ٱبْنُ مَرْيَمَ قَوْلَ ٱلْحَقِّ ٱلَّذِي فِيهِ يَمْتَرُونَ ۝

It is not conceivable that God should beget a son. Limitless is He in His glory! When He wills a thing to be, He only says to it, 'Be,' and it is. (35)

مَا كَانَ لِلَّهِ أَن يَتَّخِذَ مِن وَلَدٍ سُبْحَـٰنَهُ إِذَا قَضَىٰ أَمْرًا فَإِنَّمَا يَقُولُ لَهُۥ كُن فَيَكُونُ ۝

God is my Lord and your Lord; so worship Him alone. That is a straight path.' (36)

وَإِنَّ ٱللَّهَ رَبِّي وَرَبُّكُمْ فَٱعْبُدُوهُ هَـٰذَا صِرَٰطٌ مُّسْتَقِيمٌ ۝

Yet are the sects at variance among themselves. Woe, then, to the unbelievers when a momentous day arrives. (37)

فَٱخْتَلَفَ ٱلْأَحْزَابُ مِنۢ بَيْنِهِمْ فَوَيْلٌ لِّلَّذِينَ كَفَرُوا۟ مِن مَّشْهَدِ يَوْمٍ عَظِيمٍ ۝

How well they will hear and see on the day they will appear before Us. Truly the wrongdoers are today in evident error. (38)

أَسْمِعْ بِهِمْ وَأَبْصِرْ يَوْمَ يَأْتُونَنَا لَـٰكِنِ ٱلظَّـٰلِمُونَ ٱلْيَوْمَ فِي ضَلَـٰلٍ مُّبِينٍ ۝

Hence, warn them of the Day of Distress, when everything will have been determined while they remain heedless, persisting in unbelief. (39)

وَأَنذِرْهُمْ يَوْمَ الْحَسْرَةِ إِذْ قُضِيَ الْأَمْرُ وَهُمْ فِي غَفْلَةٍ وَهُمْ لَا يُؤْمِنُونَ ۝

We alone shall remain after the earth and all who live on it have passed away. To Us they shall all return. (40)

إِنَّا نَحْنُ نَرِثُ الْأَرْضَ وَمَنْ عَلَيْهَا وَإِلَيْنَا يُرْجَعُونَ ۝

A Passionate Prayer Answered

"*Kāf. Hā. Yā. 'Ayn. Ṣād.*" (Verse 1) These are separate letters of the Arabic alphabet. A number of *sūrahs* begin with such separate letters which we explain as being some of the letters used in the composition of the Qur'ān. Yet the Qur'ān has its unique, inimitable style, the like of which human beings can never produce, despite the fact that the same letters and words are available to them. They simply cannot devise any construction that even remotely approaches the style employed by the divine power that produced this Qur'ān.

Having mentioned these letters, the *sūrah* immediately begins the first story of Zachariah and John, in which compassion provides both the central idea and the overall atmosphere. Hence grace is mentioned at the outset: "*This is an account of the grace which your Lord bestowed on His servant Zachariah.*" (Verse 2) The story begins with a scene of earnest supplication by Zachariah in total secrecy:

When he called out to his Lord in the secrecy of his heart, he prayed: 'My Lord! Feeble have become my bones, and my head glistens with grey hair. But never, my Lord, has my prayer to You remained unanswered. Now, I fear [what] my kinsmen [will do] after I am gone, for my wife is barren. Bestow, then, upon me, out of Your grace, a successor who will be my heir as well as an heir of the House of Jacob; and make him, my Lord, one with whom You are pleased.' (Verses 3–6)

329

He is alone, addressing his appeal to God, away from watching eyes and listening ears. He wants to lay his troubled heart open before his Lord, recounting his worries. He addresses Him as if he were speaking to someone who is very close, without even using the Arabic address article, *Yā*. Needless to say, his Lord hears and sees, without the need to be addressed or called upon. But a person troubled by worries finds comfort in vocalizing his concern. Most Gracious as He is, God knows this to be part of human nature. Hence, He likes that His servants pray to Him, making a clean breast of all that worries them: "*Your Lord says: Pray to Me and I will answer you.*" (40: 60) When they do, they find relief from their heavy burden. They are reassured because they have assigned such burdens to the One who is more able and powerful. They feel that they are in contact with the Most Merciful who will not disappoint anyone who appeals to Him and relies on Him.

Zachariah complains to his Lord that his bones have become feeble, and when bones are feeble, the whole body is weak. After all, the bones are the stiffest part of the body. They form the skeleton which the muscles flesh up. He also complains that his head glistens with grey hair. The Qur'ānic expression here, *ishta 'ala al-ra'su shaybā*, shows the greyness of hair like a fire being ignited, and the man's head covered with this fire, so as to leave no black hair. Both feeble bones and grey hair signify old age and the weakness associated with it. It is this weakness that is the subject matter of Zachariah's complaint as he presents his case, and his hopes, to his Lord.

He then makes a clear acknowledgement: "*Never, my Lord, has my prayer to You remained unanswered.*" (Verse 4) He is used to having his prayers answered. He was not disappointed when he prayed to Him in his time of strength and vigour. Now in his old age and weakness, the need for his prayers to be answered is even more pressing.

Having presented his case, expressed his fears and hopes, he makes his request. The point is that he fears that those who will succeed him might not be up to looking after his heritage properly. Being one of the major prophets of the Children of Israel, Zachariah's heritage involved serving God's cause as well as looking after the people of his household. One of those was Mary whose upbringing was entrusted to him. She served in the sanctuary which he managed. Again his property, which he managed properly and spent on only good purposes, was among his concerns. His worry was that those who succeeded him might not follow the course he had charted, perhaps because he knew them not to be up to that task. "*Now, I fear [what] my kinsmen [will do] after I am gone.*" (Verse 5)

What added to his worries was the fact that he was childless: "*For my wife is barren.*" (Verse 5) She had given him no child to bring up and prepare as a successor. This was his concern. As for his hope, he requested that God grant him a successor who would properly manage and look after the heritage of Jacob's household, i.e. his ancestors: "*Bestow, then, upon me, out of Your grace, a successor who will be my heir as well as an heir of the House of Jacob.*" (Verses 5–6) Zachariah, a God-fearing prophet, does not forget to specify what he hopes this successor would be like: "*And make him, my Lord, one with whom You are pleased.*" (Verse 6) He should not be arrogant, tyrannical, or greedy. He should be one who is content with what God gives him. Such contentedness should furthermore spread a sense of ease and happiness all round.

A Child Is Born Against All Probability

The moment of truth comes: the prayer is answered, bringing with it God's grace and acceptance. It is the Lord Himself that calls out to His servant from His sublime presence: "*Zachariah!*" He immediately gives him the good news: "*We bring you the happy news of [the birth of] a son.*" (Verse 7) He bestows on him further kindness, by choosing for him the name of that son: "*Whose name shall be John.*" (Verse 7) This is a special name, not previously given to anyone: "*Never have We given this name to anyone before him.*" (Verse 7)

This is but an example of God's grace as it is given in abundance to His servant whose secret supplication was passionate, and which clearly expressed his fears and hopes. Zachariah's prayer was motivated by fear that his heirs would not be able to look after the heritage of the true faith properly. He feared that they would not fulfil the trust in a way that earns God's pleasure. Hence, God bestowed on him what corresponded to his good intention.

Zachariah, who was deeply involved in his supplication, passionately expressing his desire and urging his case, was suddenly alerted by this speedy answer to his prayer. The reality stares him in the face: he is well advanced in years, his bones feeble, his hair completely grey, and his wife barren, having given him no child when he was in his prime. How is he to have a child of his own? He wants to be reassured and to know the means by which God will give him this son: *"My Lord! How can I have a son when my wife is barren, and I am well advanced in years?"* (Verse 8)

He is facing the reality, as well as God's promise. He certainly trusts that God's promise will be fulfilled. He only wants reassurance and to know how, considering his circumstances, the fulfilment will take place. That would give him much needed reassurance. It is a perfectly normal condition in a situation like that faced by the noble and God-fearing prophet, Zachariah. Needless to say, he was only a human being who cannot ignore the reality. Hence, he would love to know how God will reverse it.

The answer to all his enquiries is straightforward. It is all perfectly easy for God to accomplish. God reminds him of something that he knows well, namely his own bringing into existence. This is something to be considered by every living creature. It applies to everything in this universe: *"He said: Thus it is. Your Lord says, 'This is easy for Me; even as I had earlier created you when you were nothing.'"* (Verse 9)

With regard to creation, there is nothing to be classified as easy or difficult in as far as God is concerned. In all cases of creation, whether it is something large or small, trivial or gigantic, the method is the same: it is only a matter of God willing that thing to be and it comes into existence. It is God who makes a barren woman childless, and an old man unable to procreate. He is certainly able to reverse this situation, removing the cause of a woman's barrenness and renewing a man's ability to cause his wife to conceive. By human standards, this is easier than initiating life in the first place. But with God, everything is easy, whether it involves origination or rebirth.

Nevertheless, Zachariah's eagerness to be reassured motivates him to ask for a sign indicating the realization of the happy news he was given. The sign God gave him was most fitting to the general atmosphere of his prayer and how it was answered. This sign gives him a further way to thank, glorify and praise God for giving him a son in his old age. He was to isolate himself from all worldly concerns for three days and live in direct contact with God. His speech would be normal when he glorified God, but he would not be able to utter a word of normal human speech. Yet he would remain in sound health, no illness affecting him. *"He replied: Your sign will be that for full three nights [and days] you will not speak to people."* (Verse 10)

This was exactly what took place: *"He then came out to his people from the sanctuary and signified to them [by gesture] to extol God's limitless glory by day and by night."* (Verse 11) He wanted them to live in the same mental condition he was in, to feel God's grace at its most abounding, and to give thanks for the grace He had bestowed on Zachariah, and on them.

John: A Prophet in His Own Right

The *sūrah* now leaves Zachariah in complete silence dealing with other people and his glorification and praise of God. As that scene closes, the *sūrah* reveals a new one in which we see John, the child given to Zachariah, as fully grown. It is his Lord who calls out to him from on high: *"John! Hold fast to the book with [all your] strength."* (Verse 12) This follows the Qur'ānic method of highlighting only the most important events, portraying images that are full of life and vigour.

Before we have even a single word about John himself, his account commences with an address from on high. It portrays an awesome scene giving us a good idea of John's position. It also shows us how God responded to Zachariah's prayers when he requested an heir who would fulfil the trust that he himself had been fulfilling, as it related both to faith and kin. Thus the first scene in which John is involved is the one where he is elected to bear the highest responsibility: *"John! Hold fast to the book with [all your] strength."* (Verse 12) The book referred to here is the Torah, given to Moses. All the Israelite prophets were charged with its preservation and implementation. They were also given the task of educating people in the Torah, so that they would know what was lawful to them and what was unlawful. John inherited his father Zachariah. He is here told to rise to the task and fulfil his trust with all his resolve and strength. He must never weaken or slacken. He should never abdicate his responsibilities.

The *sūrah* tells us what John was given to equip him for the great tasks he was assigned: "*We granted him wisdom while he was still a youth, as well as, by Our grace, compassion and purity; and he was [always] righteous.*" (Verses 12–13) These were indeed the qualifications that suited him for his task. They provided great help in the fulfilment of his duties. Now let us look closer at these qualifications.

God granted him wisdom in his youth, which made him unique in his personality, as he was unique in his birth and name. Wisdom is normally acquired as one grows in years, but in John's case, God granted him this in his early years.

God also granted him compassion as a special gift implanted in his very nature. He did not have to train or persuade himself to be compassionate. Such compassion is necessary for a prophet who takes care of people's hearts and souls, trying always to set them on the course of goodness with ease.

John was further granted purity and cleanliness of heart and practice. Thus, he was able to counter the effects of other people's hard natures and wickedness and so help them grow in purity.

The other quality that served John well was his righteousness. He keenly sensed his close tie with God, and knew that He was not only watching him but with him in all situations, public or private. That completes the qualities that John was given to qualify him for his task. They were given to him when he was still in his youth, so that he could inherit his father, who had appealed to God to give him an heir.

Thus the account of John is brought to its conclusion with two verses highlighting the fact that he was "*kind to his parents. Never was he haughty or rebellious. So peace was upon him on the day he was born, and on the day of his death, and will be on the day when he shall be raised to life again.*" (Verses 14–15) As we see in this short passage, the line he followed throughout his life was clearly laid out. No further details of the story of Zachariah requesting a son, nor of that son John could have provided anything extra in as much as the lessons we can draw are concerned. Hence it is brought to a close.

Suspending the Law of Procreation

John's birth, remarkable as it is, is not however the most wonderful that the *sūrah* tells us about. It has another story to tell, even more remarkable and wonderful. This is the birth of Jesus. The *sūrah* gives its account of John's birth first, with its remarkable aspect of him being born to a barren mother and a father well advanced in years. Jesus, on the other hand, was born to a virgin mother who had had no intimate contact with any man in her life. This is indeed far more wonderful and remarkable.

If we leave aside for a moment the creation of man in his present form and in the way God tells us of how He created him, the birth of Jesus, son of Mary, should be considered the most remarkable event of human history. It is an event that has no parallel.

Man did not witness his own creation, a remarkable event that heralded human life. That involved the creation of the first man ever to exist, born of no father and no mother. Countless centuries then passed before divine wisdom willed to bring about a second most remarkable event. This was the birth of Jesus without a father. In this, the event does not follow the pattern that subsequently applied after the creation of the first human being. This new birth was witnessed by human beings and remained an event of great importance to which people's attentions were drawn generation after generation. Needless to say, the creation of the first human being could not have been witnessed by people, as it was this creation that first ushered in human life on earth.

Divine wisdom has determined that life continues through procreation, involving the union of a male and a female. This applies to all species without exception. Even in the case of species where there are no fully distinguished males and females, every creature has male and female cells in its body. This law of procreation continued in operation for endless periods of time. People thought it was the only method of creation, forgetting the first event that brought man into existence, because that event was special, and could not be compared with procreation.

It was God's will, then, to give them this example of the creation of Jesus, son of Mary, to remind people of His free-will and unrestrained power which cannot be subject to the laws He sets in operation. Jesus' birth has not been repeated in history, because it is only proper that God's law should come into operation and be seen with all its effects. This single event remains for all time indisputable evidence that God's will is always free, unshackled by any factor whatsoever. Hence God says of Jesus: "*We will make him a sign for mankind.*" (Verse 21)

Because the event was so remarkable and unfamiliar, some people could not conceive of how it could happen and could not appreciate the wisdom of publicizing it in this way. Hence, they attributed to Jesus, son of Mary, qualities of divinity, inventing tales and superstitions about his birth. They thus fell foul of God's purpose, distorting the pure faith based on God's oneness.

In this *sūrah*, the Qur'ān relates how this remarkable event took place, highlighting its great significance and showing such tales and superstitions to be absolutely false. The *sūrah* relates the story in a series of highly emotional scenes, which leave a profound effect on anyone who reads them: it is as though he is witnessing the events as they take place.

The Most Remarkable Birth in History

Relate in the book [the story of] Mary and how she withdrew from her family to a place in the east, where she kept herself in seclusion from them. We, then, sent to her Our angel, who appeared to her in the shape of a well-made human being. She said: 'May the Most Merciful protect me from you. [Do not come near me] if you fear God.' 'I am but an emissary of your Lord,' he said, '[and have come] to give you a son endowed with purity.' She said: 'How shall I have a child when no man has ever touched me and I have never been a loose woman?' He answered: 'Thus did your Lord speak: This is easy for Me. We will make him a sign for mankind and an act of grace from Us. It is a matter [We have] decreed.' (Verses 16–21)

This is the first scene: Mary is a young, virgin woman, a saint whose mother vowed, when she was still an unborn baby, that she would serve in the temple. No one had ever witnessed from her anything other than perfect purity and chastity. In fact people associated her with Aaron, the first of the temple's devout servants. For generations, her family were renowned for being God-fearing and a model of piety.

We see this young woman going off to be alone. The *surah* does not specify why she wanted to be alone, but there must have been something to so require her to be by herself, unseen by anyone else. It may have been a very private matter that girls normally experience.

Once she is alone, screened from everyone and assured of complete privacy, she receives a great shock. She finds in front of her a man in his prime: "*We, then, sent to her Our angel, who appeared to her in the shape of a well-made human being.*" (Verse 17) She is both shocked and shaken, which is only the normal reaction of a chaste virgin. Her immediate reaction is to seek God's protection and to appeal to Him for support. She appeals to the man's sense of fearing God. She reminds him of God so that he may be restrained from attempting anything evil. So she says to him: "*May the Most Merciful protect me from you. [Do not come near me] if you fear God.*" (Verse 18) Should he be a God-fearing person, he would respond to the mere mention of God's name and His attribute of mercy. He would then resist any evil motive and restrain his desire.

We can visualize this young woman, a pure devout virgin, and what she might have gone through in that moment when she was surprised by a young man appearing before her in her place of privacy. This was her first shock.

Yet what answer does she receive? The man tells her something she could never have imagined: "'*I am but an emissary of your Lord,*' he said, '*[and have come] to give you a son endowed with purity.*'" (Verse 19) We can imagine the panic and shock that must have overwhelmed Mary when that perfect man, whom she did not yet know to be an emissary from her Lord, spoke to her. For all she knew, he might have been an assailant playing a trick on her, exploiting her innocence. Yet what he tells her, in the privacy of that place, well away from others, is

337

that he wants to give her a child. How shocked must Mary have been? We cannot even begin to imagine. That is the second great shock for Mary.

"She said: How shall I have a child when no man has ever touched me and I have never been a loose woman?" (Verse 20) Now she speaks frankly and plainly to him. She is all alone with him, and the reason why he surprised her is now clear. She does not know yet how he will give her a child. Nor does it make matters any easier or less worrying for her that he has declared himself to be God's emissary. Nothing that he says about that child, stating that he will be pure and that nothing evil will be attached to his birth or moral conduct, is sufficient to reassure her. It is a situation where modesty is completely out of place. She must have the matter out and clear at once. How, then, could she have a child when she is a virgin, untouched by any man? She is not a loose woman about to agree to a sexual act that could produce a child.

Her questioning in this fashion suggests that up to that moment she could not conceive of any way by which that person could give her a child except the familiar way of sexual contact between a male and a female. This is the natural way, according to human perception.

"He answered: Thus did your Lord speak. That is easy for Me. We will make him a sign for mankind and an act of grace from Us." (Verse 21) This miraculous event that Mary cannot even begin to imagine is easy for God to accomplish. His is the power that says to anything, 'Be,' and it immediately exists. Hence, everything is easy for Him, whether it is accomplished according to natural laws that are familiar to man or in some other fashion. The angel, who is referred to in this instance as 'the Spirit' tells her that it is God who says that it is easy for Him, and that He wants this unique and remarkable event to be a sign for all mankind, making clear to them His power and free, unshackled will. He also wants this child to be a mercy and a blessing to the Israelites in the first place and to all humanity thereafter. It is by showing them this miraculous event that they know Him, believe in Him and worship Him, seeking to earn His pleasure.

Thus ends the dialogue between the trusted angel and the Virgin Mary. The *sūrah* does not mention what happened after that exchange, leaving a gap in the story, which frequently happens in the Qur'ān. But it does mention that what the angel said to Mary about the birth of her son is a matter that has been settled and finalized. *"It is a matter [We have] decreed."* (Verse 21) But how? Nothing is mentioned here by way of explanation.

However, we can refer here to the use of the phrase, Our Spirit, which is mentioned in this instance and in another *sūrah*. Here it occurs in the verse: *"We, then, sent to her Our Spirit, who appeared to her in the shape of a well-made human being."* (Verse 17) In the other context, the phrase occurs as follows: *"And Mary, daughter of 'Imrān, who guarded her chastity, whereupon We breathed of Our Spirit into her."* (66: 12)

Now the question arises as to whether the reference in these two *sūrahs* is to the same thing or not. From our point of view, the references would appear to be different on each occasion. In the present *sūrah*, Mary, it refers to Gabriel, the Holy Spirit, who was God's emissary to Mary. In *Sūrah* 66, The Prohibition, it refers to the spirit that God breathed into Adam when He created him to make of him a human being. He again breathed of it into Mary to bring about her conception. It is this divine breathing of the spirit that gives life with all its human characteristics. These include the qualities and faculties that enable man to be in contact with the Supreme Society, while also giving him his human feelings, intellect, thought, emotions and inspiration. In Mary's case, Gabriel carried this breath of the spirit from God to place it into her. We must also add however that we do not know anything about the nature of the spirit, neither when it refers to Gabriel himself, nor when it has a different connotation. Both belong to the realm which is beyond our perception. We simply try to understand the relevant text in the two *sūrahs* and consider that the usage differs in each case.

The story then continues, and we are shown the outcome of all this. We see this baffled virgin going through something much harder for her: *"So she conceived him, and retired to a far-off place. And the throes of childbirth drove her to the trunk of a palm-tree. [In her anguish] she cried: 'Would that I had died before this and passed into complete oblivion!'"* (Verses 22–23) This was the third great shock Mary received.

How Jesus Was Born

The *sūrah* does not mention how she conceived Jesus or the length of her pregnancy. It gives no details about whether it was an ordinary pregnancy, with the breathing of spirit into Mary starting the life process within the egg, which then goes through the growth process, with the implantation of the conceived egg that becomes a germ-cell then a morsel, to which bones are then added before they are covered with flesh. That would mean that the foetus completed its normal period of nine-months gestation. All this is possible. Equally possible in this special case is that the female egg took a different course so as to reduce the different stages of growth, and ensure the development of the foetus so rapidly that the period of pregnancy was made much shorter. There is nothing in the text of the *sūrah* to indicate either. Hence, there is no point in pursuing this avenue further.

As we read on, we see Mary in a remote place, away from her family and community. She is now in a far more terrible situation. Previously, she was up against all that her upbringing has instilled in her of moral values; but that was an internal struggle with herself. Now she is about to be faced with a public scandal. Besides, she was in great physical pain added to her psychological distress. In the midst of labour and childbirth she is driven to lean against the trunk of a palm tree. She is all alone, a true virgin and suffering the pains of childbirth, not knowing about how to cope with the situation and having none to give her even moral support. In her anguish she cries: *"Would that I had died before this and passed into complete oblivion!"* (Verse 23) We almost see her face, feel her confusion, and sense her agony as she wishes herself into oblivion.

In the midst of all this anguish, she is confronted with the greatest surprise:

> But [a voice] from below cried out to her: Do not give in to grief. Your Lord has provided a brook running beneath you. And if you shake the trunk of the palm tree towards you, it will drop you fresh ripe dates. So eat and drink and be happy. Should you see any human being, just convey this to him: 'I have vowed a fast to the Most Merciful and will not speak today to any human being.' (Verses 24–26)

O God! What is happening here! A child born this very moment crying out to her, comforting her and reaffirming her bond with her Lord, directing her as to how to obtain food and drink, and providing her with the argument and evidence to use when she sees people.

The first thing the voice says to her is that she must not grieve. *"Your Lord has provided a brook running beneath you."* (Verse 24) God has not forsaken you. Indeed, He has made this brook run at your feet, which most probably started its course at that very moment, either from a spring or from a high point nearby. Besides, the palm tree against which she leant provided food. She only need to shake it and *"it will drop you fresh ripe dates."* (Verse 25) Thus she has essential food and water. Sweet food is good for a mother who has just delivered her baby. Dates are perhaps the best food she could eat. *"So eat and drink and be happy."* (Verse 26) All the necessary reassurance is given her.

Then she is told how to deal with her predicament when she meets other people. She need only impart to anyone by signal, not words, that she has made a vow not to speak to anyone. She is in full and complete devotion which prevents her from answering any questions: *"Should you see any human being, just convey this to him: I have vowed a fast to the Most Merciful and will not speak today to any human being."* (Verse 26)

We imagine that her surprise lingered long, and that she took a while to take stock of her situation and stretch her hand to the trunk of the tree and shake it for her meal of dates. But when she fully realized what was happening, she was reassured that God would not abandon her. Indeed, He had given her all the proof she needed. He gave her a child who spoke from the moment of his birth to explain the miracle that had brought him into being.

As Mary Confronts Her People

Then we glimpse a highly dramatic scene: *"She went to her people carrying the child."* (Verse 27) We can easily imagine the great surprise on their faces. Most probably, these were her immediate family. They had known their daughter, Mary, to be exemplary in her purity. She was indeed a virgin dedicated to worship in the temple; but there she was with a baby in her arms. Hence their exclamation: *"Mary, you have indeed done an amazing thing! Sister of Aaron, your father was not a wicked man, nor was your mother a loose woman!"* (Verses 27–28)

They start by reproaching her: *"You have done an amazing thing!"* It is a wicked, most dreadful thing that you have perpetrated. But then their reproach takes a different tone, adding sarcasm and ridicule. They call her: 'Sister of Aaron!' Aaron was a prophet who was in charge of the Temple, passing this duty to his offspring. Mary was often associated with Aaron because of her exemplary devotion in the service of the Temple. How ironic that the girl associated with Aaron's perfect devotion should perpetrate such an enormity: *"Your father was not a wicked man, nor was your mother a loose woman!"* (Verse 28) Such a sin is only committed by loose women and prostitutes.

In her own defence, Mary says nothing other than carrying out what her amazing child has instructed her to say: *"But she pointed to the child."* (Verse 29) Again we are left to imagine their amazement, anger and fury at this young woman, virgin as she was, carrying her child openly in her arms, and then refusing to answer their questions, only pointing to the child and indicating that they should ask him. *"They said: How can we talk to a babe in the cradle?"* (Verse 29) But then a supernatural event occurs again and the baby speaks out:

> *Whereupon he said: 'I am a servant of God. He has vouchsafed to me revelations and made me a prophet, and made me blessed wherever I may be. He has enjoined on me prayer and charity as long as I live. He has made me kind to my mother, not haughty or bereft of grace. Peace was on me on the day when I was born, and [will be on me] on the day of my death and on the day when I shall be raised to life again.'* (Verses 30–33)

Thus Jesus declared his status: a servant of God. He is not God's son, as some sects claim; nor was he divine as claimed by others, nor one of a Trinity constituting one God while being three, as claimed by others. He declares that God has made him a prophet, which means that he was neither God's son nor partner. God has blessed him and enjoined him to keep his prayers and be charitable throughout his life.

He is also enjoined to be very kind towards his mother and to show humility to his people. This means that he has a limited life duration, he dies and will be resurrected. God has bestowed on him peace, security and reassurance on the day of his birth, the day of his death and the day of his resurrection. The statement is very clear here in respect of the death and resurrection of Jesus. It admits no argument or different interpretation.

The Qur'ān does not add anything beyond painting this scene. It does not tell us how the people reacted to this miraculous event. Nor does it inform us what happened to Mary and her remarkable son after that. It does not mention anything about the time when he became a prophet. It simply says, quoting Jesus: "*He has vouchsafed to me revelations and made me a prophet.*" (Verse 30) The theme here is the birth of Jesus. Hence, when the *sūrah* has given its account of his birth, culminating in that miraculous scene, with Jesus talking to Mary's family, the scene is drawn to a close. This is followed by an emphatic statement of the truth concerning Jesus:

> Such was, in the words of truth, Jesus the son of Mary, about whose nature they still dispute. It is not conceivable that God should beget a son. Limitless is He in His glory! When He wills a thing to be, He only says to it, 'Be,' and it is. God is my Lord and your Lord; so worship Him alone. That is a straight path. (Verses 34–36)

The Full Truth about Jesus

This is the whole truth about Jesus. It has nothing of the claims advanced by those who assign to him a divine nature, or those who make false accusations against his mother. What God states here is the complete truth, giving details of his origin and birth. There is no room for doubt or argument. It is not for God to take for Himself a son. Most sublime is He in His glory. He needs no son, because offspring are only needed by mortals, so that their line of existence is continued. Alternatively, offspring are needed by the weak so that they have the support of their children against their enemies. But God is immortal, and able to do what He wills, having power over all things. All creatures come into existence when He says to them, 'Be'. This means that He accomplishes any purpose of His merely by willing it to take place, not by having help from a son or partner.

Jesus concludes his words by declaring the truth that God is his Lord and the Lord of all mankind. Hence, they must worship Him alone, assigning to Him no partners: *"God is my Lord and your Lord; so worship Him alone. That is a straight path."* (Verse 36) With this statement made by Jesus himself, and with this account of his birth there is no room left for legend or myth in the whole affair. This is the full import of his statement and the way it is phrased.

The *sūrah* then refers to the conflicting views and beliefs advanced by various groups concerning Jesus, his birth, nature and status. All are highly objectionable as compared with the clear and simple truth.

"Yet are the sects at variance among themselves." (Verse 37) Constantine, the Roman Emperor, held one of three famous synods, attended by 2,170 bishops. They differed a great deal about Jesus. Each group expressed a certain view. Some said that he was God who descended to earth in person, giving life to whomever He willed and caused others to die, before returning to heaven. Some said that he was God's son, while others claimed that he was one of the three entities forming the Godhead: the Father, the Son and the Holy Spirit. A different group claimed that he was one of three deities: God was one, Jesus another and his mother the third. However, another group said that Jesus was God's servant, messenger, spirit and word. Others made yet different claims. All in all, no more than 308 agreed on any one view. The Emperor decided to support that view, expelling all those who did not agree, and persecuting those who opposed it, particularly those who advocated God's oneness.

Since such deviant beliefs were established by synods composed of large numbers of bishops, the *sūrah* warns unbelievers about what happens to those who deviate from the faith based on God's oneness. This warning tells them of a scene that will take place on a great and eventful day witnessed by much larger numbers:

Woe, then, to the unbelievers when a momentous day arrives. How well they will hear and see on the day they will appear before Us. Truly the wrongdoers are today in evident error. Hence, warn them of the Day of Distress, when everything will have been determined while they remain heedless, persisting in unbelief. (Verses 37–39)

Woe to them when they witness a momentous day, referred to here in an indefinite mode to impart to it a more awesome air. It is a day witnessed by all human beings and *jinn*, as well as the angels. All shall stand in the presence of God Almighty, to whom the unbelievers ascribe partners.

The *sūrah* then derides them for turning away from all the pointers to the right guidance in this present life. On that day theirs will be the sharpest of hearing and seeing: *"How well they will hear and see on the day they will appear before Us. Truly the wrongdoers are today in evident error."* (Verse 38) Their situation is amazing: they do not hear or see when hearing and seeing are the means to discern guidance and follow it in order to escape doom. Yet they hear and see extremely well when these faculties are used to stress their humiliation. They will be made to hear what they dislike and see what they are wont to avoid.

"Hence, warn them of the Day of Distress." (Verse 39) That is a day when distress will be at its most acute, when distress will be a quality of the day itself. They need to be warned, because such distress is of no use to anyone: *"When everything will have been determined while they remain heedless, persisting in unbelief."* (Verse 39) It is as though the day is directly linked to their unbelief and heedlessness.

God's Messenger is commanded to warn people against that day, which will come, no doubt. For, everything and everyone on earth shall return to God, like inheritance that reverts to the Only Heir: *"We alone shall remain after the earth and all who live on it have passed away. To Us they shall all return."* (Verse 40)

2

A Long Line of Prophets

Mention in the Book Abraham. He certainly was a man of truth and a prophet. (41)

وَٱذْكُرْ فِي ٱلْكِتَٰبِ إِبْرَٰهِيمَ إِنَّهُۥ كَانَ صِدِّيقًا نَّبِيًّا ﴿٤١﴾

He said to his father: 'My father! Why do you worship something that neither hears nor sees and can be of no avail whatever to you? (42)

إِذْ قَالَ لِأَبِيهِ يَٰٓأَبَتِ لِمَ تَعْبُدُ مَا لَا يَسْمَعُ وَلَا يُبْصِرُ وَلَا يُغْنِي عَنكَ شَيْـًٔا ﴿٤٢﴾

My father! There has come to me knowledge which you do not have. Follow me, and I shall guide you along a straight path. (43)

يَٰٓأَبَتِ إِنِّي قَدْ جَآءَنِي مِنَ ٱلْعِلْمِ مَا لَمْ يَأْتِكَ فَٱتَّبِعْنِيٓ أَهْدِكَ صِرَٰطًا سَوِيًّا ﴿٤٣﴾

My father! Do not worship Satan, for Satan has indeed rebelled against [God] the Most Merciful. (44)

يَٰٓأَبَتِ لَا تَعْبُدِ ٱلشَّيْطَٰنَ إِنَّ ٱلشَّيْطَٰنَ كَانَ لِلرَّحْمَٰنِ عَصِيًّا ﴿٤٤﴾

My father! I dread lest a scourge will fall upon you from the Most Merciful, and then you will become one of Satan's friends.' (45)

يَٰٓأَبَتِ إِنِّيٓ أَخَافُ أَن يَمَسَّكَ عَذَابٌ مِّنَ ٱلرَّحْمَٰنِ فَتَكُونَ لِلشَّيْطَٰنِ وَلِيًّا ﴿٤٥﴾

He answered: 'Are you renouncing my gods, Abraham? If you do not desist, I shall most certainly have you stoned. Now begone from me for good!' (46)

قَالَ أَرَاغِبٌ أَنتَ عَنْ ءَالِهَتِى يَـٰٓإِبْرَٰهِيمُ لَئِن لَّمْ تَنتَهِ لَأَرْجُمَنَّكَ وَٱهْجُرْنِى مَلِيًّا ﴿٤٦﴾

Abraham replied: 'Peace be on you. I shall pray to my Lord to forgive you; for He has always been very kind to me. (47)

قَالَ سَلَـٰمٌ عَلَيْكَ سَأَسْتَغْفِرُ لَكَ رَبِّىٓ إِنَّهُۥ كَانَ بِى حَفِيًّا ﴿٤٧﴾

But I shall withdraw from you all and from whatever you invoke instead of God, and I shall pray to my Lord alone. Perhaps, by my prayer to my Lord I shall not be unblest.' (48)

وَأَعْتَزِلُكُمْ وَمَا تَدْعُونَ مِن دُونِ ٱللَّهِ وَأَدْعُواْ رَبِّى عَسَىٰٓ أَلَّآ أَكُونَ بِدُعَآءِ رَبِّى شَقِيًّا ﴿٤٨﴾

When he had withdrawn from them and from all that they were worshipping instead of God, We bestowed on him Isaac and Jacob, each of whom We made a prophet. (49)

فَلَمَّا ٱعْتَزَلَهُمْ وَمَا يَعْبُدُونَ مِن دُونِ ٱللَّهِ وَهَبْنَا لَهُۥٓ إِسْحَـٰقَ وَيَعْقُوبَ وَكُلًّا جَعَلْنَا نَبِيًّا ﴿٤٩﴾

We bestowed on them of Our mercy and We granted them the high honour of [conveying] the truth. (50)

وَوَهَبْنَا لَهُم مِّن رَّحْمَتِنَا وَجَعَلْنَا لَهُمْ لِسَانَ صِدْقٍ عَلِيًّا ﴿٥٠﴾

And mention in the Book Moses, who was a chosen one, a messenger of God and a prophet. (51)

وَٱذْكُرْ فِى ٱلْكِتَـٰبِ مُوسَىٰٓ إِنَّهُۥ كَانَ مُخْلَصًا وَكَانَ رَسُولًا نَّبِيًّا ﴿٥١﴾

We called out to him from the right side of Mount Sinai and drew him near [to Us] in mystic communion. (52)

وَنَادَيْنَاهُ مِن جَانِبِ الطُّورِ الْأَيْمَنِ وَقَرَّبْنَاهُ نَجِيًّا ۝

We gave him, out of Our grace, his brother Aaron, to be a prophet. (53)

وَوَهَبْنَا لَهُ مِن رَّحْمَتِنَا أَخَاهُ هَارُونَ نَبِيًّا ۝

And mention in the Book Ishmael who was always true to his promise, and was a messenger of God, a prophet. (54)

وَاذْكُرْ فِي الْكِتَابِ إِسْمَاعِيلَ إِنَّهُ كَانَ صَادِقَ الْوَعْدِ وَكَانَ رَسُولًا نَبِيًّا ۝

He used to enjoin on his people prayer and charity, and his Lord was well pleased with him. (55)

وَكَانَ يَأْمُرُ أَهْلَهُ بِالصَّلَوٰةِ وَالزَّكَوٰةِ وَكَانَ عِندَ رَبِّهِ مَرْضِيًّا ۝

And mention in the Book Idrīs, who was a man of truth, a prophet. (56)

وَاذْكُرْ فِي الْكِتَابِ إِدْرِيسَ إِنَّهُ كَانَ صِدِّيقًا نَبِيًّا ۝

We raised him to a lofty station. (57)

وَرَفَعْنَاهُ مَكَانًا عَلِيًّا ۝

These were some of the prophets upon whom God bestowed His blessings – of the seed of Adam, and of those whom We carried in the ark with Noah, and of the seed of Abraham and Israel, and of those whom We had guided

أُو۟لَٰٓئِكَ الَّذِينَ أَنْعَمَ اللَّهُ عَلَيْهِم مِّنَ النَّبِيِّـۧنَ مِن ذُرِّيَّةِ ءَادَمَ وَمِمَّنْ حَمَلْنَا مَعَ نُوحٍ وَمِن ذُرِّيَّةِ إِبْرَٰهِيمَ وَإِسْرَٰٓءِيلَ وَمِمَّنْ هَدَيْنَا

and chosen. When the revelations of [God] the Most Merciful were recited to them they fell down prostrating themselves [before Him] and weeping. (58)

وَاجْتَبَيْنَاۤ إِذَا نُتْلَىٰ عَلَيْهِمْ ءَايَٰتُ الرَّحْمَٰنِ خَرُّوا۟ سُجَّدًا وَبُكِيًّا ۩ ۝

They were succeeded by generations who neglected their prayers and followed only their lusts; and these will, in time, meet with utter disillusion. (59)

فَخَلَفَ مِنۢ بَعْدِهِمْ خَلْفٌ أَضَاعُوا۟ ٱلصَّلَوٰةَ وَٱتَّبَعُوا۟ ٱلشَّهَوَٰتِ فَسَوْفَ يَلْقَوْنَ غَيًّا ۝

Excepted, however, shall be those who repent, believe and do righteous deeds. These will enter the Garden and will not be wronged in any way: (60)

إِلَّا مَن تَابَ وَءَامَنَ وَعَمِلَ صَٰلِحًا فَأُو۟لَٰئِكَ يَدْخُلُونَ ٱلْجَنَّةَ وَلَا يُظْلَمُونَ شَيْـًٔا ۝

the gardens of Eden which [God] the Most Merciful has promised to His servants, in the realm that lies beyond the reach of human perception. Indeed, His promise is certain of fulfilment. (61)

جَنَّٰتِ عَدْنٍ ٱلَّتِى وَعَدَ ٱلرَّحْمَٰنُ عِبَادَهُۥ بِٱلْغَيْبِ إِنَّهُۥ كَانَ وَعْدُهُۥ مَأْتِيًّا ۝

There they will hear no idle talk, but only the voice of peace. And their sustenance shall be given them there morning and evening. (62)

لَّا يَسْمَعُونَ فِيهَا لَغْوًا إِلَّا سَلَٰمًا وَلَهُمْ رِزْقُهُمْ فِيهَا بُكْرَةً وَعَشِيًّا ۝

Such is the paradise which We shall give the righteous among Our servants to inherit. (63)

تِلْكَ ٱلْجَنَّةُ ٱلَّتِى نُورِثُ مِنْ عِبَادِنَا مَن كَانَ تَقِيًّا ۝

We descend only by the command of your Lord. To Him belongs all that is before us and all that is hidden from us and all that is in between. Never does your Lord forget anything. (64)

وَمَا نَتَنَزَّلُ إِلَّا بِأَمْرِ رَبِّكَ لَهُ مَا بَيْنَ أَيْدِينَا وَمَا خَلْفَنَا وَمَا بَيْنَ ذَلِكَ وَمَا كَانَ رَبُّكَ نَسِيًّا ۝

He is the Lord of the heavens and the earth and all that is between them. Worship Him alone, then, and remain steadfast in His worship. Do you know any whose name is worthy to be mentioned side by side with His? (65)

رَبُّ السَّمَوَاتِ وَالْأَرْضِ وَمَا بَيْنَهُمَا فَاعْبُدْهُ وَاصْطَبِرْ لِعِبَادَتِهِ هَلْ تَعْلَمُ لَهُ سَمِيًّا ۝

A Son's Passionate Appeal

The account given in this *surah* of the birth of Jesus is concluded with a statement showing the fallacy and singularity of the myth making Jesus God's son. This is a fabrication upheld by some Christians in their distorted beliefs. The *surah* now gives an account of part of Abraham's story, demonstrating the singularity and fallacy of pagan beliefs. Abraham is the great ancestor from whom the Arabs claim to descend. In fact the pagan Arabs claimed the custodianship of the Ka'bah, built by Abraham and his son, Ishmael.

In this account, Abraham's contented, patient and gentle character is shown in sharp relief. We see these aspects of his character in his approach and language. They are also clearly apparent in his behaviour and how he responds to his father's overbearing attitude. We also feel how God has bestowed His grace on Abraham, compensating him for his father and people, all unbelievers, with goodly offspring that beget a whole nation which has its generous share of prophets and saintly divines. Yet these are followed by generations who neglected prayers and deviated from the path shown them by Abraham to pursue their desires. Those were the unbelievers.

351

God describes Abraham in the Qur'ān as being 'a man of truth and a prophet'. The Arabic word, *ṣiddīq*, translated here as 'a man of truth' has a wider sense than merely being truthful. It connotes that he was always truthful and a firm believer in the truth. Both qualities fit well with his character:

> *Mention in the Book Abraham. He certainly was a man of truth and a prophet. He said to his father: 'My father! Why do you worship something that neither hears nor sees and can be of no avail whatever to you? My father! There has come to me knowledge which you do not have. Follow me, and I shall guide you along a straight path. My father! Do not worship Satan, for Satan has indeed rebelled against [God] the Most Merciful. My father! I dread lest a scourge will fall upon you from the Most Merciful, and then you will become one of Satan's friends.'* (Verses 41–45)

It is with such a passionate appeal that Abraham addresses his father, trying to guide him to the goodness God had taught him and to which He had directed him. His appeal is an endearing one, stressing his position as a loving son. He asks him: "*Why do you worship something that neither hears nor sees and can be of no avail whatever to you?*" (Verse 42) The normal practice is that people address their worship to someone who is more exalted, knowledgeable and stronger than man. Indeed worship is always presented to someone exalted above man's position. How is it, then, that in this case it is presented to something below the level of man, and indeed below the level of animals; something that does not hear or see anything and can cause no benefit or harm. This was the case of Abraham's father and community. They worshipped idols, just like the Arabs of the Quraysh who opposed Islam.

This is the first point in Abraham's appeal to his father. He follows it with a statement that he does not make this claim at his own behest. Rather, he makes it on the basis of true knowledge that has been vouchsafed to him by God to set him on the path of true guidance. He was certainly younger and less experienced than his father, but what had been bestowed on him from on high gave him a clear recognition of the truth. Hence he gives his advice to his father who had not received such knowledge. He wanted his father to follow suit so that he would be on the road of truth: "*My father! There has come to me knowledge which you do not have. Follow me, and I shall guide you along a straight path.*" (Verse 43)

There is nothing wrong with a father following his son when this son has a direct recourse to a higher source able to give true guidance. In this case, the son is the one who follows the right way, leading only to what is good.

Having shown his father the fallacy of idol worship and outlined the source of guidance he received, which is the cornerstone of his appeal to his father, Abraham makes it clear that the way followed by his father is that of Satan. His own aim is to guide his father to the way acceptable to God, the Most Merciful. He fears that his father may incur God's anger and thus become a close friend of Satan:

> *My father! Do not worship Satan, for Satan has indeed rebelled against [God] the Most Merciful. My father! I dread lest a scourge will fall upon you from the Most Merciful, and then you will become one of Satan's friends.* (Verses 44–45)

It is Satan who tempts people to worship idols. This means that whoever worships idols is in the same position as one who worships the devil himself. Satan, it must not be forgotten, is a rebel who disobeys God in every way. Abraham warns his father against incurring God's displeasure. For if he does, he will become Satan's friend and follower and so liable to God's punishment. This shows clearly that when God guides a servant of His to obey Him, that in itself is a blessing, while befriending Satan is a scourge leading to God's punishment and a position of utter ruin on the Day of Judgement.

Insolent Answer to a Compassionate Appeal

Abraham's appeal, made in the most compassionate language, cannot however find its way to his father's hardened heart. The father retorts with rejection and threats:

Are you renouncing my gods, Abraham? If you do not desist, I shall most certainly have you stoned. Now begone from me for good! (Verse 46)

His father's answer was harsh, arrogant and threatening. He considered Abraham's rejection of idols to be impertinent. It was a crime for which Abraham deserved a cruel punishment: i.e. death by stoning. Hence, he advised him to stay away, or else punishment would be forthcoming.

It is with such ignorance and cruelty that the father replies to the son's passionate and polite appeal. No regard is given for the son's care and concern for his father. This is indeed the pattern of response that advocates of faith receive from those who are hardened by disbelief and lack of guidance.

Abraham, however, does not allow anger to dictate his attitude. He does not lose sight of his dutifulness to his father. Hence, he continues to address him with respect and compassion:

Abraham replied: Peace be on you. I shall pray to my Lord to forgive you; for He has always been very kind to me. But I shall withdraw from you all and from whatever you invoke instead of God, and I shall pray to my Lord alone. Perhaps, by my prayer to my Lord I shall not be unblest. (Verses 47–48)

Abraham makes it clear that he will not respond to the threat, nor will he indulge in futile argument. He promises his father to pray to God to forgive him and not to punish him by allowing him to go further astray. He will pray to God to have mercy on his father and guide him to the truth. He tells him that he is used to God's generous favours, as He answers his prayers. Then he adds that if his own presence and appeal irritate his father, then he will withdraw, leave his father and people, abandoning the deities they invoke instead of God. He will only worship God alone, hoping that by doing so he will avoid being unblest. Such is a believer's politeness and humility. Abraham does not feel that he is deserving of favours from God more than being spared misery, unhappiness and withdrawal of blessings.

Thus Abraham left his father, his community and homeland, as well as their idols and worship practices. God, however, blessed him with offspring and gave him what was better than that which he had sacrificed.

> *When he had withdrawn from them and from all that they were worshipping instead of God, We bestowed on him Isaac and Jacob, each of whom We made a prophet. We bestowed on them of Our mercy and We granted them the high honour of [conveying] the truth.* (Verses 49–50)

Isaac was Abraham's son, born to him by his wife Sarah who, prior to his birth, was childless. Jacob was Isaac's son, but he is mentioned here as though he were Abraham's own son, because he was born during his grandfather's lifetime, growing up under his care. Thus, he was close to his grandfather, just as though he were his own son. He learnt faith from him directly and he taught it to his own children. Both Isaac and Jacob were prophets.

"*We bestowed on them of Our mercy.*" (Verse 50) This is a reference to Abraham, Isaac and Jacob, as well as to their offspring. They were all recipients of God's mercy, which is mentioned here as the most bounteous gift granted by God in the general ambience of the *surah*. Furthermore, it was the quality of God's bounty that compensated Abraham for the loss of his people and homeland, giving him reassurance in his new solitary environment. "*We granted them the high honour of [conveying] the truth.*" (Verse 50) They were truthful in their mission, enjoying trust and honour among their people. Their word was listened to and received well.

The *surah* moves on, speaking about the same branch of Abraham's seed and reminding us of Moses and Aaron: "*And mention in the Book Moses, who was a chosen one, a messenger of God and a prophet. We called out to him from the right side of Mount Sinai and drew him near [to Us] in mystic communion. We gave him, out of Our grace, his brother Aaron, to be a prophet.*" (Verses 51–53)

Moses is described here as one who was chosen for the task of dedication to God's call. He is identified as a prophet who is entrusted with a message that he must deliver to people. A prophet is not given the same task. He is an advocate of faith which he receives from God directly. Among the Children of Israel there were many prophets who were given the task of advocating the message delivered by Moses and judging among people according to the Torah revealed to him by God: *"Indeed, it is We who revealed the Torah, containing guidance and light. By it did the prophets, who had surrendered themselves to God, judge among the Jews, and so did the divines and the rabbis: [they gave judgement] in accordance with what had been entrusted to their care of God's Book and to which they themselves were witnesses."* (5: 44)

The grace granted to Moses is highlighted as he was called out from the right side of Mount Sinai. [That was the right side of Moses as he stood at that moment facing the Mount.] He was drawn so close as to be spoken to in communion. We do not know how this communication took place, or how Moses understood it. Was it a voice heard by Moses through his ears in the normal way, or was it an address received by his whole being. Nor do we know how God prepared Moses to receive His own words. But we believe that all this took place. It is simply very easy for God to accomplish it, bringing His servant into communion with Him while at the same time retaining his humanity. We must not forget that man acquired his status with the breathing in of God's spirit into him.

The *sūrah* mentions how God bestowed His mercy on Moses by giving him the support of Aaron, his brother, whom God also made a prophet. It was Moses who requested this help and God granted it: *"My brother Aaron is far better in speech than I am. Send him, therefore, as a helper, so that he might bear witness to my speaking the truth; for I fear indeed that they will accuse me of lying."* (28: 34) Indeed, throughout the *sūrah* there is an unmistakeable air of divine mercy.

More Prophets

Now the *sūrah* refers to the other branch of Abraham's seed, bringing in Ishmael, the father of the Arabs, for special mention:

And mention in the Book Ishmael who was always true to his promise, and was a messenger of God, a prophet. He used to enjoin on his people prayer and charity, and his Lord was well pleased with him. (Verses 54–55)

The *sūrah* highlights a special quality of Ishmael's, which was his being true to his promise. This is a characteristic common to all prophets and all God-fearing men and women. The fact that it is highlighted here suggests that in Ishmael's case it must have had very special significance. Moreover, Ishmael is given the status of messenger of God, which means that he preached God's message to the Arabs of old. Indeed he was their highest grandfather. We know that even shortly before the advent of the message of the Prophet Muḥammad, there were some individual Arabs who believed in one God. Most probably they were the last remnants of Ishmael's followers.

The *sūrah* also mentions that the fundamentals of his faith included prayer and *zakāt*, which he ordered his family and his people to observe. Moreover, the *sūrah* leaves us in no doubt that Ishmael earned God's pleasure, which imparts a sense of contentment and satisfaction to anyone. This contentment is another aspect that permeates the whole *sūrah*, in the same way as mercy. In fact the two aspects of mercy and contentment are mutually related.

The last prophet to be mentioned in this *sūrah* is Idrīs: "*And mention in the Book Idrīs, who was a man of truth, a prophet. We raised him to a lofty station.*" (Verses 56–57) We have no way of determining during which period of history Idrīs lived. Most probably he was ahead of Abraham. He was not one of the Jewish prophets. There is no mention of him in the Jewish books. The Qur'ān describes him as a man of truth and a prophet. It records the fact that God granted him honour and made him worthy of praise, elevating him to a lofty position.

There is a view we would like to mention here without suggesting whether it is true or false. Some Egyptologists suggest that Idrīs is an Arabicized form of Osiris in the same way as Yohanna is Arabicized as Yaḥyā, and Eliesha as Al-Yasaʿ. We know that around Osiris many a legend has been woven. It is said that old Egyptians believed that he was elevated to heaven where he was established on a throne. Whoever, after death, is found to have to his credit more good deeds in this life than bad ones will join Osiris who has become an Egyptian deity. He is also said to have taught the Egyptians all that they knew before he was elevated to heaven.

Be that as it may, we confine ourselves to what the Qur'ān states about Idrīs, without indulging in speculation. We only say that it is more probable that he lived before the time of Abraham.

The *sūrah* mentions all these prophets in order to compare them, a group of God-fearing believers, with later generations of pagan Arabs and unbelieving Israelites. The gulf separating the two is vast. There is nothing to bring the newcomers close to their ancestors.

> *These were some of the prophets upon whom God bestowed His blessings – of the seed of Adam, and of those whom We carried in the ark with Noah, and of the seed of Abraham and Israel, and of those whom We had guided and chosen. When the revelations of [God] the Most Merciful were recited to them they fell down prostrating themselves [before Him] and weeping. They were succeeded by generations who neglected their prayers and followed only their lusts; and these will, in time, meet with utter disillusion.* (Verses 58–59)

In this scene of the role of prophethood in human history, we see only the main features delineated: *'of the seed of Adam,'* and *'of those whom We carried in the ark with Noah,'* and also *'of the seed of Abraham and Israel.'* Adam's seed includes all, and Noah refers to all who came after him, while Abraham combines the two major branches of prophethood: Jacob as the head of the Israelite tree and Ishmael to whom the Arabs belong and from among whom came the last of all prophets.

Those prophets together with those from among their offspring whom God guided and chose of pious people share a main quality in common: *"When the revelations of [God] the Most Merciful were recited to them they fell down prostrating themselves [before Him] and weeping."* (Verse 58) They are truly God-fearing, very sensitive to what pleases or displeases God. They shudder when His revelations are recited. This sensation is so strong that they cannot express their inner feelings in words. Their eyes are tearful and they fall down prostrating themselves before God and weep.

Yet such highly God-fearing people are succeeded by generations that are distant from God, by people who neglect their prayer and deny it as a duty incumbent on them. Instead, they follow only their lusts and indulge in every loose activity. The difference is so clear and the contrast complete.

The *sūrah* warns those who turned away from the path followed by their God-fearing forefathers, and shows them that they are bound to lose their way and end in ruin. Indeed, their end looms large: "*These will, in time, meet with utter disillusion.*" (Verse 59) Disillusion will lead them into error, and error will take them to utter destruction.

God's Door Remains Open

The *sūrah* makes it clear that the door remains wide open for all who wish to repent and mend their ways. Through that door comes the scent of God's mercy and the aura of abounding grace:

> *Excepted, however, shall be those who repent, believe and do righteous deeds. These will enter the Garden and will not be wronged in any way: the gardens of Eden which [God] the Most Merciful has promised to His servants, in the realm that lies beyond the reach of human perception. Indeed, His promise is certain of fulfilment. There they will hear no idle talk, but only the voice of peace. And their sustenance shall be given them there morning and evening. Such is the paradise which We shall give the righteous among Our servants to inherit.* (Verses 60–63)

Repentance that initiates a sincere acceptance of the divine faith and good works, thus making its positive significance a clear reality, ensures escape from that ruinous fate. Those who resort to such repentance will not end up in disillusion, but will rather go to heaven, where they are subjected to no wrong. They go there for permanent abode. God has promised entry into this garden to His servants and they believed in it before they could ever see it, because God's promise always comes true.

The *sūrah* then draws an image of heaven and its dwellers: "*There they will hear no idle talk, but only the voice of peace.*" (Verse 62) Their talk is free of idle remarks, loud noise, futile argument. It is a conversation when only one type of voice is heard. It is the type that fits in with this pleasant atmosphere, full of contentment. That is the voice of peace. Provisions are certain to come in this heaven, without the need for hard work, worry or anxiety. They will never be exhausted: "*Their sustenance shall be given them there morning and evening.*" (Verse 62) In such a blissful atmosphere, requests, demands and worries are out of place.

"*Such is the paradise which We shall give the righteous among Our servants to inherit.*" (Verse 63) Anyone who wishes to share in this inheritance is aware of the way to ensure it: repentance, firm belief and good works. Descent and ancestry are of no avail. Certain people descended from those God-fearing prophets and the goodly people who followed divine guidance and whom God selected for honour, but their descendants neglected their prayers and followed their own wanton desires. Their descent benefited them nothing. They are certain to end in disillusion.

God's Absolute Lordship

This passage of the *sūrah* ends with a declaration of God's total Lordship of the universe. Hence, people are directed to worship Him alone and to bear with patience the hard tasks involved. Furthermore, the possibility of anyone having something in common with God is absolutely negated.

> We descend only by the command of your Lord. To Him belongs all that is before us and all that is hidden from us and all that is in between. Never does your Lord forget anything. He is the Lord of the heavens and the earth and all that is between them. Worship Him alone, then, and remain steadfast in His worship. Do you know any whose name is worthy to be mentioned side by side with His? (Verses 64–65)

Reports are unanimous that the angel Gabriel was ordered to say the first statement to the Prophet: "*We descend only by the command of your Lord.*" (Verse 64) This was in reply to the Prophet when he felt that revelation was slow in coming. In fact Gabriel had not come to see him for some time, and he experienced a feeling of loneliness, keenly missing the angel whom he loved. Gabriel was then ordered by God to tell him: "*We descend only by the command of your Lord.*" He conducts all our affairs: "*To Him belongs all that is before us and all that is hidden from us and all that is in between.*" (Verse 64) He forgets nothing. Revelations are bestowed when He in His wisdom wills that they be bestowed.

The verse ends with the statement: "*Never does your Lord forget anything.*" (Verse 64) It is fitting that this comment should be followed with the injunction to worship God alone and remain steadfast, declaring at the same time His Lordship over all things: "*He is the Lord of the heavens and the earth and all that is between them.*" (Verse 65) No one else has any share in this Lordship.

"*Worship Him alone, then, and remain steadfast in His worship.*" (Verse 65) Worship Him and persevere in shouldering the responsibilities that such worship entails. These include the responsibility of attaining the high standard that allows one to present oneself before Him and of maintaining this high standard. Worship Him alone and mobilize all your abilities and potential for meeting Him and for learning from that sublime source. This is a hard task, requiring one to free oneself of all restrictions and responsibilities, activities and distractions. Yet this task is coupled with a pleasure that cannot be fully appreciated except by those who have experienced it. Yet the pleasure cannot be gained except by those who rise to the task and fulfil it with the determination it deserves. Dedication is the key word here, and without dedication, the pleasure will not be forthcoming, nor the results one hopes for.

"*Worship Him alone, then, and remain steadfast in His worship,*" remembering that worship in Islam does not denote merely the rituals of worship. It includes all activities, feelings, intentions and thoughts. It is hard to direct all these towards heaven and make their aim the winning of God's pleasure. As it is hard, it requires perseverance. It requires that one directs every human activity on earth to pleasing God, ensuring that it remains free of all restrictions, temptations and desires.

Thus we see how Islam is truly a comprehensive system for life. When man implements this system, feeling that whatever he does, large or small, is meant as worship of God, he rises to the pure and enlightened level of worship. Such a system requires, for its proper fulfilment, perseverance and endurance at the time of suffering.

The command is given to us all that we must *"worship Him alone."* He is the only One in the universe who deserves to be the recipient of our worship. The passage concludes with the rhetorical question: *"Do you know any whose name is worthy to be mentioned side by side with His?"* (Verse 65) This question also asks whether we know any equal to God. Supreme is He above all things!

3

Two Interlinked Lives

'What!' says man, 'When I am once dead, shall I be raised up alive?' (66)

وَيَقُولُ ٱلْإِنسَٰنُ أَءِذَا مَا مِتُّ لَسَوْفَ أُخْرَجُ حَيًّا ۝

Does not man remember that We earlier created him, when he was nothing? (67)

أَوَلَا يَذْكُرُ ٱلْإِنسَٰنُ أَنَّا خَلَقْنَٰهُ مِن قَبْلُ وَلَمْ يَكُ شَيْئًا ۝

By your Lord, We shall most certainly bring them forth together with the evil ones, and then We shall most certainly gather them, on their knees, around hell; (68)

فَوَرَبِّكَ لَنَحْشُرَنَّهُمْ وَٱلشَّيَٰطِينَ ثُمَّ لَنُحْضِرَنَّهُمْ حَوْلَ جَهَنَّمَ جِثِيًّا ۝

and thereupon We shall drag out from every group those who had been most obstinate in their rebellion against the Most Merciful. (69)

ثُمَّ لَنَنزِعَنَّ مِن كُلِّ شِيعَةٍ أَيُّهُمْ أَشَدُّ عَلَى ٱلرَّحْمَٰنِ عِتِيًّا ۝

For, indeed, We know best who most deserve to be burnt in the fire of hell. (70)

ثُمَّ لَنَحْنُ أَعْلَمُ بِٱلَّذِينَ هُمْ أَوْلَىٰ بِهَا صِلِيًّا ۝

There is not one among you who shall not pass over it: this is, for your Lord, a decree that must be fulfilled. (71)

وَإِن مِّنكُمْ إِلَّا وَارِدُهَا ۚ كَانَ عَلَىٰ رَبِّكَ حَتْمًا مَّقْضِيًّا ﴿٧١﴾

But We shall save those who are God-fearing, and leave the wrongdoers there, on their knees. (72)

ثُمَّ نُنَجِّي الَّذِينَ اتَّقَوا وَّنَذَرُ الظَّالِمِينَ فِيهَا جِثِيًّا ﴿٧٢﴾

When Our revelations are recited to them in all their clarity, the unbelievers say to those who believe: 'Which of the two sides has a better position and a superior community?' (73)

وَإِذَا تُتْلَىٰ عَلَيْهِمْ ءَايَٰتُنَا بَيِّنَٰتٍ قَالَ الَّذِينَ كَفَرُوا لِلَّذِينَ ءَامَنُوا أَيُّ الْفَرِيقَيْنِ خَيْرٌ مَّقَامًا وَأَحْسَنُ نَدِيًّا ﴿٧٣﴾

How many a generation have We destroyed before their time, who were superior in material riches and in splendour. (74)

وَكَمْ أَهْلَكْنَا قَبْلَهُم مِّن قَرْنٍ هُمْ أَحْسَنُ أَثَٰثًا وَرِءْيًا ﴿٧٤﴾

Say: 'As for those who live in error, may the Most Merciful lengthen their span of life!' But when they see the fulfilment of that of which they have been forewarned, be it suffering or the Last Hour, they will realize who is worst in position and weaker in forces. (75)

قُلْ مَن كَانَ فِي الضَّلَٰلَةِ فَلْيَمْدُدْ لَهُ الرَّحْمَٰنُ مَدًّا ۚ حَتَّىٰ إِذَا رَأَوْا مَا يُوعَدُونَ إِمَّا الْعَذَابَ وَإِمَّا السَّاعَةَ فَسَيَعْلَمُونَ مَنْ هُوَ شَرٌّ مَّكَانًا وَأَضْعَفُ جُندًا ﴿٧٥﴾

God advances in guidance those who seek His guidance. Good deeds of lasting merit are, in your Lord's sight, worthy of greater recompense, and yield far better returns. (76)

وَيَزِيدُ اللَّهُ الَّذِينَ اهْتَدَوْا هُدًى وَالْبَاقِيَاتُ الصَّالِحَاتُ خَيْرٌ عِندَ رَبِّكَ ثَوَابًا وَخَيْرٌ مَّرَدًّا ۞

Have you ever considered [the case of] the one who denies Our signs and boasts: 'I shall surely be given wealth and children!' (77)

أَفَرَأَيْتَ الَّذِى كَفَرَ بِآيَاتِنَا وَقَالَ لَأُوتَيَنَّ مَالًا وَوَلَدًا ۞

Has he, perchance, attained to a realm which is beyond the reach of a created being's perception? Or has he concluded a covenant with the Most Merciful? (78)

أَطَّلَعَ الْغَيْبَ أَمِ اتَّخَذَ عِندَ الرَّحْمَٰنِ عَهْدًا ۞

By no means! We shall record what he says, and We shall long extend his suffering, (79)

كَلَّا سَنَكْتُبُ مَا يَقُولُ وَنَمُدُّ لَهُ مِنَ الْعَذَابِ مَدًّا ۞

and We shall divest him of all that he is now speaking of, and he shall appear before Us all alone. (80)

وَنَرِثُهُ مَا يَقُولُ وَيَأْتِينَا فَرْدًا ۞

They have taken to worshipping deities other than God, hoping that they will give them power and glory. (81)

وَاتَّخَذُوا مِن دُونِ اللَّهِ آلِهَةً لِّيَكُونُوا لَهُمْ عِزًّا ۞

By no means! They will renounce their worship and turn against them. (82)

كَلَّا سَيَكْفُرُونَ بِعِبَادَتِهِمْ وَيَكُونُونَ عَلَيْهِمْ ضِدًّا ۞

Have you not seen how We let loose satanic forces upon the unbelievers to repeatedly incite them to evil? (83)

أَلَمۡ تَرَ أَنَّآ أَرۡسَلۡنَا ٱلشَّيَٰطِينَ عَلَى ٱلۡكَٰفِرِينَ تَؤُزُّهُمۡ أَزّٗا ۝

So, be not in haste: We only allow them a fixed number of days. (84)

فَلَا تَعۡجَلۡ عَلَيۡهِمۡۖ إِنَّمَا نَعُدُّ لَهُمۡ عَدّٗا ۝

The day [will surely come] when We shall gather the God-fearing before [God] the Most Merciful, as honoured guests, (85)

يَوۡمَ نَحۡشُرُ ٱلۡمُتَّقِينَ إِلَى ٱلرَّحۡمَٰنِ وَفۡدٗا ۝

and drive those who are lost in sin to hell as a thirsty herd. (86)

وَنَسُوقُ ٱلۡمُجۡرِمِينَ إِلَىٰ جَهَنَّمَ وِرۡدٗا ۝

None will have power to intercede for them except one who has received permission from [God] the Most Merciful. (87)

لَّا يَمۡلِكُونَ ٱلشَّفَٰعَةَ إِلَّا مَنِ ٱتَّخَذَ عِندَ ٱلرَّحۡمَٰنِ عَهۡدٗا ۝

They say: 'The Most Merciful has taken to Himself a son!' (88)

وَقَالُواْ ٱتَّخَذَ ٱلرَّحۡمَٰنُ وَلَدٗا ۝

Indeed you have said a most monstrous falsehood, (89)

لَّقَدۡ جِئۡتُمۡ شَيۡـًٔا إِدّٗا ۝

at which the heavens might be rent into fragments, and the earth be split asunder, and the mountains fall down in ruins! (90)

تَكَادُ ٱلسَّمَٰوَٰتُ يَتَفَطَّرۡنَ مِنۡهُ وَتَنشَقُّ ٱلۡأَرۡضُ وَتَخِرُّ ٱلۡجِبَالُ هَدًّا ۝

That people should ascribe a son to the Most Merciful, (91)

أَن دَعَوْا لِلرَّحْمَٰنِ وَلَدًا ۝

although it is inconceivable that the Most Merciful should take to Himself a son. (92)

وَمَا يَنۢبَغِى لِلرَّحْمَٰنِ أَن يَتَّخِذَ وَلَدًا ۝

Not one of all [the beings] that are in the heavens or on earth but shall appear before the Most Merciful as a servant. (93)

إِن كُلُّ مَن فِى ٱلسَّمَٰوَٰتِ وَٱلْأَرْضِ إِلَّآ ءَاتِى ٱلرَّحْمَٰنِ عَبْدًا ۝

Indeed, He has full cognizance of them. He has kept a strict count of their numbers, (94)

لَّقَدْ أَحْصَىٰهُمْ وَعَدَّهُمْ عَدًّا ۝

and, on the Day of Resurrection, every one of them will appear before Him all alone. (95)

وَكُلُّهُمْ ءَاتِيهِ يَوْمَ ٱلْقِيَٰمَةِ فَرْدًا ۝

God will certainly bestow love on those who believe and do righteous deeds. (96)

إِنَّ ٱلَّذِينَ ءَامَنُوا۟ وَعَمِلُوا۟ ٱلصَّٰلِحَٰتِ سَيَجْعَلُ لَهُمُ ٱلرَّحْمَٰنُ وُدًّا ۝

And so have We made [the Qur'ān] easy to understand, in your own tongue, so that you may give good tidings to the God-fearing and give warning to those who are given to futile contention. (97)

فَإِنَّمَا يَسَّرْنَٰهُ بِلِسَانِكَ لِتُبَشِّرَ بِهِ ٱلْمُتَّقِينَ وَتُنذِرَ بِهِۦ قَوْمًا لُّدًّا ۝

How many a generation have We destroyed before their time! Can you find a single one of them now, or hear so much as a whisper of them? (98)

وَكَمْ أَهْلَكْنَا قَبْلَهُم مِّن قَرْنٍ هَلْ تُحِسُّ مِنْهُم مِّنْ أَحَدٍ أَوْ تَسْمَعُ لَهُمْ رِكْزًا ۝

Overview

So far the *sūrah* has given us accounts of a number of prophets, including Zachariah and the birth of John, his son, Mary and the birth of Jesus, Abraham and his split from his community and their false deities. We have also heard about the generations that followed them, and whether they lived in accordance with the guidance God gave them or they fell into error. The *sūrah* comments on these accounts declaring that Lordship belongs solely to God, who alone deserves to be worshipped, without partners. This is the essential truth that these histories of earlier prophets bring out in full relief.

Now we look at this final passage which discusses the pagan beliefs that ascribe divinity to other beings beside God and deny resurrection. It portrays a number of scenes of the Day of Judgement and people's different destinies. These are drawn very vividly, full of action, incorporating the reactions of the whole universe, whether the heavens, earth, human beings, *jinn*, believers or unbelievers. The *sūrah* alternates scenes of the Day of Judgement with scenes of this life, so as to establish a real link between the two lives. Thus, our beginnings are shown to take place in this world and we see the results in the life to come, as though the gulf between them is covered in a few short verses, or even a few words. This gives us the sense that the two worlds are interlinked.

The Reality of Resurrection

The passage begins with a scene in which man is shown to be astonished about the reality of resurrection. "*'What!' says man, 'When I am once dead, shall I be raised up alive?'*" (Verse 66) The first point here is that this surprise is attributed to mankind in general. In fact, this same comment was expressed by many peoples during different periods of history. Hence, it is only normal that it should be attributed to the human kind in general. The surprise, or the objection results from man being oblivious of how he came into being. Where and what was he before entering this life? The fact is that he had no existence and then he began to exist. Had man remembered this fact, it would have been easier for him to visualize his return to life after death. Hence, the answer comes in the form of a rhetorical question: *"Does not man remember that We earlier created him, when he was nothing?"* (Verse 67)

This denial of the truth of resurrection is followed by an oath implying a stern warning. God, in His glory, swears by Himself, which makes this the most solemn and serious oath, that they will all be resurrected and gathered together. This is, then, a forgone conclusion: *"By your Lord, We shall most certainly bring them forth."* (Verse 68) But they will not be alone. They will be driven *"together with the evil ones."* (Verse 68) This shows them to be one category with the evil ones who always incite them to deny the truth of faith. Thus the two groups are leaders and followers.

At this point, a vivid picture is drawn showing them sitting on their knees around hell, in total misery and humiliation: *"Then We shall most certainly gather them, on their knees, around hell."* (Verse 68) It is a fearsome scene, with multitudes upon multitudes of people brought together to the vicinity of hell and made to sit on their knees around it, suffering its heat and watching its fierce fire burn. They expect to be thrown into it at any time. They, thus, feel their misery to be compounded with humiliation.

The humiliation is even worse in the case of those who are proud and arrogant in this life. Hence, this image is followed with one in which we see the most hardened of these evil-doers being pulled and dragged towards it: *"Thereupon We shall drag out from every group those who had been most obstinate in their rebellion against the Most Merciful."* (Verse 69) The sound here is stressed heavily, so that it gives an even more graphic and lifelike picture of how they are dragged out. Although the next image is left to our imagination, we nonetheless see them being thrown into hell.

God certainly knows best which people are more deserving of punishment in hell. No one is taken at random, or by chance from that huge multitude. It is God who has brought them here and He knows them all, one by one. He knows what each and every one of them deserves: "*For, indeed, We know best who most deserve to be burnt in the fire of hell.*" (Verse 70) Those, then, are the ones who will be chosen first for the fire.

The believers witness this fearful scene as they too are brought near to it: "*There is not one among you who shall not pass over it: this is, for your Lord, a decree that must be fulfilled.*" (Verse 71) They arrive there, look at hell as it burns fiercely, asking for more feed. They also see the tyrants and the hardened sinners as they are made to enter into it. The believers, however, have a different end: "*But We shall save those who are God-fearing, and leave the wrongdoers there, on their knees.*" (Verse 72)

What Gives Better Returns

Now the *sūrah* leaves with us this scene of the Day of Judgement to paint an image of this world in which the unbelievers are shown behaving arrogantly towards the believers, branding them as poor and weak, and boasting about their own wealth and petty social values.

"*When Our revelations are recited to them in all their clarity, the unbelievers say to those who believe: 'Which of the two sides has a better position and a superior community?'*" (Verse 73) These people have their own social clubs demonstrating all the material values which the wealthy and powerful are keen to emphasize in their corrupt world. By contrast, we see humble gatherings where there are no such material riches or adornments. Instead, there are only the values of faith which unite people in these other groups. The two are juxtaposed so as to fully demonstrate their contrast.

The first side stands out with its wide variety of temptations: wealth, beauty, power and influence. It uses all these to serve people's interests, and provide them with all manner of pleasures. The second side appears too humble by comparison, yet it looks with disdain at wealth and beauty and it ridicules power and influence. It calls on people to join its ranks, without offering them any personal gain, material interest or favours that rulers and governments can provide. It simply offers them the faith, pure and simple, without adding to it any adornment. It seeks strength through being on God's side, nothing else. In fact, it makes clear to mankind that accepting it will involve hardship, effort and struggle. Also clear is the fact that none will be rewarded for anything in this life. The reward to be expected will be in the form of being close to God, enjoying His pleasure in the life to come.

The elders of the Quraysh at the time of the Prophet used to listen to God's revelations being recited to them, but then they would say to the believers who lacked all riches: "*Which of the two sides has a better position and a superior community?*" (Verse 73) Which side: the elders who denied Muhammad's message, or the humble who responded to him? Al-Nadr ibn al-Hārith, 'Amr ibn Hishām, al-Walīd ibn al-Mughīrah and their powerful clique, or Bilāl, 'Ammār, Khabbāb and their brothers, poor and deprived as they were? Had the message preached by Muhammad been any good, would his followers be those who had no power or influence in the Quraysh society? Would they have met in a humble place like al-Arqam's house? Would his opponents be those who enjoyed all the luxuries and social prominence?

Such is worldly logic, advanced by those who have no aspiration to any truly high horizon. It is divine wisdom that keeps faith free of all adornment and superficial attraction, offering no temptation. Thus, only those who take it for its real value, without hope of immediate gain, will accept it. By contrast, those who are after wealth, worldly interests, pleasures and the like will turn away from it.

The *sūrah* comments on the boasts of those arrogant unbelievers, speaking proudly about what they enjoy in this life of pleasures and luxuries. The comment draws their attention to how earlier peoples were destroyed, despite the great riches they enjoyed: "*How many a generation have We destroyed before their time, who were superior in material riches and in splendour.*" (Verse 74) They benefited nothing by all their splendour, nor were their material privileges of any avail to them when God visited His punishment upon them.

Human beings always forget! Had they remembered and reflected, they would not have been deceived by appearances. The end suffered by one generation after another of the unbelievers of old should serve as a clear warning but people remain heedless. They continue to ignore the destiny awaiting them, should they follow in the footsteps of those who preceded them. After all, those earlier unbelievers were of greater strength and enjoyed larger followings and more wealth.

The *surah* then instructs the Prophet to pray against them in the form of a joint appeal to God to add to the misery to be suffered by the side which persisted in error. This is to continue until God fulfils His promise either in this life or in the life to come:

Say: 'As for those who live in error, may the Most Merciful lengthen their span of life!' But when they see the fulfilment of that of which they have been forewarned, be it suffering or the Last Hour, they will realize who is worst in position and weaker in forces. God advances in guidance those who seek His guidance. Good deeds of lasting merit are, in your Lord's sight, worthy of greater recompense, and yield far better returns. (Verses 75–76)

They claim that they follow better and superior guidance to that advocated by Muḥammad and his followers, and their evidence is their wealth and luxuries. Be that as it may! Muḥammad will appeal to his Lord to give increase to each side: the one in error and the one following right guidance. Then when what Muḥammad promises comes to pass, which is the triumph of the believers over those in error, or the final punishment they receive on the Day of Judgement, they will realize which of the two sides is worse in position, weaker in forces. On that day, the believers will rejoice and feel their superiority: "*God advances in guidance those who seek His guidance. Good deeds of lasting merit are, in your Lord's sight, worthy of greater recompense, and yield far better returns.*" (Verse 76) This is certainly better than all that in which human beings find pleasure and enjoyment.

A Promise Coming True

The *sūrah* then picks up on another type of boast and decries it also:

> *Have you ever considered [the case of] the one who denies Our signs and boasts: 'I shall surely be given wealth and children!' Has he, perchance, attained to a realm which is beyond the reach of a created being's perception? Or has he concluded a covenant with the Most Merciful? By no means! We shall record what he says, and We shall long extend his suffering, and We shall divest him of all that he is now speaking of, and he shall appear before Us all alone.* (Verses 77–80)

The immediate cause of the revelation of these verses is reported by Khabbāb ibn al-Aratt who said: "I was an ironmonger, and I had money due to be paid to me by al-'Āṣ ibn Wā'il. I went to him to demand payment. He said, 'By God! I am not going to repay you until you reject Muḥammad and his message.' I said, 'I shall not reject Muḥammad until you have died and been resurrected.' He said to me, 'Well! Wait then. For, when I have been resurrected after my death, I will have wealth and children. You can come to me then and I will pay you what I owe you.' God then revealed these verses."

Al-'Āṣ's words serve merely as an example of the ridicule with which the unbelievers responded to the call of Islam and their derision of the whole concept of resurrection. The Qur'ān highlights the singularity of his claims: "*Has he, perchance, attained to a realm which is beyond the reach of a created being's perception?*" (Verse 78) That would be a good source of information, giving him knowledge of what may happen in that world. "*Or has he concluded a covenant with the Most Merciful?*" (Verse 78) In such a case, he would be certain that God's covenant will be fulfilled. This is followed by an expression of categorical negation which, in Arabic, adds connotations of a prohibition: "*By no means!*" (Verse 79) He neither attained to any such realm, nor made any covenant with God. He merely rejects the truth and derides its promise.

A stern warning is, then, very apt here to stop such arrogant claims: "*By no means! We shall record what he says, and We shall long extend his suffering.*" (Verse 79) We will write down whatever he says, so that it is not forgotten, admitting no dispute on the Day of Judgement. This is again a merely descriptive image, because no dispute or argument is possible as God's knowledge encompasses every little detail. Moreover, the punishment meted out to such sinners will be increased manifold, in time and volume, so as to continue without interruption.

A further image of warning is added: "*and We shall divest him of all that he is now speaking of, and he shall appear before Us all alone.*" (Verse 80) Thus, everything that he speaks about of his wealth and children will be taken away from him, so that he is left with nothing. The Arabic text here, *narithuhū mā yaqūl*, gives an image of inheritance, in order to make the deprivation total, just as when an heir takes away all that a deceased person has left behind, discarding nothing. "*He shall appear before Us all alone.*" (Verse 80) He will have nothing of what gave him his standing in society. Thus, he will have no money, property, relatives, followers or supporters as he appears before God all alone, a powerless individual.

Have you, then, considered this person who denies God's revelation, yet speaks about his fortunes on a day when he has no position or influence? It is a day when he will be deprived of all that gave him power in this life. This is just one type of unbelief, false claims and ridicule of the truth.

The *sūrah* continues its discussion of different aspects of unbelief:

> *They have taken to worshipping deities other than God, hoping that they will give them power and glory. By no means! They will renounce their worship and turn against them. Have you not seen how We let loose satanic forces upon the unbelievers to repeatedly incite them to evil? So, be not in haste: We only allow them a fixed number of days. The day [will surely come] when We shall gather the God-fearing before [God] the Most Merciful, as honoured guests, and drive those who are lost in sin to hell as a thirsty herd. None will have power to intercede for them except one who has received permission from [God] the Most Merciful.*
> (Verses 81–87)

Those who deny God's revelations ascribe divinity to beings other than God, and they will worship such false deities hoping that they will give them power, victory and glory. Some worshipped angels, while others worshipped *jinn*. They called on those whom they worshipped, appealing to them for support against their enemies. But the very angels and *jinn* they worship now denounce their action, disassociate themselves of their worship and condemn their attitude. As the Qur'ān describes their position, those who were worshipped in this present life will on the Day of Judgement *"turn against them,"* and will give a testimony that condemns the unbelievers who worshipped them.

Satanic forces, or devils, will always incite them to commit sinful actions. These forces have been given the chance to tempt and misguide human beings, ever since Satan, or *Iblīs*, requested God to allow him such opportunity. The Prophet is instructed not to precipitate matters: *"So, be not in haste."* (Verse 84) He should not be over-grieved about them. They are given a chance, with a definite time limit, during which everything they do or say is counted and recorded. The verse here describes the accuracy of the reckoning: *"We only allow them a fixed number of days."* (Verse 84) Perhaps we should add that this is an inadequate translation of the Arabic statement, *na ʿddu lahum ʿaddā.* In the Arabic text, the object of what is being numbered is deleted so as to give us an impression of the meticulous counting and recording of everything. This is an awesome image, because when the recording is made by God, it does not overlook or miss anything out. Someone who feels that his boss is carefully monitoring his actions so as to identify any mistake will inevitably feel uneasy and worried. So how does the person who knows that God Almighty is watching him feel?

The outcome of all this reckoning is shown in yet another image of the Day of Judgement. The believers will come to God in a procession met with honour and hospitality: *"The day [will surely come] when We shall gather the God-fearing before [God] the Most Merciful, as honoured guests."* (Verse 86) On the other hand, the unbelievers will be driven like cattle until they arrive at their last abode: *"And drive those who are lost in sin to hell as a thirsty herd."* (Verse 86) There will be no intercession on that day, except for one who has done a good deed in this worldly life. Such a deed will be like a promise from God which He will honour. God has promised those who do good works to give them an abundant reward, and God does not fail to honour His promises.

Monstrous Claims by the Unbelievers

The *sūrah* then refers to another monstrous claim often made by different unbelievers. The Arab idolaters of the past used to claim that the angels were God's daughters, while the unbelievers among the Jews claimed that Ezra was the son of God, and the unbelievers among the Christians made the same claim for Jesus. The whole universe shudders as such false claims are alleged, because monotheism is inherent in the nature of the whole universe.

> *They say: 'The Most Merciful has taken to Himself a son!' Indeed you have said a most monstrous falsehood, at which the heavens might be rent into fragments, and the earth be split asunder, and the mountains fall down in ruins! That people should ascribe a son to the Most Merciful, although it is inconceivable that the Most Merciful should take to Himself a son.* (Verses 88–92)

The very sound of these verses and their rhythm add to the air of anger at this false claim. In fact the whole universe rejects this claim most vehemently. It shudders and quivers with abhorrence as it hears this falsehood against God Almighty. It is a reaction similar to that of a person who feels that his very integrity is attacked, or that the honesty of someone he loves is assailed. The shudder is common to the heavens, the earth and the mountains. In their beat, the words here show the movement of a violent quake.

As soon as the offensive word is uttered, "*They say: The Most Merciful has taken to Himself a son,*" the expression of horror immediately follows: "*Indeed you have said a most monstrous falsehood.*" (Verse 89) Everything that is settled and stable is thus shaken. The whole universe is in anger at this false allegation against God, the Creator. The statement is shocking to everything in nature. The universe is created

376

and functions on the basis of the basic principle of God's oneness: *"Indeed you have said a most monstrous falsehood, at which the heavens might be rent into fragments, and the earth be split asunder, and the mountains fall down in ruins! That people should ascribe a son to the Most Merciful, although it is inconceivable that the Most Merciful should take to Himself a son."* (Verses 89–92)

In the midst of this universal anger, a clear and definitive statement is issued:

> *Not one of all [the beings] that are in the heavens or on earth but shall appear before the Most Merciful as a servant. Indeed, He has full cognizance of them. He has kept a strict count of their numbers, and, on the Day of Resurrection, every one of them will appear before Him all alone.* (Verses 93–95)

All beings that live anywhere in the heavens and on earth are servants of God, subject to His will, submitting to Him willingly. He has neither son nor partner. All are His creatures and servants.

Fear creeps into our hearts as we contemplate the significance of this statement by God, the Most High: *"Indeed, He has full cognizance of them. He has kept a strict count of their numbers."* (Verse 94) None is forgotten and none will be able to escape. *"On the Day of Resurrection, every one of them will appear before Him all alone."* (Verse 95) God watches everyone. They will all come to Him on the Day of Resurrection, each on his or her own. None will have the support or encouragement of anyone else. Indeed, all community feeling is gone, for in front of God, everyone speaks for oneself.

In contrast with this loneliness and isolation, the believers are given a comforting, friendly surrounding: *"God will certainly bestow love on those who believe and do righteous deeds."* (Verse 96) The mention of love in this context is bound to comfort and penetrate people's hearts. It is a type of love that spreads in heaven and spills over to fill the earth and comfort people. The whole universe is given a full share of it.

Abū Hurayrah, a companion of the Prophet, reports that God's Messenger said: "When God loves a human being, He calls in Gabriel and says to him: 'Gabriel, I love this person, so you love him too.'

Gabriel then loves that person and calls out to all those living in heaven, saying: 'God loves this person, so you all love him too.' Thus all those who live in heaven start to love that person. He will also be loved on earth. But if God dislikes someone, He also calls in Gabriel and says: 'Gabriel, I dislike this person, so you hate him too.' Gabriel then hates that person and calls out to all those living in heaven, saying: 'God dislikes this person, so you all hate him too.' Thus all those who live in heaven start to hate that person. He will also be hated on earth." [Related by al-Bukhārī, Muslim and Aḥmad]

This happy news to the believers and this warning to those who deny the truth and argue against it are the message the Qur'ān gives. God has made the Qur'ān easy for the Arabs to read and understand, as He has put it in His Messenger's own language: *"And so have We made [the Qur'ān] easy to understand, in your own tongue, so that you may give good tidings to the God-fearing and give warning to those who are given to futile contention."* (Verse 97)

The *sūrah* concludes with a scene that we contemplate in our minds for a long time, hardly able to shift our gaze:

> *How many a generation have We destroyed before their time! Can you find a single one of them now, or hear so much as a whisper of them?* (Verse 98)

This scene begins with a violent shock before overwhelming us with a total and deep silence. It is as though it takes us to the valley of death to show us how earlier people met their fate. In that great valley which stretches much further than the eyes can see, our minds imagine the life that used to prosper on earth, the people that moved about everywhere, their feelings, hopes and aspirations. But all that is gone. Complete silence pervades. For death has overtaken all, leaving only a host of rotting cadavers. Not a single one stirs, not a single sound, not even a breath. *"Can you find a single one of them now?"* (Verse 98) Look around and see. *"Or can you hear so much as a whisper of them?"* (Verse 98) Listen as much as you wish. There is nothing but a deadly silence. None remain except the One who never dies. Eternal He is and limitless in His glory.

SŪRAH 20

Ṭā Hā

Prologue

This *sūrah* begins and ends with an address to the Prophet explaining his task and outlining the limits of his duties. It is not a mission of distress that has been imposed on him, nor is it an affliction which he has to endure. It is a mission of advocacy and admonition, giving good news and warning against wrongdoing. The ultimate judgement over people is exercised by God, the One, who has no partners, and who controls the whole universe, with all that appears of it and what remains hidden. God is the One who is fully aware of all hearts' secrets, and to whom all people prostrate. It is to Him that all people, obedient and sinners, refer. Hence, the Prophet should not be bothered by whoever chooses the path of unbelief. He should not be distressed over their denial of the truth.

Between the opening and the close, the *sūrah* relates the history of Moses from the point when he received his first revelations to the adoption by the Israelites of the calf as an object of worship. All is related here in full detail, especially the discourse between God and His servant Moses, the argument between Moses and Pharaoh, and the contest between Moses and the Egyptian sorcerers. Within the story, we see how God takes good care of Moses, whom He brought up the way He wanted. It was to Moses and his brother that He said: *"Have no fear; for I shall be with you: I hear all and I see all."* (Verse 46)

Adam's story is given in a short, quick account, highlighting the grace God bestowed on him after he committed his offence. It speaks of the guidance God gave him as also how He allowed his offspring to make their own free choice, whether to follow divine guidance or fall into error, after they were repeatedly warned.

This story is surrounded by scenes of the hereafter, which makes it sound as though it is a complement to what happened on high, right at the very beginning of human life. Thus God's obedient servants will return to heaven, while those who disobey Him are destined for the fire, in confirmation of what was said to Adam at the time he descended to earth. Thus the *sūrah* is made of two parts: the first includes the opening address to the Prophet: "*We did not bestow this Qur'ān on you from on high to cause you distress, but only as an admonition to the God-fearing.*" (Verses 2–3) This is followed by the story of Moses, which is given as an example of the care God takes of those whom He chooses to convey His message to people. They will not suffer distress on account of their task, as they receive His care.

The second part of the *sūrah* provides some scenes of the Day of Judgement as well as Adam's story. Both fit in well with the opening of the *sūrah* and the story of Moses. The end of the *sūrah* is thus similar to its beginning, providing a consistent and distinctive atmosphere.

The *sūrah*, however, is distinguished by a special, sublime and majestic air which touches our hearts. It generates a sense of reassurance and submission to God Almighty. This air is generated by the scene when God, the Most Merciful, makes His presence felt by His servant Moses in the sacred valley, and the long discourse in the deep silence of the night, when Moses is totally alone, except for his Lord's presence. The whole universe responds to this long discourse. This is further amplified by the scene of God's presence on the Day of Resurrection when all creatures are gathered: "*All sounds will be hushed before the Most Merciful, and you will hear nothing but a faint sough in the air.*" (Verse 108) "*All faces will be humbled before the Ever-Living, the Self-Subsisting Lord.*" (Verse 111)

The rhythm of the whole *sūrah* employs the same beat, from start to finish, providing a pleasant, relaxing feeling that opens up to the universe. It is further enhanced by the choice of a long 'a' sound for verse endings, throughout the entire *sūrah*, excepting a small number of verses.

I

The Purpose of Revelation

Ṭā Hā

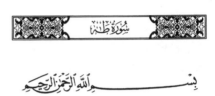

In the Name of God, the Merciful, the Beneficent

Ṭā Hā. (1)

We did not bestow this Qur'ān on you from on high to cause you distress, (2)

but only as an admonition to the God-fearing. (3)

It is a revelation from Him who has created the earth and the high heavens, (4)

the Most Merciful, established on the throne of His almightiness. (5)

To Him belongs all that is in the heavens and on earth, as well as all that is between them, and underneath the soil. (6)

لَهُۥ مَا فِى ٱلسَّمَٰوَٰتِ وَمَا فِى ٱلْأَرْضِ وَمَا بَيْنَهُمَا وَمَا تَحْتَ ٱلثَّرَىٰ ﴿٦﴾

If you say anything aloud, then [know that] He knows all that is secret, as well as all that is yet more hidden. (7)

وَإِن تَجْهَرْ بِٱلْقَوْلِ فَإِنَّهُۥ يَعْلَمُ ٱلسِّرَّ وَأَخْفَى ﴿٧﴾

[He is] God; there is no deity other than Him. His alone are all the attributes of perfection. (8)

ٱللَّهُ لَآ إِلَٰهَ إِلَّا هُوَ لَهُ ٱلْأَسْمَآءُ ٱلْحُسْنَىٰ ﴿٨﴾

Have you learnt the story of Moses? (9)

وَهَلْ أَتَىٰكَ حَدِيثُ مُوسَىٰٓ ﴿٩﴾

When he saw a fire, he said to his family: 'Wait here! I perceive a fire. Perhaps I can bring you a lighted torch, or find some guidance at the fire.' (10)

إِذْ رَءَا نَارًا فَقَالَ لِأَهْلِهِ ٱمْكُثُوٓا إِنِّىٓ ءَانَسْتُ نَارًا لَّعَلِّىٓ ءَاتِيكُم مِّنْهَا بِقَبَسٍ أَوْ أَجِدُ عَلَى ٱلنَّارِ هُدًى ﴿١٠﴾

But when he came close to it, a voice called out to him: 'Moses, (11)

فَلَمَّآ أَتَىٰهَا نُودِىَ يَٰمُوسَىٰٓ ﴿١١﴾

I am your Lord! Take off your sandals, for you are in the sacred valley of Ṭuwā. (12)

إِنِّىٓ أَنَا۠ رَبُّكَ فَٱخْلَعْ نَعْلَيْكَ إِنَّكَ بِٱلْوَادِ ٱلْمُقَدَّسِ طُوًى ﴿١٢﴾

Know that I have chosen you. Listen, then, to what is being revealed. (13)

وَأَنَا ٱخْتَرْتُكَ فَٱسْتَمِعْ لِمَا يُوحَىٰٓ ﴿١٣﴾

Indeed, I alone am God; there is no deity other than Me. So, worship Me alone, and establish regular prayer to celebrate My praise. (14)

إِنَّنِي أَنَا ٱللَّهُ لَآ إِلَٰهَ إِلَّآ أَنَا۠ فَٱعْبُدْنِي وَأَقِمِ ٱلصَّلَوٰةَ لِذِكْرِيٓ ١٤

Although I have chosen to keep it hidden, the Last Hour is bound to come, so that every soul may be rewarded in accordance with what it strove for. (15)

إِنَّ ٱلسَّاعَةَ ءَاتِيَةٌ أَكَادُ أُخْفِيهَا لِتُجْزَىٰ كُلُّ نَفْسٍ بِمَا تَسْعَىٰ ١٥

Hence, let not anyone who does not believe in its coming and follows only his own desires turn your thoughts from it, lest you perish. (16)

فَلَا يَصُدَّنَّكَ عَنْهَا مَن لَّا يُؤْمِنُ بِهَا وَٱتَّبَعَ هَوَىٰهُ فَتَرْدَىٰ ١٦

Now, what is this in your right hand, Moses?' (17)

وَمَا تِلْكَ بِيَمِينِكَ يَٰمُوسَىٰ ١٧

He answered: 'It is my staff; upon it I lean, and with it I beat down the leaves for my sheep; and other uses have I for it.' (18)

قَالَ هِيَ عَصَايَ أَتَوَكَّؤُا۟ عَلَيْهَا وَأَهُشُّ بِهَا عَلَىٰ غَنَمِي وَلِيَ فِيهَا مَـَٔارِبُ أُخْرَىٰ ١٨

Said He: 'Throw it down, Moses.' (19)

قَالَ أَلْقِهَا يَٰمُوسَىٰ ١٩

So he threw it down, and thereupon it was a snake, moving rapidly. (20)

فَأَلْقَاهَا فَإِذَا هِىَ حَيَّةٌ تَسْعَىٰ ﴿٢٠﴾

Said He: 'Take it up and have no fear. We shall restore it to its former state. (21)

قَالَ خُذْهَا وَلَا تَخَفْ سَنُعِيدُهَا سِيرَتَهَا الْأُولَىٰ ﴿٢١﴾

Now put your hand under your armpit. It will come out [shining] white, without blemish: another sign. (22)

وَاضْمُمْ يَدَكَ إِلَىٰ جَنَاحِكَ تَخْرُجْ بَيْضَاءَ مِنْ غَيْرِ سُوءٍ ءَايَةً أُخْرَىٰ ﴿٢٢﴾

We shall show you some of Our most wondrous signs. (23)

لِنُرِيَكَ مِنْ ءَايَٰتِنَا الْكُبْرَىٰ ﴿٢٣﴾

Go to Pharaoh; for he has indeed transgressed all bounds.' (24)

اذْهَبْ إِلَىٰ فِرْعَوْنَ إِنَّهُ طَغَىٰ ﴿٢٤﴾

Said [Moses]: 'My Lord, open up my heart [to Your light], (25)

قَالَ رَبِّ اشْرَحْ لِى صَدْرِى ﴿٢٥﴾

and make my mission easy for me, (26)

وَيَسِّرْ لِى أَمْرِى ﴿٢٦﴾

and free my tongue from its impediment, (27)

وَاحْلُلْ عُقْدَةً مِّن لِّسَانِى ﴿٢٧﴾

so that people may understand what I say. (28)

يَفْقَهُوا قَوْلِى ﴿٢٨﴾

Appoint for me a helper from among my kinsmen, (29)

وَاجْعَل لِّى وَزِيرًا مِّنْ أَهْلِى ﴿٢٩﴾

Aaron, my brother. (30)

هَٰرُونَ أَخِى ۝

Grant me strength through him, (31)

ٱشْدُدْ بِهِۦ أَزْرِى ۝

and let him share my task, (32)

وَأَشْرِكْهُ فِىٓ أَمْرِى ۝

so that together we may extol Your limitless glory (33)

كَىْ نُسَبِّحَكَ كَثِيرًا ۝

and remember You always. (34)

وَنَذْكُرَكَ كَثِيرًا ۝

You are surely watching over us.' (35)

إِنَّكَ كُنتَ بِنَا بَصِيرًا ۝

Said He: 'You are granted all that you have asked for, Moses. (36)

قَالَ قَدْ أُوتِيتَ سُؤْلَكَ يَٰمُوسَىٰ ۝

And indeed We bestowed Our favour upon you in a time gone by, (37)

وَلَقَدْ مَنَنَّا عَلَيْكَ مَرَّةً أُخْرَىٰٓ ۝

when We inspired your mother, saying: (38)

إِذْ أَوْحَيْنَآ إِلَىٰٓ أُمِّكَ مَا يُوحَىٰٓ ۝

"Place [your child] in a chest and throw it into the river. The river will cast him ashore, and one who is an enemy to Me and an enemy to him will pick him up." I lavished My love on you, so that you may be reared under My watchful eye. (39)

أَنِ ٱقْذِفِيهِ فِي ٱلتَّابُوتِ فَٱقْذِفِيهِ فِي ٱلْيَمِّ فَلْيُلْقِهِ ٱلْيَمُّ بِٱلسَّاحِلِ يَأْخُذْهُ عَدُوٌّ لِّي وَعَدُوٌّ لَّهُ وَأَلْقَيْتُ عَلَيْكَ مَحَبَّةً مِّنِّي وَلِتُصْنَعَ عَلَىٰ عَيْنِي ﴿٣٩﴾

Then your sister went forth and said [to Pharaoh's people]: "Shall I direct you to one who might take care of him?" Thus did We restore you to your mother, so that her mind might be set at ease and that she might not grieve. And [when you came of age,] you killed a man; but We saved you from all grief, although We tested you with various trials. You then stayed for years among the people of Madyan; and now you have come here, Moses, as ordained [by Me]; (40)

إِذْ تَمْشِي أُخْتُكَ فَتَقُولُ هَلْ أَدُلُّكُمْ عَلَىٰ مَن يَكْفُلُهُ فَرَجَعْنَاكَ إِلَىٰ أُمِّكَ كَيْ تَقَرَّ عَيْنُهَا وَلَا تَحْزَنَ وَقَتَلْتَ نَفْسًا فَنَجَّيْنَاكَ مِنَ ٱلْغَمِّ وَفَتَنَّاكَ فُتُونًا فَلَبِثْتَ سِنِينَ فِي أَهْلِ مَدْيَنَ ثُمَّ جِئْتَ عَلَىٰ قَدَرٍ يَٰمُوسَىٰ ﴿٤٠﴾

for I have chosen you for Myself. (41)

وَٱصْطَنَعْتُكَ لِنَفْسِي ﴿٤١﴾

Go forth, then, you and your brother, with My signs, and never slacken in remembering Me. (42)

ٱذْهَبْ أَنتَ وَأَخُوكَ بِـَٔايَٰتِي وَلَا تَنِيَا فِي ذِكْرِي ﴿٤٢﴾

Go forth, both of you, to Pharaoh; for he has transgressed all bounds of equity! (43)

اَذْهَبَآ إِلَىٰ فِرْعَوْنَ إِنَّهُۥ طَغَىٰ ۝

But speak to him mildly, so that he may yet take heed, or may be filled with apprehension.' (44)

فَقُولَا لَهُۥ قَوْلًا لَّيِّنًا لَّعَلَّهُۥ يَتَذَكَّرُ أَوْ يَخْشَىٰ ۝

They said: 'Our Lord! We fear lest he hasten with insolence or tyranny against us.' (45)

قَالَا رَبَّنَآ إِنَّنَا نَخَافُ أَن يَفْرُطَ عَلَيْنَآ أَوْ أَن يَطْغَىٰ ۝

Answered He: 'Have no fear. I shall be with you. I hear all and see all. (46)

قَالَ لَا تَخَافَآ إِنَّنِي مَعَكُمَآ أَسْمَعُ وَأَرَىٰ ۝

Go, then, you two to him and say, "We are the emissaries of your Lord. Let the Children of Israel go with us, and oppress them no more. We have now come to you with a message from your Lord. Peace to all who follow [God's] guidance. (47)

فَأْتِيَاهُ فَقُولَآ إِنَّا رَسُولَا رَبِّكَ فَأَرْسِلْ مَعَنَا بَنِىٓ إِسْرَٰٓءِيلَ وَلَا تُعَذِّبْهُمْ قَدْ جِئْنَٰكَ بِـَٔايَةٍ مِّن رَّبِّكَ وَالسَّلَٰمُ عَلَىٰ مَنِ اتَّبَعَ الْهُدَىٰٓ ۝

It has been revealed to us that the suffering shall befall those who deny the truth and turn away from it." (48)

إِنَّا قَدْ أُوحِىَ إِلَيْنَآ أَنَّ الْعَذَابَ عَلَىٰ مَن كَذَّبَ وَتَوَلَّىٰ ۝

[Pharaoh] said: 'Who, now, is this Lord of you two, Moses?' (49)

قَالَ فَمَن رَّبُّكُمَا يَٰمُوسَىٰ ۝

He replied: 'Our Lord is He who gives everything its distinctive nature and form, and further guides them.' (50)

قَالَ رَبُّنَا ٱلَّذِىٓ أَعْطَىٰ كُلَّ شَىْءٍ خَلْقَهُۥ ثُمَّ هَدَىٰ ﴿٥٠﴾

Said [Pharaoh]: 'And what of all the past generations?' (51)

قَالَ فَمَا بَالُ ٱلْقُرُونِ ٱلْأُولَىٰ ﴿٥١﴾

[Moses] answered: 'Knowledge of that rests with my Lord alone, recorded in a Book. My Lord does not err, and neither does He forget. (52)

قَالَ عِلْمُهَا عِندَ رَبِّى فِى كِتَٰبٍ لَّا يَضِلُّ رَبِّى وَلَا يَنسَى ﴿٥٢﴾

He it is who has made the earth your cradle, and has traced on it paths for you to walk on, and who sends down waters from the sky with which We bring forth diverse pairs of plants. (53)

ٱلَّذِى جَعَلَ لَكُمُ ٱلْأَرْضَ مَهْدًا وَسَلَكَ لَكُمْ فِيهَا سُبُلًا وَأَنزَلَ مِنَ ٱلسَّمَآءِ مَآءً فَأَخْرَجْنَا بِهِۦٓ أَزْوَٰجًا مِّن نَّبَاتٍ شَتَّىٰ ﴿٥٣﴾

Eat, then, and graze your cattle. In all this there are signs for those who are endowed with reason. (54)

كُلُوا۟ وَٱرْعَوْا۟ أَنْعَٰمَكُمْ إِنَّ فِى ذَٰلِكَ لَءَايَٰتٍ لِّأُو۟لِى ٱلنُّهَىٰ ﴿٥٤﴾

Out of this [earth] have We created you, and into it shall We return you, and out of it shall We bring you forth once again. (55)

مِنْهَا خَلَقْنَٰكُمْ وَفِيهَا نُعِيدُكُمْ وَمِنْهَا نُخْرِجُكُمْ تَارَةً أُخْرَىٰ ﴿٥٥﴾

And, indeed, We showed Pharaoh all Our signs, but he denied them and refused [to take heed]. (56)

وَلَقَدْ أَرَيْنَٰهُ ءَايَٰتِنَا كُلَّهَا فَكَذَّبَ وَأَبَىٰ ﴿٥٦﴾

He said: 'Have you, Moses, come to drive us out of our land with your magic? (57)

قَالَ أَجِئْتَنَا لِتُخْرِجَنَا مِنْ أَرْضِنَا بِسِحْرِكَ يَٰمُوسَىٰ ۝

In that case, we shall most certainly produce for you magic to match it. Set, then, for us an appointment which neither we nor you shall fail to keep, at a suitable, open place.' (58)

فَلَنَأْتِيَنَّكَ بِسِحْرٍ مِّثْلِهِ فَٱجْعَلْ بَيْنَنَا وَبَيْنَكَ مَوْعِدًا لَّا نُخْلِفُهُ نَحْنُ وَلَآ أَنتَ مَكَانًا سُوًى ۝

Answered Moses: 'Your appointment shall be the day of the Festival; and let the people assemble when the sun is risen high.' (59)

قَالَ مَوْعِدُكُمْ يَوْمُ ٱلزِّينَةِ وَأَن يُحْشَرَ ٱلنَّاسُ ضُحًى ۝

Thereupon Pharaoh withdrew and put together the artful scheme which he would pursue; and then turned up. (60)

فَتَوَلَّىٰ فِرْعَوْنُ فَجَمَعَ كَيْدَهُ ثُمَّ أَتَىٰ ۝

Moses said to them: 'Woe betide you! Do not invent any falsehood against God, lest He afflict you with most grievous suffering. He who contrives such a lie is sure to come to grief.' (61)

قَالَ لَهُم مُّوسَىٰ وَيْلَكُمْ لَا تَفْتَرُواْ عَلَى ٱللَّهِ كَذِبًا فَيُسْحِتَكُم بِعَذَابٍ وَقَدْ خَابَ مَنِ ٱفْتَرَىٰ ۝

So they debated among themselves as to what to do; but they kept their counsel secret. (62)

فَتَنَٰزَعُوٓاْ أَمْرَهُم بَيْنَهُمْ وَأَسَرُّواْ ٱلنَّجْوَىٰ ۝

389

They said: 'These two are surely sorcerers intent on driving you away from your land by their sorcery, and on doing away with your exemplary way of life. (63)

قَالُوٓاْ إِنْ هَٰذَٰنِ لَسَٰحِرَٰنِ يُرِيدَانِ أَن يُخْرِجَاكُم مِّنْ أَرْضِكُم بِسِحْرِهِمَا وَيَذْهَبَا بِطَرِيقَتِكُمُ ٱلْمُثْلَىٰ ﴿٦٣﴾

Hence, decide on the scheme you will pursue, and then come forward in one single body. For, indeed, he who prevails today shall ever be successful.' (64)

فَأَجْمِعُواْ كَيْدَكُمْ ثُمَّ ٱئْتُواْ صَفًّا وَقَدْ أَفْلَحَ ٱلْيَوْمَ مَنِ ٱسْتَعْلَىٰ ﴿٦٤﴾

Said [the sorcerers]: 'Moses! Either you throw [first], or we shall be the first to throw.' (65)

قَالُواْ يَٰمُوسَىٰٓ إِمَّآ أَن تُلْقِىَ وَإِمَّآ أَن نَّكُونَ أَوَّلَ مَنْ أَلْقَىٰ ﴿٦٥﴾

He answered: 'You throw first!' And by virtue of their sorcery, their ropes and staffs seemed to him to be moving rapidly. (66)

قَالَ بَلْ أَلْقُواْ فَإِذَا حِبَالُهُمْ وَعِصِيُّهُمْ يُخَيَّلُ إِلَيْهِ مِن سِحْرِهِمْ أَنَّهَا تَسْعَىٰ ﴿٦٦﴾

And in his heart Moses became apprehensive. (67)

فَأَوْجَسَ فِى نَفْسِهِۦ خِيفَةً مُّوسَىٰ ﴿٦٧﴾

But We said [to him]: 'Have no fear! It is you who shall certainly prevail. (68)

قُلْنَا لَا تَخَفْ إِنَّكَ أَنتَ ٱلْأَعْلَىٰ ﴿٦٨﴾

Now throw that which is in your right hand and it shall swallow up all that they have wrought. For, they have wrought nothing but a sorcerer's deceitful trick; and sorcerers can never come to any good, whatever they may do.' (69)

وَأَلْقِ مَا فِى يَمِينِكَ تَلْقَفْ مَا صَنَعُوٓاْ إِنَّمَا صَنَعُواْ كَيْدُ سَٰحِرٍ وَلَا يُفْلِحُ ٱلسَّاحِرُ حَيْثُ أَتَىٰ ﴿٦٩﴾

So down fell the sorcerers, prostrating themselves, and declared: 'We do believe in the Lord of Aaron and Moses.' (70)

فَأُلْقِيَ ٱلسَّحَرَةُ سُجَّدًا قَالُوٓاْ ءَامَنَّا بِرَبِّ هَٰرُونَ وَمُوسَىٰ ۝

Said [Pharaoh]: 'Do you believe in him before I have given you permission? Surely, he must be your master who has taught you witchcraft! I shall most certainly cut off your hands and feet on opposite sides, and I shall most certainly crucify you on the trunks of the palm trees. You will then come to know for certain which of us can inflict a more severe and longer lasting punishment.' (71)

قَالَ ءَامَنتُمْ لَهُۥ قَبْلَ أَنْ ءَاذَنَ لَكُمْ إِنَّهُۥ لَكَبِيرُكُمُ ٱلَّذِى عَلَّمَكُمُ ٱلسِّحْرَ فَلَأُقَطِّعَنَّ أَيْدِيَكُمْ وَأَرْجُلَكُم مِّنْ خِلَٰفٍ وَلَأُصَلِّبَنَّكُمْ فِى جُذُوعِ ٱلنَّخْلِ وَلَتَعْلَمُنَّ أَيُّنَآ أَشَدُّ عَذَابًا وَأَبْقَىٰ ۝

They answered: 'Never shall we prefer you to all the evidence of the truth that has come to us, nor to Him who has brought us into being! Decree, then, whatever you are going to decree. You can only decree on what pertains to this worldly life. (72)

قَالُواْ لَن نُّؤْثِرَكَ عَلَىٰ مَا جَآءَنَا مِنَ ٱلْبَيِّنَٰتِ وَٱلَّذِى فَطَرَنَا فَٱقْضِ مَآ أَنتَ قَاضٍ إِنَّمَا تَقْضِى هَٰذِهِ ٱلْحَيَوٰةَ ٱلدُّنْيَآ ۝

As for us, we have come to believe in our Lord, hoping that He may forgive us our faults and all that magic to which you have forced us. God is certainly the best and He is Everlasting.' (73)

إِنَّآ ءَامَنَّا بِرَبِّنَا لِيَغْفِرَ لَنَا خَطَٰيَٰنَا وَمَآ أَكْرَهْتَنَا عَلَيْهِ مِنَ ٱلسِّحْرِ وَٱللَّهُ خَيْرٌ وَأَبْقَىٰ ۝

He who shall appear before his Lord [on Judgement Day] laden with sin shall be consigned to hell, where he shall neither die nor live. (74)

وَإِنَّهُ مَن يَأْتِ رَبَّهُ مُجْرِمًا فَإِنَّ لَهُ جَهَنَّمَ لَا يَمُوتُ فِيهَا وَلَا يَحْيَىٰ ۝

But he who shall appear before Him as a believer, having done righteous deeds, shall be exalted to the highest ranks, (75)

وَمَن يَأْتِهِ مُؤْمِنًا قَدْ عَمِلَ الصَّٰلِحَٰتِ فَأُوْلَٰٓئِكَ لَهُمُ الدَّرَجَٰتُ الْعُلَىٰ ۝

abiding in the gardens of Eden, through which running waters flow. Such shall be the recompense of those who keep themselves pure. (76)

جَنَّٰتُ عَدْنٍ تَجْرِى مِن تَحْتِهَا الْأَنْهَٰرُ خَٰلِدِينَ فِيهَا ۚ وَذَٰلِكَ جَزَآءُ مَن تَزَكَّىٰ ۝

Then We thus inspired Moses: 'Go forth with My servants by night, and strike out for them a dry path through the sea. Have no fear of being overtaken, and dread nothing.' (77)

وَلَقَدْ أَوْحَيْنَآ إِلَىٰ مُوسَىٰٓ أَنْ أَسْرِ بِعِبَادِى فَاضْرِبْ لَهُمْ طَرِيقًا فِى الْبَحْرِ يَبَسًا لَّا تَخَٰفُ دَرَكًا وَلَا تَخْشَىٰ ۝

Pharaoh pursued them with his hosts, but they were overwhelmed by the power of the sea. (78)

فَأَتْبَعَهُمْ فِرْعَوْنُ بِجُنُودِهِ فَغَشِيَهُم مِّنَ الْيَمِّ مَا غَشِيَهُمْ ۝

For Pharaoh had led his people astray and had not guided them aright. (79)

وَأَضَلَّ فِرْعَوْنُ قَوْمَهُ وَمَا هَدَىٰ ۝

Children of Israel! We saved you from your enemy, and then We made a covenant with you on the right flank of Mount Sinai. We sent down manna and quails for you. (80)

يَٰبَنِىٓ إِسْرَٰٓءِيلَ قَدْ أَنجَيْنَٰكُم مِّنْ عَدُوِّكُمْ وَوَٰعَدْنَٰكُمْ جَانِبَ ٱلطُّورِ ٱلْأَيْمَنَ وَنَزَّلْنَا عَلَيْكُمُ ٱلْمَنَّ وَٱلسَّلْوَىٰ ﴿٨٠﴾

Eat of the wholesome things which We have provided for you and do not transgress, lest you should incur My wrath. He that incurs My wrath has indeed thrown himself into utter ruin; (81)

كُلُوا۟ مِن طَيِّبَٰتِ مَا رَزَقْنَٰكُمْ وَلَا تَطْغَوْا۟ فِيهِ فَيَحِلَّ عَلَيْكُمْ غَضَبِى وَمَن يَحْلِلْ عَلَيْهِ غَضَبِى فَقَدْ هَوَىٰ ﴿٨١﴾

but I certainly forgive all sins for anyone who repents, believes and does righteous deeds, and thereafter keeps to the right path. (82)

وَإِنِّى لَغَفَّارٌ لِّمَن تَابَ وَءَامَنَ وَعَمِلَ صَٰلِحًا ثُمَّ ٱهْتَدَىٰ ﴿٨٢﴾

[And God said]: 'Now what has caused you, Moses, to leave your people behind in so great a haste?' (83)

وَمَآ أَعْجَلَكَ عَن قَوْمِكَ يَٰمُوسَىٰ ﴿٨٣﴾

He answered: 'They are treading in my footsteps, while I have hastened to You, my Lord, so that You might be well-pleased with me.' (84)

قَالَ هُمْ أُو۟لَآءِ عَلَىٰٓ أَثَرِى وَعَجِلْتُ إِلَيْكَ رَبِّ لِتَرْضَىٰ ﴿٨٤﴾

Said He: 'Then [know that] in your absence We have put your people to a test, and the Sāmiriy has led them astray.' (85)

قَالَ فَإِنَّا قَدْ فَتَنَّا قَوْمَكَ مِنۢ بَعْدِكَ وَأَضَلَّهُمُ ٱلسَّامِرِىُّ ﴿٨٥﴾

393

Thus Moses returned to his people full of wrath and sorrow: 'My people,' he said, 'Did not your Lord hold out a goodly promise to you? Did, then, [the fulfilment of] this promise seem to you too long in coming? Or are you determined to see your Lord's condemnation fall upon you, and so you broke your promise to me?' (86)

فَرَجَعَ مُوسَىٰ إِلَىٰ قَوْمِهِ غَضْبَـٰنَ أَسِفًا قَالَ يَـٰقَوْمِ أَلَمْ يَعِدْكُمْ رَبُّكُمْ وَعْدًا حَسَنًا أَفَطَالَ عَلَيْكُمُ ٱلْعَهْدُ أَمْ أَرَدتُّمْ أَن يَحِلَّ عَلَيْكُمْ غَضَبٌ مِّن رَّبِّكُمْ فَأَخْلَفْتُم مَّوْعِدِي ۝

They answered: 'We did not break our promise to you of our own free-will, but we were loaded with the burdens of the [Egyptian] people's ornaments, and so we threw them [into the fire], and likewise this Sāmiriy threw.' (87)

قَالُواْ مَآ أَخْلَفْنَا مَوْعِدَكَ بِمَلْكِنَا وَلَـٰكِنَّا حُمِّلْنَآ أَوْزَارًا مِّن زِينَةِ ٱلْقَوْمِ فَقَذَفْنَـٰهَا فَكَذَٰلِكَ أَلْقَى ٱلسَّامِرِيُّ ۝

Thus he produced for them the effigy of a calf, which made a lowing sound. 'This,' they said, 'is your deity and the deity of Moses; but he has forgotten.' (88)

فَأَخْرَجَ لَهُمْ عِجْلًا جَسَدًا لَّهُ خُوَارٌ فَقَالُواْ هَـٰذَآ إِلَـٰهُكُمْ وَإِلَـٰهُ مُوسَىٰ فَنَسِيَ ۝

Why! Did they not see that it could not give them any response, and that it could neither harm nor benefit them? (89)

أَفَلَا يَرَوْنَ أَلَّا يَرْجِعُ إِلَيْهِمْ قَوْلًا وَلَا يَمْلِكُ لَهُمْ ضَرًّا وَلَا نَفْعًا ۝

And, indeed, Aaron had said to them earlier: 'My people! You are but being tempted to evil by this calf. Your only Lord is the Most Merciful! Follow me, then, and do as I bid you.' (90)

وَلَقَدْ قَالَ لَهُمْ هَٰرُونُ مِن قَبْلُ يَٰقَوْمِ إِنَّمَا فُتِنتُم بِهِۦ وَإِنَّ رَبَّكُمُ ٱلرَّحْمَٰنُ فَٱتَّبِعُونِى وَأَطِيعُوٓاْ أَمْرِى ۝

But they had replied: 'By no means shall we cease worshipping it until Moses comes back to us.' (91)

قَالُواْ لَن نَّبْرَحَ عَلَيْهِ عَٰكِفِينَ حَتَّىٰ يَرْجِعَ إِلَيْنَا مُوسَىٰ ۝

[Moses] said: 'Aaron! What has prevented you, when you saw that they had gone astray, (92)

قَالَ يَٰهَٰرُونُ مَا مَنَعَكَ إِذْ رَأَيْتَهُمْ ضَلُّوٓاْ ۝

from following me? Why have you disobeyed me?' (93)

أَلَّا تَتَّبِعَنِ أَفَعَصَيْتَ أَمْرِى ۝

'Son of my mother,' he replied, 'do not seize me by my beard, or by my head! I was afraid that you might say, "You have caused a split among the Israelites and did not wait for my orders."' (94)

قَالَ يَبْنَؤُمَّ لَا تَأْخُذْ بِلِحْيَتِى وَلَا بِرَأْسِىٓ إِنِّى خَشِيتُ أَن تَقُولَ فَرَّقْتَ بَيْنَ بَنِىٓ إِسْرَٰٓءِيلَ وَلَمْ تَرْقُبْ قَوْلِى ۝

Said [Moses]: 'What is then your case, Sāmiriy?' (95)

قَالَ فَمَا خَطْبُكَ يَٰسَٰمِرِىُّ ۝

He answered: 'I have gained insight into something which they were unable to see; and so I took a handful of dust from the trail of the messenger and flung it away; for thus has my mind prompted me to act.' (96)

قَالَ بَصُرْتُ بِمَا لَمْ يَبْصُرُواْ بِهِۦ فَقَبَضْتُ قَبْضَةً مِّنْ أَثَرِ ٱلرَّسُولِ فَنَبَذْتُهَا وَكَذَٰلِكَ سَوَّلَتْ لِى نَفْسِى ۝

Said [Moses]: 'Begone, then! It shall be your lot to say throughout your life, "Do not touch me." But you shall be faced with a destiny from which you shall have no escape. Now look at this deity of yours to whose worship you have become so devoted: we shall most certainly burn it, and then scatter it far and wide over the sea.' (97)

قَالَ فَٱذْهَبْ فَإِنَّ لَكَ فِي ٱلْحَيَوٰةِ أَن تَقُولَ لَا مِسَاسَ وَإِنَّ لَكَ مَوْعِدًا لَّن تُخْلَفَهُ وَٱنظُرْ إِلَىٰ إِلَٰهِكَ ٱلَّذِي ظَلْتَ عَلَيْهِ عَاكِفًا لَّنُحَرِّقَنَّهُ ثُمَّ لَنَنسِفَنَّهُ فِي ٱلْيَمِّ نَسْفًا ۝

Your only deity is God, other than whom there is no deity. His knowledge encompasses all things. (98)

إِنَّمَآ إِلَٰهُكُمُ ٱللَّهُ ٱلَّذِي لَآ إِلَٰهَ إِلَّا هُوَ وَسِعَ كُلَّ شَيْءٍ عِلْمًا ۝

Knowledge Going Deeper than Secrets

Ṭā Hā. *We did not bestow this Qur'ān on you from on high to cause you distress, but only as an admonition to the God-fearing. It is a revelation from Him who has created the earth and the high heavens, the Most Merciful, established on the throne of His almightiness. To Him belongs all that is in the heavens and on earth, as well as all that is between them, and underneath the soil. If you say anything aloud, then [know that] He knows all that is secret, as well as all that is yet more hidden. [He is] God; there is no deity other than Him. His alone are all the attributes of perfection.* (Verses 1–8)

These opening verses give the *sūrah* a tender start beginning with two letter sounds, Ṭā Hā, to indicate that this *sūrah*, like the entire Qur'ān, is made up of letters from the Arabic alphabet, as we have explained in earlier volumes. The two letters chosen here have the same sound-ending as the verses of the *sūrah*.

We then have a reference to the Qur'ān, in the same way as other *sūrahs* commencing with separate letters, but the reference here is made in the form of an address to the Prophet [peace be on him]. "*We did not bestow this Qur'ān on you from on high to cause you distress.*" (Verse 2) We have not revealed this Qur'ān so that it leads you to a state of distress. We do not want to make things hard for you requiring that you recite it in worship going beyond the limits of human ability. In fact, the Qur'ān is made easy for remembrance, and whatever requirements and duties it imposes are easy for people to fulfil. It only imposes duties that are well within human ability. Reciting it during worship is a blessing, providing us with an opportunity to be in touch with the Supreme Society from whom we derive strength, reassurance, contentment and a feeling of companionship.

Nor did We reveal this Qur'ān so that you would become distressed when people refused to accept it as divine revelation. You are not required to force them to faith, nor to overstretch yourself in trying to convince them of the truth of your message. This Qur'ān is bestowed from on high to you as a reminder and a warning: "*But only as an admonition to the God-fearing.*" (Verse 3)

When God's Messenger gives such an admonition, reminding people of God and warning them against disbelief and disobedience of God's orders, his mission is fulfilled. God's Messenger is not required to open sealed hearts, nor is it his task to overpower minds and souls. This can only be done by God, who has bestowed this Qur'ān from on high. He is the One who is in full control of the whole universe and who knows every heart's secrets: "*It is a revelation from Him who has created the earth and the high heavens, the Most Merciful, established on the throne of His almightiness. To Him belongs all that is in the heavens and on earth, as well as all that is between them, and underneath the soil.*" (Verses 4–6)

The One who has revealed this Qur'ān is God who created the earth and the high heavens. This shows that the revelation of the Qur'ān is a universal phenomenon, like the creation of the heavens and earth. It is a revelation from on high. The *sūrah* thus links the laws that govern the universe with those that bring revelation. There is thus perfect harmony here between the high heavens, the earth and the Qur'ān, revealed as it is from on high to the earth.

The One who bestowed the Qur'ān from on high, and created the earth and the high heavens is God, the 'Most Merciful'. Hence, He has not given it to His servant, Muḥammad, to cause him distress. His attribute of limitless grace is highlighted here to emphasize this. Besides, He is the One in control of the whole universe, God, "*the Most Merciful, established on the throne of His almightiness.*" This is an expression indicating complete control and total power. So, the fate of all people is in His hands, while His Messenger's role is only to admonish those who are God-fearing.

But in addition to His control of the universe, He has complete dominion: "*To Him belongs all that is in the heavens and on earth, as well as all that is between them, and underneath the soil.*" (Verse 6) Scenes of the universe are used to highlight the concepts of dominion and knowledge in a way that can be understood by human intellect. Otherwise, the reality is much greater than this. God is the owner of all existence, and this is greater by far than all creatures in the heavens, the earth, and in between them and what is under the soil.

God's knowledge encompasses everything in His dominion: "*If you say anything aloud, then [know that] He knows all that is secret, as well as all that is yet more hidden.*" (Verse 7) Again there is perfect harmony between the inferences from this verse speaking about God's knowledge of secrets and what is more deeply hidden on the one hand and the verse speaking of God's dominion on the other. We note the contrast between what is visible in the universe and what is open of people's words, and also between what is hidden under the soil and that which is hidden in people's thoughts: that is, secret thoughts and things more deeply hidden. A secret is covered in shrouds, and what is 'more hidden' denotes further degrees of covering, as in the case of something buried very deep underground.

This address provides the Prophet with reassurance, comfort and knowledge that God listens to him. He does not leave him alone to feel distressed by his task of delivering the message of the Qur'ān, or facing the unbelievers alone without support. If the Prophet appeals to his Lord aloud, he should know that God knows all secrets and what is buried deeper than secrets. When we realize that God is near to us, knowing our thoughts and secret appeals, we are reassured and content. We no longer feel our isolation in the midst of hostile opponents who reject our faith and entertain different views.

This section concludes with a declaration of God's oneness, after stating His total dominion, control and perfect knowledge: *"He is God; there is no deity other than Him. His alone are all the attributes of perfection."* (Verse 8) The Arabic term, *ḥusnā*, rendered here as 'perfection' is specially selected to contribute to the rhythm while also adding to the general ambience of grace and care which is characteristic of the whole *sūrah* and of its opening in particular.

More Details about Moses

Now God begins to tell His Messenger, Muḥammad, the story of Moses, as an example of the care He takes of those whom He chooses to bear His message. Accounts of Moses are more frequent in the Qur'ān than those of all other messengers. This history is given in the Qur'ān in episodes, each of which fits perfectly with the general theme of the *sūrah* in which it occurs. So far, we have seen such episodes in *Sūrah* 2, The Cow; 5, The Repast; 7, The Heights; 10, Jonah; 17, The Night Journey; and 18, The Cave. Other references are also made in later *sūrahs*.

The account given in *Sūrah* 5, The Repast, tells how the Children of Israel stood at a distance from the Holy Land, refusing to enter it because of the powerful residents living there. In *Sūrah* 18, The Cave, also in this volume, we saw Moses' encounter with the pious man and what occurred when the two travelled together. Here, however, we have a long and detailed history covering several episodes, as was the case in *Sūrahs* 2, 7, and 10. The episodes given in each *sūrah* may be totally different, but where there are similarities, these are portrayed from different angles, so that they fit more perfectly with the general line of the *sūrah* in which they occur.

Thus, in *Sūrah* 2, The Cow, Moses' story is preceded by that of Adam and how he was honoured in heaven, how he was given charge of the earth and the grace God bestowed on him when He granted him forgiveness. In the same vein, the story of Moses and the Children of Israel provides a reminder of God's grace, God's covenant with them, their salvation from Pharaoh, their prayer for rain and how they were given manna and quails for food. It also mentions Moses' appointment with his Lord and how the Children of Israel took to worshipping the calf in his absence, God's forgiveness and binding covenant under the mountain, their breach of the Sabbath and the story of the cow.

In *Sūrah* 7, The Heights, Moses' story is preceded by warnings and an outline of the fate suffered by earlier communities who denied God's messages after they were given different signs and miracles. Hence, the story in this *sūrah* begins at the point when Moses was given his message. It refers to the various signs given to him, such as his staff and hand, as well as the floods, locusts, ants, frogs and blood, and speaks in detail about the encounter with the sorcerers, the fate of Pharaoh and his people. It then mentions how the Israelites worshipped the calf in Moses' absence. It culminates with an announcement of the heritage of God's grace and guidance being passed over to those who follow the last Messenger, the unlettered Prophet.

In *Sūrah* 10, Jonah, Moses' story is preceded by a short account of the destruction of earlier communities for rejecting God's guidance despite the clear evidence provided for them. The account of Moses given in this *sūrah* again begins with his message and his encounter with the sorcerers, followed by a detailed picture of the destruction of Pharaoh and his army. In the present *sūrah*, this comes immediately after the opening verses which speak about the grace God bestows on those whom He selects to convey His message. The story has the same aura of divine grace, starting with the dialogue between Moses and God. It includes examples of the care God took of Moses and the support He gave him. It mentions that such care started long before his message, during his early childhood, when God provided him with protection and love: "*I lavished My love on you, so that you may be reared under My watchful eye.*" (Verse 39)

An Address from On High

Have you learnt the story of Moses? When he saw a fire, he said to his family: 'Wait here! I perceive a fire. Perhaps I can bring you a lighted torch, or find some guidance at the fire.'" (Verses 9–10)

The Prophet is asked a rhetorical question about whether or not he had heard of Moses' history and how it reflects God's grace and the guidance He provides for those whom He chooses as His messengers.

Here we see Moses (peace be upon him) on the road between Madyan and Egypt, close to Mount Sinai, returning with his wife after he had completed the term he had agreed with the Prophet Shu'ayb. This agreement meant that Shu'ayb would give him one of his two daughters in marriage in return for eight or ten years during which he would be his assistant. He most probably spent ten years before he felt that he could leave with his wife to return to the country where he grew up. There the Children of Israel, Moses' people, lived in subjugation.[1]

Why is he returning to Egypt having fled there after killing an Egyptian whom he found quarrelling with an Israelite? He had after all found safe refuge with Shu'ayb, his father-in-law. So why would he leave that place of security and return to Egypt? Here we see human homesickness as the tool used by God to bring Moses to the place where he was to play an important role. Thus is life. We are motivated by feelings, passions, aspirations, hopes and memories, but all these are merely the outward causes of the desired result. They are what we see on the surface, but below them is the will that no sight can see. It is God's will, and He is the Almighty who accomplishes everything He wants.

Thus we see Moses on his way back to Egypt, losing his way in the desert, accompanied only by his wife, and perhaps a servant. He loses his way in the darkness of the night in the open desert. We sense this from the way he says to his companions: *"Wait here! I perceive a fire.*

---

1. An account of the situation the Children of Israel lived under occurs in *Sūrah* 28, The Story, which was revealed earlier than the present *sūrah*.

Perhaps I can bring you a lighted torch, or find some guidance at the fire." (Verse 10) People living in the desert normally lit their fires on high ground so that those travelling at night could see it, find their way or come over to it where they would find a welcome and hospitality, as well as directions to continue their journey.

Moses saw the fire as he was walking through the desert and he was warmed by hope. He moved towards it in order to fetch a firebrand, as night in the desert is normally cold. He also felt he might find some guidance as to which direction to travel in. He went there to bring back a torch, but was in for a great surprise. For he found the fire that warms souls and spirits, and provides guidance for the greatest journey of all:

> *But when he came close to it, a voice called out to him: 'Moses, I am your Lord! Take off your sandals, for you are in the sacred valley of Ṭuwā. Know that I have chosen you. Listen, then, to what is being revealed. Indeed, I alone am God; there is no deity other than Me. So, worship Me alone, and establish regular prayer to celebrate My praise. Although I have chosen to keep it hidden, the Last Hour is bound to come, so that every soul may be rewarded in accordance with what it strove for. Hence, let not anyone who does not believe in its coming and follows only his own desires turn your thoughts from it, lest you perish.'* (Verses 11–16)

This is an awe-inspiring scene. We shudder as we imagine Moses alone in the open desert, engulfed in the complete darkness and silence of the night, making his way towards the fire by the side of the mountain. Then suddenly, the whole universe echoes the great address: "*Moses, I am your Lord! Take off your sandals, for you are in the sacred valley of Ṭuwā. Know that I have chosen you. Listen, then, to what is being revealed.*" (Verses 12–13)

That small, insignificant particle that is a human being is here faced with that great majesty which no human can envisage. Compared with such majesty, the heavens and earth shrink into insignificance. Nevertheless, that human being received a divine address from on high. How? We only say: by God's grace! How else? At that moment, all humanity, represented by Moses (peace be upon him), is elevated.

It is sufficient for a human being to receive this grace for one moment. Humanity as a whole is honoured by simply having the ability to sustain such a communication in some way. Yet how does it occur? We do not know. It is not the function of the human mind to judge. All that we can do is to look on in admiration and believe what we see.

"*When he came close to it, a voice called out to him: Moses.*" (Verse 11) The calling out is expressed in the original Arabic text in the passive voice with no reference to who or what made the address. In English we say, 'a voice called out'. We cannot define the source of this address, its direction, form or nature; nor can we be sure how Moses heard or received it. There was simply an address of a certain nature and it was received accordingly. We accept that this has taken place, without asking how, because that is part of the way in which God accomplishes His business.

"*Moses, I am your Lord! Take off your sandals, for you are in the sacred valley of Ṭuwā.*" (Verse 12) You are in the presence of God Almighty, so take off your shoes. You must not step with your shoes in the valley over which God's presence is made. "*Know that I have chosen you.*" (Verse 13) What honour is granted to the man chosen directly by God. Moses is, after all, merely one servant among the great multitude living on a planet that is no more than a small particle in a much larger group. Yet this group is merely a small particle in the great universe. This universe came into existence when God willed it to exist. We can thus imagine the great care God has taken of man.

When this announcement of God's honour, reflected in God's selection of Moses as His messenger is made, he is asked to prepare for what is coming by taking off his sandals. Then he is told to be ready to learn: "*Listen, then, to what is being revealed.*" (Verse 13)

This brief revelation sums up three crucial aspects of the divine faith: belief in God's oneness, addressing all worship to Him alone, and belief in the Last Hour. These are the foundation of God's message that remained the same throughout human history: "*Indeed, I alone am God; there is no deity other than Me. So, worship Me alone, and establish regular prayer to celebrate My praise. Although I have chosen to keep it hidden, the Last Hour is bound to come, so that every soul may be rewarded in accordance with what it strove for. Hence, let not anyone who does not believe in its coming and follows only his own desires turn your thoughts from it, lest you perish.*" (Verses 14–16)

God's oneness is the cornerstone of faith. In His address to Moses, God emphasizes it in different forms: first in a statement bearing a strong emphasis, "*Indeed, I alone am God.*" (Verse 14) Then Godhead is clearly stated as applicable to no one else: "*There is no deity other than Me.*" (Verse 14) When Godhead is thus established, worship follows. Worship means that every activity should aim to please God. Singled out among all human activity is prayer: "*Establish regular prayer to celebrate My praise.*" (Verse 14) Prayer is the most complete and perfect of all types of worship celebrating God's praise. In fact its sole purpose is such. It discards everything else. Thus in prayer we are prepared for contact with God.

The Last Hour is the time appointed for administering rewards, in all justice and fairness. People think of this time and make sure that they keep it in mind. They move on in life, looking with watchful eyes, fearing to slip. God makes it clear that this Last Hour is certain to come: "*Although I have chosen to keep it hidden, the Last Hour is bound to come.*" (Verse 15) What people know about this Last Hour is limited to the information God has given them. This is all that they need to know, as determined by divine wisdom. That something should remain unknown is essential in human life. For we need to have something unknown to aspire towards. With human nature as it is, if everything were clearly exposed, activity would cease and life would become sterile. In fact, we continuously seek the unknown: we watch carefully, entertain hopes and aspirations, experiment and learn, and uncover what we can of our own potentials and those of the universe around us. We contemplate God's signs all around us. We invent and produce new things. When we think of the Last Hour, whose timing remains unknown, we do not lose sight of it. Since we do not know its timing, we remain conscious of it, ready for its arrival. Needless to say, this applies only to those of us who preserve our sound human nature. Those who distort it however are bound to fall and fail: "*Let not anyone who does not believe in its coming and follows only his own desires turn your thoughts from it, lest you perish.*" (Verse 16)

Indeed, pursuing one's desire is the cause of denying the Last Hour. Sound human nature believes that humanity cannot attain its super status during this present life, where justice is not seen to be done. There must then be another life where man attains perfection and absolute justice is carried out.

Moses' Mission Defined

This was an address to which the whole universe responded. In it, God gave His chosen messenger the fundamental truth of His oneness. Moses must have forgotten all about himself and the purpose for which he aimed towards the fire. He was now only following this voice coming to him from on high. He was attentive to the divine instructions being given to him. As he is so absorbed, with his mind and soul fully attentive to it, he is asked a question which requires no answer from him: "*Now, what is this in your right hand, Moses?*" (Verse 17)

Of course Moses had his staff in his hand, but where was his mind at that moment? Well, he remembers and gives his reply: "*He answered: It is my staff; upon it I lean, and with it I beat down the leaves for my sheep; and other uses have I for it.*" (Verse 18) The question did not ask about the uses he had for his staff, but rather about the object he was holding. Nevertheless, Moses realizes that he was not being asked to name the object in his hand, but to state what he did with it. Hence his answer outlining the purposes for which he used it. He used it for support when walking and beat the leaves of the trees so that they fell and were eaten by his sheep. We know that Moses tended sheep for Shu 'ayb, his father-in-law. It is also reported that he had a number of sheep given him as his share. Furthermore, he had other uses for his staff to which he refers in general without going into specifics, because what he has already stated gives a clear indication of them.

The omnipotent power, however, does with his staff what he could have never imagined. This comes as part of his preparation for his task: "*Said He: 'Throw it down, Moses.' So he threw it down, and thereupon it was a snake, moving rapidly. Said He: 'Take it up and have no fear. We shall restore it to its former state.'*" (Verses 19–21)

Thus he saw in front of his eyes the great miracle that occurs every moment while people remain oblivious to it. That is the miracle of life: the staff became a rapidly moving snake. Millions and millions of lifeless atoms or objects are transformed into living things all the time, but they do not fill man with wonder and amazement like a staff being transformed into a snake. Man lives in a world demarcated by his senses and experiences. He cannot go far beyond what he can perceive. To see a staff made of wood transformed into a snake that moves quickly was bound to shock his senses. He was thus profoundly alert. The hidden aspects of how life first came about and the miraculous nature of life springing up at every moment are too subtle to capture man's mind and imagination. This is particularly the case when something becomes too familiar; it thus goes unnoticed.

The miracle of life took place, and Moses was full of amazement, with fear tearing at his heart. But the command was given: "*Take it up and have no fear. We shall restore it to its former state.*" (Verse 21) It will once again be a staff. The *sūrah* does not mention Moses' other reaction, which in another *sūrah* shows him running away. Here we have only a subtle reference to the fear that overwhelmed him. This is because the general atmosphere in this *sūrah* is one of safety and reassurance. It is not to be disturbed by speaking about such overwhelming fear that causes a man to run away.

Thus Moses was reassured, he picked up the snake and it was a staff again, regaining its original shape and form. Thus the other aspect of the miracle took place, with life departing from a living creature.

Another command was issued to Moses from on high: "*Now put your hand under your armpit. It will come out [shining] white, without blemish: another sign.*" (Verse 22) Moses did as he was told. It should be noted that the Qur'ān uses a different expression to denote the position where Moses was to put his hand, his armpit. It is described as his 'wing' which gives an air of freedom of movement and freedom from the earth's gravity. Thus his hand came out shining white, but its whiteness indicates no illness or malignancy. This is indeed another sign to be added to that of his staff. He is thus made to see some of the great miracles God works out: "*We shall show you some of Our most wondrous signs."* (Verse 23) When he has seen these with his own eyes, he will be reassured and able to carry out his great task with greater determination.

"Go to Pharaoh; for he has indeed transgressed all bounds." (Verse 24) Up to this point Moses was unaware that he was chosen for this very hard task. He has first hand knowledge of Pharaoh, since he himself was brought up in Pharaoh's own palace, witnessing his tyranny and how he treated his people with unabating cruelty. Since he is now in audience with his Lord, feeling the great honour God has bestowed on him, he asks for assistance and reassurance to better execute his mission: *"Said [Moses]: 'My Lord, open up my heart [to Your light], and make my mission easy for me, and free my tongue from its impediment, so that people may understand what I say. Appoint for me a helper from among my kinsmen, Aaron, my brother. Grant me strength through him, and let him share my task, so that together we may extol Your limitless glory and remember You always. You are surely watching over us.'"* (Verses 25–35)

Requests Granted

So, Moses requests his Lord to open up his heart, so that the hard task before him would be a pleasure to undertake. It would also motivate him to carry on with it without impediment. He further prays to God to facilitate his task. When God facilitates a task for anyone, it is certain to succeed. For, what can man accomplish on his own, unless God facilitates matters for him? How can he achieve success when he has only limited ability and deficient knowledge while the road ahead is long, difficult and unknown.

The first thing Moses prayed for was heart reassurance that he would clearly feel, and then that God should facilitate things for him. What can man do without such help, relying on his little ability and limited knowledge? But Moses requests more to help him with his task. He wanted his tongue to be freed so that people could understand him easily when he spoke. It has been reported that he suffered from some sort of speech impediment. Most probably this is what he means here. It is further supported by what he is quoted as saying: *"My brother*

Aaron is far better in speech than I am." (28: 34) The prayer Moses said here was made first in general terms. Now he adds details which he feels necessary for the task ahead.

First he asks for a helper from his own family, and that was Aaron. He knew Aaron to be outspoken, courageous and yet someone who could control his feelings. Moses himself was passionate and rather hot-tempered. Therefore, he requested his Lord for support, letting his brother share in the fulfilment of his task. He realized that his task required much glorification of God, constant remembering of Him and contact with Him through prayers. Thus we see Moses requesting God to open up his heart and facilitate his task, to free him of his speech difficulty, and give him a helper from among his family. All this he needed not to carry on the task entrusted to him, but rather so that he and his brother could glorify God and remember Him often as He should be remembered and glorified. Thus, they would be able to receive His guidance, as He is the One who knows their situation best. *"You are surely watching over us."* (Verse 35) You know our limited resources and our need for Your help.

God, benevolent and compassionate as He is, does not let His guest go back empty-handed. Nor does He delay answering his prayer: *"Said He: You are granted all that you have asked for, Moses."* (Verse 36)

Just a simple word, without the need for detail, sums up the positive and immediate response. Moses has been granted all that he requested. The way this response is phrased indicates that all that Moses requested became a reality immediately. Then, Moses hears his Lord addressing him by name. What is more honourable than that God in His majesty should mention one of His servants by name?

This is more than anyone can hope for of God's grace and compassion. The meeting took its time and the address was made in full, with a complete and positive response to Moses' prayer. Yet God's grace continues to be bestowed in abundance. There is no check to slow down or prevent God's mercy when He grants it. Therefore, He gives Moses even further reassurance as He reminds him that His grace has been shown to him for a long time. Moreover, every moment longer he stays in his Lord's presence gives him further happiness and greater strength to pursue his mission.

*And indeed We bestowed Our favour upon you in a time gone by,
when We inspired your mother, saying: 'Place [your child] in a chest
and throw it into the river. The river will cast him ashore, and one
who is an enemy to Me and an enemy to him will pick him up.' I
lavished My love on you, so that you may be reared under My watchful
eye. Then your sister went forth and said [to Pharaoh's people]: 'Shall
I direct you to one who might take care of him?' Thus did We restore
you to your mother, so that her mind might be set at ease and that
she might not grieve. And [when you came of age,] you killed a
man; but We saved you from all grief, although We tested you with
various trials. You then stayed for years among the people of Madyan;
and now you have come here, Moses, as ordained [by Me]; for I have
chosen you for Myself.* (Verses 37–41)

Moses was going to meet the most powerful man on earth, a tyrant
who knew no mercy. Against him he was to conduct the battle between
faith and unfaith. He would be in the thick of things, facing all sorts of
difficulties, against Pharaoh at first, then against his own people whose
nature had been corrupted by long subjugation. They did not have the
necessary qualities to fulfil the mission entrusted to them after they
were liberated from Pharaoh's tyranny. Hence, God tells him that he,
Moses, has been fully equipped for the task, as he was reared under
God's watchful eye, given the necessary skills for taking on seemingly
impossible tasks, right from the time of his infancy. God took care of
him in his formative years when he placed him right under Pharaoh's
nose, without any other care or support. Yet Pharaoh's hand could not
harm him, because it was God who took care of him. He need not
worry now about Pharaoh's power, as he still enjoys God's help and
care in his adulthood. It is God who has chosen him for His mission.

Reminder of Past Favours

God responded by saying that all Moses' requests were granted.
This was an act of grace by the One who is Most Merciful. But with
this he is also given a reminder of God's past favours. Such a reminder
is certain to reassure Moses that with God's support he can face any

power or dictator. "*And indeed We bestowed Our favour upon you in a time gone by.*" (Verse 37) The One who granted him all this protection and support will not let him down now. In the past, His favours were continuous, so it is unlikely that they will stop now after Moses has been assigned a mission by God. The favour mentioned first is that given to his mother which any woman in her condition would have needed. Her inspiration then told her: "*Place [your child] in a chest and throw it into the river. The river will cast him ashore.*" (Verse 39)

We note here that the text describes rough and violent actions: a child being pushed into a wooden chest, and the chest thrown into the river. Then the river casts the box and the child inside onto the shore. But what then? To whose care will this child be entrusted? The answer is: "*One who is an enemy to Me and an enemy to him will pick him up.*" (Verse 39) Amidst all this Moses is also told: "*I lavished My love on you, so that you may be reared under My watchful eye.*" (Verse 39)

All this is an aspect of divine providence which transforms love and compassion into a shield to protect the child from all the blows, waves and currents. None of the powers of evil is able to harm the recipient of such love, even though he is no more than an infant of only a few days who cannot indicate his needs or express his feelings.

We have in this image a rare contrast between the great tyrannical forces lying in wait for the tiny infant and the hard circumstances engulfing him on the one hand and, on the other, the flowing compassion guarding him from all fears and protecting him against all dangers. His protection comes about as tender love, without the need for fighting or confrontation: "*I lavished My love on you, so that you may be reared under My watchful eye.*" (Verse 39) Nothing further can be added to explain such gentle, loving tenderness than this most perfect Qur'ānic expression of how Moses was reared under God's watchful eye. How can human expression describe a creature reared under such care? The most that we can do is contemplate the situation and what it meant for Moses' development. It is a great honour for any human being to have direct divine care for just a moment in his life. What honour is then bestowed on one who is reared under such care? Perhaps this is what made Moses able to receive this address direct from God.

Thus Moses is reared under God's protection right under Pharaoh's nose, and Pharaoh is the enemy of both God and Moses. Thus, as a young child, he is always within an arm's reach of Pharaoh, without any human guard or protector. Nevertheless, Pharaoh's evil hand is restrained by the fact that God has lavished His love on Moses, the child, so that he attracts love by all who see him. Needless to say, with Moses being reared under God's watchful eye, no harm could come to him from Pharaoh or anyone else.

But this is not all. Not only was Moses taken care of, but his mother could not be left at home worrying about her child. The two were soon reunited. "*Then your sister went forth and said [to Pharaoh's people]: 'Shall I direct you to one who might take care of him?' Thus did We restore you to your mother, so that her mind might be set at ease and that she might not grieve.*" (Verse 40) That was part of God's design. He prevented the little baby from taking just any woman's breast. No wet nurse would breast-feed him. Pharaoh and his wife, who had adopted the baby cast to them by the river, were searching for a wet nurse, and this became well known. On instructions from her mother, Moses' sister went to them saying that she knew the best woman to take care of the baby. [All this is described in detail in *Sūrah* 28.] She brought them the baby's own mother and he took her breast immediately. Thus, God's design for mother and child was accomplished, for the mother had done as she was told, throwing her baby into a wooden chest in the Nile. This action brought the baby to the enemy who was killing all Israelite children. Thus, the safety of this child was accomplished by giving him to his enemies to remain with them, with no other support or guardianship.

The next favour Moses is reminded of is his escape after having killed a man: "*And you killed a man; but We saved you from all grief, although We tested you with various trials. You then stayed for years among the people of Madyan; and now you have come here, Moses, as ordained [by Me]; for I have chosen you for Myself.*" (Verses 40–41)

The killing of this man took place some time during Moses' early adult years, having grown up in Pharaoh's palace. He had gone to the market one day and found two people quarrelling, one an Israelite the other an Egyptian. The Israelite appealed to him for help, and Moses pushed the Egyptian, but rather too strongly for the latter fell and was killed. Moses did not intend to kill the man, but simply to push him away. When he saw him dead, he was full of grief. It is good to remember here that Moses was brought up under God's own care, right from his early childhood. Hence, it was only natural that he was filled with remorse, blaming himself for over-reacting. God reminds him here of His favour, as He directed him to seek forgiveness, which alleviated his sorrow.

However, God did not let him simply get away with this without a lesson to learn and benefit from in his future task. Hence, He set him the test of fearing the consequences of his offence and his subsequent attempt to escape punishment. The test took then another form, forcing him to flee the land where he was born and brought up, departing alone without friend or companion. Moreover, having been brought up in the palace of the greatest ruler of the time, enjoying every comfort and luxury, he now had to earn a living. Thus, he had to serve others, and work as a shepherd.

At the appointed time, when he attained maturity, after passing the tests to which God subjected him, and when circumstances in Egypt were most suited, with the Israelites subjected to much oppression, Moses was brought in from Madyan. He might have thought that he had chosen to travel at that time himself, but the fact of the matter was that stated in the Qur'ānic verse: *"Now you have come here, Moses, as ordained [by Me]."* (Verse 40) So his return was at a time God had determined as most suitable.

"I have chosen you for Myself." (Verse 41) Thus, Moses was trained and prepared so as to be completely devoted to God's message and to serving His cause. He was purged of all the temptations of this worldly life, so as to be purely dedicated to the task God appointed for him. All that had passed in his life was part of his training to fulfil the mission that was about to be entrusted to him. Here God tells him that neither himself, nor his family, nor anyone else had any claim on his time or services. He was chosen by God for whatever God wanted him to do.

Moses' Mission Outlined

Having made this very clear to Moses, God gives him his first instructions:

> *Go forth, then, you and your brother, with My signs, and never slacken in remembering Me. Go forth, both of you, to Pharaoh; for he has transgressed all bounds of equity! But speak to him mildly, so that he may yet take heed, or may be filled with apprehension.* (Verses 42–44)

Moses is told to go with his brother Aaron, equipped with the signs God has given them. He has seen two of these in the transformation affecting his staff and his hand. They are told not to slacken in remembering God, for such remembrance is the best equipment and support they can have. Moses is reminded that God protected him from Pharaoh and his wickedness even when he was a helpless child, thrown in the Nile. Nothing of that hardship caused him any harm. Now that he has completed his training, he can approach his task with ease and reassurance, trusting to God's care.

As Moses is directed to go to Pharaoh, he is told that Pharaoh has transgressed all bounds and resorted to tyranny and oppression. Nevertheless, his instruction is that he and his brother are to *"speak to him mildly."* (Verse 44) Mild and gentle words which do not trigger a hardening of attitude or insolence and arrogance, which is commonly adopted by tyrants, may yet reawaken Pharaoh's heart and alert him to the consequences of his actions. Thus, Moses and Aaron were to go about their task, hoping that Pharaoh might take heed, and never despairing of his reform and positive response to God's guidance. An advocate of faith who gives up on people and thinks that they never respond positively to his message cannot deliver it in the way it should be delivered. Nor is he able to hold on to it in the face of rejection and denial.

God certainly knew how Pharaoh would respond, but taking the necessary measures in preaching God's message is prerequisite. God takes people to account after they act, even though He is aware of their actions before they are made. His knowledge of future events is the same as His knowledge of the present and the past.

How to Confront a Tyrant

So far we have discussed what Moses was told when God addressed him directly alone in the desert. The *sūrah* then takes us across time and place, covering an indeterminable period of time and distance, to show us both Moses and Aaron expressing their concerns to their Lord about their forthcoming confrontation with Pharaoh. They feared most that he might be quick to punish and harm them severely when they called on him to believe in God.

> *They said: 'Our Lord! We fear lest he hasten with insolence or tyranny against us.' Answered He: 'Have no fear. I shall be with you. I hear all and see all. Go, then, you two to him and say, "We are the emissaries of your Lord. Let the Children of Israel go with us, and oppress them no more. We have now come to you with a message from your Lord. Peace to all who follow [God's] guidance. It has been revealed to us that the suffering shall befall those who deny the truth and turn away from it."'* (Verses 45–48)

For certain, Aaron was not with Moses when his Lord first spoke to him, favouring him with a long interactive discourse, clarifying all necessary issues and allowing him to ask questions and giving him the answers he needed. The fact that now both Moses and Aaron make the reply together, saying, *"We fear lest he hasten with insolence or tyranny against us"*. This, then, suggests that this statement was made at a later time. This is part of the Qur'ānic method of skipping over time and place, leaving gaps in the scenes and events of a story, which are gathered and understood as one reads on. Thus, the Qur'ān concentrates on events, actions and attitudes which inspire the reader and listener.

So, some time after Moses left the place where he received God's long address, close to Mount Sinai, he met with his brother, Aaron. The latter also received God's revelation commanding him to be with his brother and that together they should address Pharaoh. Hence, the two together express their concerns to their Lord: "*We fear lest he hasten with insolence or tyranny against us.*" (Verse 45) They feared Pharaoh's impulsive reaction, which might be too strong, and they feared his tyranny, which was much more profound than mere physical harm. In his power, Pharaoh could be expected to resort to either of these or to both of them.

At this point they receive God's decisive answer which leaves no room for fear or worry: "*Answered He: Have no fear. I shall be with you. I hear all and see all.*" (Verse 46) Thus, God Almighty who has power over all creatures and who creates the universe and all creatures in it, using nothing more than His will to bring them into existence, tells them that He is with them. This should have been sufficient, but God adds to this what increases their certainty of help. This is evidenced by the fact that He hears all and sees all. What could Pharaoh do against the power of the Almighty, whether in a precipitate reaction or a well considered one?

Coupled with this reassurance Moses and Aaron are given guidance on the form of address they should make to Pharaoh and on how to argue their case: "*Go, then, you two to him and say, 'We are the emissaries of your Lord. Let the Children of Israel go with us, and oppress them no more. We have now come to you with a message from your Lord. Peace to all who follow [God's] guidance. It has been revealed to us that the suffering shall befall those who deny the truth and turn away from it.'*" (Verses 47–48)

Thus they should start by stating the foundation of their message: "*We are the emissaries of your Lord.*" (Verse 47) This would give him right from the first moment the understanding that it is God who is his and all people's Lord. He is not the Lord of Moses and Aaron, or the Children of Israel alone. It was a superstition of the days of pagan ignorance that each group of people, or each tribe, had its own deity or deities. Moreover, it was commonly held during some periods of history that Pharaoh was a deity, of godly descent, and as such, he was to be worshipped.

When the basic element of their message was thus outlined, Moses and Aaron explained their immediate concern: "*Let the Children of Israel go with us, and oppress them no more.*" (Verse 47) This was the limit of their message to Pharaoh, to save the Children of Israel and bring them back to their monotheistic faith. They would then lead them to the blessed land which God had assigned to them for settlement, up to the time when they would sink into corruption and be destroyed in consequence.

They further showed Pharaoh a sign to prove that they were telling the truth when they said that they were messengers from his Lord: "*We have now come to you with a message from your Lord.*" (Verse 47) They follow this with an element of encouragement, hoping that he might respond: "*Peace to all who follow [God's] guidance.*" (Verse 47) It might be that when he had listened to this that he would respond to the greeting of peace and accept God's guidance.

They then add an element of implicit warning, in order not to stir his arrogance and hostility: "*It has been revealed to us that the suffering shall befall those who deny the truth and turn away from it.*" (Verse 48) It might be that he would decide not to include himself among those who deny the truth and turn away from it.

We see here how God gave Moses and Aaron reassurance and showed them the way to follow. He indeed outlined their course for them so that they would approach their task with peace, reassurance and clear guidance.

At this point the curtains are drawn, only to rise again when we see Moses and Aaron in confrontation with the tyrant.

Calling on a Tyrant to Believe

The *sūrah* does not mention how Moses and Aaron were admitted into Pharaoh's presence, but nonetheless they were. For certain, their Lord was with them hearing and seeing what took place, and no doubt guiding their communication. But what power, and what authority was at the disposal of Moses and Aaron to enable them to communicate to Pharaoh, great as he might have been, what God, their Lord, commanded them to convey to him? The *sūrah* paints a vivid picture of the dialogue between Moses and Pharaoh, starting with this question and answer: "*[Pharaoh] said: 'Who, now, is this Lord of you two, Moses?' He replied: 'Our Lord is He who gives everything its distinctive nature and form, and further guides them.'"* (Verses 49–50) It is clear that Pharaoh does not wish to acknowledge God's Lordship, which the two prophets had made clear to him saying they were *'the emissaries of your Lord.'* Pharaoh realized that Moses was the main advocate of the message. Hence, he puts his question to him: *"Who, now, is this Lord of you two, Moses?"* (Verse 49) In whose name are you addressing me to demand the release of the Israelites?

Moses replies emphasizing God's attributes of creation, initiation and providing guidance and balance: *"Our Lord is He who gives everything its distinctive nature and form, and further guides them."* (Verse 50) Thus it is: our Lord is the one who has given everything its existence in the form and the nature it has. He then guides each and everyone to fulfil their respective roles, providing them all with the means for such fulfilment. The Arabic text of this verse uses the conjunctive, *thumma*, or then, separating the creation of everything and imparting guidance to it. This conjunctive is rendered in the translation as 'further' to indicate the true meaning of the verse. There is no lapse of time between creating a creature and giving it guidance. The conjunctive is used to indicate the difference in rank between the mere creation of something and giving it the necessary knowledge to fulfil its role. Providing such guidance is more elevated than leaving creatures to their own devices.

This description of God given by Moses sums up the highest and most perfect attributes of God the Creator who controls everything in the universe. It is He who gives every creature its form, nature and role. When man casts his eye and contemplates as best he can this endless universe, he sees the results of what the great power of God makes of every existence, great or small, starting with the minute atom up to the largest creature, spanning life between a one-celled creature to the most sophisticated form of life, i.e. man.

The great universe is made up of countless atoms, cells, substances, creatures and living things. Every atom in the universe interacts, every cell has a life, every living being moves, and every creature influences and is influenced by others. But all work, individually and collectively, within the boundaries of the laws God has planted in their natures and constitutions, without conflict, defect, or slackening at any moment. Yet every individual creature is, on its own, a complete world:

its cells, organs and systems work in accordance with its nature, within the overall law God operates in the universe, in perfect order and perfect complementarity.

Let us leave aside the great universe and look for a moment at each creature on its own. Human knowledge and endeavour is limited in its ability to study and understand such a creature. We are talking here of studying the characteristics, role, illnesses and treatment of creatures in our world. We are not speaking about creating these creatures or guiding them to fulfil their respective roles. This is something totally beyond man's knowledge or ability. Man himself is one of God's creatures. God has given him existence in the form he has, and assigned to him his role like all other creatures. The One who gives every creature its nature and form and further guides them to perform their roles is God, the only deity in the universe.

Here Pharaoh puts another question: *"And what of all the past generations?"* (Verse 51) Where have all those past generations gone? Who was their Lord? What happened to them since they died unaware of the Lord Moses spoke about?

"[Moses] answered: Knowledge of that rests with my Lord alone, recorded in a Book. My Lord does not err, and neither does He forget." (Verse 52) Thus Moses refers all this unknown matter to his Lord whose knowledge is perfect, encompassing every single detail of every little creature, and who never forgets anything. It is He alone who knows about all those generations, their past and future. The realm that lies beyond the reach of human perception belongs totally to God, who alone determines the eventual outcome of mankind and their life.

Moses continues to draw Pharaoh's attention to some of the results of God's action in the universe and how these results affect human life. He selects results which could be seen close by, and which were well-known in Egypt with its rich soil, abundant water, and plentiful crops and cattle:

> He it is who has made the earth your cradle, and has traced on it paths for you to walk on, and who sends down waters from the sky with which We bring forth diverse pairs of plants. Eat, then, and graze your cattle. In all this there are signs for those who are endowed with reason. (Verses 53–54)

An Argument Too Powerful

The whole earth is a cradle for mankind at all places and in all times. It is indeed the same as a child's cradle; for human beings are the children of the earth in whose lap they grow up and on whose produce they feed. At the same time, it has been levelled for them so that they can walk on it, pursue their life affairs, cultivate it and benefit by its treasures. God made it so on the day He gave nature and forms to all His creatures. Thus, He gave the earth its structure which enables it to sustain the type of life He assigned to prosper on it. Similarly, He gave human beings their nature and form which make them able to live on the earth He made a cradle for them. The two senses imparted by the verse are closely interlinked.

Both the cradle image and the quality of being level are most clearly seen in Egypt, with its highly fertile valley which requires only the minimum effort from its people to yield its rich produce. The whole valley of Egypt is like a warm cradle nurturing a small child.

The wise Creator who has levelled the earth has also opened up on it paths for people to travel and has sent down waters from the sky. It is from the rain pouring from the sky that rivers form and run to provide irrigation. One of these is, of course, the Nile running close to where Pharaoh had his palace. With such plentiful water, plants are brought forth in a great variety of pairs.

God in His wisdom has willed that, like all living things, plants should grow in pairs. Indeed this duality is a consistent phenomenon that applies to all living creatures. In most cases, plants carry the male and female cells in the same shoot, but there are types where one shoot has only male cells and another female, in the same way as in most animal species. This provides perfect harmony that applies to all living things. Hence, the statement: *"In all this there are signs for those who are endowed with reason."* (Verse 54) Indeed, no sound mind could reflect on such phenomena without concluding that it is the work of the wise Creator who has given every living thing its nature and form, and guided them all.

The *sūrah* continues the reporting of what Moses said, but uses the form of a direct address by God Himself: *"Out of this [earth] have We created you, and into it shall We return you, and out of it shall We bring you forth once again. And, indeed, We showed Pharaoh all Our signs, but he denied them and refused [to take heed].*" (Verses 55–56) It is from this earth, made as a cradle for mankind, and which supports the diverse cultivation of plants for food and grazing, that mankind are created, and to it they shall return and then from it again they are resurrected after death.

Man is certainly created from the same substance as this earth. All the components of his body are largely the same as the components of the earth. Furthermore, he eats of its produce, drinks its waters, breathes its air, and benefits from it as his cradle. Then, he goes back to it a dead corpse, when his remains become part of its soil and atmosphere. From the earth he is resurrected for a second life, just as he was created for the life of this world.

This reminder of the relationship between man and the earth fits well with the exchange between Moses and Pharaoh, the tyrant who arrogantly claims a godly position when he too originated from the earth and to it he will certainly return. He is no more than any object God has created on earth and guided to fulfil its assigned role. "*We showed Pharaoh all Our signs, but he denied them and refused to take heed.*" (Verse 56) God showed him all sorts of signs in the great universe, and Moses pointed these out to him. The two signs of Moses' staff and hand are not specified here since they are included among the general category of God's signs. The signs in the universe are far greater and more permanent. It is implied however that Pharaoh has already been shown Moses' own special signs. His reply to all God's signs is mentioned in detail, and we realize that he is actually referring to these two signs: "*Have you, Moses, come to drive us out of our land with your magic? In that case, we shall most certainly produce for you magic to match it. Set, then, for us an appointment which neither we nor you shall fail to keep, at a suitable, open place.*" (Verses 57–58)

Ready to take up the challenge, Moses delivered a straight answer: "*Your appointment shall be the day of the Festival; and let the people assemble when the sun is risen high.*" (Verse 59)

How to Avoid a Losing Argument

Pharaoh simply stopped arguing. He realized that Moses had the stronger case, supported by the clearest proof, namely, God's signs seen everywhere in the universe, as well as his own two special signs. Hence, he resorted to an old ploy, often used by tyrants and opponents of God's messages. He pointed an accusing finger at Moses, describing him as a sorcerer, claiming that it was through sorcery that Moses turned the staff into a snake and made his hand look shining white, without blemish. Magic was the thought presenting itself immediately to Pharaoh, because it was widely practised in Egypt. The two signs given to Moses seemed, on the surface, similar to magic, which is no more than the deception of the senses that could sometimes lead to false feelings so as to produce tangible effects. Thus, under the influence of magic, a man may see things that are not present, or he may see them in a form other than their own. At times a person who is under a magical spell may be physically and psychologically affected, as though the spell has had its effect on him in reality. But Moses' signs were not of this sort. They were signs given to him by God, the Creator of all things, the One who can bring about both temporary and permanent transformations.

"He said: Have you, Moses, come to drive us out of our land with your magic?" (Verse 57) It appears that the persecution of the Israelites was motivated by political reasons, with Pharaoh fearing that their numbers would increase to give them numerical strength. For the sake of retaining power and maintaining their rule or kingdom, tyrants will commit the most ghastly and inhumane crimes, paying no heed to moral or ethical considerations. They are prepared to silence the voice of even their own conscience and honour. Thus, Pharaoh pursued a policy of weakening and humiliating the Israelites, killing their male offspring and sparing the females, while forcing the adults among them into hard labour. Therefore Moses and Aaron demanded their release, saying to him: *"Let the children of Israel go with us, and oppress them no more."* (Verse 47) His reply to their request was indicative of his fears: *"Have you, Moses, come to drive us out of our land with your*

magic?" (Verse 57) To Pharaoh, such a release was a step towards ousting him from government.

According to Pharaoh's thinking, Moses made this demand for the release of the Israelites for no other reason, and the only thing he was prepared to put forward in support of his demand was an act of sorcery. It was easy, therefore, to reply to him in kind: *"In that case, we shall most certainly produce for you magic to match it."* (Verse 58) Tyrannical rulers cannot see beyond the obvious. They think that those who advocate a divine faith use it as a cover for worldly aims. They imagine that they want to take over the reins of government. When they realize that such advocates of faith have something miraculous, either of the type given to Moses or something that touches people's hearts and wins them over, they respond with something of an apparently similar nature. Their thoughts run along the following lines: if the advocate of a message resorts to magic, then we will produce similar magic; if he uses fine words, these are also at our command; if he advocates moral values, we will support high moral values; if he does good and benevolent works, we will do the same. Such tyrants do not understand that advocates of a divine message rely on their faith and on God's support. These are the weapons which ensure their triumph.

With such thinking and motivation, Pharaoh asks Moses to set an appointment for his confrontation with the sorcerers. In order to give the appearance of power, Pharaoh leaves it to Moses to choose the time: *"Set, then, for us an appointment."* (Verse 58) In order to give an even stronger impression of his confidence, he re-emphasizes the importance of that appointment *"which neither we nor you shall fail to keep."* (Verse 58) He only asks for the match to be in an open area for the challenge to be seen, *"at a suitable, open place."* (Verse 58)

Moses accepts Pharaoh's challenge and sets the appointment for a festival day when the people are in the mood to celebrate, gathering in the main squares and open areas: *"Answered Moses: Your appointment shall be the day of the Festival; and let the people assemble when the sun is risen high."* (Verse 59) Thus he sets the best time when everything is at its clearest and people will be out and about in numbers. He does not set a very early time when people would still be at home, nor at midday when the heat could prevent their gathering, nor in the evening when darkness might discourage their attendance or impair their vision.

Thus ends the first scene of confrontation between faith and tyranny. The curtains fall to be raised again and we see the match in full view.

In Confrontation with the Sorcerers

"*Thereupon Pharaoh withdrew and put together the artful scheme which he would pursue; and then turned up.*" (Verse 60) In this short verse the *sūrah* sums up all that Pharaoh said, the advice he was given by the powerful elite among his government, the discussion with the sorcerers and his encouragement and promises of rich reward to them, as well as the schemes he and his advisers finally plotted. Indeed, this short verse, comprising only six words in the Arabic text, shows three successive movements: Pharaoh's withdrawal into his own quarters, mapping out his strategy and turning up for the confrontation.

Before the confrontation began, Moses felt that he should give the sorcerers some honest and sincere advice. Thus, he warned them against attributing false fabrications to God. So doing, he hoped that they would accept God's guidance and abandon sorcery, which is blatant falsehood: "*Moses said to them: Woe betide you! Do not invent any falsehood against God, lest He afflict you with most grievous suffering. He who contrives such a lie is sure to come to grief.*" (Verse 61)

A sincere piece of advice can touch the hearts of those it addresses. This might have been the case here, for some of the sorcerers were touched by Moses' words and began to have second thoughts. Those who were keen to go through with the showdown however began to argue with them in whispers, fearing that Moses would overhear them. "*So they debated among themselves as to what to do; but they kept their counsel secret.*" (Verse 62)

The more hardened of them tried to encourage those who were reluctant, and warned them against a gloomy future under Moses and Aaron. They described the two prophets as being driven by a desire for power, hoping to rule Egypt and change the faith of its people. To forestall their schemes, they needed to demonstrate their unity and confront them as one body, without hesitation. It was a day of outright and decisive confrontation, and the winner would take all.

> They said: These two are surely sorcerers intent on driving you away from your land by their sorcery, and on doing away with your exemplary way of life. Hence, decide on the scheme you will pursue, and then come forward in one single body. For, indeed, he who prevails today shall ever be successful. (Verses 63–64)

One sincere word motivated by faith falls like a powerful explosive in the camp of falsehood. It shakes unbelievers' hearts and weakens their ranks. They are no longer sure of their own ability, and they entertain doubts about their own beliefs. Hence the doubters needed such encouragement. They were reminded that Moses and Aaron were merely two men, against a much larger group of sorcerers, backed by Pharaoh, his kingdom, wealth and army. They forgot however that Moses and Aaron were supported by God who hears and sees all.

Perhaps this gives us an explanation of the attitude of Pharaoh and his arrogant tyranny, as well as the attitude of the sorcerers who enjoyed his support. To start with, who are those two men, Moses and Aaron, to be given such importance, with Pharaoh himself putting a challenge to them and accepting their own challenge? What is their position which compels him to put together a deceitful strategy, mustering in the process a large force of skilful sorcerers, who were the best in his land, and bringing all the people to witness the confrontation? How come that he himself comes along and sits with his full entourage to see the confrontation? How is it that Pharaoh is prepared to listen to Moses' argument, which denies him all the privileges he claims for himself, when Moses is no more than an Israelite whose people are continually persecuted under his own rule? This was all due to the dignity God has imparted to Moses and Aaron which inspired awe among all those who listened to them. Moreover, God was with them, listening and seeing all that was taking place.

It was also that awe-inspiring dignity that made one word of Moses sufficient to cause much confusion among the sorcerers, requiring them to hold secret council, magnifying the dangers and motivating one another to remain firm, steady and united.

After all this, they came forward, giving Moses the choice: "*Said [the sorcerers]: Moses! Either you throw [first], or we shall be the first to throw.*" (Verse 65) This is a challenge aiming to show a united, powerful front and a commendable degree of fairness. Hence, his answer was to accept the challenge: "*You throw first.*" (Verse 66) He allowed them to start and produce whatever they wanted so that he could have the final say. And what was the result? They apparently produced a magnificent piece of magic, taking the whole multitude by surprise and even affecting Moses.

"*And by virtue of their sorcery, their ropes and staffs seemed to him to be moving rapidly. And in his heart Moses became apprehensive.*" (Verses 66–67) The Qur'ānic expression, *awjasa fī nafsihī khīfatan*, suggests a truly mighty magic, which filled the whole arena. Moses felt fear creep into his heart, even though God was with him hearing and seeing everything as it took place. Needless to say, Moses would not have entertained any fear unless the whole thing was so awesome that for a moment he became oblivious to the fact that he was much stronger. Hence, he needed reminding that he relied on a much superior power:

> But We said [to him]: Have no fear! It is you who shall certainly prevail. Now throw that which is in your right hand and it shall swallow up all that they have wrought. For, they have wrought nothing but a sorcerer's deceitful trick; and sorcerers can never come to any good, whatever they may do. (Verses 68–69)

You are the one supporting the truth, while they enjoin nothing but falsehood. You have the faith, while they have their tricks and craft. You believe in the truth of your message, while they have nothing but the reward they hope to receive from Pharaoh and the pleasures of this life. You are the one who derives his strength from God Almighty while they serve a human creature who will die despite his tyrannical power.

Thus God reassures Moses telling him to have no fear. He further tells him: "*Now throw that which is in your right hand.*" (Verse 69)

What he has in his hand is not specified so as to give an air of awe. *"And it shall swallow up all that they have wrought."* (Verse 69) For it is all sorcery and witchcraft. Sorcerers can never achieve ultimate success, no matter what they do, what device they use or which way they follow. They rely on trickery and deception. There is no real substance to what they do. Hence they fare no better than anyone else who confronts the truth with false appearances. They may put up quite a show and may inspire awe and fear, but then the power of the truth, steady, factual, unboastful, will strike. With that blow falsehood will be defeated immediately, left to retreat into oblivion.

Then Moses threw down his staff. The *sūrah* describes the magnitude of the surprise which then occurred by mentioning how it affected the sorcerers who had come full of hope to win the challenge. Only a few moments earlier, their sorcery, which was of the highest standard, had generated fear among all the spectators, including Moses himself. He, a messenger of God, thought that their ropes and staffs turned into snakes, alive and moving rapidly.

Now the surprise Moses produced completely transformed their feelings and thoughts. So much so that words could not express their reaction: *"So down fell the sorcerers, prostrating themselves, and declared: We do believe in the Lord of Aaron and Moses."* (Verse 70) That was like a touch on a very raw nerve, and the whole body is shaken violently. It was like a light being switched on to dispel all darkness. Such power is felt by reawakened hearts, filling them, in a split second, with unshakeable faith.

A Tyrant's Threat

Do tyrants understand this inner reaction? Do they realize how hearts can be transformed? With a long history of tyranny and injustice, during which they see their subordinates bow to their every command, hasten to fulfil their desire at the slightest indication, tyrants forget that it is God who changes hearts and minds. They cannot appreciate that when a heart responds to contact with God, the bond is complete. The believer, then, derives strength and light from Him alone. Thus, no one can subjugate such a believer to his own power. Hence, Pharaoh's reaction: *"Said [Pharaoh]: Do you believe in him before I have given you permission? Surely, he must be your master who has taught you witchcraft! I shall most certainly cut off your hands and feet on opposite sides, and I shall most certainly crucify you on the trunks of the palm-trees. You will then come to know for certain which of us can inflict a more severe and longer lasting punishment."* (Verse 71)

"Do you believe in him before I have given you permission?" (Verse 71) Such is the retort of a tyrant who cannot understand how others feel faith touch their hearts such that they cannot turn it away. After all, people's hearts are, as the Prophet says, held between two of God's, the Most Merciful's, fingers and He turns them around as He wills.

"Surely, he must be your master who has taught you witchcraft!" (Verse 71) For Pharaoh, this was the only reason for the sorcerer's submission to Moses. He could not perceive of faith touching their hearts. He could not understand that God's hand had lifted the cover blurring their vision and that they could now see things for what they were.

Pharaoh follows this with the normal kind of threat tyrants use when they feel they have no power over others' hearts and souls. They threaten physical torture and punishment on those who do not submit to their tyranny: *"I shall most certainly cut off your hands and feet on opposite sides, and I shall most certainly crucify you on the trunks of the palm-trees."* (Verse 71) Arrogant and boastful, he continues with his claims to authority and power. His is a brutal force, ready to tear human bodies apart. Thus brute force is utilized to counter solid, logical argument: *"You will then come to know for certain which of us can inflict a more severe and longer lasting punishment."* (Verse 71)

Hearts Touched by Faith

But it was too late for Pharaoh. Faith had touched the hearts of those sorcerers and the small, insignificant person within each of them was now in firm contact with the great source of real power. Hence, they were now very strong, while all earthly powers were weak. Indeed the whole life on earth is too small when compared to the broad, bright horizons to which those believing hearts now looked up. All that pertains to life on earth is of no consequence: *"They answered:*

Never shall we prefer you to all the evidence of the truth that has come to us, nor to Him who has brought us into being! Decree, then, whatever you are going to decree. You can only decree on what pertains to this worldly life. As for us, we have come to believe in our Lord, hoping that He may forgive us our faults and all that magic to which you have forced us. God is certainly the best and He is Everlasting." (Verses 72–73)

This is the sort of change faith brings about in the hearts of people who, until a moment earlier, were submissive to Pharaoh, considering their highest achievement to be close to him, receiving his favours. Now they are ready to confront him with a determination that puts his power, throne and wealth in proper perspective: *"Never shall we prefer you to all the evidence of the truth that has come to us, nor to Him who has brought us into being!"* (Verse 72) Such evidence is much more precious in our view, and God, our Creator, is far dearer to us than anything else. *"Decree, then, whatever you are going to decree."* (Verse 72) This is a challenge to Pharaoh to do his worst. He cannot stop them. *"You can only decree on what pertains to this worldly life."* (Verse 72)

This is as far as Pharaoh's power extends. They tell him clearly that he has no authority over them anywhere other than in this worldly life, which is short, momentary and of little value. Whatever punishment he may inflict on them is too trivial to be feared by a heart that has established close contact with God and hopes to receive His reward in the hereafter. *"As for us, we have come to believe in our Lord, hoping that He may forgive us our faults and all that magic to which you have forced us."* (Verse 73) They tell him that in the past they could not disobey him when he forced them to practise magic. Now that they have faith, they hope to be forgiven by God who, they realize, is the best and the everlasting. His reward is far more plentiful and enjoyed for much longer than any worldly reward.

The sorcerers who came to believe in God were inspired by their faith to adopt an attitude that looked down on Pharaoh and his power:

He who shall appear before his Lord [on Judgement Day] laden with sin shall be consigned to hell, where he shall neither die nor live. But he who shall appear before Him as a believer, having done righteous deeds, shall be exalted to the highest ranks, abiding in the gardens of Eden, through which running waters flow. Such shall be the recompense of those who keep themselves pure. (Verses 74–76)

Pharaoh had originally threatened them, saying that his punishment was more severe and longer lasting. Their reply provides an image of one who comes on the Day of Judgement to meet his Lord, being fully laden with sin. The punishment such a person receives is indeed the longer lasting and more painful, because such a person *"shall be consigned to hell, where he shall neither die nor live."* (Verse 74) He does not enjoy the termination of pain that a dead person normally has, nor is he living so as to enjoy life's pleasures. He simply receives a painful punishment that leads to neither life nor death. On the opposite side the highest ranks are shown. These are the gardens of bliss, irrigated by running waters. Such is *"the recompense of those who keep themselves pure,"* purging themselves of all sin.

Thus these new believers take no notice of a despot's threats, and instead stand up to him with the powerful words of faith. They are profoundly confident, issue a warning based on faith and express their hopes based on a newly-found faith.

This confrontation is recorded in the history of mankind as a declaration of man's freedom, after throwing away the shackles of this worldly life, its powers, worries and aspirations. No human heart can adopt such a confrontational attitude unless it believes in God and relies on His support.

The Drowning of Pharaoh and His Army

The curtains are drawn only to lift again on a new scene in Moses' history. Now we see the triumph of faith and truth in practical life, after their victory as an idea and belief. What we have seen so far is the triumph of the sign given to Moses over sorcery, the new faith in the sorcerers' hearts over their hopes of gain and fears of loss as well as over Pharaoh's threats and punishment. Now we see a related victory for truth over falsehood, guidance over error, and faith over tyranny. All this takes place in real life after it has been achieved in people's consciences. In fact advocates of the truth cannot openly demonstrate

429

their high moral ground until they have triumphed within themselves over all temptation.

Truth and faith have a certain reality which, once materialized within one's conscience, finds its way into real life. Should faith remain an outward appearance that does not touch the heart, and truth remain a raised slogan that has not sunk deep into people's hearts and minds, then tyranny and falsehood may be victorious. They can achieve such a victory with the physical power under their command, one which cannot be matched by the mere appearance of faith and slogans of truth. It is only when the latter are truly established in hearts and minds that they become stronger than the physical might which falsehood and tyranny can muster. This is the fact which we clearly see in Moses' attitude towards the sorcerers and their ploys, and later in the sorcerers' attitude towards Pharaoh and his noblemen. This is the prelude to victory as we see in the next scene in the *sūrah*.

> *Then We thus inspired Moses: 'Go forth with My servants by night, and strike out for them a dry path through the sea. Have no fear of being overtaken, and dread nothing. Pharaoh pursued them with his hosts, but they were overwhelmed by the power of the sea. For Pharaoh had led his people astray and had not guided them aright.* (Verses 77–79)

The *sūrah* does not mention here what happened after the confrontation between faith and tyranny, nor what measures Pharaoh took against the sorcerers after they declared their belief in God, defying his power and tyranny, as well as all earthly temptation. It simply paints this scene of total victory so that the triumph in one's own conscience is directly related to triumph in real life. We also see here how God provides total care for His servants. By the same token, the *sūrah* does not dwell on the scene of departure from Egypt, and the standing before the sea, as these are painted in detail in other *sūrahs*. In fact, it shows the victory scene here without preliminaries, because these concerned people's hearts.

All we have here is the inspiration given to Moses to depart from Egypt at night with the Children of Israel, and to strike out for them a dry path across the sea. We see Moses with complete reassurance as he and his followers receive God's care. Thus, he has no fear of his people being overtaken by Pharaoh or of being overwhelmed by the parted sea. God's will which made the sea such a great volume of water with all its characteristics is able to part it for a while to give those believers a dry path through so as to continue their journey.

"*Pharaoh pursued them with his hosts, but they were overwhelmed by the power of the sea. For Pharaoh had led his people astray and had not guided them aright.*" (Verses 78–79) Thus the *sūrah* sums up how Pharaoh and his host were overwhelmed by the sea. It gives no further details. In this way, it retains its total effect. We realize that Pharaoh had led his people into error in their way of life in the same way as he led them into error by pursuing the believers into the sea. In both cases, he led them to utter ruin.

We prefer not to dwell on the details of what happened to Pharaoh and his people, so that we move on with the *sūrah* as it relates the story. We will, however, reflect for a moment on the lessons that we can derive from this scene.

When God Intervenes

It was God who conducted the battle between faith and tyranny. The believers were not required to do anything other than follow the inspiration received by Moses and to move out at night. The believers were no match for the unbelievers in terms of material power. Moses and his men were weak and powerless, while Pharaoh and his army held all the material power. Hence, a battle between the two parties could not take place. Therefore, God took over, but only after the truth of faith was fully engrained in the hearts of those whose only strength was that which they derived from faith. Thus we see the tyrant delivering his threat and warning the believers of doom: "*I shall most certainly cut off your hands and feet on opposite sides, and I shall most certainly crucify you on the trunks of the palm trees.*" (Verse 71) To this, the believers, with their hearts full of faith, reply: "*Decree, then, whatever you are going to decree. You can only decree on what pertains to this worldly life.*" (Verse 72)

The simple truth of the matter is that when the battle between faith and tyranny reached this level in people's hearts, God himself took up the banner of truth and hoisted it high, leaving the banner of falsehood trampled upon. All this took place without the believers exerting any effort whatsoever.

We also learn from this account that when the Children of Israel accepted the humiliation Pharaoh imposed on them, by virtue of his persecution campaign, killing their men and sparing their women, God did not interfere on their side. They simply accepted their subjugation, fearing Pharaoh and his power. But when faith was paramount in the hearts of those who believed in Moses and his message, and when they were ready to withstand the torture with their heads held high, declaring their rejection of Pharaoh and their belief in God, then God intervened and conducted the battle. Thus, victory was achieved on the battlefield as it was earlier achieved within their hearts and souls.

Such is the lesson driven home in this *sūrah* as it portrays the two scenes in quick succession, without dwelling on further detail. This is what people of faith should understand, so that they know when to expect God's help to achieve their victory.

The Price for God's Intervention

Yet to those who were saved and granted victory a reminder and a warning are given so that they do not forget or abandon their most important weapon:

> *Children of Israel! We saved you from your enemy, and then We made a covenant with you on the right flank of Mount Sinai. We sent down manna and quails for you. Eat of the wholesome things which We have provided for you and do not transgress, lest you should incur My wrath. He that incurs My wrath has indeed thrown himself into utter ruin; but I certainly forgive all sins for anyone who repents, believes and does righteous deeds, and thereafter keeps to the right path.* (Verses 80–82)

They have passed the danger zone and have surged on towards
Mount Sinai, leaving Pharaoh and his army drowned. Their
deliverance was a recent event which they remember well, but it is
recorded here as a reminder, so that they may give thanks.

The appointment at the right hand side of Mount Sinai is mentioned
here as though it is an accomplished event, when it was a meeting for
which Moses had to prepare himself for over a period of forty nights.
He would then receive the tablets and the laws recorded therein. This
was a law to regulate the lives of the people entrusted with a mission
in the Holy Land after their departure from Egypt.

The fact that they were given manna, a sweet type of food that
gathers on leaves, and quails, a type of bird that is easy to catch and
eat, was another aspect of God's grace, of His taking care of them in
the barren desert where they found themselves. God was looking after
them, even to the point of providing them with their daily food, and
in such a way that required no hard effort.

God reminds them of all these favours and warns them against
transgression, in the form of indulgence in physical pleasure and
neglect of the duties they left Egypt to fulfil. God is preparing for
them an assignment which they must undertake. The Arabic word
used here for transgression, *tatghaw*, is the same word that signifies
the tyranny they experienced in their very recent past. Hence, they
are warned: *"Eat of the wholesome things which We have provided for
you and do not transgress, lest you should incur My wrath. He that incurs
My wrath has indeed thrown himself into utter ruin."* (Verse 81) Pharaoh
had thrown himself into such ruin only recently, falling off his throne
and drowning in the sea. To experience such ruin is to fall from high,
which contrasts with tyranny that exalts the tyrant and assumes for
him a high position of power. The Qur'ān here juxtaposes such
contrasting elements in word and meaning to achieve both heightened
effect and perfect harmony.

With this warning against indulgence in easy pleasures and neglect
of the task assigned for them, the door for repentance is left open for
anyone who slips so that he may return to the proper path. *"But I
certainly forgive all sins for anyone who repents, believes and does righteous
deeds, and thereafter keeps to the right path."* (Verse 82)

Repentance is not merely a word we say with our mouths. It is a resolve in one's mind that manifests itself in strong faith and good deeds, as well as practical behaviour. So when faith is settled in a person's heart, faith is purged of all alien traces, and confirmed by good deeds. In this way, man sets himself on the right path, guided by faith and benefiting by the guarantee provided by good action. Achieving guidance is shown here as the result of strong faith and determined action.

Thus ends the scene of victory and the comments the *sūrah* has to make on it. The curtains fall and lift again to show us the second scene of an address made directly to God by the side of Mount Sinai.

Promises Fulfilled or Broken

God has appointed a time for Moses to meet Him at the Mount after forty days, when he would be given the commandments outlining the tasks his people have to fulfil after the victory they were given. Victory carries with it its own responsibilities, as does faith. Hence, it was necessary for Moses to be psychologically prepared and ready to receive God's commandments.

Thus, Moses went up the Mount, leaving his people at the bottom, after asking his brother Aaron to deputize for him. Moses longed dearly for this encounter, when he would stand in front of his Lord and address Him. He had had this experience once before and was keen to experience it again. Hence, he made haste to stand in the presence of his Lord. He was however totally unaware of what his people had perpetrated after he had left.

His Lord tells him the news, pointing out what has taken place. The scene is shown to us and we listen to the conversation:

[And God said]: 'Now what has caused you, Moses, to leave your people behind in so great a haste?' He answered: 'They are treading in my footsteps, while I have hastened to You, my Lord, so that You might be well-pleased with me.' Said He: 'Then [know that] in your absence We have put your people to a test, and the Sāmiriy has led them astray.' (Verses 83–85)

434

Thus Moses is faced with a terrible shock. He was in haste to meet his Lord, after forty days of diligent preparation, eager to listen to His directives and commandments which would constitute the basis of the new way of life for the Children of Israel. It was to be a way of life suited for a community that had been freed from the shackles of subjugation so that it would become the bearer of a divine message.

The long period they had spent in subjugation and humiliation under Pharaoh's rule and his idolatrous beliefs had had a damaging effect on the nature of the Israelites. Their ability to withstand the difficulties that attend the fulfilment of a hard task, and to remain true to their promises in the face of hardship, was certainly suspect. Psychologically, they suffered an impairment which made them always keen to have a comfortable life, even if this meant a willingness to be led without troubling to think. No sooner did Moses leave them under Aaron's stewardship than they allowed their faith to collapse at the first hurdle. Hence, they needed repeated tests and trials in a process of psychological rebuilding. The first test to which they were subjected was that of the golden calf which the Sāmiriy had produced. "*In your absence We have put your people to a test, and the Sāmiriy has led them astray.*" (Verse 85) Moses did not know about this test until his appointment with his Lord.

The *sūrah* sums up the scene of the direct address between God and Moses very briefly in order to describe Moses' reaction to what he learnt, his speedy return, his anger and his sorrow. How could his people do this after God had saved them from humiliating subjugation by tyrannical idolatry, and favoured them with easy provisions and care in the desert? He had only very recently reminded them of God's favours, warning them against going astray. Yet now they follow the first one to call them back to paganism and the worship of a calf!

The *sūrah* does not tell us any details about how they were led to this situation. It moves on to the scene of Moses hurriedly returning to his people. However, the way this is described tells us something of these details. Moses has returned, angry, sad, remonstrating with his people and scolding his brother. He must have known the magnitude of their ghastly deed:

Thus Moses returned to his people full of wrath and sorrow: 'My people,' he said, 'Did not your Lord hold out a goodly promise to you? Did, then, [the fulfilment of] this promise seem to you too long in coming? Or are you determined to see your Lord's condemnation fall upon you, and so you broke your promise to me?' They answered: 'We did not break our promise to you of our own free-will, but we were loaded with the burdens of the [Egyptian] people's ornaments, and so we threw them [into the fire], and likewise this Sāmiriy threw.' Thus he produced for them the effigy of a calf, which made a lowing sound. 'This,' they said, 'is your deity and the deity of Moses; but he has forgotten. Why! Did they not see that it could not give them any response, and that it could neither harm nor benefit them? And, indeed, Aaron had said to them earlier: 'My people! You are but being tempted to evil by this calf. Your only Lord is the Most Merciful! Follow me, then, and do as I bid you.' But they had replied: 'By no means shall we cease worshipping it until Moses comes back to us.' (Verses 86–91)

Such was the trial to which the Israelites were put. It is revealed to us as Moses confronts his people. It is not reported in the scene of the meeting between Moses and his Lord. It is left to the scene of inquiry undertaken by Moses upon his return.

Justifying Deliberate Error

Enraged and full of sorrow, Moses asked his people: "*Did not your Lord hold out a goodly promise to you?*" (Verse 86) God had promised them victory and to enter the Holy Land as a community believing in His oneness. Only very recently had they witnessed the initial steps towards the complete fulfilment of this promise. Hence, he remonstrated with them: "*Did, then, [the fulfilment of] this promise seem to you too long in coming? Or are you determined to see your Lord's condemnation fall upon you?*" (Verse 86) Their action was akin to that perpetrated by one who wants to bring God's condemnation on his head, so he wilfully and deliberately does what incurs it. Moses asked them if this was why they broke their promise to him to maintain the path he had shown them until his return.

They gave him a singular excuse which exposed the effects on their mentality of their long time living in subservience. It is a ludicrous excuse: "*We did not break our promise to you of our own free-will.*" (Verse 87) It was beyond our ability and control. "*But we were loaded with the burdens of the [Egyptian] people's ornaments, and so we threw them [into the fire].*" (Verse 87) They had carried with them loads of jewellery borrowed from Egyptian women. Now they say they wanted to get rid of all these because they were taken unlawfully. The Sāmiriy took these gold articles and made of them the golden calf. The Sāmiriy was either a man from Samaria accompanying them or one of them known by this appellation. When he made the calf, he purposely placed some holes in it, so that when the wind blew, it produced a lowing sound, despite the fact that it had no life or soul. It was merely an inanimate object. But no sooner did they see such a golden calf making such a noise than they forgot their true Lord who had saved them from their humiliation. Most stupidly and inexcusably they started to worship the calf, repeating the ludicrous statement that Moses had been misled when he went to the mountain looking for his deity, while the deity was there with them, as they claimed. They said: "*This is your deity and the deity of Moses; but he has forgotten.*" (Verse 88)

Their stupid remarks also detract from the position of their prophet, Moses, who was the one to accomplish their salvation under God's guidance. What they said about the calf alleged that Moses had no guiding relationship with his Lord. Hence, he did not know how to find Him, taking the wrong path and looking for him in the wrong place.

Yet they were fooled by a simple trick, which they should have easily recognized for what it was. "*Why! Did they not see that it could not give them any response, and that it could neither harm nor benefit them?*" (Verse 89) It was not even a living calf that could hear them and respond in the way that cows and calves respond. It could not aspire to the status of an ordinary animal. It could not bring them the least harm or benefit, not even fighting with its horns or drawing water from a stream.

Moreover, Aaron, their other prophet who deputized for his brother Moses, their saviour, had given them honest and sincere advice, pointing out to them that it was all a test: *"And, indeed, Aaron had said to them earlier: My people! You are but being tempted to evil by this calf. Your only Lord is the Most Merciful! Follow me, then, and do as I bid you."* (Verse 90) He assured them that the proper course for them to take was to follow him as they had promised Moses. He told them that Moses was certain to return when his Lord had finished His business with him. Rather than follow his advice, they evaded their responsibility and abandoned their commitment to obey their prophets, saying: *"By no means shall we cease worshipping it until Moses comes back to us."* (Verse 91)

Thus Moses returned, sorrowful and angry. He listened to his people's excuses which revealed the extent of their twisted logic. In his anger, he turned to his brother dragging him by his head and beard, crying in his anger: *"Aaron, what has prevented you, when you saw that they had gone astray, from following me? Why have you disobeyed me?"* (Verses 92–93) He scolded him for allowing them to worship the calf without taking effective action to prevent them. But Aaron was merely obeying his brother's orders when he had told him not to do anything serious until he returned. Did Aaron, then, disobey his brother by doing so?

The *sūrah* has already stated Aaron's attitude. Now he explains to his brother what he did, trying to calm his fury and awaken his compassion. He reminds him of their close relationship: *"'Son of my mother,' he replied, 'do not seize me by my beard, or by my head! I was afraid that you might say: You have caused a split among the Israelites and did not wait for my orders.'"* (Verse 94)

Here we find Aaron to be far more in control of his emotions. He touches on a tender point in Moses' feelings, reminding him of their being siblings. He also explains to him that he simply wished to do what his brother had bid him. He feared that should he adopt strong measures the Children of Israel might split into factions, some worshipping the calf, and others following his advice. Since his brother wanted him to take care of them all, keeping them together, he felt that his attitude was simply one of following the orders he had been given.

Temptation of the Golden Calf

Now Moses addresses all his anger to the Sāmiriy, the perpetrator of the whole trouble. He did not speak to him first because the people themselves should have known better than to follow someone who came up with an outrageous idea. Aaron, as their trusted leader, was also responsible for making sure that they did not slip, should they be faced with temptation. The Sāmiriy takes less importance, since he did not use brute force to compel them to follow his lead, nor did he cast a screen over their faculties of thinking. He simply presented a temptation and they fell for it. They could very easily have remained true to the guidance of their first prophet, Moses, and benefited by the counsel of their second prophet, Aaron. Hence, responsibility lay with them in the first place, then with their leader, and finally with the perpetrator of the trouble.

"Said [Moses]: What is then your case, Sāmiriy?" (Verse 95) How come all this has happened because of you? The way the question is phrased is indicative of the seriousness of the whole affair.

> *He answered: I have gained insight into something which they were unable to see; and so I took a handful of dust from the trail of the messenger and flung it away; for thus has my mind prompted me to act.* (Verse 96)

There are countless reports that try to explain the Sāmiriy's answer: What did he see? Who was the messenger of whose trail he took a handful? What did this have to do with the calf he made and how did throwing this handful affect the calf he made? It is frequently mentioned in these reports that he saw Gabriel the angel in the form he takes when he descends to earth. So he took a handful of dust from underneath his foot or his horse's hoof and threw the dust at the golden calf to produce the lowing sound, or that this was the cause behind making the jewellery into a lowing calf.

The Qur'ān does not tell us here what really happened; it simply quotes what the Sāmiriy said. We are inclined to consider this an excuse the Sāmiriy concocted in order to evade responsibility for what actually happened. We feel that it was he who made the calf out of the jewellery the Israelites threw away, having taken it deceptively and unlawfully from the Egyptian women. As he made it, he deliberately ensured that as the wind went through its hollow inside it produced such a noise. When questioned about it, he sought an excuse, hence his suggestion that he had seen Gabriel and took a handful of his trail.

Be that as it may, Moses punished him by expelling him for life from the Israelite community, leaving his destiny in the hereafter to God Almighty. He further took a strong and effective measure concerning the deity he had made with his own hands, aiming to show his people that it was an inanimate object, unable to protect its maker or to save itself: "*Said [Moses]: Begone, then! It shall be your lot to say throughout your life, 'Do not touch me.' But you shall be faced with a destiny from which you shall have no escape. Now look at this deity of yours to whose worship you have become so devoted: we shall most certainly burn it, and then scatter it far and wide over the sea.*" (Verse 97)

Thus the Sāmiriy was ostracized: no one could go near him either to harm or benefit him. Nor was he allowed to touch anyone either. This was one of the penalties prescribed in Moses' faith: expelling the offender and ostracizing him to the extent that no one went near him. The other aspect is that of God's punishment at His own time.

Still angry and furious, Moses ordered the calf to be burnt, cast away and its ashes thrown in the sea. Such a strong action seems to be a characteristic of Moses. In this instance, however, his anger is in defence of God's faith. In such a situation, strong action is commendable.

With the false deity being burnt and blown away, Moses declared the basic principle of true faith: "*Your only deity is God, other than whom there is no deity. His knowledge encompasses all things.*" (Verse 98)

With this declaration we come to the end of the story of Moses as related in this *sūrah*. The overriding tone here is that of the grace God bestows on His servants, His care and forgiveness, even when they err. The *sūrah* does not add any other episode of Moses' history, because subsequent events tell of the punishment God metes out to them for their sinful and corrupt ways. The overall atmosphere of this *sūrah* is one of mercy, compassion and grace, and later episodes do not fit with such an atmosphere.

2

Man's Long Drawn Battle

Thus do We relate to you some of the history of past events; and thus have We given you, out of Our grace, a reminder. (99)

كَذَٰلِكَ نَقُصُّ عَلَيْكَ مِنْ أَنۢبَآءِ مَا قَدْ سَبَقَ ۚ وَقَدْ ءَاتَيْنَٰكَ مِن لَّدُنَّا ذِكْرًا ۝

All who shall turn away from it will certainly bear a heavy burden on the Day of Resurrection. (100)

مَّنْ أَعْرَضَ عَنْهُ فَإِنَّهُۥ يَحْمِلُ يَوْمَ ٱلْقِيَٰمَةِ وِزْرًا ۝

For ever shall they bear it; and grievous for them will be its weight on the Day of Resurrection, (101)

خَٰلِدِينَ فِيهِ ۖ وَسَآءَ لَهُمْ يَوْمَ ٱلْقِيَٰمَةِ حِمْلًا ۝

the day when the Trumpet is blown. For on that day We shall assemble all the guilty ones, their eyes dimmed [by terror], (102)

يَوْمَ يُنفَخُ فِى ٱلصُّورِ ۚ وَنَحْشُرُ ٱلْمُجْرِمِينَ يَوْمَئِذٍ زُرْقًا ۝

whispering to one another, 'You have spent but ten days on earth.' (103)

يَتَخَٰفَتُونَ بَيْنَهُمْ إِن لَّبِثْتُمْ إِلَّا عَشْرًا ۝

We know best what they will be saying when the most perceptive of them shall say: 'You have spent there but one day!' (104)

نَّحْنُ أَعْلَمُ بِمَا يَقُولُونَ إِذْ يَقُولُ أَمْثَلُهُمْ طَرِيقَةً إِن لَّبِثْتُمْ إِلَّا يَوْمًا ﴿١٠٤﴾

They ask you about the mountains. Say: 'My Lord will scatter them far and wide, (105)

وَيَسْـَٔلُونَكَ عَنِ ٱلْجِبَالِ فَقُلْ يَنسِفُهَا رَبِّى نَسْفًا ﴿١٠٥﴾

and leave the earth level and bare, (106)

فَيَذَرُهَا قَاعًا صَفْصَفًا ﴿١٠٦﴾

with no curves or ruggedness to be seen. (107)

لَّا تَرَىٰ فِيهَا عِوَجًا وَلَآ أَمْتًا ﴿١٠٧﴾

On that day, all will follow the summoning voice from which there will be no escape. All sounds will be hushed before the Most Merciful, and you will hear nothing but a faint sough in the air. (108)

يَوْمَئِذٍ يَتَّبِعُونَ ٱلدَّاعِىَ لَا عِوَجَ لَهُۥ وَخَشَعَتِ ٱلْأَصْوَاتُ لِلرَّحْمَٰنِ فَلَا تَسْمَعُ إِلَّا هَمْسًا ﴿١٠٨﴾

On that day, intercession will be of no avail to any except a person in whose case the Most Merciful will have granted permission, and whose word He will have accepted. (109)

يَوْمَئِذٍ لَّا تَنفَعُ ٱلشَّفَٰعَةُ إِلَّا مَنْ أَذِنَ لَهُ ٱلرَّحْمَٰنُ وَرَضِىَ لَهُۥ قَوْلًا ﴿١٠٩﴾

He knows all that lies open before them and all that is hidden from them, whereas they cannot have thorough knowledge of Him. (110)

يَعْلَمُ مَا بَيْنَ أَيْدِيهِمْ وَمَا خَلْفَهُمْ وَلَا يُحِيطُونَ بِهِۦ عِلْمًا ﴿١١٠﴾

All faces shall be humbled before the Ever-Living, the Self-Subsisting Lord; and undone shall be he who is burdened with evildoing; (111)

وَعَنَتِ ٱلْوُجُوهُ لِلْحَيِّ ٱلْقَيُّومِ وَقَدْ خَابَ مَنْ حَمَلَ ظُلْمًا ۞

but anyone who will have done righteous deeds, being a believer, need have no fear of being wronged or deprived. (112)

وَمَن يَعْمَلْ مِنَ ٱلصَّٰلِحَٰتِ وَهُوَ مُؤْمِنٌ فَلَا يَخَافُ ظُلْمًا وَلَا هَضْمًا ۞

And thus have We bestowed from on high the Qur'ān in the Arabic tongue, and have given in it many facets to all manner of warnings, so that they may be God-fearing or that it may be for them a source of remembrance. (113)

وَكَذَٰلِكَ أَنزَلْنَٰهُ قُرْءَانًا عَرَبِيًّا وَصَرَّفْنَا فِيهِ مِنَ ٱلْوَعِيدِ لَعَلَّهُمْ يَتَّقُونَ أَوْ يُحْدِثُ لَهُمْ ذِكْرًا ۞

Sublimely exalted is God, the Ultimate Sovereign, the Ultimate Truth. Be not in haste with the Qur'ān before it has been revealed to you in full, but always say: 'My Lord, increase my knowledge.' (114)

فَتَعَٰلَى ٱللَّهُ ٱلْمَلِكُ ٱلْحَقُّ وَلَا تَعْجَلْ بِٱلْقُرْءَانِ مِن قَبْلِ أَن يُقْضَىٰ إِلَيْكَ وَحْيُهُۥ وَقُل رَّبِّ زِدْنِي عِلْمًا ۞

Long ago, We made a covenant with Adam; but he forgot it, and We found him lacking in firmness of purpose. (115)

وَلَقَدْ عَهِدْنَآ إِلَىٰٓ ءَادَمَ مِن قَبْلُ فَنَسِىَ وَلَمْ نَجِدْ لَهُۥ عَزْمًا ۞

And when We said to the angels, 'Prostrate yourselves before Adam,' they all prostrated themselves; except *Iblīs*, who refused. (116)

وَإِذْ قُلْنَا لِلْمَلَٰئِكَةِ ٱسْجُدُوا۟ لِءَادَمَ فَسَجَدُوٓا۟ إِلَّآ إِبْلِيسَ أَبَىٰ ﴿١١٦﴾

'Adam,' We said, 'this is indeed a foe to you and your wife; so let him not drive the two of you out of the Garden, for then you will be plunged into affliction. (117)

فَقُلْنَا يَٰٓـَٔادَمُ إِنَّ هَٰذَا عَدُوٌّ لَّكَ وَلِزَوْجِكَ فَلَا يُخْرِجَنَّكُمَا مِنَ ٱلْجَنَّةِ فَتَشْقَىٰٓ ﴿١١٧﴾

It is guaranteed that you shall not hunger here or feel naked, (118)

إِنَّ لَكَ أَلَّا تَجُوعَ فِيهَا وَلَا تَعْرَىٰ ﴿١١٨﴾

and you shall not thirst here or suffer from the blazing sun.' (119)

وَأَنَّكَ لَا تَظْمَؤُا۟ فِيهَا وَلَا تَضْحَىٰ ﴿١١٩﴾

But Satan whispered to him, saying: 'Adam, shall I lead you to the tree of life eternal, and to a kingdom that will never decay?' (120)

فَوَسْوَسَ إِلَيْهِ ٱلشَّيْطَٰنُ قَالَ يَٰٓـَٔادَمُ هَلْ أَدُلُّكَ عَلَىٰ شَجَرَةِ ٱلْخُلْدِ وَمُلْكٍ لَّا يَبْلَىٰ ﴿١٢٠﴾

They both ate of its fruit; and thereupon their shameful parts became visible to them, and they began to cover themselves with pieced-together leaves from the Garden. Thus did Adam disobey his Lord, and thus did he stray into error. (121)

فَأَكَلَا مِنْهَا فَبَدَتْ لَهُمَا سَوْءَٰتُهُمَا وَطَفِقَا يَخْصِفَانِ عَلَيْهِمَا مِن وَرَقِ ٱلْجَنَّةِ وَعَصَىٰٓ ءَادَمُ رَبَّهُ فَغَوَىٰ ﴿١٢١﴾

Then his Lord elected him [for His grace], accepted his repentance, and bestowed His guidance upon him. (122)

ثُمَّ ٱجْتَبَٰهُ رَبُّهُۥ فَتَابَ عَلَيْهِ وَهَدَىٰ ﴿١٢٢﴾

'Get down, both of you, and be out of it;' He said, 'each of you shall be an enemy to the other. When guidance shall come to you from Me, he who follows My guidance will not go astray, nor will he suffer misery; (123)

قَالَ ٱهْبِطَا مِنْهَا جَمِيعًۢا بَعْضُكُمْ لِبَعْضٍ عَدُوٌّ فَإِمَّا يَأْتِيَنَّكُم مِّنِّي هُدًى فَمَنِ ٱتَّبَعَ هُدَايَ فَلَا يَضِلُّ وَلَا يَشْقَىٰ ﴿١٢٣﴾

but he who turns away from My message shall have a straitened life and We shall raise him up blind on the Day of Resurrection.' (124)

وَمَنْ أَعْرَضَ عَن ذِكْرِي فَإِنَّ لَهُۥ مَعِيشَةً ضَنكًا وَنَحْشُرُهُۥ يَوْمَ ٱلْقِيَٰمَةِ أَعْمَىٰ ﴿١٢٤﴾

'Lord,' he will say, 'why have You raised me up blind, while I was endowed with sight?' (125)

قَالَ رَبِّ لِمَ حَشَرْتَنِيٓ أَعْمَىٰ وَقَدْ كُنتُ بَصِيرًا ﴿١٢٥﴾

He will reply: 'Thus it is: Our revelations were brought to you, but you were oblivious to them. So today shall you be consigned to oblivion.' (126)

قَالَ كَذَٰلِكَ أَتَتْكَ ءَايَٰتُنَا فَنَسِيتَهَا وَكَذَٰلِكَ ٱلْيَوْمَ تُنسَىٰ ﴿١٢٦﴾

For thus shall We reward him who transgresses and does not believe in his Lord's revelations. Indeed the suffering in the life to come shall be most severe and most enduring. (127)

وَكَذَٰلِكَ نَجْزِي مَنْ أَسْرَفَ وَلَمْ يُؤْمِنۢ بِـَٔايَٰتِ رَبِّهِۦ وَلَعَذَابُ ٱلْأَخِرَةِ أَشَدُّ وَأَبْقَىٰٓ ﴿١٢٧﴾

Can they not see how many generations We have destroyed before their time? They walk about in the very places where they dwelt. In this there are signs for people of wisdom. (128)

أَفَلَمْ يَهْدِ لَهُمْ كَمْ أَهْلَكْنَا قَبْلَهُم مِّنَ الْقُرُونِ يَمْشُونَ فِي مَسَاكِنِهِمْ إِنَّ فِي ذَٰلِكَ لَآيَاتٍ لِّأُولِي النُّهَىٰ ۝

Now, were it not for a decree from your Lord already gone forth, setting a term, their destruction would have been inescapable. (129)

وَلَوْلَا كَلِمَةٌ سَبَقَتْ مِن رَّبِّكَ لَكَانَ لِزَامًا وَأَجَلٌ مُّسَمًّى ۝

Hence, bear with patience whatever they may say, and extol your Lord's limitless glory and praise Him before the rising of the sun and before its setting; and extol His glory, too, during the hours of the night as well as during the hours of the day, so that you may attain a state of contentment. (130)

فَاصْبِرْ عَلَىٰ مَا يَقُولُونَ وَسَبِّحْ بِحَمْدِ رَبِّكَ قَبْلَ طُلُوعِ الشَّمْسِ وَقَبْلَ غُرُوبِهَا وَمِنْ آنَاءِ اللَّيْلِ فَسَبِّحْ وَأَطْرَافَ النَّهَارِ لَعَلَّكَ تَرْضَىٰ ۝

Do not turn your eyes covetously towards whatever splendour of this world's life We have allowed many of them to enjoy in order that We may test them thereby. Whatever provisions your Lord may give are indeed better and longer lasting. (131)

many

وَلَا تَمُدَّنَّ عَيْنَيْكَ إِلَىٰ مَا مَتَّعْنَا بِهِ أَزْوَاجًا مِّنْهُمْ زَهْرَةَ الْحَيَاةِ الدُّنْيَا لِنَفْتِنَهُمْ فِيهِ وَرِزْقُ رَبِّكَ خَيْرٌ وَأَبْقَىٰ ۝

Enjoin prayer on your people, and be diligent in its observance. We do not ask you for any provisions. It is We who provide for you. The future belongs to the God-fearing. (132)

وَأْمُرْ أَهْلَكَ بِالصَّلَوٰةِ وَاصْطَبِرْ عَلَيْهَا لَا نَسْئَلُكَ رِزْقًا نَّحْنُ نَرْزُقُكَ وَالْعَٰقِبَةُ لِلتَّقْوَىٰ ﴿١٣٢﴾

They say: 'Why does he not bring us a sign from his Lord?' Has there not come to them a clear evidence of the truth in the earlier scriptures? (133)

وَقَالُوا لَوْلَا يَأْتِينَا بِئَايَةٍ مِّن رَّبِّهِۦ أَوَلَمْ تَأْتِهِم بَيِّنَةُ مَا فِى الصُّحُفِ الْأُولَىٰ ﴿١٣٣﴾

Had We destroyed them with a calamity before his coming, they would have said, 'Our Lord, if only You had sent us a Messenger, we would have followed Your revelations rather than be humiliated and disgraced.' (134)

وَلَوْ أَنَّا أَهْلَكْنَٰهُم بِعَذَابٍ مِّن قَبْلِهِۦ لَقَالُوا رَبَّنَا لَوْلَا أَرْسَلْتَ إِلَيْنَا رَسُولًا فَنَتَّبِعَ ءَايَٰتِكَ مِن قَبْلِ أَن نَّذِلَّ وَنَخْزَىٰ ﴿١٣٤﴾

Say: 'Everyone is hopefully waiting; so wait, if you will. You will certainly come to know who has followed the even path, and who has been rightly guided.' (135)

قُلْ كُلٌّ مُّتَرَبِّصٌ فَتَرَبَّصُوا فَسَتَعْلَمُونَ مَنْ أَصْحَٰبُ الصِّرَٰطِ السَّوِىِّ وَمَنِ اهْتَدَىٰ ﴿١٣٥﴾

Overview

The *sūrah* started with a discussion on the Qur'ān, making it clear that the purpose of its revelation to the Prophet Muḥammad (peace be upon him) was not that he might be afflicted by it. Part of the Qur'ān covers the story of Moses and how it reflects the care God took of Moses, his brother Aaron and their people. Now that the story has been told, the *sūrah* resumes speaking about the Qur'ān, the role it is intended to play and the fate which is bound to be suffered by those who turn their backs to it. This fate is shown in a scene of the Day of Judgement in which the days of this present life are seen to be infinitesimal, the earth loses its mountains and is seen flat and bare; sounds are hushed before God the Most Merciful; and faces are humbled before God, the Ever-Living. This scene, and the warnings made in the Qur'ān, are intended to arouse feelings of God-consciousness, reminding people of their relationship with God. This passage concludes by giving the Prophet renewed comfort with respect to the Qur'ān which was being revealed to him. He must not hasten to repeat its words during the process of receiving it as he used to do fearing that he might forget some parts of it. He need not entertain any such fear, because God has taken it upon Himself to preserve the Qur'ān and make it easy for recitation and study. In this context, the Prophet is instructed to pray to God to give him more knowledge.

Since the Prophet was keen to repeat the Qur'ānic revelations as they were given to him, for fear of forgetting them, the *sūrah* mentions how Adam forgot God's covenant. This is followed by the declaration of hostility between him and Satan, stating the different ends of the people who remember their covenant with God and those who forget it. These two different ends are shown in one of the scenes of the Day of Resurrection the Qur'ān portrays, as though the Day gives the end of the journey which started in heaven and aims to return there.

The *sūrah* concludes with fine touches aiming to comfort the Prophet so that he is not afflicted by those who deny the truth of his message or those who turn away from it. They have their appointed term. He should not attach any importance to the worldly riches they may have been given, because this is all a test which they have to pass.

Instead, he should be more preoccupied with his worship and with glorifying and praising God so that he can find reassurance and contentment. Generations were destroyed before these and they provided the example and the warning, but God now willed to send them His last Messenger so that they had no excuse for rejecting the truth. Since they turned away from him, he should leave them alone to face their inevitable end: "*Say: Everyone is hopefully waiting; so wait, if you will. You will certainly come to know who has followed the even path, and who has been rightly guided.*" (Verse 135)

Reasons for Qur'ānic History

Thus do We relate to you some of the history of past events; and thus have We given you, out of Our grace, a reminder. All who shall turn away from it will certainly bear a heavy burden on the Day of Resurrection. For ever shall they bear it; and grievous for them will be its weight on the Day of Resurrection, the day when the Trumpet is blown. For on that day We shall assemble all the guilty ones, their eyes dimmed [by terror], whispering to one another, 'You have spent but ten days on earth.' We know best what they will be saying when the most perceptive of them shall say: 'You have spent there but one day!' (Verses 99–104)

Just as Moses' history is related in the Qur'ān, so do We also relate other past events. The Qur'ān is described here as 'a reminder', because it reminds us of God, His signs and messages, as well as other signs given to people of old.

Those who turn away from this reminder are described here as guilty, and they are shown in a scene from the Day of Judgement. We see them carrying their burdens like a traveller carries his luggage, but theirs are foul, troublesome burdens. When the trumpet is blown to gather all creatures, the guilty come forward with blue faces showing their grief and worry. Terrified, they speak to one another in whispers: they cannot raise their voices. All this describes the fear that overwhelms them at that moment when all the dead are raised. But what is the subject of their whispers? They simply try to guess the duration of their life on earth, for that life has become so short in their view that they imagine it to have lasted only a few days. Some of them say: "*You have spent but ten days on earth.*" (Verse 103) However, those with a better judgement and a more accurate view feel life on earth to have been much shorter than that. They tell the others: "*You have spent there but one day.*" (Verse 104)

Thus their life on earth, with all its pleasures, comforts, grief and worries, shrinks into insignificance. It lasted only a brief period of time, and was of little value to anyone. For what is the value of ten days, even when they bring all sorts of happiness and enjoyment? And what price may be attached to one night, even though its every minute was one of pleasure and happiness? How could these compare with the endless time which awaits them after the Day of Resurrection?

All Submit to God

This awesome scene is further enhanced by returning to a question they had asked during their life on earth about the mountains and what would happen to them. The answer vividly describes the state of fear in which they find themselves:

> *They ask you about the mountains. Say: 'My Lord will scatter them far and wide, and leave the earth level and bare, with no curves or ruggedness to be seen. On that day, all will follow the summoning voice from which there will be no escape. All sounds will be hushed before the Most Merciful, and you will hear nothing but a faint sough in the air. On that day, intercession will be of no avail to any except a person in whose case the Most Merciful will have granted permission, and whose word He will have accepted. He knows all that lies open before them and all that is hidden from them, whereas they cannot have thorough knowledge of Him. All faces shall be humbled before the Ever-Living, the Self-Subsisting Lord; and undone shall be he who is burdened with evildoing; but anyone who will have done righteous deeds, being a believer, need have no fear of being wronged or deprived.' (Verses 105–112)*

These images come clearly to our eyes, and we see the great mountains, which we have known to be firmly rooted and stable, being blown and scattered. They are raised no more; indeed they are flat, level with no curves or any rugged surface. The whole earth is flat, level, having neither hills nor valleys.

But after the blowing away of the mountains, the storm dies down and the gathered multitudes listen attentively. Every movement and every little sound is hushed. They all listen to the voice that calls them to group together, and they follow its commands submissively, acting promptly, turning neither here nor there. This is a totally different reaction from the one they showed in this life when they were called on to follow divine guidance, but they turned away and refused. We note the perfect harmony of expression when the response to the summoning voice is total, with no escape, while the old mountains are now part of the flat, level earth that has no curve or elevation.

This is followed by a state of perfect silence, with no sound to be heard: "*All sounds will be hushed before the Most Merciful, and you will hear nothing but a faint sough in the air... All faces shall be humbled before the Ever-Living, the Self-Subsisting Lord.*" (Verses 108 and 111)

The whole scene is majestic, whereas the whole place, vast and infinite, is still, silent, and quiet. Whenever anyone speaks, they only whisper. Questions are raised very quietly, for all feel their humility. God's majesty imparts an air of great reverence. No one can intercede except a person whose words are acceptable to God. All knowledge belongs to God, while creatures cannot have full knowledge of Him. The wrongdoers will be burdened with the wrongs they have perpetrated, which will lead them to ruin, while the believers are reassured, fearing no injustice or lack of appreciation of their good works. The whole scene is one of great majesty, witnessed by God, the Most-Merciful.

And thus have We bestowed from on high the Qur'ān in the Arabic tongue, and have given in it many facets to all manner of warnings, so that they may be God-fearing or that it may be for them a source of remembrance." (Verse 113)

It is in the same pattern that the Qur'ān gives a whole variety of warnings, painting scenes of awesome and reverential fear to remind those who reject its message of what they will face in the life to come. Perhaps they will take heed, or realize that they need to act before it is too late. Hence, at the beginning of the *sūrah* God says to His Messenger: "*We did not bestow this Qur'ān on you from on high to cause you distress, but only as an admonition to the God-fearing.*" (Verses 2–3)

At the beginning of his message, the Prophet used to repeat the words of God's revelations before the angel had finished them. He did so because he was very keen that he should not forget a word. This was not easy for him. Hence, his Lord reassures him that he will not forget what is entrusted to him.

"*Sublimely exalted is God, the Ultimate Sovereign, the Ultimate Truth. Be not in haste with the Qur'ān before it has been revealed to you in full, but always say: 'My Lord, increase my knowledge.'*" (Verse 114) Most sublime is God, the true King of the whole universe. Before Him all heads are hung down, and all perpetrators of injustice are powerless, while believers who have done well are reassured. It is He who has bestowed this Qur'ān from on high. Therefore, you, Muḥammad, need not hasten to repeat its words. He has sent it down for a definite purpose, and He will not allow it to be lost. All you need to do is to pray to Him for increased knowledge, reassured that what He has given you will not be taken away. True knowledge is that imparted by God. It is a knowledge that lingers, brings benefit, yields good fruits and is never wasted.

Man's Lack of Purpose

The *sūrah* gives a brief account of Adam's story, when he forgot the commitment he made to God. When he was tempted by the prospect of immortality, he yielded, listening to Satan and his promptings. This was a test which God wanted him to go through before he was placed in charge of the earth. It also provided an example of what Satan can do, so that Adam's offspring would learn the lesson. When the test was completed, God bestowed His mercy on Adam, assigning his role to him, and providing him with guidance.

452

Every story related in the Qur'ān is made to fit with the context in which it is given. In this *sūrah*, Adam's story follows soon after the reference to the Prophet's hasty repetition of Qur'ānic revelations, for fear of forgetting them. Hence, Adam's forgetting of his commitment is referred to at the outset. Moreover, the story is given in a *sūrah* which reveals many aspects of God's grace bestowed on those chosen servants whom He places under His care. Therefore, in this story the point is made that God chose Adam, accepted his repentance and provided him with guidance. This is followed by a scene of the Day of Resurrection portraying the two different ends of God's obedient servants on the one hand and, on the other, those who persist in disobedience. This is shown like a journey back from earth to the first abode where everyone is given their rightful reward. Let us now look at the story as it is related in this *sūrah*.

"Long ago, We made a covenant with Adam; but he forgot it, and We found him lacking in firmness of purpose," (Verse 115) God's covenant with Adam was that he could eat of all the fruits in the Garden except for one tree that represented the prohibition necessary to strengthen willpower, assert one's personality and liberate oneself of the oppressive pressure of desire. All this is necessary to give the human soul the freedom to do without its supposed needs, so that it is not enslaved by desire. This is indeed the true measure of human excellence. Whenever man's will weakens under the pressure of desire, he sinks closer to the level of animals.

Hence, God so tested man initially in order to prepare him for his role of building human life on earth. Thus the test is seen to be part of God's grace which He bestows on man in abundance: his power to resist temptation is alerted and enhanced. His eyes are opened to the struggle awaiting him between the pleasures raised before him by Satan and his will to honour his commitment to God. The results of this first test are made public: *"He forgot it [i.e. his commitment], and We found him lacking in firmness of purpose."* (Verse 115) The result is declared before the details of the test have been given.

"And when We said to the angels, 'Prostrate yourselves before Adam,' they all prostrated themselves; except Iblīs, who refused." (Verse 116) This first episode of the story is given in very general terms, without

453

the details given in other *sūrahs*. The general context here is one of mercy, care and blessings. Hence, these aspects are brought forth very quickly: *"'Adam,' We said, 'this is indeed a foe to you and your wife; so let him not drive the two of you out of the Garden, for then you will be plunged into affliction. It is guaranteed that you shall not hunger here or feel naked, and you shall not thirst here or suffer from the blazing sun.'"* (Verses 117–119)

We see how God takes care to alert Adam to the wicked designs employed by his enemy, warning him against Satan's treachery, after he disobeyed God's command to prostrate himself before Adam. The warning is very precise, showing the inevitable result of listening to Satan and his promptings: *"Let him not drive the two of you out of the Garden, for then you will be plunged into affliction."* (Verse 117) Once Adam is thrown out of heaven, all he will have is affliction: hard labour, going astray, worry, indecision, endless waiting, agony, deprivation, etc. As long as he is in Paradise, he is immune to all affliction: *"It is guaranteed that you shall not hunger here or feel naked, and you shall not thirst here or suffer from the blazing sun."* (Verses 118–119) All that man needs is available in plenty in Paradise, which means that man should ensure he stays there. We note here how hunger and nakedness are shown to be parallel to thirst and intense heat. These four represent man's initial concerns as he tries to find food, clothing, drink and shade.

Adam however was without experience. Moreover, he was burdened by weakness, such as his desire for survival and his other desire to feel himself powerful. It was through these weaknesses that Satan was able to tempt him: *"But Satan whispered to him, saying: 'Adam, shall I lead you to the tree of life eternal, and to a kingdom that will never decay?'"* (Verse 120)

We see here how Satan touches Adam's raw nerve. Man's life and power are limited. Hence, he longs for survival and lasting power. These two desires provided Satan with suitable openings. As we have said, Adam had all human weaknesses planted in him for a definite purpose. Hence, he forgot his commitment and transgressed the permitted limits: *"They both ate of its fruit; and thereupon their shameful parts became visible to them, and they began to cover themselves with pieced-together leaves from the Garden. Thus did Adam disobey his Lord, and thus did he stray into error."* (Verse 121)

It appears that what Adam and his wife saw were their genitals, which had thus far been covered. This is the more likely explanation, since they started to cover themselves again, piecing together leaves from the trees in heaven. On the other hand, the expression may mean that their action aroused their sexual desire. Prior to sexual feelings, man does not feel any shame in leaving his private parts exposed. Indeed, he may not be aware of them unless he feels such urges. It is then that he experiences shame and feels too shy to expose himself.

It may be that the tree was forbidden to Adam and his wife because its fruits could awaken their sexual desire. Perhaps it was intended to leave this desire dormant for a time. It could be, on the other hand, that their forgetting of their commitment to God and their disobedience of His orders resulted in a weakening of their willpower and a break of their bond with the Lord Creator, giving way to the emergence of sexual and reproductive desires. It is only in this way that man can extend his life beyond his own term. All these are possible explanations for the association between their eating of the forbidden tree and their becoming aware of their nakedness. The Qur'ān does not say, "their shameful parts became visible"; rather, these parts became visible "to them". This suggests that these parts were screened from them and then became exposed through their own inner feelings. In another *sūrah* the Qur'ān says: *"Satan whispered to them both, so that he might show them their nakedness, of which they had previously been unaware."* (7: 20) *"[Satan] stripped them of their garment in order to make them aware of their nakedness."* (7: 27) Perhaps the clothing that Satan removed was not physical, but rather, a protective feeling of innocence, purity and closeness to God. These are mere hypotheses which we neither emphasize nor give weight to. We state them only to make the first human experience with temptation clearer.

But God extended His grace to Adam and his wife after he had disobeyed Him. This was only the first experience: *"Then his Lord elected him [for His grace], accepted his repentance, and bestowed His guidance upon him."* (Verse 122) Realizing the enormity of his error,

Adam repented and sought God's forgiveness, but this is not mentioned here in order to leave God's grace to be seen most clearly.

Drawing the Lines of Battle

The order was then given to the two combatants to descend to earth, which would be the battleground in this long-lasting war: "*Get down, both of you, and be out of it; each of you shall be an enemy to the other.*" (Verse 123) Thus, the enmity was declared the whole world over. This means that there is no excuse for Adam and his progeny. None can claim to have been taken unawares. Everyone knows the score and the unabating hostility. The whole universe is aware of it: "*Each of you shall be an enemy to the other.*" (Verse 123)

Along with this declaration which resounded throughout the heavens and the earth, and which was witnessed by all the angels, God has willed, out of His grace, to send His messengers bringing guidance to mankind, before He punishes them for their sins. Thus, at the same time He alerts His servants to this enmity between Adam and Satan, He announces to them that He will provide them with guidance. He will then give them their reward according to whether they follow His guidance or reject it:

> When guidance shall come to you from Me, he who follows My guidance will not go astray, nor will he suffer misery; but he who turns away from My message shall have a straitened life and We shall raise him up blind on the Day of Resurrection. 'Lord,' he will say, 'why have You raised me up blind, while I was endowed with sight?' He will reply: 'Thus it is: Our revelations were brought to you, but you were oblivious to them. So today shall you be consigned to oblivion.' For thus shall We reward him who transgresses and does not believe in his Lord's revelations. Indeed the suffering in the life to come shall be most severe and most enduring. (Verses 123–127)

This promise of the guidance mankind will receive from God is made immediately after Adam's story, as though it constitutes a part of it. It is declared there in heaven at the conclusion of the story. It is, then, final, determined long ago, admitting no cancellation or amendment.

"*He who follows My guidance will not go astray, nor will he suffer misery.*" (Verse 123) When human beings follow divine guidance, they are immune from going astray and suffering misery. Both eventualities however exist, but God protects those of His servants who follow His guidance from them. Misery is attendant on following error, even though a person has all the pleasures the world can give. Indeed, such pleasures are part of his misery both in this life and in the life to come. For every forbidden pleasure is succeeded by pain and negative consequences. When human beings stray from God's guidance, they sink into worry, confusion and instability. They swing from one extreme to the other. Misery will always be the result of such worry and confusion, even though a person enjoys all the riches life can give. But the ultimate misery is that suffered in the hereafter. However, those who follow God's guidance are protected from error and misery in this earthly life. This compensates them for their lost Paradise until they return to it on the appointed day.

"*But he who turns away from My message shall have a straitened life and We shall raise him up blind on the Day of Resurrection.*" (Verse 124) When human life severs its links with God, depriving itself of His abundant grace, it becomes straitened, even though it may be materially affluent. It is a type of stress attendant on being isolated from God and the reassurance of His mercy. It is a stress that demonstrates itself in worry, doubt and confusion; holding tight to what one owns and fearing unexpected loss; coveting all manner of comfort and pleasure; nurturing aspirations and ambitions, etc. People do not feel true reassurance except when they place their trust in God, holding tight to their bond with Him. The reassurance generated by faith in God adds much to life's dimensions in length, breadth, depth and expanse. Without such reassurance, life is nothing but a continuous misery and is far harder than what man suffers through poverty and deprivation.

"*We shall raise him up blind on the Day of Resurrection.*" (Verse 124) This is the same type of going astray as that which man went through in the life of this world. It comes by way of recompense for his turning

457

away from God's message in this first life. Hence, he asks: *"Lord, why have You raised me up blind, while I was endowed with sight?"* (Verse 125) The answer is not long coming: *"Thus it is: Our revelations were brought to you, but you were oblivious to them. So today shall you be consigned to oblivion. For thus shall We reward him who transgresses and does not believe in his Lord's revelations. Indeed the suffering in the life to come shall be most severe and most enduring."* (Verses 126–127)

Anyone who turns his back on God's message certainly transgresses. He walks away from the guidance brought to him by God's Messenger when it is the richest blessing and the most valuable resource. He transgresses as he turns his sight to objects he was not meant to look at, yet remains oblivious to God's revelations. It is not surprising that he lives a straitened life. Moreover, on the Day of Resurrection he will be raised up blind.

We note here how the wording and the images drawn provide complementary and contrasting scenes: the fall from heaven is followed by misery and going astray. It contrasts with the return to heaven where one is free from all such misery. A life of ease contrasts with a straitened life, and guidance contrasts with blindness. All this comes by way of comment on Adam's story, which is the story of all mankind. It starts and ends in heaven, as we saw earlier in *Sūrah* 7, The Heights. However the scenes here are different. In each case, they fit the general emphasis of the *sūrah* in which they are drawn.

The Lessons of History

The *sūrah* now moves us along to look at how earlier communities met their fate, which is much closer to us than the Day of Judgement. Moreover, we can see their destruction and what is left of them with our own eyes, while we cannot see resurrection.

> Can they not see how many generations We have destroyed before their time? They walk about in the very places where they dwelt. In this there are signs for men of wisdom. Now, were it not for a decree from your Lord already gone forth, setting a term, their destruction would have been inescapable. (Verses 128–129)

When we look with our eyes and minds at the fate of earlier communities; when we look closely at the lands were they lived and prospered; when we imagine their dwellings and how they became empty with no one living in them; when we stretch our imagination to see them walking through their lands, going here and there, moving along, taking rest, looking to their futures, dealing with their worries, and then open our eyes to see nothing but emptiness, we realize that we are at the edge of a precipice that threatens to engulf us like it did earlier communities. We know that the great power that overwhelmed earlier generations is able to overwhelm the present ones as well. We understand then the meaning of the warning given to us, because the lesson is there for us to see. How come, then, that people do not recognize divine guidance when the fate of earlier generations provides every guiding indication to anyone who has a mind to use: *"In this there are signs for people of wisdom."* (Verse 128)

Divine wisdom has willed that God will not eliminate them by a calamity that befalls them in this present world. This is the reason why they do not meet a similar fate. This is a situation God has decreed, giving them respite up to a term appointed for them. Otherwise they too would have been punished for their rejection of the truth: *"Now, were it not for a decree from your Lord already gone forth, setting a term, their destruction would have been inescapable."* (Verse 129)

The Way to Contentment

We mentioned that the unbelievers had been given respite. They will have their term, but they have definitely not been abandoned. The Prophet is told not to pay much attention to them or to the luxuries and comforts they have been given in this life. All this is a test for them. What God has given him of His blessings is much better and greater. He is to remain patient and steadfast:

> *Hence, bear with patience whatever they may say, and extol your Lord's limitless glory and praise Him before the rising of the sun and before its setting; and extol His glory, too, during the hours of the night as well as during the hours of the day, so that you may attain*

a state of contentment. Do not turn your eyes covetously towards whatever splendour of this world's life We have allowed many of them to enjoy in order that We may test them thereby. Whatever provisions your Lord may give are indeed better and longer lasting. Enjoin prayer on your people, and be diligent in its observance. We do not ask you for any provisions. It is We who provide for you. The future belongs to the God-fearing. (Verses 130–132)

The Prophet is instructed to bear with patience whatever the unbelievers say. He is not to answer their blasphemy, rejection or ridicule. He should be neither distressed by what they say, nor grieved at what may await them. He is to turn to his Lord, glorifying Him before sunrise and sunset: early with the fresh breath of dawn as life awakens, and late as everything begins to cool down when the sun is about to set and the whole universe seems to close its eyes, ready to sleep. He is to glorify God and praise Him intermittently through the day and the night, so as to keep his link with Him throughout.

Such glorification is urged on the Prophet, and all his followers, "*so that you may attain a state of contentment.*" (Verse 130) When we glorify God, we have a direct link with Him, and the person who maintains such a link is contented, reassured. He is in a state of contentment as everything around him feels content; and he is reassured because he knows that, with God's help, he is safe and secure. Thus, contentedness is the fruit of worship and God's glorification. In itself, it is a reward that is generated within one's heart.

So the Prophet is instructed to turn his face to God offering his worship. He is further instructed: "*Do not turn your eyes covetously towards whatever splendour of this world's life We have allowed many of them to enjoy.*" (Verse 131) There is plenty of splendour in this life which may appear very tempting. There are luxuries, pleasures, wealth, children, high position and power. But all this is merely a 'flower', to use the exact word of the Qur'ān; and like a flower, all this splendour will fade within a very brief period. Hence, they are given all this splendour to enjoy "*in order that We may test them thereby.*" (Verse 131) Thus, their true metal will be known by the way they use what God has favoured them with of the splendour of this life. But then they must realize that at the end of the day, *"whatever provisions your Lord may give are indeed better and longer lasting."* (Verse 131) This refers to what the believers are given in the life to come. These provisions are for enjoyment, not a test. They have no special lure to turn people away from what is better. They are the better provision and they are everlasting.

We must not understand this verse as encouraging self-denial or disdain for the comforts of this life. It is rather an encouragement to hold on to true and lasting values, to maintain one's ties with God and be contented. This is the best way to resist the temptation of the splendour and attractions of this life. When we maintain such values, we are free to rise above the lure of false temptations, splendid as they may appear.

"Enjoin prayer on your people." (Verse 132) The first duty of a Muslim is to make his home a Muslim home, enjoining his family to attend to their prayers so that they all maintain their ties with God. Thus, they are united in their approach to life. Life in a home where all members turn to God for worship is certainly a happy one.

"And be diligent in its observance." (Verse 132) Be diligent so that you offer your prayers complete and its effect becomes a reality. Prayer restrains man from loathsome deeds and indecency. This is its true effect. To attain the level where prayer provides such restraint requires diligence in its observance. Unless we reach the stage that our prayer yields this fruit, it remains a mere sequence of phrases and movements.

Prayer and worship generally are duties assigned to the Prophet and believers. God does not gain anything by them. He is in need of no one: *"We do not ask you for any provisions. It is We who provide for you."* (Verse 132) Worship nurtures God-consciousness within the worshipper. Hence, *"the future belongs to the God-fearing."* (Verse 132) It is man who benefits by prayer, both in this life and in the life to come. He offers his worship to God and he enjoys, as a result, a state of contentment. He is comfortable, reassured. Furthermore, he ultimately receives a much greater reward in the hereafter. As for God, He needs nothing from anyone.

As the *sūrah* draws to its close, it refers again to those people who, enjoying position and power, reject God's revelations and demand

461

that the Prophet deliver a miracle. They make such demands even after the Prophet has given them the Qur'ān which explains in all clarity what previous messages from God were like.

"*They say: 'Why does he not bring us a sign from his Lord?' Has there not come to them a clear evidence of the truth in the earlier scriptures?*" (Verse 133) They need no physical miracle. Hence, their demands betray their arrogance. The Qur'ān is more than sufficient as proof. It links the new message with God's previous messages, uniting them all and clarifying what was left in general terms in previous messages.

God has given those who deny the truth everything they need to recognize the truth and believe in it when He sent them His last Messenger: "*Had We destroyed them with a calamity before his coming, they would have said, 'Our Lord, if only You had sent us a Messenger, we would have followed Your revelations rather than be humiliated and disgraced.'*" (Verse 134)

At the time when this verse was recited, they had been neither humiliated nor disgraced. The verse describes their inevitable end which will bring them humiliation and disgrace. It may be that they will then say: '*Our Lord, if only You had sent us a Messenger.*' Now a Messenger is sent to them and they have no excuse to justify their rejection.

As the *sūrah* describes their end, the Prophet is commanded to leave them alone, without grieving for them. He should announce to them that he will await the end, and let them await it as they wish: "*Say: Everyone is hopefully waiting; so wait, if you will. You will certainly come to know who has followed the even path, and who has been rightly guided.*" (Verse 135)

Thus the *sūrah* ends. It started with assuring the Prophet that the Qur'ān was not revealed to him to cause him any distress. It defined the role of the Qur'ān as '*an admonition to the God-fearing.*' (Verse 3) The end is in full harmony with the beginning. It provides a reminder and an admonition for those who may benefit thereby. As the Prophet conveyed his message complete, the only thing that remains is to await the end, which is determined by God.

Index

463